Spreading the Gospel in
Colonial Virginia

Spreading the Gospel in Colonial Virginia

Preaching Religion and Community

With Selected Sermons
and Other Primary Documents

Introduction and Notes by Edward L. Bond

LEXINGTON BOOKS
Lanham • Boulder • New York • Toronto • Oxford

Published in association with

Colonial Williamsburg
The Colonial Williamsburg Foundation
Williamsburg, Virginia

LEXINGTON BOOKS

Published in the United States of America
by Lexington Books
An imprint of The Rowman & Littlefield Publishing Group, Inc.
4501 Forbes Boulevard, Suite 200, Lanham, Maryland 20706

PO Box 317
Oxford
OX2 9RU, UK

Published in association with The Colonial Williamsburg Foundation
P.O. Box 1776, Williamsburg, Virginia 23187-1776
www.colonialwilliamsburg.org

British Library Cataloguing in Publication Information Available

Library of Congress Cataloging-in-Publication Data

Spreading the gospel in colonial Virginia : preaching religion and community :
   with selected sermons and other primary documents / introduction and notes by
   Edward L. Bond.
      p. cm.
   Includes bibliographical references.
   ISBN 0-7391-0721-6 (pbk. : alk. paper)
      1. Virginia—Church history.   2. Sermons, American—Virginia.   3.
   Virginia—Church history—Sources.   I. Bond, Edward L.
   BR555.V8S66 2004
   277.55'07—dc22

                                                                    2004018663

Printed in the United States of America

⊗™ The paper used in this publication meets the minimum requirements of American
National Standard for Information Sciences—Permanence of Paper for Printed Library
Materials, ANSI/NISO Z39.48–1992.

For
Thomas Finn,
James Morris,
Charles Royster,
and Kathleen Bond

~

Contents

~

Foreword

Religious histories of colonial Virginia usually include descriptions of the Church of England establishment in Virginia weakened by lack of support from the Crown, too few parish ministers before the eighteenth century, the supposed lackluster spiritual inclinations of Anglican clergy and parishioners alike, and the mid-eighteenth-century religious revival historians call the Great Awakening. Also well-documented are mounting opposition to constraints on the free exercise of religion in prerevolutionary Virginia and widespread support for the disestablishment of Anglican religious authority after the war. On the other hand, religious thought and practice in everyday life in Virginia have garnered less scholarly interest, except as they related to the conversion experience and religious discipline of dissenters and the "rational" religious views of some of the Founding Fathers.

What, then, is to be made of the mounting evidence for genuine religious sentiment and spiritual development in colonial Virginia? A more nuanced portrait of religious life in the Old Dominion is warranted. In his previous book and articles, Edward L. Bond, one among a small number of historians who have taken up that challenge, has made the case that religious belief in colonial Virginia was more diverse and heartfelt than previously recognized.

In *Spreading the Gospel in Colonial Virginia: Preaching Religion and Community*, Bond writes an engaging narrative history of religion in Virginia from 1607 to the revolutionary era. To be sure, the tried and true themes are there, now given better dimension with new evidence and the author's appreciation for a variety of devotional approaches. Selections of sermons and private devotional writings composed by people from various religious traditions living in Virginia are accompanied by background information about the individuals who wrote the sermons and devotional prose and the circumstances that gave rise to the writings. (A larger selection of writings can be found in the book's hardcover edition, published in 2004.) The author gives additional perspective on the texts in exquisitely detailed footnotes that ground the documents in theology, Anglican and otherwise, and explain the denominational and scriptural underpinnings of religious traditions in Virginia. As new evidence for religion in everyday life of Virginians surfaces and older sources are reexamined, historians will consult *Spreading the Gospel in Colonial Virginia* again and again for information and the texts themselves.

Spreading the Gospel in Colonial Virginia has another important legacy: it is designed to spur further research into religion in colonial Virginia. The Special Collections section of the John D. Rockefeller, Jr. Library at The Colonial Williamsburg Foundation and the other repositories represented in this collection have among their holdings many more religious works and writings than could be included here.

Meantime, historians, professors, museum professionals, students, and readers of history have a new resource for the study of religion in the colony of Virginia and for delving firsthand into sermons and other religious materials Virginians wrote and read over two centuries under British rule and Christian instruction.

Linda H. Rowe
Historian
Colonial Williamsburg Foundation

Preface

The documents in this collection represent the wide variety of extant materials on religion in colonial Virginia. They include the sermons of established as well as dissenting ministers, a layman's devotional work, and an account of the Baptists in Virginia during the Great Awakening. The sermon literature includes typical discourses that congregations might have heard on a typical Sunday as well as sermons composed for a particular occasion such as a funeral or to preach before the colony's General Assembly. Anglicans, Presbyterians, Baptists, and evangelical Anglicans are all represented.

In choosing which documents to include, two principles guided my decisions. First, manuscript sources, in general, took precedence over published materials. Second, sources that are less generally available to researchers took precedence over those that are more readily available. Some omissions may surprise readers. Sermons by Samuel Henley and Devereux Jarratt, all of which are fairly well known already, do not appear. Many of Samuel Henley's sermons are political in nature and were not included for that reason. Some are also already available in modern facsimile editions. William Stith's *A Sermon, Preached Before the General Assembly at Williamsburg, March 2, 1745/46*[1] is dedicated solely to politics as well and, like Henley's political discourses, has little to do with "spreading the Gospel." The decision not to include any of Jarratt's discourses was difficult, but his works are widely known and the sermons of Charles Clay, the collection's representative of evangelical Anglicanism, can be clearly dated to the period before the coming of the American Revolution. Other discourses were excluded for different reasons. The

Presbyterian John Todd's sermon on psalmody is both off topic and, at over 100 pages, far too long; the sermons of John Thompson of St. Mark's Parish in Orange County are simply handwritten copies of portions of John Tillotson's sermons; and the discourses of Henry Jacob, a Brownist who died on his way to the colony in the early 1600s, are extraordinarily long, thus including one of his works would have meant deleting four or five other sermons.

A note about my editorial method is necessary. With the exception of silently expanding the numerous abbreviations in Charles Clay's "Sermon on Canticles 2:13," I have reproduced the documents as they appeared in the seventeenth and eighteenth centuries. Original page numbers and my corrections to the original texts appear in brackets. In those places where I guessed at a particular word, the word appears in brackets with a question mark. Obvious printer's errors have been corrected silently. Thorns have been brought down to the line, and I have changed the few instances of "ye" to "the." Readers will find footnotes indicated by both numbers and letters. Numbered notes are mine. Lettered notes are the author's original footnotes, or, in the case of a manuscript sermon, his original margin notes. In some cases I have expanded upon the author's note to clarify a reference. My words should be obvious from the context. Unless otherwise noted, all scriptural references are to the King James version of the Bible.

Note

1. William Stith, A Sermon, Preached Before the General Assembly at Williamsburg, March 2, 1745/46 (Williamsburg, 1746), Virginia Historical Society.

~

Acknowledgments

This project began several years ago when Susan Berg, then director of the John D. Rockefeller, Jr. Library at The Colonial Williamsburg Foundation, asked me to look at the various books related to religion in the Foundation's rare book collection. She introduced me to John Turner, director of the Foundation's Religious Studies Program, and we began to discuss what a book of documents on religion in colonial Virginia should look like. The book has grown far beyond what we originally envisioned. Susan and John have been strong supporters of this project as has Joe Rountree, The Colonial Williamsburg Foundation's Director of Publications. In addition to negotiating with presses, finding outside readers to evaluate the manuscript, and all of the other mysterious things that publications directors do, he has patiently and tactfully dealt with my many and sometimes panicked queries about when this book would make it to press. Serena Krombach, my editor at Lexington Books, has also been an enthusiastic supporter of the book. Funding for the project was provided by the generous financial support of F.G. and Kathy O. Summitt and the Summitt Christian History Scholarship Fund.

Most of my research was done at Colonial Williamsburg's Rockefeller Library, and the staff there helped smooth many paths for me. Del Moore, who is the model reference librarian, George Yetter, and Gail Greve were especially helpful. Sebastian Nwaneri, Alabama A&M's interlibrary loan librarian, kept me supplied with books during the academic year. Ronnie Nettles, dean of the Natchez branch of Copiah-Lincoln Community College, made my work easier by granting me permission to use the college's interlibrary loan system during summers spent in Mississippi. Joan McLemore, Co-Lin's librarian, filled my numerous interlibrary loan requests.

Part I, "A Brief History of Religion in Colonial Virginia," benefited from close readings by several people. James Morris, Jewel Spangler, Thomas Buckley, Joan Gundersen, Charles Royster, and Kathleen Bond all made suggestions that improved this section tremendously. Kathleen Bond and James Morris also saved me from committing several sins of commission against the English language. Linda Rowe, who is one of the great treasures of the Colonial Williamsburg Historical Research Department, gave the entire manuscript a close reading and, in addition to saving me from committing several sins of omission against Hening's *Statutes*, made many suggestions that helped to make this a much better book. Thad Tate read the entire manuscript as well and pointed out its strengths and weaknesses with a keen eye. The final draft benefited tremendously from his comments on an earlier version and his conversations with me about religion in early Virginia. His willingness to read, comment on, and criticize my work has meant a great deal to me. Since first learning of this project, Linda and Thad have been among the book's most enthusiastic supporters.

My parents, Robert and Jean Bond, have encouraged my scholarship for years. Working on this project allowed me the opportunity to visit them in Virginia far more often than I might have been able to otherwise. We are all grateful for that opportunity.

The abridged version of *Spreading the Gospel in Colonial Virginia* is dedicated to four people. Three of them are former teachers who helped shape my academic career—Thomas Finn, James Morris, and Charles Royster. During the fall term of my senior year I took Professor Finn's course, "The Gospels." It met in the afternoon on Mondays, Wednesdays, and Fridays. I can still recall sitting in his classroom on several Friday afternoons, professor and students engaged in discussion, all of us unaware that the class's official ending time had passed ten or fifteen minutes earlier. Professor Finn was then, is now, and, I suspect, will remain for me the model of an undergraduate teacher. It's been over ten years since James Morris urged me to return to graduate school to work on my Ph.D. I don't regret following his advice. He has read many drafts of my work and has tried to help me become a better writer as well. Charles Royster has shaped my academic career in more ways than he realizes. During my first month as a Ph.D. student, another instructor assigned my class one of Professor Royster's books. After reading it I knew the type of history I wanted to pursue. His advice, his encouragement, and his criticism have helped make me a better historian; his example is one I continue to set before me. I am grateful to Tom, Jim, and Charlie. This book is my way of saying thank you.

The fourth person the abridged version of *Spreading the Gospel in Colonial Virginia* is dedicated to is my wife, Kathleen, for all the things we share.

PART ONE

INTRODUCTION

~

CHAPTER ONE

A Brief History of
Religion in Colonial Virginia

On 5 July 1705 a crowd of people braved the summer's heat and assembled at the great hall in Colonel William Bridger's home in Chuckatuck, Virginia. Justices of the peace, small farmers, planters, military officers, and others gathered there to witness a disputation between Joseph Glaister (d. 1718/19), a Quaker missionary, and the Reverend Andrew Monro, the Anglican[1] minister of Newport Parish in Isle of Wight County. The proposed agenda of the debate (one of several disputations held between Quakers and Anglicans that year) included fourteen propositions that touched upon a wide range of controversial issues, from "Whether can Mankind, by any Means, be free from Sin on this Side the Grave?" to "Whether is there any Example in the Scripture, where any Apostle of Christ ever forced or received any Maintenance, either by any human Law, or without such Law, from any who did not receive their Ministry, or from such as did?"[2] The disputants began with a significant point of disagreement between the two religious persuasions: whether the Great Commission at the close of Matthew's Gospel was to be understood as an "outward visible Baptism with Water" or an "invisible Baptism of the Holy Ghost."[3] Anglicans traditionally baptized infants by pouring a small amount of water on the child's head in the name of the Father, the Son, and the Holy Ghost, and the colony's laws required that all newborns be brought to the local parish minister for baptism in a timely manner. Quakers found this practice illegitimate and mocked it as "sprinkling" or "dipping."

Over the next hour or so, Glaister and Monro sparred verbally with each other, first about the meaning of baptism, and, second, about the possibility of human beings living a sinless life on earth. Both men demonstrated a wide knowledge of the scriptures and the Jewish context of early Christianity. Onlookers crowded around the men. Supporters shouted approval of their favorite; they refreshed him with tobacco and ale; sometimes they hooted at his opponent. Other people in the crowd, no doubt, held no such allegiances. They had come to Bridger's house not to support one side or the other, but in order to learn more about which persuasion spoke to their own spiritual longings. Before entertaining a third proposition on the legitimacy of requiring all citizens to provide monetary support for an established church regardless of their adherence, Monro, an older man, was overcome by the heat. The disputants then agreed to break off their debate and continue at another time.[4]

The scene portrays a situation at odds with the traditional interpretation of religion in colonial Virginia. Often the description devolves into a caricature of pious dissenters and nominally Anglican planters more concerned with their next crop of tobacco, the price of slaves, or a wager on a horse race than on the things of God. Nor does the disputation depicted above suggest the Anglican "hegemony" over religion in colonial Virginia that is so often asserted.[5] It shows a very different Virginia, one in which all ranks of people were desirous of religion and interested in the finer points of theology. Religious leaders showed a willingness to debate the truths of religious doctrines and practices with one another in disputes which edified and entertained significant numbers of colonists. Longtime Commissary James Blair (1655–1743), in fact, encouraged debates between people of different religious persuasions, so long as these were "done in a friendly and peaceable Manner, and with a Design to find out the Truth"[6] and bemoaned the tendency of all Christians to "lay greater Stress upon some of those little Points, in which they differ, than upon the great Points of Christianity in which they are agreed."[7] In short, the scene portrays a Virginia more tolerant, more concerned about religion, and more religiously diverse than the traditional stereotype suggests.

That is not to say that Virginians were always tolerant of other faiths, that the established Anglican Church did not have legal advantages, or that dissenters were not harassed from time to time both by private individuals and the state. Ambiguity and paradox marked religion and the religious life of Virginians during the colonial period. Like other European polities of the era Virginia had an established church, but that church was often so ineffectual that both leaders and the populace cared little if dissenters brought a religious presence to the colony.[8] Colonists desired religious materials and leaders, but often a formal religious presence seemed missing from the colony's public life. Toleration and contention vied for preeminence. Puritans, Quakers, Presbyterians, Moravians, and Baptists all at one time or another endured persecution at the hands of the establishment, although intradenominational strife, such as that between Commissary James Blair and his clergy, often overshadowed conflict between denominations and between the state and dissenting groups. Beneath all of the ambiguities and paradoxes, however, we must recognize what lay at the heart of religion in colonial Virginia, the desire, too little regarded by historians, of Virginians for a religious presence in their lives. This is what colonists meant when they complained about the shortage of clergy and devotional books; it is what Quakers, Presbyterians, and Baptists meant when they pleaded first for toleration then for religious freedom; it is what many Anglicans meant when they defended the privileges of their established Church of England; it is what Joseph Glaister, Andrew Monro, and the people who attended their disputation illustrate.

⌒

The story of English religion in Virginia predates the successful establishment in 1607 of a settlement at Jamestown. Members of the Virginia Company of London, a trading company committed to founding English colonies and profiting from them, as well as other supporters of colonization, believed God had preordained English possession of the North American continent. The belief had roots in the wider notion that the English nation shared a special relationship with God. Protestant English people in particular could see evidence in the half century prior to settling Jamestown of England's chosen status. Elizabeth's accession to the English throne in 1558, the defeat in 1588 of the Spanish Armada sent by the Roman Catholic King of Spain Philip II to destroy England, and the discovery of the Gunpowder Plot, a conspiracy by several Roman Catholics to blow up James I (1566–1625) and the government at the opening of Parliament in 1605, all offered proof of God's inordinate concern for England. Although Protestants held the belief in God's special relationship with England with particular prejudice, Roman Catholic Englishmen shared it as well. Indeed, by the eve of colonization, England's status as an early modern chosen people had become something of an article of faith and the hope of settling overseas colonies in North America a design English people assumed blessed by an Anglophile deity.[9]

Belief in the nation's relationship with God came easily to the "God-centered" people of Tudor-Stuart England. They lived in a world permeated with the divine and believed in an active and immanent deity concerned with even the most trivial of daily events. They could escape neither the divine nor religion. A successful voyage to the New World indicated God's favor, while a storm at sea, a poor harvest, or the untimely death of one's cat-tle revealed His displeasure.[10] Even in seventeenth-century Virginia, where the spotty extant sources make documenting religion difficult, one catches glimpses of the importance of God and religion to the settlers. Michael Lap-worth offered up a typical prayer of thanksgiving after reaching the colony in 1621: "thankes be to god I escaped sickness at sea."[11] A portion of one of the colony's earliest law codes, the strict *Lawes Divine, Morall and Martiall*, did not use the exact words but nonetheless reflected the Ten Commandments in exact order.[12] John Rolfe wrestled with whether it was God's will that he wed the Indian princess Pocahontas, knowing full well that English ministers had decried the "abominable mixture" resulting from Native American–English unions.[13] And the colonists wasted little time after settling at Jamestown before setting aside a space in which they could worship God. John Smith described their makeshift church: "Wee did hang an awning (which is an old saile) to three or foure trees to shadow us from the Sunne, our walls were rales of wood, our seats unhewed trees, till we cut plankes, our Pulpit a bar of wood nailed to two neighbouring trees, in foule weather we shifted into an old rotten tent, for we had few better . . . this was our Church."[14]

Successfully planting a settlement in Virginia not only helped demon-strate God's support of English colonization efforts to those inclined to in-terpret things this way but also brought the established Church of England to the New World. It was England's national church, one of the many state churches that defined institutional religion among the nations of early mod-ern Europe. State churches established not only "the principal forms of Christian worship, doctrine, and moral teachings" but also "the ecclesiastical order and theological configuration that the state would permit its laity to follow." In theory the church supported the state and the state in turn sup-ported the church, in England's case by granting vestries the authority to levy taxes in order to defray church expenses.[15]

One of the more peculiar churches that developed out of the Protestant Reformation, the Church of England traces its history back to the 1530s when Henry VIII (1491–1547) and Parliament threw off papal leadership of the Church in England, replacing it with a Church of England headed by the king rather than the pope. Despite severing the relationship with Rome, however, Henry oversaw little reform of theology or practice during his reign, and the Church of England maintained most of the devotional and liturgical practices of the medieval Catholic Church, although during his reign the Church of England attacked both pilgrimages and the adoration of images as popish superstitions. Henry himself opposed clergy marriage and accepted private masses, auricular confession, and the Roman Catholic eucharistic doctrine of transubstantiation.[16] Not until his death did serious reformation take place in England.[17]

As with other European nations in the sixteenth and seventeenth centuries, the ruler's religion dictated the religion of the national church. Thus the Church of England lurched back and forth from Catholicism to Protestantism for several decades after Henry's death, depending upon the religious sympathies of the reigning monarch: Protestantism under Edward VI (1537–1553), Roman Catholicism under Mary (1542–1587), and back to a more moderate Protestantism under Elizabeth I (1533–1603).[18]

Seeking political legitimacy and internal peace, Elizabeth and her bishops hoped to end the chaos in the national church by following a middle way. The result was a hybrid creation, part Roman Catholic, part Calvinist.[19] The Church of England retained an episcopal form of church government (meaning rule by bishops) and combined Calvinist theology with the yearly Christological cycle of the Roman Catholic liturgical calendar purged of some of its Marian festivals[20] offensive to all Protestants and, with the exception of St. Paul, limiting celebrations of saints' days to those Biblical saints who had witnessed Christ's resurrection. United more by shared forms of worship set down in the *Book of Common Prayer*, the most important document of the English Reformation, than by a clearly defined theology, the Church of England allowed for a wide variety of Protestant beliefs, from Anglicans generally content with the extent of reform in England to the more Calvinist-minded Puritans who wanted to push England's reformation further and remove all vestiges of Roman Catholicism from the national church. Puritans opposed the set liturgies in the *Book of Common Prayer*, using the sign of the cross at baptism, kneeling to receive communion, clergy wearing vestments, and other practices they thought smacked too much of Catholicism. Despite the well-known antagonism that later developed between the two groups, at the time of Virginia's founding and for nearly a decade thereafter, it is nonetheless improper to speak of Puritans and Anglicans because "Puritans then were Anglicans." True, their enthusiasm for Calvinism and sermons far surpassed that of other members of the Church of England, but they nevertheless remained members of the national church, content for a time to pursue additional reform from within.[21]

By the late 1610s, however, the struggle between Puritans and Anglicans moved beyond reform to the question of which group would control the Church of England. Dissatisfied with the Anglican establishment, Puritan groups began to leave England. Most simply wished to worship God in their own way without the legal restrictions that King James I had begun to place on them. Others, fearing for their own safety, fled because they believed God would soon punish the English people for their sins and their failure to adequately reform the Church and hoped to be far away from England when the inevitable judgment came. The Pilgrim fathers, a group of Separatist Puritans who had already abandoned communion with the Church of England, immigrated to Plymouth in 1620. A decade later in 1630 a more moderate group of non-Separatist Puritans, Puritans who remained members of the Church of England, albeit with great misgivings about its form of leadership and the extent of reform, founded the Massachusetts Bay colony. The largest number of Puritan exiles settled in the West Indies.[22]

Conditions for religious minorities deteriorated further in England following the death of James I in 1625 and the accession to the throne of his son, Charles I (1600–1649). James had believed that Christian unity rested upon a "very limited number of crucial Catholic doctrines." Beyond those few points, on divisive matters such as predestination and the theology of grace, for instance, reasonable people could disagree—so long as their disagreements did not disrupt the nation's internal peace. Charles viewed things differently. Where James had found unity in his ambiguous ecclesiastical policies, Charles saw only illusions and inconsistency. He believed that the lack of doctrinal and ceremonial uniformity his father had tolerated had allowed Puritans, whom he viewed as a menace, to challenge the very concept of monarchy. On the whole, Charles replaced his father's flexibility and accommodation to all but the most extreme nonconformists and recusants (Roman Catholics who refused to attend the Church of England) with policies emphasizing order, deference, and authority. In addition, Charles increased the influence of Bishop William Laud (1573–1645), an anti-Puritan zealot, eventually appointing him archbishop of Canterbury in 1633. Laud pursued conformity with a vengeance, using the power of not only his office but also the Privy Council and the Star Chamber as well to attack those who disagreed with him about ceremonials, doctrine, and church government. At his trial for treason in 1644, Laud defended his actions: "Ever since I came in place, I laboured nothing more than that the external worship of God, too much slighted in most parts of this kingdom, might be preserved, and that with as much decency and uniformity as might be, being still of opinion that unity cannot long continue in a Church where uniformity is shut out at the church door." He especially angered Puritans by elevating the importance of the communion table at the expense of the pulpit. Laud insisted that the table be fenced with rails and placed against the east wall of the church, thus making it seem more like an altar where a Roman Catholic priest might offer the sacrifice of the mass than a table where Protestants might share a meal. Puritan-minded English people saw Catholicism lurking beneath many of Laud's innovations: when he demanded that the people receive the elements of communion while kneeling, Puritans saw transubstantiation; when Laud brought back the sign of the cross at baptism, Puritans saw the reintroduction of popish superstition. Confronted by Laud's persecution and possessed of the belief that the Reformation in England was retrogressing rather than proceeding, thousands of Puritans fled their homeland in the so-called Puritan migration of the 1630s. For many of these men and women, like Roger Williams, flight was a desperate measure of last recourse: "It was death to me when Bishop Laud pursued me out of this land, and my conscience was persuaded against the national church, and ceremonies and bishops."[23] Other religious persuasions also found themselves unwelcome in Charles's England and sought refuge in America. In 1632, George Calvert, Lord Baltimore (ca. 1580–1632), gained permission to establish a colony for Roman Catholics in Maryland. The first settlers arrived in 1634 and, even then, Protestants outnumbered Roman Catholics. In 1702, the Church of England became Maryland's established church.[24]

The 1630s marked a period of religious turmoil in England, and by the end of the decade the conflict between Anglicans and Puritans had skipped the bounds of religion and entered politics. Again, a significant part of the problem lay with Charles I. After Parliament passed the Petition of Right in 1628, the first law since the beginning of the Tudor reign to limit the powers of a sovereign, he prorogued the assembly and ruled on his own. Seeking support against the Puritan-dominated Parliament, Charles embraced the Church of England's "Anglo-Catholic" party, represented by men like Bishop William Laud and the recently deceased Bishop of Winchester, Lancelot Andrewes (1555–1626). "At each point Charles and his friends diverged sharply from the Puritan party within the establishment." When Charles convened Parliament again in 1640, the body repudiated nearly every portion of his government in the Grand Remonstrance of 1641. In the fall of 1642, Civil War broke out between the Puritan supporters of Parliament and the Anglican adherents of Charles and divine right monarchy. Parliament abolished deans and bishops and in 1645 outlawed use of the *Book of Common Prayer*, forcing Anglican spirituality to retreat into the private conscience. A week later, Laud was executed for treason. Charles's own execution came four years later.[25]

Virginia's peculiar circumstances led the Church of England to develop very differently there and, consequently, Virginians avoided much of the religious conflict that rocked the English-speaking world in the first half of the seventeenth century. Unlike Plymouth and Massachusetts Bay in New England, the Quaker colony of Pennsylvania, or Maryland (where Roman

Catholics could settle peaceably), Virginia was not established as a haven for any particular religious minority. Virginia's early settlers did not leave England in order to escape religious persecution or to create a more godly society. Nor did they think of themselves as the chosen remnant of God's elect, for they lived in an age when God's elect still meant the English nation as a whole rather than one particular religious group within the nation. From the colony's earliest days, religious mixture had been the norm. Nonetheless, whatever religious persuasion they supported, English colonists who came to Virginia assumed that religion would form a significant part of the fabric of their lives.[26]

Most of Virginia's early settlers were probably sympathetic to the Anglican wing of the Church of England. John Smith was; so were John Rolfe and Thomas West, the Lord De la Warr.[27] A foreign spy even reported in 1609 that a majority of the settlers refused to attend the services of one minister whom they considered "somewhat a puritane," eventually forcing him to return to England with the hope of finding a more agreeable congregation.[28] Based on the crucifixes, rosary beads, and religious medallions unearthed by the Association for the Preservation of Virginia Antiquities's Jamestown Rediscovery dig, several Roman Catholics lived in the colony as well, although these objects may have been the possessions of Roman Catholics brought back to the colony as prisoners by Samuel Argall when he destroyed the French settlement at Mount Desert in 1613. In 1620 John Pory (1572–1636), a former member of Parliament and Virginia planter, wrote to Sir Edwin Sandys, then treasurer of the Virginia Company of London, to tell him of his concerns about one "Mr. Chanterton [who] smells to much of Roome . . . as he attempts to work miracles with his Crucyfixe." Brownists and other Separatist Puritans also made their homes in Virginia during the 1610s.[29]

Colonial leaders formally established the Church of England in 1619 at the first meeting of the General Assembly, although previous charters granted to the Virginia Company had assumed that it would be in place and had directed colonists to follow the English Church "in all fundamentall pointes."[30] Additional statutes passed in 1619 urged ministers to catechize "suche as are not yet ripe to come to the Communion"; prescribed penalties for those who violated God's moral laws; charged ministers with keeping accurate records of "all the Christenings, burials, & marriages," thus giving the Church legal responsibility for maintaining these vital statistics; and required each town to help proselytize native children, the last a goal that typically declined in importance the further one journeyed from England toward Virginia. The burgesses soon expanded upon these demands. In 1624 they ordered each settlement to set aside "some decent howse or sittinge roome" as a place to hold regular worship services. At the same session, they reaffirmed their desire that "there be an uniformitie in our Church kept as neere as may be to the Canons of *Englande* both in Substance and Circumstance."[31]

Despite Crown admonitions to follow the practices of the English Church as closely as the colony's circumstances permitted, during Virginia's early years Company leaders and colonial authorities often disregarded both Company instructions and their own votes in the colony's General Assembly reiterating the same goal. Peopling the colony rated higher with them than maintaining religious party unity. Virginia's notorious death rate (over 80 percent between 1607 and 1624)[32] made any settler, whatever his or her religious persuasion, a treasured commodity, for only by keeping up the colony's population could the Virginia Company preserve England's experiment in empire. The burden of finding people to settle in Virginia fell largely upon Sir Edwin Sandys, an "assistant" or director of the Virginia Company of London by 1616 and later its treasurer, a position roughly equivalent to a modern chairman of the board. Sandys held extraordinarily tolerant and forward-looking opinions about religion. In his published works, he argued that any hopes of re-creating a united Christendom out of the various state churches wrought by the Reformation were illusory. He advocated instead "what today we would call peaceful coexistence," and was likely the first person in post-Reformation Europe to do so.[33] Sandys encouraged both Anglican and dissenting groups to come to Virginia, including the Separatist-Puritan Pilgrims whose voyage took them to Plymouth instead. Other groups of Separatist Puritans came to Virginia and established settlements on the south side of the James River in what would become Nansemond and Lower Norfolk Counties. Even such an enemy to the established church as Henry Jacob, who had founded one of England's first Independent Congregational Churches, was welcome in the colony, although he died before he could reach Virginia to establish his particular plantation, "Jacobopolis."[34]

Colonists' discovery of a cash crop helped encourage the development of the "peaceful coexistence" Sandys favored. The earliest attempts to make the colony pay all resulted in failure as the profits expected from lumber, sassafras, silkworms, and wine never materialized. The settlers finally turned to tobacco. Local natives had long planted the weed, but this tobacco had an unpleasant taste and found few takers on the European market. John Rolfe, however, successfully experimented with growing better-quality West Indian tobacco in the colony, and when settlers learned that the land's promise lay in tobacco, they took to planting it with a vengeance. Soon they had accommodated themselves to the demands of tobacco culture. Instead of settling in towns like people in England or New England did, they scattered about the countryside in order to plant as much of the yellow weed as possible, often settling near one of the many rivers that still divide the Tidewater and Piedmont regions into a series of peninsulas. Francis Wyatt complained in 1622 that the colony's settlements were "so dispersed & [the] people so straglingly seated, that we were not only bereft of the friendly comerce and mutuall societie one of another in religious duties, the first fruites of Civility, but were also disabled any way to prouide for the common safety either against forraigne or domesticke invasion, the carefullest charge of Christian charity."[35] Virginia's diffuse settlement pattern made it possible for different religious factions to settle far enough away from each other to avoid daily contact and potential conflict. Puritans in the colony, for example, established settlements on the south side of the James River, an area where the lands were less fertile than in the James River Valley and the tobacco, as a result, of lesser quality. They lived there, as an Anglican minister later put it, "in their place," where they did not bother other colonists and other colonists left them to themselves.[36] At a time when Puritan and Anglican wings of the Church of England were becoming more and more hostile toward each other in the mother country, the amount of space in Virginia afforded an opportunity for both groups to coexist peacefully in the same polity. The people the settlers took the land from also helped to shape Virginia's tolerant ecclesiastical polity. Whatever English settlers may have thought about rival religious factions, they soon realized that they shared far more in common with each other than they did with Native Americans. The Powhatan uprising of 1622, in which approximately three hundred colonists were killed, only underscored the point.[37]

Virginia's "peaceful coexistence" nearly collapsed in the early 1640s. When Governor William Berkeley (1605–1677) arrived in 1642 civil war had already broken out in England. Berkeley, as a royalist, a friend of Charles I, and a staunch Anglican, distrusted Puritans and took his instructions to uphold the Church of England more literally than previous governors. Like his king, Berkeley distrusted the ambiguities of Jacobean religious polity. For a brief period he acted against Virginia's Puritans, forcing them to take an oath of allegiance and banishing three Massachusetts clergymen who had come to the colony to minister to Puritan congregations on the traditionally Puritan south side of the James River. Berkeley's actions marked a shift in the government's attitude toward Puritans. The ministers he expelled, in fact, had come to the colony in response to a letter people in Lower Norfolk County had sent to Boston in the summer of 1642 explicitly requesting three ministers to lead their parishes, even though the county had but one parish at the time. Members of the colony's General Assembly apparently knew of the plan, for they divided Upper Norfolk County into three parishes during their 1642/43 session. Faced with overt and unexpected hostility from the colony's new governor, some Virginia Puritans fled to Maryland. Berkeley changed his course, however, following a year-long trip to England in 1644 and 1645 during which he fought alongside Charles I against Parliament's armies. Perhaps he realized that religious persecution had no place in a strong polity; perhaps he came to accept the colony's decades-old practice of practical toleration. Certainly, Berkeley retained his hatred of Puritans throughout his life, but following his return to Virginia he avoided persecuting religious minorities for the remainder of his terms as governor.[38] Anthony Langston probably characterized the Virginia of the 1650s accurately when he described the colony as a place where men could "take up Land (untaken before) and there seat, build, clear, and plant without any manner of restraint from the Government in relation to their Religion, and god's Service."[39] In addition, commissioners of the Commonwealth (all familiar with Virginia) sent by Parliament to subdue the colony disregarded their instructions and allowed Anglican Virginians to continue using the *Book of Common Prayer* throughout Parliament's reign.[40]

Langston's Edenic description of Virginia's moderate ecclesiastical polity and the commissioners' indulgence of Anglicans highlight the significant degree of religious toleration Virginians enjoyed by midcentury, but there were nonetheless some serious problems in the colony's religious life, particularly the inability of the established Church of England to provide adequate pastoral care for Virginia's settlers. Three factors contributed to the crisis: the colonists' settlement pattern, the shortage of clergy, and the Church of England's failure to establish ecclesiastical leadership in the New World. Although the way Virginians accommodated their settlement patterns in order to plant as much of their staple crop as possible had helped to create a context in which the "peaceful coexistence" of different religious groups could take root, the colonists' manner of planting their settlements also contributed to the colony's crisis in pastoral care. The widely scattered settlements vexed immigrant clergymen. The colonists' scattered manner of settling hindered the public practice of religion since it meant that most people lived a significant distance from the local parish church. Virginians lived like "*Hermites* . . . dispersedly and scatteringly seated upon the sides of Rivers," the Reverend Roger Greene complained, "as might make their due and constant attendance upon the publick worship and Service of God impossible to them."[41] The Reverend Alexander Forbes, minister of Isle of Wight Parish in the 1720s, echoed Greene's criticism: "the distance of the way may hinder many at sometimes who cannot be prepared to come X. XII. or XV miles [to church], tho' they might and would if they had but V. or VI."[42]

Parishes in Virginia were very large, and in most cases the parish's central or "mother" church was situated so far away from many of the inhabitants that they could not reasonably travel to and from church each Sabbath day. In order to take the church to the people, most parishes constructed smaller church buildings, or chapels of ease, at convenient spots in outlying areas, thus making it easier for many parishioners to attend church regularly. Still, this did not suit everyone. On one occasion in the 1730s some residents of Spotsylvania County showed the high regard they held for traveling shorter rather than longer distances to church in a perverse way. Angry that an additional church building had been constructed in another area of the parish instead of in their neighborhood, they set fire to the new edifice, successfully damaging the structure enough to render it useless.[43]

Colonial parsons served their churches and chapels of ease on a rotating basis, officiating and preaching first at one church and then at the others in their turn on successive Sundays. In many areas of the colony, especially during the eighteenth century, this arrangement meant that many Virginians did not come into contact with the local minister more than once every three or four weeks. In the minister's absence vestries hired clerks to read prayers and a sermon from either the *Book of Homilies* or the published works of an English divine.[44] Nonetheless, the surviving evidence suggests that Virginians frequently did not attend church if the weather was bad or if the parish minister was not preaching that day. "Extremities of heat in Summer, frost and Snow in Winter, and tempestuous weather in both," as Roger Greene put it, often prevented settlers from traveling to church, as did "Rivers & Streams rendered impassable with much rain." The law, in fact, only required church attendance once every four weeks. Church attendance in eighteenth-century Virginia probably hovered at just over 50 percent.[45]

Mediocre church attendance, however, did not necessarily indicate a lack of desire for traditional religious patterns. Colonists wanted their children baptized, and when a minister came into their area they were happy to go and hear him preach. Writing in 1729 about the group of surveyors who ran the line dividing Virginia and North Carolina, Lieutenant Governor William Gooch (1681–1751) indicated how much people in that remote territory wanted the presence of the church when he described the work of the group's chaplain, Peter Fontaine (1691–1757): "he Christened above an hundred Children, a great many adult Persons, and preached to Congregations who have never had publick Worship since their first Settlement in those Parts."[46]

Conscientious ministers worried about the impact that the colony's accommodation to tobacco culture had both on the religious life of the laity and on their own abilities to serve their parishioners adequately. Roger

Greene grew anxious about colonial laypeople whom he described as "grow[ing] wilde in that Wildernesse" untended by a gardener, or in this case a minister. Their refusal to settle in towns meant that settlers endured the want "of Christian Neighborliness, of brotherly admonition, of holy Examples of religious Persons, of the Comfort of theirs, and the Ministers Administrations in Sicknesse, and Distresses, of the benefit of Christian Civil Conference and Commerce." Writing nearly a century after Greene, the Reverend James Maury (1718–1769) gave some indication of the toll a large parish could take on a dedicated clergyman: "[M]ine is the most extensive & inconvenient Parish in the Colony; that is regularly served. In it are three Churches & a Chappel, and Each of which equal Attendance is given. The Distances between these & the Glebe are 7, 12, 16 & 24 Miles; which, besides many long Rides to baptize & marry & bury, together with several others to Court & Warehouse on my own private Business, you'll find, upon a little Reflection, afford such an abundant Employment, that Intervals of Leisure & Repose are as short, as they are rare; which must unavoidably be still further diminished & curtailed by the necessary cares of a Family of no less than 8 children."[47]

A shortage of clergy also contributed to the Church of England's problems in Virginia. As early as 1611 the Reverend Alexander Whitaker (1575–1617) expressed a concern that would linger for over a century: "Our harvest [of souls] is froward and great for want" of ministers. Seventy-five years later William Fitzhugh, an attorney and tobacco planter from Stafford County, made a similar charge, writing that what "bears the greatest weight with me . . . is the want of spirituall help & comforts, of which this fertile Country, in every thing else, is barren and unfruitful."[48] Statistics tell a grim tale. In 1616, four ministers served the colony's 350 settlers. By 1661, nearly 25,000 people lived in the colony; perhaps ten or twelve were clergymen. Three-and-a-half decades later in 1697, only twenty-two of Virginia's approximately fifty parishes had ministers—and that for a population approaching 60,000 souls.[49] Writing in 1653, Governor Richard Bennett (ca. 1609–1675) gave voice to the regrets of many devout Virginians: "the greatest want that Virginia hath is in the power[,] purity[,] & spirituality of its Ministry of the word, for want whereof we know not God, we Live as without God in the world."[50]

Although Virginia's crisis in pastoral care predated the dissolution of the Virginia Company of London in 1624, the problem grew worse thereafter. The Company had worked hard to fill colonial cures. They recruited clergy and required each candidate for missionary work in Virginia to preach a sample sermon before the Company membership, who then assessed the minister's worthiness. Between 1607 and 1624, they sent twenty-two ministers to the colony. The Company's efforts contrast sharply with the actions of Charles I's Privy Council a few years later. Governor John Harvey (d. 1646) repeatedly forwarded to the Council requests for "grave and conformable" ministers, suggesting in 1629 that paying for the transportation of clergy traveling to Virginia might encourage more ministers to attempt the journey. The Privy Council did not return a sympathetic response: "such voluntary ministers may go over as will transport themselves at their own charge."[51] Colonial pleas for a greater ecclesiastical presence in Virginia fell on English ears more interested in hearing of the size of the next tobacco harvest than of the spiritual state of the men and women who spread the English empire into North America.

Virginia's Church of England also suffered from an absence of ecclesiastical leadership. No bishop resided in North America during the colonial period, nor did one ever make an episcopal visitation of the colonies. Lack of a resident bishop thus disrupted Anglican religious life. Clergy went without the traditional measure of supervision, guidance, and advocacy. And since only a bishop could ordain men to the deaconate or to the priesthood, colonial men who wanted to pursue a career in the church had to travel to England for holy orders. Failure of the Church of England to settle a bishop in North America had an impact on the laity as well. Children could not be confirmed and, therefore, technically could not receive the sacrament of Holy Communion, although most colonial ministers overlooked the requirement and admitted unconfirmed people to the Lord's Supper anyhow, a practice in keeping with a caveat in the 1662 *Book of Common Prayer* that made confirmation unnecessary as a condition for receiving the sacrament in some cases: "And there shall none be admitted to the holy Communion, until such time as he be confirmed, or be ready and desirous to be confirmed." Before the early 1800s, according to one authority on Christian initiation in the Anglican tradition, "confirmation was more often ignored than observed."[52] Consecrating church buildings was also an episcopal function, and although some Virginia ministers agreed to perform this duty, the practice went beyond the bounds set by canon law. Not until the mid-1680s when Henry Compton (1632–1713), the bishop of London, sent the Reverend John Clayton (1657–1725) to the colony as his commissary or representative did a member of the church hierarchy reside in North America. In fact, most previous bishops of London, to whom jurisdiction of the colonial church had fallen by tradition since a previous bishop of London had been a member of the Virginia Company of London, had paid little attention to the colonial portion of their episcopal charge, hoping that the next incumbent of the see would take on the responsibility. Even commissaries found that their powers were limited, first by Virginia's tradition of lay authority over the Church, and second by the lack of power invested in the office. Commissaries, for instance, could neither confirm nor ordain, and the shortage of clergy made it difficult for them to discipline the occasional wayward minister.[53]

Proposals to settle a bishop in Virginia or one of the other English colonies met with no success. At least five times between the dissolution of the Virginia Company in 1624 and Clayton's appointment as commissary, various people put forward plans to send a bishop to the colonies. Conflict over religion and taxation between the Crown and a Puritan-dominated Parliament unwilling to expand royal authority doomed plans advanced in 1634, 1636, and 1638. Efforts to establish a bishopric in Virginia in the early 1660s following the Restoration of King Charles II (1630–1685) ran afoul of the colonists's growing sense of their own identity and their own interests. By the 1660s Virginians had not only established their own form of ecclesiastical organization but also begun to resent imperial authority, and even Anglican settlers were reluctant to introduce further avenues of English power into the colony. In 1672 Charles II introduced yet a fifth attempt to transplant traditional English ecclesiastical authority to the colony when he nominated the incumbent of Ware Parish in Gloucester County, the Reverend Alexander Moray, a Scottish clergyman who had fought alongside the king at the Battle of Worcester in 1650, to become bishop of a proposed diocese in Virginia. Charles, however, never signed the charter establishing the overseas diocese, so no bishop ever filled the see. When he became bishop of London following Compton's death in 1713, Edmund Gibson thought of appointing a suffragan bishop[54] for America, apparently convinced that the existence of the commissary system would make it easy to sneak a suffragan past colonists already zealous of their own perceived rights: "They having been already used to a Commissary, A Bishop will come in upon them more insensibly." Leaders of the Society for the Propagation of Christian Knowledge suspected that Gibson wanted Virginia's own Commissary James Blair to fill the post: "His L[or]d[shi]p seems fully convinced of the Expediency of having Suffragan B[isho]ps on your Side of the Water, and if Mr. Blair were on this Side now, I believe he would not return without such a Character if he would accept it." At any rate, the plan came to nothing. Thomas Sherlock (1678–1761), bishop of London, raised the issue of a North American episcopate again in the 1740s in an effort to rid himself of what he considered a vexatious, costly, and paperwork-producing portion of his episcopal charge. Nonconformists in New England, however, roared their opposition, fearful that they would be forced by a bishop to conform to the Church of England. The episcopacy question lingered on without resolution into the 1770s when it became increasingly drawn into the crisis leading up to the American

Revolution. By then even some Anglican clergy, including a few from Virginia, opposed introducing a bishop into North America. In fact, "resistance to an American episcopate was greatest" in the Chesapeake.[55]

English neglect of the colonists' religious lives forced settlers to take responsibility for the day-to-day operations of the Church of England in Virginia, in the process lending an American form to the English institution. Lacking centers of theological education, ecclesiastical courts, bishops, and the other institutional structures that supported the Church in the mother country, colonial laypeople had no choice but to take a greater role in church affairs than did lay people back in England. The laity, in fact, governed Virginia's established church, a practice church historian John Woolverton has described as "laicization."[56]

Although historians have often blamed the extent of laicization in Virginia for weakening the colony's established Church of England, this process can be interpreted in another way. Most lay Virginians wanted the Church of England in their lives. They wanted the spiritual presence it brought, and they wanted it as one of the traditional units of local government that oversaw important civic responsibilities. When the English Church hierarchy and the Lords of the Privy Council neglected the colonists' spiritual welfare, Virginians did not flee the established church. Instead, lay Virginians took steps to recruit clergy for the colony. Some people, like Richard Bennett, wrote to friends in England to ask for help in securing ministers.[57] The General Assembly went further and offered financial incentives to clergymen willing to serve in Virginia. In 1656 the Assembly granted colonial ministers tax breaks in the form of exemptions from "publique levies" for themselves and up to six servants. Burgesses also agreed to award any settler who successfully recruited a minister for the colony a bounty of £20 in addition to a reimbursement of the clergyman's transportation costs. County justices likewise used the power of their offices to urge colonists traveling abroad to recruit ministers. When the Lower Norfolk County Court, for example, learned in 1655 that Captain Thomas Willoughby planned to sail for England, they asked him to help "p[ro]vide a Minister of God's word for us."[58] Vestries in the mid-seventeenth century sometimes offered ministers generous contracts if they would serve their parishes. In 1652, for instance, the Reverend Alexander Cooke's agreement with the people of Lancaster County allowed him "double tythes confirmed to me for the first year."[59] And in a decision born out of desperation, Governor William Berkeley took it upon himself to ordain deacons for Virginia parishes, an action with no standing in canon law.[60]

These efforts did not always work out for the best. While Joan Gundersen has argued convincingly that the vast majority of eighteenth-century Anglican clergymen were beyond reproach, the same cannot be said of some of their seventeenth-century brethren.[61] Ministers who served the colony between the dissolution of the Virginia Company in 1624 and Henry Compton's appointment as bishop of London in 1675 were a mixed bag. Men such as Morgan Godwyn, Roger Greene, John Hammond, and Lionel Gatford brought credit to the established church. Others did not. Writing in 1656, John Hammond portrayed Virginia's ministers as men who "could babble in the Pulpet, roare in a Tavern, exact from their Parishioners, and rather by their dissoluteness destroy then [sic] feed their Flocks."[62] Other anecdotal evidence suggests that his claims have merit.[63] Nor did Governor Berkeley's decision to ordain deacons redound to the church's credit in the long run. These noncanonical deacons were probably among the men holding irregular orders whose removal from office Bishop Compton demanded in the late 1670s. Nonetheless, the efforts of laypeople to find ministers for Virginia parishes reveal on the part of the colonial laity a desire to have the Church of England as a presence in their lives that the English Church and Crown did not provide in the seventeenth century.

Lay control of the Church functioned on two levels. The General Assembly of Virginia made laws governing the Church, and local vestries oversaw the operation of individual parishes. The General Assembly set ministers' salaries, defined parish boundaries, established new parishes as the colony expanded, set minimum requirements for church attendance, defined activities legal on Sundays, and delegated local authority over church matters to vestries and county courts.[64] The Assembly's powers could be immense. In 1623/24 it passed laws modifying the traditional liturgical calendar of the Church of England, instructing colonists that when two holy days fell together during tobacco season, "betwixt the feast of the annuntiation of the blessed virgin [25 March] and St. Michael the archangell [29 September], then only the first to be observed."[65] English history, however, offered precedent for the Virginia statute. During August 1536 Thomas Cromwell, Henry VIII's "Viceregent in spirituals," had announced an act abolishing all but four holy days between early July and late September on the grounds that stopping work to celebrate the numerous holy days damaged the economy.[66] In 1631/32, the burgesses formalized the process of choosing churchwardens and outlined their duties, which included presenting to the authorities "all adulterers or fornicators, such as shall abuse their neighbors by slanderinge, tale carryinge or backbitinge, or that shall not behave themselves orderlie and soberlie in the churche duringe devine service." Swearers, drunkards, and profaners of the Sabbath could also expect to find themselves on the court docket. The burgesses prescribed the duties of clergy as well, taking on part of the role of an English diocesan bishop. They directed ministers to preach at least one sermon each week, to celebrate the Eucharist three times a year, to catechize children in their parishes, and not to "give themselves to excesse of drinkinge or ryott, spending theire time idelie by day or by night playinge at dice, cards, or other unlawful game."[67]

As in the mother country, local governance of the Church of England fell to groups known as vestries. The Assembly had established a vestry system in Virginia by 1636, although a semblance of the later system can be seen as early as 1611. Colonial vestry members were "always white, always male, and usually wealthy."[68] A statute of 1662 fixed their number at twelve.[69] Like their English counterparts out of which they evolved, Virginia vestries functioned as a unit of local government. Historian John Nelson, in fact, has perceptively described local government in colonial Virginia as "parish-county," noting that we should think of the parish and the county as "linked institutions sharing, dividing up, and intermingling their interests and responsibilities." Rarely larger than a county and usually much smaller (many counties contained at least two parishes), the parish and its vestry leaders formed the layer of government closest to the people. Vestrymen presented moral offenders to the proper authorities (which in Virginia meant to county rather than ecclesiastical courts), cared for the poor, provided for bastard and orphaned children, processioned lands, hired ministers, and maintained church buildings and lands. Vestries in colonial Virginia also acted as the colony's chief providers of social welfare. Thus, when vestries met to lay the annual parish levy, "the largest tax paid" by most colonists, they included not only the minister's salary but also funds spent on poor widows, orphans, and individuals who could not care for themselves. In 1760, for example, the vestry of St. Paul's Parish in Hanover County ordered the following payment: "That William Hughes keep John Fox the Ensuing year for 1,200 pounds of Tobacco." The fact that Virginia's established Church of England provided the colony's main form of social welfare for the poor offered the most important justification for imposing the parish levy on dissenters. Nor were these distributions on behalf of the poor merely token payments. In 1760, St. Paul's, Hanover County, spent over half its budget on relief of orphaned children, bastards, and the poor. Outlays of 25 percent to 33 percent may have been more typical, although that still represented a substantial portion of any parish's budget.[70]

As part of the "parish-county" government, vestries engaged in a number of other civil responsibilities as well. They maintained roads and often provided ferry service over the colony's many rivers, although by the 1730s these functions had been largely taken over by the county courts. Vestries in the

1720s also appointed people to serve as "tobacco viewers," a task that over-production of tobacco and the resulting low price of this staple made necessary. "Tobacco viewers" inspected planters' crops to ensure that no one planted more tobacco than the law prescribed. While tedious, the work was not necessarily as difficult as it may seem. "Viewers" usually counted just the plants in four rows of a man's fields, divided that total by four in order to find an average number of plants per row, then multiplied the average number and the total number of tobacco rows to arrive at the grand total.[71] One of the vestries' most important civil functions was processioning or "going round" every four years "the bounds of every person's land" in the parish and renewing the landmarks separating one man's property from his neighbor's. Bounds processioned three times without complaint gained legal status as the formal boundaries of an individual's property.[72]

Circumstances allowed Virginia vestries to assume powers unknown to their English and colonial counterparts. The greatest power granted vestries was the right to "elect and make choyce of their ministers," a practice confirmed by the General Assembly in 1643.[73] While the practice is commonplace in contemporary Episcopal parishes, early modern English custom recognized no such lay authority over the clergy. Rather, the parish patron typically nominated a minister as rector, and the diocesan bishop then inducted the clergyman into his cure. Inducted ministers enjoyed the equivalent of tenure and could only be removed if they committed serious moral offenses. Colonial practice nullified this tradition. Not only were Virginia vestries reluctant to present ministers to the governor for induction (the absence of a bishop forcing the governor to take on this episcopal function), but they also retained the right to "hire [ministers] from yeare to yeare," allowing their clergy salary and use of the glebe for a set term only. Colonial vestries gained additional powers in 1658 when the burgesses passed a statute directing that "all matters concerning the vestrey, their aggreements with their ministers, touching the church-wardens, the poore and other things concerninge the parishes or parishoners respectively be referred to their owne ordering and disposeing from time to time as they shall think fitt."[74]

The other local institution with authority over religious matters in colonial Virginia was the county court. In Virginia, these tribunals held jurisdiction over offenses that English ecclesiastical courts tried and prescribed penalties for. Throughout the colonial period, county courts tried individuals presented by local grand juries for a variety of activities that violated Virginia's behavioral norms: failing to attend church, swearing, drunkenness, and adultery, among other offenses. Some people found themselves in court for working on the "Lord's Day" or for profaning the Sabbath in some other way. Grand jurors in Northampton County presented several men in 1751 for "fiddling, dancing & fireing Guns" on a Sunday, while Avury Naylor of Richmond County was presented for "hanging Tobacco on the Sabbath Day." Punishments ranged from fines and doing penance in church during public worship to whippings or, in the cases of gossip and slander during the early seventeenth century, a trip to the ducking stool. Throughout the 1650s justices in the colony often prescribed some form of penance for moral offenses in addition to a fine or whipping. Found guilty of fornication in 1626, Jane Hill was ordered to stand up in James City Parish while wearing a white sheet, one of the traditional penalties for sexual sins. Duckings, asking forgiveness during divine service on the Sabbath in front of the congregation, and similar punishments were all forms of penance, proceedings designed not so much for retribution as "for the soul's health," to reform sinners and to put them back in right relationship with God and their neighbors.[75] After 1660, however, penance appears far less frequently in the county records, and civil punishments became the rule. Another type of penance involved what people today would call "public service." In 1648, for example, the York County Court convicted Oliver Segar, a laborer, for "profaneing the sabath Day by going a fishing." For his failure to attend church the justices ordered Segar to pay a fine of 150 pounds of tobacco and to build a "sufficient bridge" over a nearby swamp, it, in the justices' words, "being the Church way."[76] Offenses that did not directly threaten the social fabric, such as drunkenness, common swearing, and failing to attend church, usually resulted in fines. Virginia's court system and churchwardens routinely treated adultery, fornication, and slander—since these offenses held the greatest potential for disrupting the community or, in the case of bastard bearing, forced members of the parish to pay additional taxes to support the child—as the most serious offenses.[77] Virginia's county courts also had responsibility for probating wills, another power maintained by English church courts.[78]

Lay authority over the Church of England in Virginia was not entirely unwarranted. Ministers came and went in seventeenth-century Virginia with astonishing frequency. The parish in Lancaster County that hired the Reverend Alexander Cooke in 1652 for "double tythes . . . for the first year" provides a good example. After taking charge of the parish there, the Reverend Cooke soon died or departed. A successor died in 1656. Yet a third minister arrived in 1657 but died two years later.[79] Some ministers died; some ministers (like Lionel Gatford and Roger Greene) did not like Virginia and left as soon as possible; and some ministers, not of the best quality, were asked to vacate their cures. All in all, vestries offered the Church of England in Virginia one source of continuity in an otherwise unstable institution. Vigilant vestrymen also defended their parishes against the occasional incompetent or immoral clergyman. By the time the English ecclesiastical hierarchy began to take an interest in Virginia's Church of England during the 1680s, colonial vestries, supported by decades of custom, were reluctant to give up their powers.[80]

Lay control of the Church, however, vexed immigrant ministers and many found it downright oppressive. In spiritual matters such as making priests and defining theology, Virginia churchmen conceded the traditional authority of the church hierarchy, but in matters of church government Virginians believed local custom should hold sway and claimed the right to determine colonial church polity, a right, by the way, that had originally been thrust upon the colonists when the English Church and Crown refused to take an interest in the colonial church back in the 1620s. Clergy familiar with English precedent balked at colonial innovations they deemed illegitimate. The Reverend Morgan Godwyn (1641–1690?), a royalist graduate of Oxford who came to Virginia in 1666, was the most articulate seventeenth-century defender of traditional clergy rights against lay authorities. He decried the onerous power of vestries, damning them as "Plebian Juntos" and "hungry Patrons." Vestries that chose to hire lay readers, whom he called "leaden lay-Priests of the vestries ordination," at salaries far lower than it would have cost to hire ministers, Godwyn accused of an uncharitable frugality that damaged religion even as it kept more of parishioners' tobacco crops in their own hands. Disillusionment turned into bitterness when he suggested to Virginians who had supported Charles I against the Puritans that the Church of England had suffered less at the hands of Oliver Cromwell than at the hands of Virginia's vestries: "our Discouragements there [Virginia] are much greater, than ever they were here in England, under the Usurpers." Not surprisingly, Godwyn's tenure in the colony was rocky—three parishes in four years. The Reverend James Wallace of Elizabeth City Parish expressed another of the clergy's fears about vestry powers when he complained that "Clergy-men here have 12 Lay patrons (Vestrymen) whom we must humour or run the risque of Deprivation." Some ministers, such as the Reverend John Monro of King and Queen Parish, found themselves shut out of their churches by their vestries following disputes over contracts. The Sunday after a meeting during which Monro's vestry had turned down his request to be inducted into his cure, he showed up to preach and read divine service only to find the church locked and a confused congregation milling around outside. When queried by the governor's Council about the incident, the vestrymen explained that they believed Monro had vacated the parish and that they had only locked the church doors in order to keep cows from wandering in and defiling the altar. While most conflicts between parsons and lay people involved vestries, salaries, and the contentious issue of induction, a few cases involved other members of the laity. In one extreme case a parishioner who opposed the parish levy assaulted James Wallace before various onlookers in open court.[81]

The struggle was not one simply between Virginians and the Church of England over authority. It symbolized instead the birth of a new institutional structure with a new understanding of authority. The result was a new form of outward identity for the Church of England in which vestries shared control of the church with bishops 3,000 miles away. By the 1680s Virginia's established church was English in theology and colonial in form.[82]

⌇

English concern for Virginia's established church increased in 1675 as a result of Henry Compton's appointment as bishop of London. Unlike previous incumbents of the see, Compton intended to take an active interest in the Church of England abroad. He explained his intentions in a letter to an unnamed correspondent: "As the care of your churches, with the rest of the plantations [colonies], lies upon me as your diocesan, so to discharge that trust, I shall omit no occasions of promoting their good and interest."[83] His investigation of conditions in the colonial church uncovered numerous abuses in need of correction: vestries sometimes intentionally left parishes vacant in order to save money; some persons serving Anglican parishes in both Virginia and Barbados "exercised the Ministeriall function w[i]thout [holy] orders" from an English bishop;[84] many wealthy Virginians continued the "profane Custome of burying in their gardens [or] orchards" rather than in the churchyard; and ministers endured both low pay and, in defiance of the colony's laws, uncertain tenure in their cures.[85]

More so than any previous bishop of London since the demise of the Virginia Company in 1624, Compton worked to remedy the deficiencies under which the colonial Church of England labored. He acted first to increase the number and quality of clergy serving the colonies.[86] He not only found good men to serve colonial parishes, but also, in the case of Virginia, attempted to act against disreputable ministers whose immoral lives had tarnished the Church's reputation. In 1677 Compton instructed Lieutenant Governor Herbert Jeffreys (d. 1678) to inquire into the "lives, licence, abilities, and qualifications" of Virginia's clergy and to suspend or remove all "scandalous, unworthy Ministers."[87] Three years later Compton consolidated the authority to approve ministers for colonial parishes in his own hands when he instructed all colonial governors to allow no minister to serve a parish "without a Certificate from the Lord Bp. of London" affirming the man's orthodoxy and good moral character.[88] In addition, at

Compton's insistence Charles II established a fund which granted each minister who filled a colonial cure a payment of £20 to help defray the costs of traveling from England to North America. This so-called Royal Bounty helped hundreds of ministers make their way to parishes in the colonies.[89]

Shortly after the accession to the throne of James II (1633–1701) in 1685, Compton also gained permission to appoint commissaries, or representatives, for each of the colonies, thus making it possible for the first time to introduce formal ecclesiastical authority into the Church of England in the North American colonies. Virginia's first commissary, John Clayton, remained in the colony for only a brief period and therefore had little impact upon the Church there. His successor, James Blair, however, led Virginia's Church of England from his appointment in 1689 until his death in 1743 and exerted tremendous influence over the church establishment.[90]

Blair had originally come to Virginia in 1685 when Bishop Compton offered the young man an opportunity to revive his career as a minister by becoming a missionary at Varina Parish (south of present-day Richmond) in Virginia's Henrico County on what was then the colonial frontier. This was quite a turn of events for a thirty-year-old man whose chosen career had seemed to hold few opportunities for him just a few months earlier.[91]

Born in 1655 in Banffshire in Scotland, Blair followed his father into the ministry. In 1669 he entered the University of Edinburgh, where he was graduated four years later. Blair completed his theological studies there in 1679, passed the presbytery's examination, and was ordained into the ministry of the Church of Scotland. Within months he took charge of his first parish, Cranston, about ten miles outside of Edinburgh. Two years later Blair was deprived of his living for refusing to swear a test oath that would have made the Roman Catholic James II head of the Scottish Church upon his accession to the English throne. Blair left Scotland and moved to London, where another Scottish clergyman who had lost his appointment, the Reverend Gilbert Burnet (1643–1715), then chaplain of the Rolls—a chapel on the grounds of the Public Records Office—found him work as a scribe recording legal records. There he remained until Bishop Compton offered him a post in North America.[92]

James Blair made the best of his assignment in Virginia. In addition to serving the Church of England, he began to purchase land. He married into the colony's political and economic elite when he took Benjamin Harrison's daughter Sarah as his bride. He was appointed the bishop of London's commissary, or representative, in 1689. He wrangled himself the presidency of the College of William and Mary. He served on the governor's Council, was the rector of James City Parish, and later served as the rector of Bruton Parish in Virginia's capital city, Williamsburg.

Blair was an ambitious man, and his appointment to the commissariat proved fortuitous since the doors of opportunity in England and Scotland had been shut. A Scot, his native country was no place to seek riches, and anti-Scots prejudice in England limited opportunities for preferment there. If Blair hoped to achieve wealth, position, or fame, then Virginia offered him the best shot.

Blair played a leading role in founding the College of William and Mary, an institution intended in part to educate colonial men for colonial cures. In 1697 optimistic trustees wrote to Thomas Tension, the Archbishop of Canterbury: "wee have . . . all reason to believe it will prove the Seminary of the Church of England in this part of the world." Postulants, however, still had to travel across the Atlantic Ocean to seek ordination from an English bishop, usually the bishop of London.[93]

Many of the commissary's other efforts proved less successful. Proposals to introduce ecclesiastical courts for both clergy and laity as well as a plan to supervise Virginia's ministers more closely met with great resistance from all concerned. The House of Burgesses allowed these proposals to die quietly without coming to a final vote. Nor could the colony's vestries be convinced to budge on the issue of induction. Blair himself eventually took their side in the matter against his clergy and was never formally inducted at Bruton Parish, where he served for thirty-three years. On the other hand, he did manage to convince the General Assembly to raise ministers' salaries to 16,000 pounds of tobacco per year and to pass an act requiring all parishes to "purchase and lay out a tract of land for the glebe . . . [a]nd likewise to build and erect a convenient dwelling house for the reception and aboad of the minister of such parish." A statute of 1727 ordered parishes to increase their glebe lands to no less than 200 acres.[94]

Despite these modest successes, the General Assembly's compensation for the clergy fell far below what Blair had hoped for. Possessed of a keen eye for the pound sterling and its equivalent in tobacco, the commissary had wanted a minimum salary for his clergy of 16,000 pounds of tobacco. In parishes with more than 400 tithables, however, he suggested that the inhabitants pay the same forty pounds of tobacco per tithable as in smaller parishes, thus allowing ministers in more populous parishes to earn greater wages. In a move that revealed his financial acumen more than his pastoral regard for clergymen serving large parishes, Blair suggested merging small parishes so that the population of the new larger parish "would be great enough to give Sufficient encouragement to a Minister."[95] Burgesses, however, refused to amend the law providing for the clergy's support, noting that 16,000 pounds of tobacco, which was supposed to approximate £80, surpassed "most of their own circumstances and of the Country in Generall."[96]

Contention marked Blair's commissariat. For the most part, the clergy disliked him. English ministers disliked him because they thought he was trying to pack the College and the Church with Scotsmen whom they considered "so basely educated . . . that their lives and conversation are [more likely] to make heathens than Christians." Ministers in general disliked him because they thought he was power hungry and prone to self-aggrandizement. Wrote one: "the said Commissary has cast an odium upon himself by his great worldly concerns."[97] Nor did he find it easy to get along with the colony's governors. Three times he traveled to England to seek the recall of governors who threatened his, the College's, the Church's, or the colony's interests. Three times the governor Blair opposed lost his position. Lieutenant Governor Alexander Spotswood (1676–1740), who lost his own battle with Blair, referred to the commissary as "the constant Instrument of Faction against all former Governors."[98] Perhaps the most charitable thing that can be said of Blair is that he guarded his own interests zealously.

Although he has been judged harshly by most historians, James Blair, along with Henry Compton and Edmund Gibson, helped bring about an "Anglican Renaissance" in Virginia between 1680 and 1720. Both the quality and number of ministers in the colony improved. By 1703, ministers filled 80 percent of Virginia's parishes and only a series of clergy deaths coupled with the establishment of several new parishes in 1724 slowed the steady progress. Vacancies, of course, occurred throughout the remainder of the colonial period, but these were the result of "normal attrition" and the expansion of the church into new territories rather than the debilitating shortages of the seventeenth century. With the General Assembly, Blair spread the Church of England into all the new counties established in Virginia between 1690 and 1740. By the 1730s the College of William and Mary, now safely through a series of crises that had threatened its existence earlier in the century, began to graduate candidates for holy orders who wanted to serve Virginia parishes. After 1730, even as the colony grew, the crisis in pastoral care abated as Blair and the commissaries who succeeded him found an adequate supply of good clergymen for the colony's vacant cures. In short, both the presence and the strength of Virginia's Church of England expanded in the years before 1775. Only when the American Revolution broke out and parishioners turned on loyalist clergy and the bishop of London, Richard Terrick, refused to ordain rebels, did the established Anglican Church face a crisis that weakened it substantially.[99]

⌒

The ambiguous elements in the religious life of colonial Virginia extended beyond an established church possessed of a pastoral crisis and controlled by laypeople. Although the Anglican establishment held legal advantages that gave it a privileged position, the establishment often showed dissenters a significant degree of "practical toleration." Many dissenters, however, resented the Church of England's privileges, and they seldom forgot that the same power that set aside the statute book and let them practice their religion could in theory and with the backing of the state become coercive. Anglicans, on the other hand, resented it when some dissenters criticized the Church of England, attempted to establish additional meetinghouses, or refused to comply with what members of the establishment considered mild laws regarding licenses or the payment of parish levies that helped to support not only the clergy but the poor as well. When these things happened Anglicans saw ingratitude, a failing many people in seventeenth- and eighteenth-century Virginia counted among the gravest of sins.

Small but vocal groups of dissenters disaffected with the Church of England lived in the colony from the 1650s on. Quakers, Presbyterians, Moravians, Methodists, and Baptists all contributed to the religious life of Virginia prior to the American Revolution. Although the General Assembly attempted to limit dissent as much as possible, the burgesses usually recognized the value of practical toleration and thus tried to make some accommodations for Christians outside the established church.

The first major movement of religious dissent in Virginia took place in the 1650s when Quaker missionaries arrived in the colony.[100] Members of the Society of Friends, or Quakers, so-called because of the spiritual "trembling" they often experienced during religious meetings, emphasized a quiet meditative faith based on the existence within each individual of what Quakers termed the "Inner Light." They rejected religious establishments and saw no need for ministers to act as spiritual intermediaries or superiors for the laity. Likewise, they required neither formal religious spaces nor formal religious rituals. Given the shortage of clergy in seventeenth-century Virginia, Quakers offered a viable pastoral alternative to the Church of England. Their simple faith and direct appeal to God won converts in the colony among slaves, elites, servants, and middle-class farmers alike.[101]

Yet Quakerism was more than a religious movement. Most Americans today probably associate Quakers with pacifism or Friends schools known for tolerance and solid academic programs. In the 1650s, however, Quakerism carried with it a not-unjustified reputation for radicalism and violence. Early English adherents of the sect included agrarian radicals, participants in anti-tithe riots, and men and women who had protested manorial rents and dues. Their religious claims could be extreme as well. One woman maintained that George Fox, the movement's founder, had resurrected her from the dead. Another English Quaker, James Nayler, said he was Christ and rode into Bristol on an ass while his female followers threw palms in his path. Quakers sometimes protested the established church by showing up naked at Anglican services. Most English people despised the sect.[102]

Reputation rather than reality shaped the response of Virginia's government to the Quakers' presence. There is no evidence to suggest that Virginia Friends wanted anything more than to worship in peace. Nevertheless, the General Assembly's description of the sect still rings with fear over three hundred and fifty years: an "unreasonable and turbulent sort of people . . . teaching and publishing lies, miracles, false visions, prophecies, and doctrines which have influence upon the communities of men both ecclesiastical and civil[,] endeavouring and attempting thereby to destroy religion, lawes, communities and all bonds of civil societie, leaveing it arbitrarie to everie vaine and vitious person whether men shall be safe." For a brief period during the late 1650s and early 1660s, Virginia's government vigorously persecuted members of the sect. The Quaker practice of meeting in private residences or in the woods raised suspicions about their intentions. They were whipped and fined, if not for their religious beliefs then for their suspected revolutionary activities. The General Assembly in 1663 even expelled a burgess from Lower Norfolk County, John Porter, for his support of the Quakers, and one Quaker missionary died in prison.[103]

This persecution faded, however, by late 1663 or early 1664 after it became clear that Virginia Friends took seriously the so-called peace testimony of 1661 by which Quakers renounced the use of violence. By the 1670s and for the remainder of the colonial period official harassment of Quakers extended little beyond the authorities' insistence that Quakers contribute to the colony's defense and pay their parish levies, since all individuals, no matter their religious persuasion, were taxed to support the established church and the social welfare programs it was charged with overseeing.[104] Even the English Act of Toleration, quietly and belatedly recognized in Virginia in 1699, required dissenters to support the Church of England with their taxes since all Virginians, no matter their faith, were considered parishioners of the established church.[105]

Despite forcing Quakers to pay their parish levies, the General Assembly did make other efforts to accommodate the Friends. By February 1690, for example, nearly a decade before the colony recognized the English Act of Toleration, the governor's Council indicated that Quakers would be allowed to practice their religion as long as they complied with the requirements of that statute.[106] Several years later in 1705, burgesses granted Quakers the right to give evidence in court "by way of solemn affirmation and declaration" instead of by swearing an oath, a practice Friends believed contrary to the Bible's teachings.[107] A few years later, acting Governor Edmund Jennings (1659–1727) and his Council placed patriarchy over religious conformity when they turned down a petition filed by Anne Walker of Kecoughtan (present-day Hampton), who complained that her husband, a Quaker, prevented her and the couple's children from worshipping at the local Church of England parish. They informed Mrs. Walker that Quaker or not, her husband possessed "that authority over his Childr. that properly Belongs to Every Christian man: that is to Bring up his Childr. in whatever Christian Religion he may Be of that is privileged By our Christian Laws."[108] In 1718, Lieutenant Governor Alexander Spotswood repealed a 1663 statute, then rarely enforced, that prohibited Quakers from meeting.[109] And by the late 1730s one minister, Anthony Gavin of St. James Parish in Goochland County, complained of the excessive indulgence shown to the Friends by influential members of the laity: "I strugle with many Difficulties from Quakers who are Countenanced by high Minded Men."[110]

If one considers their numbers alone, then Quakers were not a major presence in colonial Virginia. Writing in 1705 in his *History and Present State of Virginia*, Robert Beverley reported the existence of just "three small meetings of Quakers" in the colony.[111] The Friends' influence, however, was greater than their numbers suggest. They were energetic proselytizers, and they sought to draw converts from the established church not only by taking part in public disputations with Anglican clergy but also by distributing Quaker religious tracts to the colony's many unchurched and underchurched settlers. Quakers also challenged the statutory advantages granted to the colony's established Church of England, especially the compulsory payment of parish levies. Often they simply petitioned county or colonial authorities and asked to be exempted from what they believed was an illegal and unjust tax. Other Quakers engaged in acts of "civil disobedience," refusing to pay either their parish levies or taxes that provided for the colony's defense.[112] Although few Quakers lived in colonial Virginia, they nonetheless stood as witnesses to the hope that one day an ecclesiastical polity might embrace freedom of religion rather than mere religious toleration.

Members of several other denominations came to Virginia between 1680 and 1740. Presbyterians established a few congregations in the colony, most prominently near the Elizabeth River on the South Side in 1683 and in Accomac County on the Eastern Shore in the 1690s, both as a result of the efforts of Francis Makemie (1658–1708), often called the founder of Presbyterianism in America. In 1699 he became the first dissenting minister in Virginia to receive a license to preach under the Act of Toleration. The Pres-

byterians expanded little beyond these initial efforts, however, in part because Virginia's so-called Anglican Renaissance between 1680 and 1720
strengthened the hold of the Church of England over the colony's populace
and in part because Makemie's frequent trips abroad and his early death
robbed the denomination of its most vital leader. In the 1730s Lieutenant
Governor William Gooch encouraged the Scots-Irish in Pennsylvania to settle in Virginia's Shenandoah Valley. They accepted the governor's invitation
and came to the colony in large numbers, frequently establishing Presbyterian congregations soon after their arrival. Gooch assured Presbyterians that
they would be allowed to practice their religion as long as they "conform[ed]
themselves to the rules prescribed by the Act of Toleration, by taking the
oaths enjoined thereby, and registering their places of meeting, and behave
themselves peaceably towards the government." In frontier regions of the
colony, Presbyterians even served on Anglican vestries. Not until the Great
Awakening came to Virginia in the mid-1740s, however, did Presbyterianism
become a significant force in the colony's religious life.[113]

Presbyterian theology reflected the teachings of John Calvin (far more so
than the theology of the Church of England). Their style of worship was simple
and dignified and they stressed the centrality of preaching in their worship services. Like Anglicans—and unlike the later Separate Baptists—Presbyterians
valued an educated clergy. The term Presbyterian refers to a form of church
polity in which presbyters (ministers and representative lay elders) rather than
bishops (the episcopate) govern the church. At the lowest level of church administration, the minister and selected elders presided over each local congregation. Above the individual congregation was the Presbytery, a group comprised of ministers and selected elders from all the congregations in a particular
area. The Synod, a still broader category of Presbyterian church government, included representatives from several Presbyteries. In the colonial period, Virginia
formed part of the Synod of Philadelphia.[114]

Huguenots, Calvinist French Protestants, came to Virginia in significant
numbers for the first time in 1700. They had become a persecuted minority
in France again after 1685 when King Louis XIV revoked the Edict of
Nantes, a 1598 statute that had granted toleration and civil rights to this religious minority. Between 100,000 and 500,000 Huguenots fled their French
homeland between 1685 and 1690, often finding refuge in Switzerland, England, Holland, or Ireland. The leaders of the group of Huguenots who came
to Virginia—Olivier de la Muce, Charles Sailley, and their first parson,
Claude Phillipe de Richebourg—had spent several years trying to gain title
to a tract of land in British North America where they could establish a settlement. Virginia authorities eventually agreed to let the Huguenots found a

colony between Virginia and North Carolina. Yet more than altruism informed Virginia's decision to allow the Huguenots to emigrate. The colony's leaders planned to use the immigrants as a buffer between Indians in the west and the colony's more settled regions. Due to disputes with North Carolina over the border between the two colonies, however, the Virginia government refused to honor the Huguenots' title to the land and the group ended up settling in Manakin Town instead on land abandoned by the Monacan Indians near present-day Richmond. The General Assembly soon created a separate parish for the Huguenots, King William Parish, and exempted the immigrants from all colonial taxes and levies and, because the parish was so small, allowed the Huguenot settlers to pay their minister less than the colony's legal rate. Within a decade the Huguenots at Manakin Town had been assimilated into Virginia's established Anglican Church.[115]

Congregations of German Reformed and Lutherans were established in Virginia for the first time in the 1710s and 1720s when members of both groups immigrated to the colony to work at the iron mines established at Germanna by Lieutenant Governor Alexander Spotswood. Three waves of immigrants came to Germanna. German Reformed groups arrived in 1714; Lutherans comprised the second and third waves in 1717 and 1720. As the groups finished their four-year terms of indenture, they moved to other areas of the colony, the German Reformed to Germantown in what is now Fauquier County and the Lutherans to the eastern ridge of the Blue Ridge Mountains near the fork of the Robinson and Conway Rivers where they established Hebron Congregation. At their new home in Fauquier County the German Reformed group constructed a small village with a church and a school. Their elderly minister, the Reverend Henry Haeger, led worship services for the settlers until his death. Thereafter, unable to attract another ordained minister, the local schoolmaster, Jacob Holtzclaw, led worship services until 1760, when he also died. On a few occasions a pastor from Philadelphia traveled to Germantown to administer communion to the settlers there. By 1732 Germans from Pennsylvania moved into the colony and established settlements in the Ketoctin Valley in what was then Prince William County. This settlement, near the Potomac River on the east side of the Blue Ridge Mountains, sustained two congregations, one Lutheran and one German Reformed. Lutherans settled in the Shenandoah Valley on the west side of the Blue Ridge Mountains in the 1730s and organized congregations near the present-day towns of Luray and Elkton. The Reverend George Samuel Klug, who in 1739 became the first long-term pastor of Hebron Congregation, served the Valley Lutherans as well. He also ministered to English families in the region. In 1752 Lieutenant Governor Robert Dinwiddie (1692–1770) and his council recognized Klug's "services for many years past to the neighbouring English Inhabitants" by granting him a gift of £25. German Reformed settlers organized their first congregations in the Shenandoah Valley near Winchester in the 1740s and 1750s.

Members of a number of smaller German religious groups also came to the colony: Dunkers in 1723, Moravians in the 1740s, and, later, the Mennonites. The Dunkers, now known as the Church of the Brethren, were German Baptists who rejected infant baptism and practiced baptism by full immersion. They attracted many adherents throughout Germany, Switzerland, and Holland in the early 1700s. Persecution between 1719 and 1729, however, forced them to flee to America. Moravians, the spiritual descendants of the Bohemian reformer John Huss (1372–1415), suffered severe persecution in Europe during the fifteenth and sixteenth centuries that scattered their adherents. They remained scattered until their so-called renewal in 1722 under Count Nikolaus Zinzendorf (1700–1760) in Saxony, emerging from the "renewal" possessed of a missionary urgency that took their preachers throughout the world. Moravians established themselves in Pennsylvania and North Carolina and from there sent missionaries into the other colonies. Between 1743 and 1749 Moravian missionaries made numerous trips into Virginia to evangelize the colony's many German settlements. Their itinerant preachers, however, not only raised the government's suspicions but also brought forth complaints from the legally settled Lutheran and German Reformed congregations. In 1747 Lieutenant Governor William Gooch, worried by then about the impact of the Great Awakening on the colony, issued a proclamation prohibiting the Moravians from preaching in Virginia. As a result of their persecution by colonial authorities, Moravian missionaries stopped coming to Virginia by about 1750. With the exception of the Moravians, colonial leaders welcomed German religious groups to Virginia. At various times both Lutheran and German Reformed congregations received exemptions from colonial statutes regulating the payment of parish levies. And when the Reverend Caspar Stoever (1685–1739), who had served Hebron Congregation briefly several years before the arrival of George Klug, returned to Germany in 1734 in an attempt to find another Lutheran minister to work in Virginia's missionary fields, both Lieutenant Governor Gooch and the Reverend Patrick Henry, who would later vigorously oppose the Presbyterians of the Great Awakening, offered him support and letters of recommendation.[116]

The character of religious dissent in Virginia changed in the 1740s when the Great Awakening,[117] a trans-Atlantic movement of revivalism that swept Great Britain and the North American colonies between the mid-1720s and the early 1760s, introduced to the colony religious groups that found the deference shown to the colony's government by Huguenots, Lutherans, and Presbyterians both unjust and stifling to the Gospel. The upheaval in Virginia formed part of a larger movement that began in North America in 1720 when Theodorus Freylinghusen, a Dutch Reformed minister heavily influenced by German pietism, preached a "message of moral reform, personal piety, and mystical union with God" to the Dutch Reformed congregations of New Jersey's Raritan Valley. By 1727 the movement had spread to nearby Presbyterian churches where it came to be associated with the Reverend Gilbert Tennent (1703–1764), a young minister convinced that "religion had become a matter of dead formality" and equally convinced that the best way to revive the life of the spirit was through sermons preached with fervor and enthusiasm. In 1734 the Awakening moved into Massachusetts and Pennsylvania under the influence of Jonathan Edwards (1703–1758), minister of the Congregational Church in Northampton, who began a revival in western Massachusetts's Connecticut River Valley, and Samuel Blair, who preached a revival in Chester County, Pennsylvania.[118]

Personal piety and emotional preaching, often intended to bring about immediate conversion in listeners, marked the Great Awakening. Its leaders mocked as "religious formalism" the practices of the existing Presbyterian, Congregational, Baptist, and Anglican churches. Wherever the movement spread, it brought schism, controversy, and fear. As a result, existing denominations split into those who supported the Awakening and those who opposed it. New Sides (those who supported the Awakening) and Old Sides (those who opposed the new movement) contended for control of the Presbyterian Church; Separate Baptists who supported the movement challenged the orthodoxy of the Regular Baptists; and Separatist Congregational churches developed in New England. An evangelical wing led by George Whitefield (1714–1770) and John Wesley (1703–1791) emerged within the Church of England, although it did not become a separate denomination in North America until 1784.

The religious style of the Awakeners troubled Anglicans who valued order and decorum in their devotional practices. In public as well as in private, the Book of Common Prayer was the single greatest influence shaping the devotional lives of colonial Anglicans; only the Bible surpassed it as the book most commonly appearing in the colonists' libraries. Its liturgy repeated weekly at public worship and read each day privately by many individuals provided a constant source of structure for the spiritual life. Congregations and individual worshippers in private repeated the Apostles' Creed and the Lord's Prayer at each office, and in the lessons appointed for each day the

Bible was read through each year. Anglican liturgy, in fact, echoed the Bible, with many of its prayers crafted from the words of Holy Scripture. Day after day, week after week, the *Book of Common Prayer* gave voice to the same themes in the same words that called the faithful to repentance at every office and offered them the means of grace. By repeating the same words at each office and by using the same words week after week, the set liturgies in the *Book of Common Prayer* were intended to work a gradual transformation in the lives of the faithful.[119] Unlike the evangelicals of the Great Awakening, Anglicans placed little emphasis on conversion and their style of worship reflected this difference. Both as a devotional work and as a service book, the *Book of Common Prayer* aimed less at conversion than at assisting the presumably converted to maintain and deepen their faith. It served as the liturgy for a people thought to be Christian by virtue of their membership in the English commonwealth.[120] William Beveridge, a late seventeenth-century minister and sometime bishop of St. Asaph, explained in his discourse *A Sermon concerning the Excellency and Usefulness of the Common Prayer* the design of prayer book worship to form and order the lives of English Christians. This process, however, occurred slowly, a gradual action rather than a sudden and dramatic change like that experienced by the apostle Paul on the road to Damascus or like the conversion experiences of the evangelicals of the Great Awakening. Because the set prayers worked this transformation through sound rather than through the more immediate agency of sight, necessity demanded the frequent repetition of the same words and phrases.[121] Beveridge, in fact, based his argument on the elusive epistemology of the spoken word:

In order to our being *Edified*, so as to be made better and holier, whensoever we meet together upon a Religious account, it is necessary that the same good and holy Things be always inculcated and pressed upon us after one and the same manner. For we cannot but all find by our own Experience, how difficult it is to fasten any thing that is truly good, either upon our selves or others, and that it is rarely, if ever, effected without frequent Repetitions of it. Whatsoever good things we hear only once, or now and then, though perhaps upon the hearing of them, they may swim for a while in our *Brains*, yet they seldom sink down into our *Hearts*, so as to move and sway the Affections, as it is necessary they should do, in order to our being *Edified* by them. Whereas by a *Set Form of Publick Devotions rightly composed, as* we are continually put in mind of all things necessary for us to know and do, so that it is always done by the same Words and Expressions, which by their constant use will imprint themselves so firmly in our Minds, that . . . they will still occur upon all occasions; which cannot but be very much for our *Christian Edification.*[122]

Hence, divine worship following the rites of the *Book of Common Prayer* was intended to grasp an individual's affections and thereby sway that person toward living a holy life. Not that this reorientation occurred simply by hearing or reading the offices each day or each week. Individuals had to participate willingly in the service. By opening their minds to the words they heard, they allowed the liturgy to bring their affections into a holy frame and temper.[123] Repeatedly using the same set, brief forms encouraged this process and allowed the faithful to "recollect" their prayers or, in Beveridge's words, to "look over our Prayers again, either in a Book, or in our Minds, where they are imprinted."[124] Over time, spoken prayers taken from a set form thus gained the epistemological immediacy of sight.

The awakeners saw things differently, and this revival of religion brought a new form of Presbyterianism to Virginia. The Scots-Irish settlers in the Shenandoah Valley were "strict Presbyterians" or "Old Sides," people who adhered to the traditional Presbyterian teachings about theology and religious practices. They valued order and decorum, and they expected their ministers to be university-educated men who delivered their sermons in a conservative manner. "New Sides," those Presbyterians influenced by the Great Awakening, mocked this preaching style. One critic derided the "droaning Heaviness and serene Stupidity" of Old Side sermons. New Side clergy, on the other hand, preached in a highly emotional style that often reduced their auditors to tears. And although they did not oppose education, the revivalists valued a postulant's personal piety over a classical education. Proof of "the work of sanctifying grace in their hearts" ranked higher with the New Sides than a man's knowledge of Greek or Latin. In contrast to their Old Side counterparts, who usually served as pastor to a single settled congregation and thus preached only from "their" pulpits, New Sides were willing to preach anywhere. They preferred a church, but if the local Anglican or Old Side Presbyterian minister barred them from his pulpit, New Sides would preach the Gospel in a barn, a graveyard, or any other large, vacant field.[125]

In 1743 a group of dissenters in Virginia's Hanover County "adopted" New Side Presbyterianism as their religion. The origins of the Hanover dissenters lay in their disaffection with the local Church of England minister, the Reverend Patrick Henry[126] (d. 1777) of St. Paul's Parish. Although they had no qualms with either the liturgy or the ceremony of the established church, they believed Henry's sermons were "not savouring of experimental piety, nor suitably intermingled with the peculiarities of the religion of Jesus." Sometime during the early 1740s, Samuel Morris, a bricklayer, and several other people stopped attending the local parish church. Instead, they gathered on Sunday mornings at Morris's home to read religious tracts, among these Martin Luther's *Commentary on Galatians*; works by John Bunyan (1628–1688), author of *The Pilgrim's Progress*; and the published sermons of George Whitefield, the famous evangelical Anglican minister who had preached in Williamsburg's Bruton Parish Church in 1739. Other than dissenting from the Church of England, the Hanover group during its early stages held no particular denominational affiliation. When called before the county court and asked to explain what denomination they belonged to, they could not answer right away, then "recollecting that *Luther* was a noted Reformer, and that his Doctrines were agreeable to our Sentiments . . . we called our selves *Lutherans*." In 1743, leaders of the group convinced William Robinson, a New Side minister then on a preaching mission to the Scots-Irish in the Shenandoah Valley, to come to Hanover and preach to them. A dissenter described the impact:

> 'Tis hard for the liveliest Imagination to form an Image of the Condition of the Assembly on these glorious Days of the Son of Man. Such of us as had been hungring for the Word before, were lost in an agreeable Confusion of various Passions, surprised, astonished, pleased, enraptured! so that we were hardly capable of Self-Government, and some could not refrain from publickly declaring their Transport: we were overwhelmed with the Tho'ts of the unexpected Goodness of God, in allowing us to hear the Gospel preached in a Manner that surpassed even our former Wishes, and much more our Hopes. Many that came thro' Curiosity were *pricked to the Heart*.[127]

Robinson's preaching convinced the Hanover dissenters of their identity: they began to call themselves Presbyterians.[128]

For several years the Hanover dissenters received only occasional visits from New Side preachers sent by the Synod of New York, a New Side organization established after the Synod of Philadelphia expelled the revivalists. Nonetheless, the movement grew in the colony and, as it expanded, the Presbyterian awakening challenged Virginia's traditional sources of authority. Some New Side preachers attacked both the Church of England and Virginia's law-abiding Old Side Presbyterians, in addition to speaking "pretty freely" in their sermons "of the degeneracy of the [established] clergy." The Hanover County grand jury, for instance, accused one visiting minister, the Reverend John Roan, of slandering the Church, a charge of which he was later acquitted. Another dissenting minister openly questioned whether the bishop of London had been converted. Worse yet to colonial authorities, New Side preachers were itinerants who traveled from place to place preaching wherever they found a willing audience. A group of Anglican clergymen scoffed at these itinerants as "strolling pretended Ministers." When members of Virginia's government or the established church described revivalist ministers as "itinerants" they meant it as a slur. The term conveyed a sense of motion, instability, and disorder. New Side clergy came into an area, attacked both the Church of England and Old Side ministers, stirred their listeners into a frenzy, then moved on, leaving in their wake excited crowds hungry for religion with no leader to guide them or to direct their newfound religious passions.[129]

Itinerants also threatened traditional sources of authority by defying the strictures of the Act of Toleration and refusing to seek licenses either for themselves or for the meetinghouses where they preached. Applying for a license offered tacit admission of the state's authority in religious matters. By refusing to comply with this requirement, New Side preachers denied the government's right to regulate the life of the spirit and thus put themselves in rebellion against the traditional means of organizing society. This in part is what Gooch meant in 1745 when he complained to the grand jury of "false teachers . . . who, without order or license, or producing any testimonial of their education or sect, . . . lead the innocent and ignorant people into all kinds of delusion." In place of a classical education and government sanction for their activities, dissenting clergy offered the authority of their piety and their confidence in their mission.[130]

The arrival in Hanover County in 1747 of the Reverend Samuel Davies (1723–1761), one of the most talented New Side preachers sent to Virginia, briefly brought tensions between the government and the Presbyterian revivalists to a close. Born in 1723 in Delaware's Newcastle County, Samuel Davies became the most accomplished preacher in colonial Virginia. To read his sermons is to grasp some of the vitality with which the New Light Presbyterian must have delivered his discourses, and, after reading a few, it is not difficult to understand why so many people wanted to hear him preach. They are vibrant, persuasive, and emotional while stopping short of the enthusiasm Davies deplored.

He gained his early schooling from the local Baptist minister in Newcastle County, although this probably ended by 1732 when Davies' mother was expelled from the congregation for challenging Baptist doctrine. Cast out by the Baptists, Davies' mother turned to the Presbyterians for spiritual guidance and Samuel likely continued his education at the classical school run by Newcastle's Presbyterian minister, the Reverend William Robinson, who would later play an important role in defining the Great Awakening in Virginia's Hanover County.

By the time Davies turned fifteen, about the same time he completed his training at Robinson's school, he knew that he wished to prepare for a career in the "gospel-Ministry." The young man began schooling in 1739 or 1740 at Fagg's Manor, one of the many New Light "log colleges" established by Gilbert Tennent (1703–1764) and his former students. Young men from the middle colonies who wished to pursue a formal classical education had no convenient options in the early 1700s. Harvard and Yale were too far north in New England and the College of William and Mary in Virginia was too far to the south. Nor did William and Mary necessarily offer one of the better educational possibilities for an aspiring young man; for decades after its establishment in 1693 it functioned as little more than a grammar school. And none of the earliest colonial colleges had been founded with the intention of educating men for the Presbyterian ministry.

Davies completed his education at Fagg's Manor in 1746. Following his ordination in 1747 he was sent as an evangelist to serve the New Light congregations of Virginia who lacked preachers of their own. Hanover County, however, was a special charge since the people there had helped fund Davies' studies. In 1748 the twenty-five-year-old Davies accepted the call of the New Light Presbyterians in Hanover County to become their permanent minister. He remained in Hanover until 1759 when, against the wishes of his congregation, Davies accepted an invitation to become president of the College of New Jersey, later Princeton University.[131]

Unlike many previous New Side missionaries, Davies complied with the Act of Toleration by applying to the government in Williamsburg for licenses for himself and the four meetinghouses where he intended to preach. Davies' willingness to acquire the proper licenses was fortunate for the Hanover dissenters. Itinerant preachers had ranged about the colony between 1745 and 1747 and the authorities' patience had come to an end. Less than two weeks before Davies arrived in the colony, Lieutenant Governor Gooch had issued a proclamation against "all Itinerant Preachers, whether New-Light Men, Morravians, or Methodists from teaching or holding any Meeting in this Colony." Nor did Davies preach in the enthusiastic style the colony's leaders found so disruptive. He condemned "fiery, superficial" discourses and described the model preacher as a man possessed "of ready utterance, good delivery, solid judgment, free from enthusiastic freaks, and of ardent zeal."[132] When he criticized the Church of England, which he did more often than his most recent biographer suggests, Davies nonetheless had the good sense to do so more discreetly than previous New Side clergy who had visited Virginia.[133] Some colonial authorities held the New Light minister in such high regard that in 1749 Gooch granted Davies permission to officiate at the marriages of dissenters on the condition that he publish the banns and turn over the required fees to the Anglican minister in whose parish the wedding took place, a breach with the colony's laws that only recognized the legality of marriages performed by Anglican clergy.[134]

Virginians responded to Davies' message. Commissary William Dawson (1705?–1752) complained to the bishop of London: "since Mr. Davies has been allowed to officiate in so many places . . . there has been a great defection from our [Church of England] Religious Assemblies. The generality of his followers, I believe, were born and bred in our Communion." By 1753, Davies' Hanover congregation numbered between 500 and 600 people, a significant force in eighteenth-century county politics. So great was the growth in the dissenters' numbers that in 1755 the New Side Presbytery of Hanover was established.[135] As a result of the young minister's success, however, Virginia's authorities once again attempted to restrict the activity of New Side preachers. Davies wrangled for several years with Virginia Attorney General Peyton Randolph (1721–1775), whom he called "my old Adversary," over licenses and the number of New Side meetinghouses the government would allow the New Side Presbyterians. Randolph believed that enforcing the Act of Toleration in Virginia would only lead to needless confusion and suggested that it did not apply to Davies anyhow because the Presbyterian preached at several meetinghouses, thus making him an itinerant whom the law did not protect. Davies responded by pointing out that there was no difference between the way he cared for his far-flung congregation and the practice of Anglican ministers in large parishes who preached on a rotating basis at the mother church and the parish's chapels of ease. Virginia's authorities, Davies claimed, had never slurred these Anglican parsons with "the odious epithet of an itinerant preacher." Only the later appearance of the more radical Separate Baptists made New Side Presbyterianism a respectable religion in the eyes of Virginia's political leaders.[136]

The Separate Baptists came to Virginia in the late 1750s, and their appearance initiated the most bitter phase of the Great Awakening in the colony.[137] Baptist itinerants were fined, whipped, and imprisoned. Crowds often harassed them. After his arrest for preaching without a license, James Ireland was followed to jail by a huge mob of people who shouted "such vollies of oaths and abuse as if I were a being unfit to exist on the earth."[138] The Reverend Jonathan Boucher (1738–1804) of St. Mary's Parish in Caroline County spoke for many members of the establishment when he complained of the "swarms of separatists" and likened adherents of the sect to gnats: "though they can neither give pleasure nor do any good, they do not want either the disposition or the ability [of] those little insignificant animals to tease, to sting, and to torment."[139] The *Virginia Gazette* satirized the denomination in its pages.[140] Anglican clergymen and members of the gentry were not above disrupting Baptist worship services from time to time by physically assaulting preachers in the midst of delivering a sermon.[141] Many Virginians despised the Baptists. When the Reverend Isaac Giberne of Lunenburg Parish in Richmond preached against the sect in 1773, so many people crowded into the building to hear his discourse that they caused the gallery to collapse.[142] Nonetheless, the Baptists made extraordinary numbers of converts. In 1769 there were seven Separate Baptist congregations in Virginia; five years later there were no less than fifty-four, and nearly half of those were in long-settled regions north of the James River where the people had traditionally supported the established Church of England. By the eve of the American Revolution, no religious group in Virginia was growing faster.[143]

The Separates challenged the colony's traditional order by establishing their own communities based on values that negated those of the dominant culture. In contrast to the combination of earthly pleasures and Arminian[144] theology that marked Anglican gentry culture in colonial Virginia, Baptists adhered to a mildly Calvinistic theology summed up well by the Reverend James Ireland's account of his early preaching mission: "I began first to preach . . . our awful apostasy by the fall; the necessity of repentance unto life, and of faith in the Lord Jesus Christ. . . . Our helpless incapacity to extricate ourselves therefrom I stated and urged." Their insistence on the baptism of believers by full immersion seemed peculiar and frightening to outsiders. They stood against popular amusements such as card playing, cockfighting, gambling, "Gaming, Dancing, & Sabbath-Day Diversions." Their perceived solemnity led one Virginian to describe members of the sect as "the most melancholy people" who "cannot meet a man upon the road, but they must ram a text of Scripture down his throat."[145] Nor did other dissenters always care for the Baptists. Samuel Davies complained that they "spread over Virginia like a torrent."[146] Furthermore, Baptist ecclesiology found the very idea of state church systems, like that in Virginia, repugnant. They believed in a gathered church comprised of professing believers rather than a church that included all members of a particular political society. Separate Baptists denied the state's right to legislate for the church and thus refused to seek licenses for their preachers and meetinghouses (something to which some New Side Presbyterians like Samuel Davies submitted), arguing that their authority to preach came not from colonial authorities but from God. Their itinerancy and extraordinarily emotional preaching smacked of disorder. An early Baptist historian described the Separates' preaching: "The *Separates* in New England had acquired a very warm and pathetic address, accompanied by strong gestures and a singular tone of voice. Being often deeply affected themselves while preaching, correspondent affections were frequently expressed by tears, trembling, screams, shouts and acclamations. . . . The people were greatly astonished, having never seen things on this wise before." Instead of a society of orders and betters like that in eighteenth-century Virginia, Baptists called each other "Brother" and "Sister." They actively sought converts among the lower classes and in the slave quarters, all of whom they addressed in the same manner. To the poor the Baptists offered fellowship; to slaves they offered the equality of the Gospel. In contrast to colonial society's lax enforcement of sanctions for moral offenses, Separate Baptists held members of their communities to strict standards of morality and often disciplined brethren who fell short of the mark. Quarreling, drunkenness, and slander were censured frequently. In a culture in which physical violence was commonplace and resentment of insults was expected, Baptists also admonished members for fighting, even in self-defense. Some Baptists went so far as to confess the sin of "Getting angry Tho in just Defence of himself in Despute." Slave converts were placed under the same discipline as free members.[147] Separate Baptists rebuked Virginia's society through their manner of life. Historian Rhys Isaac captured the essence of the Baptists' challenge:

> On the one hand they were heedless of how they disrupted traditional society, acknowledging that they not only sowed discord among neighbors but also turned slaves from their masters, children from their parents, wives from their husbands, since "OUR SAVIOUR told his disciples, that, he 'came not to send peace on earth but rather division.'" On the other hand, they created tight supportive communities "of persons, called by the Gospel out of the world," seeking "to live together as brethren."[148]

Persecution of Baptist preachers helped convince a young James Madison of the necessity of religious freedom. Confronted by numerous petitions from dissenting groups, the House of Burgesses in 1769 established a Committee on Religion to look into drafting a bill of toleration for Virginia. That would not happen until after the American Revolution, and it would establish religious freedom rather than mere toleration.[149]

⁓

No matter their denomination, the men who sought to do God's work in Virginia by spreading the Gospel faced numerous difficulties. Clergy in the established Church of England often acted more like missionaries than settled ministers. Most parishes in colonial Virginia had a mother church and one or more chapels of ease at convenient points in the parish where the minister preached and read divine service in turn on successive Sundays. In his absence, the clerk[150] read the service and perhaps a discourse from *The Book of*

Homilies or a published sermon by John Tillotson or another English divine. Dissenters, of course, faced various legal disabilities. Meetinghouses and preachers both required permits from the government in order to be legal; only marriages and baptisms performed by Anglican clergy had the sanction of law.[151] Dissenters nonetheless faced many of the same problems that Anglican clergy confronted. The response of Virginia's authorities to the presence of Presbyterian and Baptist preachers can give the impression that dissenting missionaries were everywhere in the colony. That is false. Like many members of the Church of England for much of the colonial period, most dissenting groups also went without clerical leadership. Due to the small size of King William Parish, Huguenots there could not afford a full-time minister. After 1715 they could secure only temporary preachers. When dissent emerged in the 1740s and 1750s, many Huguenots found a religious home beyond the bounds of the established church.[152] Even the Presbyterians in Hanover County went without a settled minister for five years until Samuel Davies arrived in 1747. And he was still but one man ministering to congregations at four or five meetinghouses. Although the Great Awakening may have brought a vigorous revivalist presence to Virginia, the crisis in pastoral care that Anglicans knew so well continued under a different guise.

Consequently, a great deal of religious instruction took place outside the public church. Governor William Berkeley reported the practice as commonplace and seemed incredulous that English authorities could think otherwise when he answered a query from Charles II in 1671 regarding how colonists were instructed in the "christian religion." He reported: "the same course that is taken in England out of towns; every man according to his ability instructing his children."[153] The Reverend Devereux Jarratt (1733–1801), the Anglican minister who brought Methodism to Virginia in the 1770s, described a similar case nearly a century later when he noted that as a young child he and his siblings had learned about religion from their parents who "made us perfect in repeating the *Church Catechism*" (and who violated the colony's laws by not attending church).[154]

Virginians turned to a variety of religious works to guide their devotions. The Bible, of course, remained the most popular religious book in colonial Virginia, but a number of other English devotional works also helped colonists direct their journeys to heaven. Many Anglicans turned first to the *Book of Common Prayer*. Philip Ludwell, Sr., kept a "poor little old [prayer] book worn from use in his closet to help order his private devotions, and John Page believed that for family or private devotions a person "cannot make a better choice than of the church prayers."[155] *The Practice of Piety*, by Puritan bishop Lewis Bayly; *The Whole Duty of Man*, likely written by

Richard Allestree, a royalist minister; *A Week's Preparation Towards a Worthy Receiving of the Lords Supper*; Jeremy Taylor's *Holy Living* and *Holy Dying*; the sermons of Archbishop John Tillotson; and the *Church Catechism*, by the Whiggish English minister John Lewis, were all widely available in Virginia.[156] Lewis's volume proved so popular that in 1738 William Parks, who then printed the *Virginia Gazette*, published an edition out of his Williamsburg press and advertised it as "being very proper for a New Year's Gift to Children."[157]

Ministers tried to expand the influence of religion by distributing religious tracts to persons unable to afford them, a practice followed by Presbyterians, Anglicans, and Quakers alike. In 1703, the Reverend John Talbot wrote from Virginia to the Society for the Propagation of the Gospel (SPG) requesting prayer books "new or old, of all sorts & sizes," explaining that if he received these volumes, he would "carry them 100 miles about and disperse them abroad to all that desired 'em . . . 'tis a comfort to the People in the Wilderness to see that some body takes care of them."[158] In addition to the SPG, the Society for the Propagation of Christian Knowledge sent books to Anglican ministers in the colonies so they could disburse the volumes among their parishioners. Quaker missionaries distributed numerous books both to adherents and persons curious about the Friends' message, among them *A Switch for the Snake*, a tract written to combat the anonymous anti-Quaker pamphlet, *The Snake in the Grass*, which also circulated in Virginia.[159] When the Reverend James Craig (ca. 1724–1795) came to Lunenburg County's Cumberland Parish in 1759 he found many people "which by Reason of their Distance from any place of Divine Worship, had never or seldom, been at Church, since they were baptized" and who often were "ignorant of the very first Principles of Christianity." Whether or not his parishioners could read is unclear, and perhaps Craig's request simply indicates a minister's overconfidence in the power of the printed word, but he seemed certain that books would help bring religion to his backcountry parish. He wrote to Commissary Thomas Dawson (d. 1761) to ask for volumes on baptism, the Lord's Supper, and the duties of godparents, as well as William Beveridge's often reprinted *Sermon concerning the Excellency and Usefulness of the Common Prayer*: "I would freely give any Consideration to have these & such other Books to distribute among the people NOW."[160] Samuel Davies likewise distributed hundreds of religious books to persons too poor to buy the volumes themselves.[161]

Spreading the Gospel to slaves and Native Americans proved difficult. Spanish Jesuits had undertaken the first efforts to convert Native Americans in Ajacán, the Spanish name for the region known to Englishmen as Virginia, back in 1570 when they had arrived in the Bahía de Santa María

(Chesapeake Bay) and established a settlement on what the English later called the York River. The Jesuits outlined their goals succinctly: the "conversion of these people and the service of Our Lord and His Majesty and [finding] the way [entrada] to the mountains and China." In short, they hoped to spread the Gospel and Spanish power and to discover the fabled Northwest Passage to the Orient. Their efforts failed. The Indians proved resistant to Christianity, ultimately murdering most of the missionary party, and there was no passage to China for the Jesuits to discover.[162]

While Christianizing the natives of North America was an honestly held goal of many members of the Virginia Company of London and other supporters of colonization, this imperative never reached the same degree of importance in Virginia as it held back in England. George Thorpe, one of the few planters[163] who felt any degree of obligation to spread the Gospel to Virginia's indigenous peoples, complained in 1621: "There is scarce any man amongst us that doth soe much as afforde [the natives] a good thought in his hart and most men with their mouthes give them nothinge but maledictions and bitter execrations."[164] Nor did Indians show much interest in becoming Christians, in part because the English in Virginia thought that Christianity needed an English cultural context in which to flourish and therefore forced Native American converts to renounce their former civilization. One member of the Virginia Company of London explained: "concerning the baptisme of Infidelle children . . . such as mak servants or bondmen to Christians, and more xpetially to remane among [the colonists] might be baptized."[165]

Commissary James Blair attempted to redress three-quarters of a century of neglect in his proposal to establish a college in Virginia, indicating that one of the institution's ends would be to ensure "that the Christian Faith may be propagated amongst the Western *Indians*." Blair also had the good fortune to secure for the new college a sizable portion of Sir Robert Boyle's "Legacy for pious uses," left by the scientist at his death in 1691. The College of William and Mary was to use the bequest for the purpose of converting Indians to Christianity. Finding natives willing to be converted, however, remained a problem. In 1697, when the Boyle funds were officially transferred to the college, a school existed but no Indians were as yet enrolled—and there was little hope of finding Native Americans willing to attend the school. Virginia Indians refused to send their children to the college, in part because the local natives believed children sent to receive an education at the college had been sold as slaves. Many of the Native Americans who later did attend William and Mary were captives from remote tribes who had been purchased from the local natives. Writing in the same year to the Board of Trade, Governor Edmund Andros (1637–1714)—possibly in an attempt to embarrass Blair, with whom he was feuding—responded to a question about Virginians' attempts to spread the Gospel to the Natives with an answer that contained more truth than hyperbole: "None ever heard of."[166]

Lieutenant Governor Alexander Spotswood was probably the public figure in early eighteenth-century Virginia who took most seriously the mission to Virginia's native peoples. During his tenure as governor, 1710–1722, Indian enrollment at William and Mary reached its peak. In addition, Spotswood established a school for the education and Christianization of the colony's tributary Indians at Fort Christanna on the south shore of the Meherrin River. He paid the schoolmaster there, the Reverend Charles Griffin, from his private funds. Griffin taught over a hundred students at Fort Christanna between 1715 and 1718, and both natives and Englishmen held the minister in high regard. William Byrd II remarked on "the innocence of his life" and "the sweetness of his temper." The Reverend Hugh Jones suggested that had Griffin let them, the natives "would have chosen him for a king." And unlike what one historian has termed "the academic confinement at William and Mary," Indian students at Christanna remained free and close to their families. The legislation that created the Indian school at Fort Christanna, however, formed part of an Act for the Better Regulation of the Indian Trade and would have given the Virginia Indian Company a monopoly on trade with the natives for twenty years. This act generated intense opposition from Virginia's rising merchant class, including that of Commissary Blair's father-in-law and brother, and was disallowed by the Crown in 1717, thus ending both the monopoly and the school.[167]

With his plan in disarray, Spotswood turned his efforts at educating and Christianizing Virginia's natives back to William and Mary. In 1718, he invited Griffin to become master of the Indian School at the college. The Indian School, however, was already in serious decline by this time and only a few students remained. In 1723 college leaders decided to use the Boyle funds that had accumulated to construct a building, the Brafferton, for the Indian students still in attendance. Within ten years the building became home to the college's library as well. A few students remained at the college's Indian School until 1777 when the Reverend Emmanuel Jones, the school's last master, resigned. For all practical purposes, the Brafferton school had ceased functioning in 1776 when the American Revolution formally began and the college lost access to the Boyle endowment. Nor did the Indian School ever adequately fulfill its original purpose of training native men so that they could "be sent abroad to preach and convert the Indians." Most Virginians did not care about the natives' salvation or education. Most Native Americans did not want to be cooped up in a school building where they learned what they considered useless skills. The Iroquois once reflected on the deficiencies of their youth educated at the college, claiming that they "were absolutely good for nothing being neither acquainted with the true methods for killing deer, catching Beaver or surprizing an enemy." One student of Indian education at William and Mary concluded that the school's efforts "brought little credit to the College, and less accomplishment."[168]

While white Virginians could easily avoid the issue of Christianizing Native Americans since the two groups lived in different societies, they could not as readily avoid the issue of spreading the Gospel to African and African-American slaves who lived within English Virginia. Both the sources and the historiography suggest ambiguous conclusions about the seriousness and success of Virginians's efforts to Christianize slaves. The topic is complex, not only because planters and parsons often disagreed so vehemently about evangelism in the slave quarters, but also because African and African-American attitudes toward Christianity changed significantly over the course of the colonial period. Unlike Native Americans, the vast majority of whom were unfamiliar with the Gospel, many of the first generation of Africans brought to the colony and their first generation African-American descendants professed the religion of Christ crucified. Ira Berlin has described the first generation of Africans in Virginia—slave, indentured, and free—as "Atlantic creoles," people who "understood the languages of the Atlantic, bore Hispanic and occasionally English names, and were familiar with Christianity and other aspects of European culture," especially its laws. Between 1619, when the first Africans arrived in Virginia, and the late 1660s, black men and women attended the colony's established church, had their children baptized, and did penance alongside white Virginians during divine service. Enslaved creoles aware that English custom and law denied Christians the right to hold other Christians as slaves sued for their freedom in the colony's courts and often won their way out of bondage.[169]

Attitudes began to change, however, during the 1660s. In that decade chattel slavery became law in Virginia and, in 1667, the General Assembly passed a statute denying the traditional correspondence of Christianity with freedom. It declared that "baptisme doth not alter the condition of the person as to his bondage or ffreedome," a position reaffirmed in 1727 in a series of pastoral letters by no less an authority than Edmund Gibson, bishop of London.[170] The first extant source outlining the conflict in Virginia between parsons and planters over efforts to Christianize slaves also dates to the 1660s. Morgan Godwyn, the same minister who denounced the power of lay vestries, condemned white Virginians for resisting parsons' efforts to baptize slaves. The blurred racial lines of the first half of the century identified by Ira

Berlin became fixed and rigid in the years after 1660; as a result, Christianity became the basis of a white cultural identity, a possession in the minds of many Virginians proper to white people alone. "These two words," Godwyn wrote, "Negro and Slave, being by custom grown Homogeneous and Convertible; even as *Negro* and *Christian*, *Englishman* and *Heathen*, are by the like corrupt Custom and Partiality made *Opposites*; thereby as it were implying that the one could not be *Christians*, nor the other *Infidels*."[171]

Black attitudes toward Christianity also started to change in the latter decades of the seventeenth century. With the success of the "plantation revolution" and with chattel slavery clearly on the books, planters turned with greater frequency to African slaves rather than white indentured servants to meet their increasing need for laborers. As the demand for slaves increased, the source of those slaves changed. No longer did the majority of slaves imported to the colony come from the Atlantic littoral; they came instead from the interior of the African continent. Unlike the Chesapeake's charter generation, later generations of slaves imported to the colony were strangers to Christianity and European culture. By 1700 Africans from the interior "composed nearly 90 percent of the slave population" in Virginia.[172]

Changes that began in the 1660s set the terms of the debate over evangelizing slaves for nearly a hundred years. Ministers and masters willing to allow proselytizing complained that the mutual incomprehension of slaves recently arrived from Africa and missionaries presented insurmountable obstacles to conversion, a complaint made by Quakers and Presbyterians as well as Anglicans.[173] Many Virginians only reluctantly accepted the 1667 law about baptism and, as a result, resisted efforts to spread the Gospel into the slave quarters. The equation of freedom with Christianity continued to shape the perceptions of many slaveholders. Some planters thought baptism made slaves "prouder," while others believed it filled their bondsmen with unfounded "thoughts of freedom." The large number of Africans unfamiliar with both the English language and the Christian religion made some people suspect the sincerity of slave conversions, that they were but a ruse to gain freedom. James Blair mused: "I doubt not some of the Negroes are sincere Converts; but the far greater part of them little mind the serious part, only are in hopes that they shall meet with so much the more respect, and that some time or other Christianity will help them to their freedom." Lieutenant Governor Gooch blamed a threatened slave insurrection in 1730 on a rumor that "his Majesty had sent Orders for setting of them free as soon as they were Christians, and that these Orders were suppressed."[174]

Ministers who attempted to proselytize slaves often met with great resistance. The Reverend John Bagg (d. 1725) of St. Anne's Parish claimed that his parishioners were "generaly not approving thereof, being led away by the notion of their [slaves] being and becoming worse slaves when Christians." The Reverend Alexander Rhonnald of Elizabeth River Parish in Norfolk County demonstrated too great a missionary zeal to suit the taste of many slaveholders in his parish. He complained: "They use Me with the most invidious Terms of ill nature for my pains, & because I baptize more Negroes than other Brethren here & instruct them, from the Pulpit, out of common road, & encourage the Good among them to come to the Communion, after a due Sense of the matter, I am vilified & branded by such as a Negro Parson."[175] Even Quaker leaders complained that among most Friends "there seems to be a general neglect in the Education of Negroes, and in the training them up in the principles of Christian Religion."[176] James Maury, Andrew White, James Marye, and Adam Dickie, whose life was threatened, all ran into trouble with white Virginians for performing integrated baptisms.[177] Between 1700 and his death in 1743, James Blair, in the opinion of some historians, hindered efforts to spread Christianity to slaves. Much of his power rested upon alliances he had established through marriage and expediency with members of Virginia's ruling elite; to attack Virginians' reluctance to baptize their slaves was therefore to attack his patrons.[178]

Nonetheless, clergymen from Morgan Godwyn to Samuel Davies to Edmund Gibson, whose 1727 pastoral letter criticized British colonists for their resistance to evangelizing their slaves, all pressed the duty. The methods they relied upon reflected those used to prepare unbaptized white people to receive the sacrament. Samuel Davies and Jonathan Boucher were among those ministers who urged the utility of teaching slaves to read and distributed religious tracts to those who could. Boucher's practice may have been typical: "I have already distributed many of [the books] amongst the poor Slaves who are very numerous in this Parish. In many of my former letters I have told You of the Difficulties Ministers are under to reconcile the Owners of Slaves to their being instructed. . . . I generally find an old Negro, or a conscientious Overseer, able to read, whom I give Books, with an Injunction to Them to instruct such & such Slaves in their respective Neighbourhoods."[179] In the 1740s the Reverend William Dawson organized public readings of devotional literature at the College of William and Mary during the penitential season of Lent. At these gatherings upperclassmen read religious tracts to groups comprised of lowerclassmen, slaves, Indians, and indentured servants.[180] These various efforts achieved moderate success. Samuel Davies, for instance, claimed to have baptized approximately 250 slaves, a figure matched or surpassed by several Anglican ministers.[181]

Anglican clergy who tried to spread the message of the Gospel to Virginia's slave population received support from the Associates of Dr. Bray, a group formed in 1723/24 to help educate and Christianize blacks in the colonies. They sent books to colonial ministers for this purpose and established schools for blacks in Philadelphia (1758); New York (1760); Williamsburg (1760); Newport, Rhode Island (1762); and Fredericksburg, Virginia (1765). The Williamsburg school had a successful run of fourteen years, closing in 1774 after the death of its teacher. The Fredericksburg school was less successful. The town's small population proved unable to sustain the experiment and the school shut down in 1770.[182]

Despite planter resistance, some slaves did learn about Christianity. In an extraordinary letter written to the bishop of London in 1723 by an anonymous Virginia slave—who obviously had read the Bible or become familiar with Exodus in some other way—the writer complained that "wee are commandded to keep holey the Sabbath day and wee doo hardly know when it comes for our task mastrs are as hard with us as the Egpttions was with the Chilldann of Issarell." The writer also knew the requirements for baptism, requesting that the bishop "Settell one thing upon us which is that our childarn may be broatt up in the way of the Christtian faith and our desire is that they may be Larnd the Lords prayer the creed and the ten commandments and that they may appeare Every Lord's day att Church."[183]

In all likelihood, attempts to evangelize slaves were as individual as the relationships among particular slaves, particular masters, and particular ministers. Some masters took the duty more seriously than others, just as some slaves no doubt desired to become Christians more than others and just as some ministers pressed the work more vigorously than others. Ministers' complaints about slave owners who did not want their slaves to become Christians must be balanced against other evidence that suggests that slaves were expected to gain at least nominal exposure to the teachings of the church. Some Virginia churches, for instance, contained slave galleries, implying that slaves would attend worship services. Philip Vickers Fithian (1747–1776), a tutor employed by Robert Carter of Nomini Hall in 1773 and 1774, described the whole parish meeting together on Sundays, "High, Low, black, white."[184] Another tutor, the indentured servant John Harrower (ca. 1734–1777), recorded in his journal the baptisms of slave infants born on William Daingerfield's plantation and noted as well that one of his own tasks was to teach the catechism to slave children when they reached the appropriate age.[185] And despite the trouble he ran into for holding integrated baptisms, the Reverend Adam Dickie of Drysdale Parish suggested that many slave owners detected a worthwhile change in their slaves' behavior after they had received catechetical training: bondsmen "who formerly were thieves, lyars, Swearers, prophaners of the Sabbath, and neglecters of their business, from a Sense of Religion and of their Duty have left off all these things."[186] Readers should also keep in mind that many ministers owned slaves themselves.[187] They attacked not the institution itself but the lack of charity on the part of slave masters who would prevent their slaves from hearing the message of salvation contained in the Gospel.

⌁

Easy acceptance of the interpretive framework grounded on the alleged Anglican hegemony in colonial Virginia has distorted historians' understanding of religion in the colony. The Church of England, to be sure, enjoyed numerous legal advantages, and every citizen was expected to attend its services and pay tithes for its support. A substantial amount of those funds, however, did not contribute to activities of a strictly religious nature but supported what many people today would consider secular concerns: helping the poor, caring for the sick and elderly without estates, employment, or family members to care for them, and binding out orphaned children to learn a trade. In this manner, the Church of England functioned as a unit of colonial government concerned with colonists' temporal welfare.

On the other hand, throughout the colonial period, most Virginians found spiritual guidance and solace within the established church. They wanted a formal religious presence in their lives, one that proved difficult for religious leaders to provide. A shortage of clergy and large parishes resulted in a pastoral crisis for the Church of England. Dissenters contended with similar obstacles, although it was usually disgruntled Anglican ministers who pointed out the problems. The difficulties of adequately providing laypeople with pastoral guidance and religious instruction lie beneath James Maury's complaint to Commissary Thomas Dawson about the practices of dissenting ministers: "A Teacher who hath 7, 8, or 10 Meeting Houses, the People hear but Seldom; A Minister Constantly Residing amongst them, within Parochial Bounds, they have the Opportunity to hear Often . . . . Besides, Personal Residence . . . is necessary to the due Discharge of all those Pastoral Offices, wch are of a more private Nature."[188]

Dissenters confronted additional problems in their efforts to spread the Gospel in colonial Virginia. Anglican ministers and prominent laypeople, some of whom held offices in county or colonial government, were jealous of the Church of England's privileged status. Establishment, for instance, helped assure the Church's survival. When adherents or missionaries of rival religious persuasions first appeared in Virginia, members of the established church often responded aggressively. Government officials and some Anglican ministers saw dissenters as harbingers of disorder who might sow the seeds of division within society. But as Baptist minister John Leland observed, the martyr's "scarlet" found no place in Virginia. Over time the colony's government came to grant dissenters a formal degree of toleration, an indulgence that often came grudgingly and usually after a more radical religious group made previous dissenters seem moderate by comparison.

The story of religion in colonial Virginia has often focused on the struggles of dissenters, particularly the Baptists, to gain religious freedom and the efforts of Anglicans to prevent this innovation. There is truth to this tale. However, one may also see the story somewhat differently, as the struggle by Anglicans and dissenters, both of whom lacked the vocabulary and the history, either to come to terms with or to accept the possibility, much less the necessity, of a religious polity guided by the "peaceful coexistence" of different religious groups that Sir Edwin Sandys had advocated.

Notes

1. The term "Anglican" can be problematic for modern readers because the word has been used to identify different groups of people at different times in the past, not always with a great deal of precision. Some people, for instance, use "Anglican" to signify those members of the Church of England who were not Puritans, a practice which is not wholly accurate, at least not until the 1640s and 1650s. Other people associate the word with the Oxford Movement and adherents of the contemporary "high church" or Anglo-Catholic wing of the Episcopal Church, a use which implies certain tendencies in churchmanship and theology. Unless otherwise noted in the text, throughout this work "Anglican" refers to the established Church of England.

2. A reference to the practice of taxing all citizens, regardless of their religious adherence, to support the established church, in Virginia's case, the Church of England.

3. At its session in 1662, the Virginia General Assembly had passed a statute "Against persons that refuse to have their Children Baptised," a law directed at Quakers, who were then being persecuted in the colony: "Whereas many schismaticall persons out of their aversenesse to the orthodox religion, or out of the new fangled conceits of their owne heticall inventions, refuse to have their children baptized, *Be it therefore enacted by the authority aforesaid*, that all persons that, in contempt of the divine sacrament of baptisme, shall refuse when they may carry their child to a lawfull minister in that county to have them baptized shalbe amerced two thousand pounds of tobacco; halfe to the informer, halfe to the publique," in William Waller Hening, ed., *The Statutes at Large: Being a Collection of All the Laws of Virginia. . . , 13 Vols. (Richmond, 1809–1823), 2:165–66.

4. Thomas Story, *A Journal of the Life of Thomas Story: Containing an Account of His Remarkable Convincement of and Embracing the Principles of Truth, as Held by the People Called Quakers* (Newcastle upon Tyme, 1747), 392–98; Edward Lewis Goodwin, *The Colonial Church in Virginia, With Biographical Sketches of the First Six Bishops of the Diocese of Virginia and Other Historical Papers, Together with Brief Biographical Sketches of the Colo-

nial Clergy of Virginia (Milwaukee: Morehouse Publishing Company, 1927), 294; John Bennett Boddie, *Seventeenth Century Isle of Wight County, Virginia: A History of the County of Isle of Wight, Virginia, during the Seventeenth Century, Including Abstracts of the County Records* (Chicago: Chicago Law Printing Company, 1938), 428; Jay Worrall, Jr., *The Friendly Virginians: America's First Quakers* (Athens, Ga.: Iberian Publishing Company, 1994), 102. Joseph Glaister continued to participate in disputations with Anglican ministers and remained active in Virginia and North Carolina as a Quaker missionary. In 1707 he wrote "A Discourse for Friends of Virginia and North Carolina." See James Branch Cabell, ed., "A Discourse for Friends of Virginia and Carolina by Joseph Glaister," *William and Mary Quarterly* 1st ser. 25 (1916–1917): 248–53. For additional evidence of Anglican-Quaker disputations, see James Dickinson, *A Journal of the Life, Travels, and Labours of Love in the Work of the Ministry, of that Worthy Elder, and Faithful servant of Jesus Christ, James Dickinson . . .* (London, 1745), in William Evans and Thomas Evans, eds., *The Friends Library: Comprising Journals, Doctrinal Treatises, and Other Writings of Members of the Religious Society of Friends*, 14 Vols. (Philadelphia, 1837–1850), 12: 389, 395.

5. For recent works advancing this view see Rhys Isaac, *The Transformation of Virginia, 1740–1790* (Chapel Hill: University of North Carolina Press, 1982); and Dell Upton, *Holy Things and Profane: Anglican Parish Churches in Colonial Virginia* (Cambridge, Mass.: MIT Press, 1986). For an outstanding survey of the deficiencies in much of the scholarship on colonial Anglicanism, see Joan R. Gundersen, *The Anglican Ministry in Virginia, 1723–1776: A Study of a Social Class* (New York: Garland Publishing, Inc., 1989), i-v. See also John K. Nelson, *A Blessed Company: Parishes, Parsons, and Parishioners in Anglican Virginia, 1690–1776* (Chapel Hill: University of North Carolina Press, 2001), 8–9. Against the still reigning orthodoxy, both Gundersen and Nelson argue for the strength and integrity of Virginia's Church of England in the eighteenth century. On Upton, see the book reviews by Joan R. Gundersen, *William and Mary Quarterly* 3d ser. 46 (1989): 379–82; and Warren M. Billings, *Virginia Magazine of History and Biography* 95 (1987): 379–81.

6. James Blair, *Our Saviour's Divine Sermon on the Mount . . . Explained; and the Practice of it Recommended in divers Sermons and Discourses*, 5 Vols. (London, 1722), 1:212–14, 223.

7. Blair, *Our Saviour's Divine Sermon on the Mount*, 5:44.

8. The argument about Virginians accepting nearly anyone who could offer them some form of supernatural guidance has been made most forcefully by Darrett B. Rutman, "The Evolution of Religious Life in Early Virginia," *Lex et Scientia: The International Journal of Law and Science* 14 (1978): 197.

9. David Cressy, *Bonfires and Bells: National Memory and the Protestant Calendar in Elizabethan and Stuart England* (Los Angeles: University of California Press, 1989), 109, 122, 125, 141–42; Karen Ordahl Kupperman, *Settling With the Indians: The Meeting of Indian and English Cultures in America, 1580–1640* (Totowa, N.J.: Rowman & Littlefield, 1980), 159–63; Edward L. Bond, "England's Soteriology of Empire and the Roots of Colonial Identity in Early Virginia," *Anglican and Episcopal History* 66 (1997): 471–74.

10. Stuart E. Prall, *Church and State in Tudor and Stuart England* (Arlington Heights, Ill.: Harlan Davidson, 1993), 1; Perry Miller, "Religion and Society in the Early Literature of Virginia," in Perry Miller, *Errand Into the Wilderness* (Cambridge, Mass.: Harvard University Press, 1956), 110–15; Keith Thomas, *Religion and the Decline of Magic: Studies in Popular Beliefs in Sixteenth and Seventeenth Century England* (London: Weidenfeld and Nicolson, 1971), ch. 4, esp. 79–82, 107.

11. Michael Lapworth to John Ferrar, 26 June 1621, Ferrar Papers, 268, Magdalene College, Cambridge University.

12. *For the Colony in Virginea Britannia. Lawes Divine, Morrall and Martiall, &c.* (London, 1612), in Peter Force, ed., *Tracts and Other Papers, Relating Principally to the Origin, Settlement, and Progress of the Colonies in North America*, 4 Vols. (Gloucester Mass.: Peter Smith, 1963), 3, no. 2:9–12.

13. David B. Smits, "'Abominable Mixture': Toward the Repudiation of Anglo-Indian Intermarriage in Seventeenth-Century Virginia," *Virginia Magazine of History and Biography* 95 (1987): 157–92. Copies of Rolfe's letter may be found in "Letter From John Rolfe to Sir Thomas Dale," *Virginia Magazine of History and Biography* 22 (1914): 150–57; and Lyon Gardiner Tyler, ed., *Narratives of Early Virginia, 1606–1625* (New York: Barnes & Noble, 1952), 239–44.

14. John Smith, *Advertisements for the Unexperienced Planters of New England, or Any-Where*, (London, 1631), in Philip L. Barbour, ed., *The Complete Works of Captain John Smith*, 3 Vols. (Chapel Hill: University of North Carolina Press, 1986), 3:295.

15. Jon Butler, *Awash in a Sea of Faith: Christianizing the American People* (Cambridge, Mass.: Harvard University Press, 1990), 11–12.

16. A eucharistic doctrine that teaches that during the consecration the elements of bread and wine become the actual body and blood of Christ.

17. David L. Holmes, *A Brief History of the Episcopal Church* (Valley Forge, Pa.: Trinity Press International, 1993), 4–11; Eamon Duffy, *The voices of Morebath: Reformation and Rebellion in an English Village* (New Haven, Conn.: Yale University Press, 2001), 94–95.

18. Holmes, *Brief History of the Episcopal Church*, 4–11.

19. Calvinism refers to a theological system based on the ideas of John Calvin (1509–1564), the French reformer, and most extensively formulated in his *Institutes of the Christian Religion* (1536). Calvinism accepts the doctrines of *sola scriptura*, or the belief that the Bible is the sole source of authority, and *sole fide*, or the idea that faith alone without works is necessary for salvation. Calvinist teachings also espouse the total depravity of man, the utter majesty of God, and absolute predestination. As understood by the sixteenth-century reformers, *sola scriptura* did not advocate the idea of Biblical literalism; rather, it rejected both the notion that the church received revelation separate from the Bible and the idea that the church was the supreme interpreter of scripture, both Roman Catholic positions.

20. Feast days devoted to the blessed Virgin Mary.

21. Cressy, *Bonfires and Bells*, 2–6, 13–33; Horton Davies, *Worship and Theology in England*, 5 Vols. (Princeton, N.J.: Princeton University Press, 1961–1975), 5:224–28;

Holmes, *Brief History of the Episcopal Church*, 7–11; David Underdown, *Fire From Heaven: Life in an English Town in the Seventeenth Century* (New Haven, Conn.: Yale University Press, 1992), 18–21.

22. Benjamin W. Labaree, *Colonial Massachusetts: A History* (Millwood, N.Y.: KTO Press, 1979), 27.

23. Davies, *Worship and Theology*, 2:224, 338–39; Kenneth Fincham and Peter Lake, "The Ecclesiastical Policies of James I and Charles I," in Kenneth Fincham, ed., *The Early Stuart Church, 1603–1642* (Stanford, Calif.: Stanford University Press, 1993), 31; Peter Lake, "The Laudian Style: Order, Uniformity, and the Pursuit of the Beauty of Holiness in the 1630s," in Fincham, ed., *Early Stuart Church*, 181–82; Leo F. Solt, *Church and State in Early Modern England, 1509–1640* (New York: Oxford University Press, 1990), 185; H. G. Alexander, *Religion in England, 1558–1662* (London: University of London Press, 1968), 151; Charles Carlton, *Archbishop William Laud* (London: Routledge & Kegan Paul Ltd., 1987), 71. Readers interested in an accessible discussion of the religious milieu of early Jacobean England and James I's efforts to create a tolerant religious polity may wish to consult Adam Nicolson, *God's Secretaries: The Making of the King James Bible* (New York: HarperCollins Publishers, 2003).

24. Aubrey C. Land, *Colonial Maryland: A History* (Millwood, N.Y.: KTO Press, 1981), 6–9, 98–99, 104–5; Sydney E. Ahlstrom, *A Religious History of the American People* (New Haven, Conn.: Yale University Press, 1972), 192–94; Edwin Scott Gaustad, *A Religious History of America* (New York: Harper & Row, 1974), 74–77; John Frederick Woolverton, *Colonial Anglicanism in North America* (Detroit: Wayne State University Press, 1984), 138–40. The Church of England was established in Maryland following the Glorious Revolution of 1688 when Maryland had its own "Protestant Revolution." In 1691, Maryland became a royal colony. In 1692, the Assembly met and passed a law establishing the "Protestant Religion." That act, however, contained a phrase England's attorney general found objectionable and was disallowed. Not until 1702 did Maryland's General Assembly pass a law establishing the Church of England absent the offending words.

25. Richard L. Morton, *Colonial Virginia*, 2 Vols. (Chapel Hill: University of North Carolina Press, 1960), 2:164; Woolverton, *Colonial Anglicanism in North America*, 48–49; William H. Seiler, "The Church of England as the Established Church in Seventeenth-Century Virginia," *Journal of Southern History* 15 (1949): 486–87.

26. Edward L. Bond, *Damned Souls in a Tobacco Colony: Religion in Seventeenth-Century Virginia* (Macon, Ga.: Mercer University Press, 2000), 58.

27. Kupperman, *Settling With the Indians*, 189–95.

28. John Beaulieu to William Trumball, 30 November 1609, in Philip L. Barbour, ed., *The Jamestown Voyages Under the First Charter, 1606–1609*, 2 Vols. (London: Cambridge University Press, 1969), 2:287, 253.

29. Morton, *Colonial Virginia*, 1:35–36; John Pory to Sir Edwin Sandys, 12 June 1620, in Susan Myra Kingsbury, ed., *The Records of the Virginia Company of London*, 4 Vols. (Washington, D.C.: U.S. Government Printing Office, 1906–1935), 3:304; William Strachey, "A True Reportory of the Wreck and Redemption of sir Thomas

Gates, Knight," in Louis B. Wright, ed., *A Voyage to Virginia in 1609* (Charlottesville: University Press of Virginia, 1964), 41–44. Brownists were Separatist Puritans who advocated a Congregational form of church government. The name comes from the Reverend Robert Browne (ca. 1550–1633), a Separatist Puritan who established some of the first independent congregations in England. He later reconciled with the Church of England and became an orthodox minister, although he may have continued to minister to some Separatist parishes.

30. David Holmes is correct in arguing that a case can be made for several dates as the year in which the Church of England was established in Virginia. For more on this point, see Holmes, *Brief History of the Episcopal Church*, 20; Richard Beale Davis, *Intellectual Life in the Colonial South, 1585–1763*, 3 Vols. (Knoxville: University of Tennessee Press, 1978), 2:633–39; Woolverton, *Colonial Anglicanism in North America*, 16; Samuel M. Bemiss, ed., *The Three Charters of the Virginia Company of London, with Seven Related Documents; 1606–1621* (Williamsburg, 1957), 57, see also 15; *Lawes Divine, Morall and Martiall*, 2, 10–11.

31. Butler, *Awash in a Sea of Faith*, 39–40; H. R. McIlwaine, ed., *Journals of the House of Burgesses of Colonial Virginia*, 13 Vols. (Richmond, 1905–1915), 1:9, 13, 11; Hening, *Statutes at Large*, 1:122–23; 2:54; H. R. McIlwaine, ed., *Minutes of the Council and the General Court of Colonial Virginia* (Richmond, 1924; 2d ed., Richmond, Virginia State Library, 1979), 105.

32. Irene D. Hecht, "The Virginia Company, 1607–1640: A Study in Frontier Growth" (Ph.D. dissertation, University of Washington, 1969); Woolverton, *Colonial Anglicanism in North America*, 246, n. 16.

33. Theodore K. Rabb, *Jacobean Gentleman: Sir Edwin Sandys, 1561–1629* (Princeton, N.J.: Princeton University Press, 1998), 36–38, 330. Sandys' book is titled *A Relation of the State of Religion, and With What Hopes and Policies it Hath Been Framed, and is Maintained, in the Several States of These Western Parts of the World* (London, 1605).

34. Butler, *Awash in a Sea of Faith*, 38; Rabb, *Jacobean Gentleman*, 330; Davis, *Intellectual Life in the Colonial South*, 2:643–44; John Bennett Boddie, "Edward Bennett of London and Virginia," *William and Mary Quarterly* 2d ser. 13 (1933): 117–30; Babette M. Levy, "Early Puritanism in the Southern and Island Colonies," *Proceedings of the American Antiquarian Society* 70 (1960): 93–94, 105–7.

35. Edmund S. Morgan, *American Slavery, American Freedom: The Ordeal of Colonial Virginia* (New York: W.W. Norton, 1975), 87–91; Morton, *Colonial Virginia*, 1:39–40; Warren M. Billings, John E. Selby, and Thad W. Tate, *Colonial Virginia: A History* (White Plains, N.Y.: KTO Press, 1986), 43; Sir Francis Wyatt, Commission to Sir George Yeardley, 20 June 1622, *Records of the Virginia Company of London*, 3:656. Similar complaints continued throughout the colonial period. After arriving in the colony in 1684 the Reverend John Clayton, who served what was then Virginia's most "urban" parish at James City, noted the colony's deficiencies: "The Country is thinly inhabited; the Living solitary & unsociable; Trading confused, & dispersed; besides other Inconveniences." See "A Letter from Mr. John Clayton to the Royal Society," in Force, *Tracts and Other Papers*, 3, no. 12:12, 21.

36. Edward Johnson to John Ferrar, 25 March 1650, Ferrar Papers, 1160.

37. Bond, *Damned Souls in a Tobacco Colony*, chs. 2 and 3.

38. Warren M. Billings, ed., *The Papers of Sir William Berkeley, 1605–1677* (forthcoming), "Biographical Sketch"; Warren M. Billings, "William Berkeley," in John T. Kneebone, J. Jefferson Looney, Brent Tarter, and Sandra Gioia Treadway, eds., *The Dictionary of Virginia Biography* (2 volumes to date, Richmond: The Library of Virginia, 1998), 1:454–58; Morton, *Colonial Virginia*, 1:151–52; Jon Butler, ed., "Two 1642 Letters from Virginia Puritans," *Massachusetts Historical Society Proceedings* 84 (1972): 90; Hening, *Statutes at Large*, 1:250–51; Jon Kukla, "Order and Chaos in Early America: Political and Social Stability in Pre-Restoration Virginia," *American Historical Review* 90 (1985): 291–92.

39. "Anthony Langston on Towns and Corporations; and on the Manufacture of Iron," *William and Mary Quarterly* 2d ser. 1 (1921): 100–6; *Virginia Magazine of History and Biography* 1 (1893–1894): 453; *Virginia Magazine of History and Biography* 28 (1920): 139–40.

40. Morton, *Colonial Virginia*, 1:170–73.

41. R[oger] G[reene], *Virginia's Cure: or an Advisive Narrative Concerning Virginia* . . . (London, 1662), Force, *Tracts and Other Papers*, 3, no. 15:4, 13–14. Greene denounced Virginians for their decision not to settle in towns, arguing that God had commanded Christians to do so and suggesting that Virginians, like the Jews of the Old Testament, had committed the sacrilege described in Haggai 1:9 and thus lay under the curse of God. Until Virginians stopped scattering about the countryside, Greene believed the colony would languish under the divine curse. See G[reene], *Virginia's Cure*, 5.

42. Alexander Forbes to Bishop Edmund Gibson, 21 July 1724, Fulham Palace Papers, vol. 13, no. 91, Lambeth Palace Library; William Stevens Perry, ed., *Historical Collections Relating to the American Colonial Church*, 4 Vols. (Hartford, 1870; reprint, New York: AMS Press, 1969), 1:328.

43. Public Records Office Colonial Office (PRO CO) 5/1323, 48. For another example, see Nelson, *Blessed Company*, 17.

44. George MacLaren Brydon, *Virginia's Mother Church and the Political Conditions Under Which it Grew*, 2 Vols. (Richmond: Virginia Historical Society, 1947–1952), 1:372–73; David L. Holmes, "The Anglican Tradition in Colonial Virginia," in Peter W. Williams, ed., *Perspectives on American Religion and Culture* (Malden, Mass.: Blackwell Publishers, Inc., 1999), 69; Parke Rouse, Jr., *James Blair of Virginia* (Chapel Hill: University of North Carolina Press, 1971), 28; Hening, *Statutes at Large*, 1:208, 241, 290; 2:44. The extant vestry books contain a great deal of evidence regarding payments to clerks and the construction of chapels of ease. Additional evidence may be found in the responses of Virginia ministers to the Bishop of London's Queries of 1724. They may be consulted most readily in Perry, *Historical Collections*, 1:261–318. In addition, see Alexander Forbes to Bishop Gibson, 21 July 1724, Fulham Palace Papers, vol. 13, no. 91; this letter is also reprinted in Perry, *Historical Collections*, 1:327. Darrett and Anita Rutman have argued that in Middlesex County some people traveled greater distances to attend the Upper Church rather than attend the Middle

Church that was closer to their homes because they did not care for the "manorial attitudes displayed by the Wormeleys" who attended the Middle Church. See Darrett B. and Anita H. Rutman, A *Place in Time: Middlesex County, Virginia, 1650–1750* (New York: W.W. Norton & Company, 1984), 123.

45. An act passed in 1699 reduced the legal requirement for church attendance to once every two months, but the once-a-month standard became law again in 1705. Hening, *Statutes at Large*, 3:170, 360; G[reene], *Virginia's Cure*, 4; Alexander Forbes to Bishop Gibson, 21 July 1724, Fulham Palace Papers, vol. 13, no. 91; Patricia U. Bonomi and Peter R. Eisenstadt, "Church Adherence in the Eighteenth-Century British American Colonies," *William and Mary Quarterly* 3d ser., 39 (1982): 254–57.

46. PRO CO 5/1322, Part I, 11; Louis B. Wright, ed., *The Prose Works of William Byrd of Westover: Narratives of a Colonial Virginian* (Cambridge, Mass.: Harvard University Press, 1966), 66, 72, 73, 76, 97, 101, 118, 123, 130, 144.

47. G[reene], *Virginia's Cure*, 5–6, 17; Woolverton, *Colonial Anglicanism in North America*, 62; James Maury to William Douglas, 31 May 1758, Sol Fienstone Collection, David Library of the American Revolution, on deposit at the American Philosophical Society, Philadelphia, Pennsylvania. Governor Alexander Spotswood thought the extent of Virginia's parishes might lead to civil faction, irreligion, and the rise of dissenters. See his prescient analysis in *Calendar of State Papers, Colonial Series, America and the West Indies, 1574–1739*, 45 Vols. (London, 1860–1994), 16:316. The glebe was the property devoted to the maintenance of the incumbent of a parish; in Virginia this usually meant land and a dwelling.

48. Alexander Whitaker to William Crashaw, 9 August 1611, in Alexander Brown, ed., *The Genesis of the United States*, 2 Vols. (New York, 1896), 1:499; William Fitzhugh to Nicholas Hayward, January 30, 1686/87, in Richard Beale Davis, ed., *William Fitzhugh and His Chesapeake World, 1676–1701: The Fitzhugh Letters and Other Documents* (Chapel Hill: University of North Carolina Press, 1963), 203. For a good discussion of how Virginians recruited ministers, see Joan R. Gundersen, "The Search for Good Men: Recruiting Ministers in Colonial Virginia," *Historical Magazine of the Protestant Episcopal Church* 47 (1979): 453–64.

49. Butler, *Awash in a Sea of Faith*, 38; G[reene], *Virginia's Cure*, 4; Patricia U. Bonomi, *Under the Cope of Heaven: Religion, Society, and Politics in Colonial America* (New York: Oxford University Press, 1986), 16. Population estimates may be found in Morgan, *American Slavery, American Freedom*, 404. For the number of clergy in Virginia at different periods, see Woolverton, *Colonial Anglicanism in North America*, 246, n. 6.

50. Richard Bennett to John Ferrar, 12 February 1652/53, Ferrar Papers, 1217. For additional background material on Bennett, see the entry for Richard Bennett in *Dictionary of Virginia Biography*, 1:445–47.

51. Butler, *Awash in a Sea of Faith*, 38; Kingsbury, *Records of the Virginia Company of London*, 1:434, 575, 591, 635; "Governor John Harvey's Propositions Touching Virginia, [1629]," and "Certaine Answeares to Capt. Harvey's Proposicons Touching Virginia," *Virginia Magazine of History and Biography* 7 (1900): 369–71; Philip

Alexander Bruce, *Institutional History of Virginia in the Seventeenth Century: An Inquiry into the Religious, Moral, Educational, Legal, Military, and Political Condition of the People, Based on Original and Contemporaneous Records*, 2 Vols. (Gloucester, Mass.: Peter Smith, 1964), 1:118–19.

52. *The Book of Common Prayer* (London, 1662), The Order of Confirmation; David R. Holeton, "Initiation," in Stephen Sykes, John Booty, and Jonathan Knight, eds., *The Study of Anglicanism* (Revised ed., Minneapolis: Fortress Press, 1988), 297–99.

53. Warren M. Billings, *Virginia's Viceroy: Their Majesties' Governor General: Francis Howard, Lord Howard of Effingham* (Fairfax, Va.: George Mason University Press, 1991), 80; Arthur Lyon Cross, *The Anglican Episcopate and the American Colonies* (Harvard Historical Studies IX, 1902; reprint, Hamden, Conn.: Archon Books, 1964), 10. On the consecration of colonial churches, see Lawrence deButts to – Berriman, 1 July 1722, Fulham Palace Papers, vol. 13, no. 133. On the consecration of churches and confirmation, see Hugh Jones, *The Present State of Virginia, From Whence is Inferred a Short View of Maryland and North Carolina*, ed. Richard L. Morton (London, 1724; Chapel Hill: University of North Carolina Press, 1956), 97; see Henry Dodwell to Archbishop Tenison, 29 August 1700, Fulham Palace Papers, Class 930, no. 38: "It is very requisite so vast tracts of lands should have Bishops of their own for Orders and Confirmations." On the lack of practical disciplinary power that Virginia's commissaries could exercise, see James Blair to Bishop Gibson, 13 May 1724, Fulham Palace Papers, vol. 15, 2d no. 70 (there are two numbered sets of items in volume 15).

54. An assistant bishop who helps the diocesan bishop perform his ecclesiastical duties.

55. Butler, *Awash in a Sea of Faith*, 42–43; Brydon, *Virginia's Mother Church*, 1:183–84; Woolverton, *Colonial Anglicanism in North America*, 220–33; Bishop of London's paper on a Suffragan for America, [1717?], Fulham Palace Papers, Class 711, no. 18; SPCK to Governor Drysdale, 2 August 1722, SPCK Archives, Miscellaneous Letters, CN 3/1, 76; Nancy L. Rhoden, *Revolutionary Anglicanism: The Colonial Church of England Clergy During the American Revolution* (London: MacMillan Press LTD, 1999), 37–63. There is evidence that as early as the 1720s some members of Virginia's Anglican clergy opposed episcopacy. See Anthony Gavin to Bishop Gibson, 5 August 1738, Fulham Palace Papers, vol. 14, no. 51.

56. Woolverton, *Colonial Anglicanism in North America*, 74–79.

57. Richard Bennett to John Ferrar, 12 February 1652/53, Ferrar Papers, 1217. See also the Reverend Edward Johnson to John Ferrar, 25 March 1650, Ferrar Papers, 1160; and William Fitzhugh to Captain Roger Jones, 18 May 1685, William Fitzhugh to John Cooper, 20 August 1690, in Davis, *William Fitzhugh and His Chesapeake World*, 168, 268.

58. Hening, *Statutes at Large*, 1:424, 418; James Horn, *Adapting to a New World: English Society in the Seventeenth-Century Chesapeake* (Chapel Hill: University of

North Carolina Press, 1994), 393; "The Church in Lower Norfolk County," *Lower Norfolk Virginia County Antiquary*, 3 (1899–1901): 31–32.

59. Alexander Cooke to [?], 26 September 1652, in Lancaster County, Deeds, Orders, Wills, Settlements of Estates, book 1 (1652–1657), 41.

60. Governor Francis Howard, Baron Howard of Effingham to Nathaniel Crew?, n.d. [between 1685 and 1690], in Warren M. Billings, ed., *The Papers of Francis Howard, Baron Howard of Effingham, 1643–1695* (Richmond: Virginia State Library and Archives, 1989), 458. "I have this Spring Convened all the clergy before me and have Inspected into their orders and qualifications. Som of them have no orders, and as little order in their lives whome I prohibited from offitiating in the holy function, others are of good lives, but not duely qualified, some only by their one own direction of themselves to the ministry, those I have permitted still to offitiate till I have your Lordships directions, as to preaching and baptisme, but not to read the absolution nor administer the blessed Sacrament of the Lords Supper, others have a qualification as to Deacons orders from Sir William Berkeley how that will qualify I beg your Lordships directions."

61. Gundersen, *Anglican Ministry in Virginia*, 119–42.

62. John Hammond, *Leah and Rachel, or, The Two Fruitfull Sisters Virginia and Maryland: Their Present Condition Impartially Stated and Related* (London, 1656), Force, *Tracts and Other Papers*, 3, no. 14: 9; Woolverton, *Colonial Anglicanism in North America*, 61.

63. For an example, see note 60.

64. Burgesses established the county court system in 1634.

65. Hening, *Statutes at Large*, 1:123.

66. Duffy, *Voices of Morebath*, 91.

67. Woolverton, *Colonial Anglicanism in North America*, 76; Hening, *Statutes at Large*, 1:155–60.

68. Woolverton, *Colonial Anglicanism in North America*, 75–78; Holmes, *Brief History of the Episcopal Church*, 20–22; Brydon, *Virginia's Mother Church*, 1:90–93. For the vestry acts of 1641/42 and 1642/43, see *Virginia Magazine of History and Biography* 9 (1901/02): 53; Hening, *Statutes at Large*, 1:246.

69. Hening, *Statutes at Large*, 2:44. For a more detailed discussion of vestries in colonial Virginia, see William H. Seiler, "The Anglican Parish in Virginia," in James Morton Smith, ed., *Seventeenth-Century America: Essays in Colonial History* (Chapel Hill: University of North Carolina Press, 1959), 126–27, 139–41; James Kimbrough Owen, "The Virginia Vestry: A Study in the Decline of a Ruling Class" (Ph.D. dissertation, Princeton University, 1947); Clive Raymond Hallman, "The Vestry as a Unit of Local Government in Colonial Virginia" (Ph.D. dissertation, University of Georgia, 1987); and especially Joan Rezner Gundersen, "The Myth of the Independent Virginia Vestry," *Historical Magazine of the Protestant Episcopal Church* 44 (1975): 133–41.

70. Borden W. Painter, Jr., "The Anglican Vestry in Colonial America," (Ph.D. dissertation, Yale University, 1965), 47–56; Bruce, *Institutional History of Virginia in the Seventeenth Century*, 1:72–93; Brydon, *Virginia's Mother Church*, 1:90–93; 2:75; Hall-

man, "The Vestry as a Unit of Local Government in Colonial Virginia," 182–214; Nelson, *Blessed Company*, 13–15; C. G. Chamberlayne, ed., *The Vestry Book of St. Paul's Parish, Hanover County, Virginia, 1706–1786* (Richmond: The Library Board, 1940), 396–400. An act of 1722 instructed anyone who killed swine roaming in the city of Williamsburg and could not identify the animal's owner to turn the dead swine over to the local vestry "for the use of the poor of the Parish." See Waverly K. Winfree, ed., *The Laws of Virginia, Being a Supplement to Hening's* The Statutes at Large, *1700–1750* (Richmond: Virginia State Library, 1971), 227–28, 139.

71. Hallman, "The Vestry as a Unit of Local Government in Colonial Virginia," 117–26, 132–34; Winfree, *The Laws of Virginia*, 247–53; 297–99.

72. Hallman, "The Vestry as a Unit of Local Government in Colonial Virginia," 126–32; William H. Seiler, "Land Processioning in Colonial Virginia," *William and Mary Quarterly* 3d ser. 6 (1949): 416–36; Hening, *Statutes at Large*, 2:101–02; 3:82, 325–27, 530–35; 5:426–30.

73. Hening, *Statutes at Large*, 1:242.

74. Hallman, "The Vestry as a Unit of Local Government in Colonial Virginia," 12–13, 37; Woolverton, *Colonial Anglicanism in North America*, 78; Hening, *Statutes at Large*, 1:433.

75. Nelson, *Blessed Company*, 273–79; McIlwaine, *Minutes of the Council and the General Court*, 142; Bond, *Damned Souls in a Tobacco Colony*, 125–27, 131–36; Martin Ingram, *Church Courts, Sex, and Marriage in England, 1570–1640* (Cambridge: Cambridge University Press), 4, 53.

76. York County Deeds, Orders, and Wills, book 2 (1645–1649), 386, The Library of Virginia. Segar's tale may also be found in Caroline Julia Richter, "A Community and its Neighborhoods: Charles Parish, York County, Virginia, 1630–1740," (Ph.D. dissertation, College of William and Mary, 1992), 211.

77. Bond, *Damned Souls in a Tobacco Colony*, 124–27.

78. Nelson, *Blessed Company*, 273.

79. Alexander Cooke to [?], 26 September 1652, in Lancaster County, Deeds, Wills, Settlements of Estates, book 1 (1652–1657), 41, The Library of Virginia; "Some Extracts from the Records of Lancaster County," *William and Mary Quarterly* 1st ser. 20 (1911): 136–37; Horn, *Adapting to a New World*, 393.

80. Woolverton, *Colonial Anglicanism in North America*, 38; "The Church in Lower Norfolk," *Lower Norfolk County Virginia Antiquary* 3 (1899–1901): 33–34; Bond, *Damned Souls in a Tobacco Colony*, 188–89, 210–13, 218–19.

81. Woolverton, *Colonial Anglicanism in North America*, 71–74; Brydon, *Virginia's Mother Church*, 1:512–14; James Wallace to the Society for the Propagation of the Gospel, 3 April 1707, SPG Archives, A/3, 315; H. R. McIlwaine, ed., *Executive Journals of the Council of Colonial Virginia*, 6 Vols. (Richmond: Virginia State Library, 1925), 1:328, 309; "Sir E. Andros no real friends [sic] to the Clergy," Perry, *Historical Collections*, 1:34–35.

82. Bond, *Damned Souls in a Tobacco Colony*, 195–213.

83. Cross, *Anglican Episcopate*, 26.

84. Some may have been ordained in the Scottish Church, although some of the Virginians probably held the irregular deacon's orders from Governor Berkeley.

85. A Memorial of Abuses that are crept into the Churches of the Plantations, PRO CO 1/41, 48–49; Cross, *Anglican Episcopate*, 24–27; Hening, *Statutes at Large*, 2:46.

86. Cross, *Anglican Episcopate*, 25–33; Billings, *Virginia's Viceroy*, 79–80; Rouse, *James Blair of Virginia*, 61; Instructions to Governor Thomas Lord Culpeper, 6 September 1679, Fulham Palace Paper, vol. 14, no. 12.

87. Rouse, *James Blair of Virginia*, 61.

88. Perry, *Historical Collections*, 1:2–3; Billings, *Virginia's Viceroy*, 79; Cross, *Anglican Episcopate*, 31.

89. Brydon, *Virginia's Mother Church*, 1:228.

90. Billings, *Virginia's Viceroy*, 80.

91. The best biographical treatment of Blair is Thad Tate, "James Blair," *Dictionary of Virginia Biography*, 1:539–43. See also Daphne Gentry and Brent Tarter, "The Blair Family of Williamsburg, A Research Note," *Magazine of Virginia Genealogy* 32 (1994): 103–112; Rouse, *James Blair of Virginia*, 16–21, 34–35; Brydon, *Virginia's Mother Church*, 2:273–86.

92. Virginia clergy opposed to Blair later questioned whether the commissary had received episcopal ordination. P. G. Scott has vindicated Blair from the charge of a nonvalid ordination in his "James Blair and the Scottish Church: A New Source," *William and Mary Quarterly* 3d ser. 33 (1976): 300–8.

93. Thad W. Tate, "The Colonial College, 1693–1782," in Susan H. Godson et al., eds., *The College of William and Mary: A History* (Williamsburg, Va.: King and Queen Press, 1993), 3–80; Rouse, *James Blair of Virginia*, 37–38, 43–44, 64–77; Gundersen, *Anglican Ministry in Virginia*, 32–33; Stephen Fouace and nine Trustees of the College of William and Mary to Archbishop Thomas Tenison, 16 April 1697, Fulham Palace Papers, vol. 15, no. 41.

94. Rouse, *James Blair of Virginia*, 39–43, 143–48, 200; McIlwaine, *Journals of the House of Burgesses*, 2:366–67; Brydon, *Virginia's Mother Church*, 1:321, 323; Hening, *Statutes at Large*, 3:152; 4:206–7. Earlier in the seventeenth century, the General Assembly had set ministers' salaries at ten pounds of tobacco and a bushel of corn per tithable, plus the twentieth calf, kid, and hog "throughout all plantations in this colony." See Hening, *Statutes at Large*, 1:159, 242. Tithables included all slaves and all males over the age of sixteen in a household.

95. Samuel Clyde McCulloch, ed., "James Blair's Plan of 1699 to Reform the Clergy of Virginia," *William and Mary Quarterly* 3d ser. 4 (1947): 70–86. In fairness to Blair, Bishop Compton allowed his clergy to make similar arrangements in rural areas of the Diocese of London. Although Compton opposed pluralism, he nonetheless recognized the necessity of allowing ministers of poor parishes to serve an additional parish or two so that they did not fall into poverty.

96. PRO CO 5/1309, 43–45. For more on the General Assembly's opposition to Blair's plan, see Edward Nott to the Committee on Trade and Plantations, 24 De-

cember 1705, PRO CO 5/1315, Part I, 26–29. The actual value of any minister's living depended on several factors: the type of tobacco grown in his parish—sweet scented fetched a better price on the market than Oronoco—the condition of the market, and the quality of the tobacco paid to them. Ministers also received perquisites for performing marriages, preaching funeral sermons, and baptizing children. Highly regarded clergyman sometimes received more than the 16,000 pounds prescribed by law. The Reverend Francis Fontaine of York-Hampton Parish, for instance, estimated his salary at "about £150 per annum arising from 20,000 pounds weight of Sweet Scented Tobacco and a few perquisites." See the answers to the bishop of London's queries in Perry, *Historical Collections*, 1:261–318; *Calendar of State Papers, Colonial Series, America and the West Indies*, 11:155. An outstanding survey of many of these issues may be found in Susie M. Ames, *Studies of the Virginia Eastern Shore in the Seventeenth Century* (Richmond: The Dietz Press, 1940), 208–42. Joan Gundersen has argued convincingly that after the General Assembly passed the Tobacco Act of 1736, a statute which introduced quality control measures for Virginia tobacco, ministers' salaries improved tremendously. See Gundersen, *Anglican Ministry in Virginia*, 90. Ministers also derived some income from their glebe lands.

97. Nicholas Moreau to the bishop of Lichfield and Coventry, 12 April 1697, Fulham Palace Papers, vol. 14, no. 59; Perry, *Historical Collections*, 1:30. Many of the documents regarding Blair's conflict with the clergy may be found in Perry, *Historical Collections*, 1:116–17, 144–79, 199–225.

98. Tate, "James Blair," *Dictionary of Virginia Biography*, 1:539–43; Rouse, *James Blair of Virginia*, 101–12, 148–74, 194–208; Alexander Spotswood to the Committee for Trade and Plantations, 22 December 1717, PRO CO 1/1318, 291–98. Blair also played a role in the recall of Governors Andros and Nicholson.

99. Butler, *Awash in a Sea of Faith*, 100; Gundersen, *Anglican Ministry in Virginia*, 33, 55, 67, 231.

100. Bruce, *Institutional History of Virginia in the Seventeenth Century*, 1:222–51.

101. Many other people, however, found Quaker worship peculiar. Joseph Pilmore, a Methodist itinerant, described his experiences at a Quaker Meeting in 1770: "Having a special regard for the Quakers, I went with a Friend to Meeting. We waited long for the word of God, but alas! Alas! How much we were disappointed. Though there were eight Public Friends present in the Assembly, not one of them opened his mouth! What strange religious worship is this! Surely those that have the life of God in their souls, will have something to say for their Master. That Christians should wait inwardly upon the Lord, is plain and clear as the light; but, for *Ministers* to sit silent when the people are perishing for lack of knowledge, is certainly wrong. The Lord hath said, *I will set watchmen upon thy walls O Jerusalem that shall never hold their peace*, and again, *Ye that make mention of the Lord keep not silence* (Isaiah 62:6)." In Frederick E. Maser and Howard T. Maag, eds., *The Journal of Joseph Pilmore, Methodist Itinerant, for the Years August 1, 1769, to January 2, 1774* (Philadelphia: Historical Society of the Philadelphia Annual Conference of the United Methodist Church, 1969), 56.

102. Barry Reay, "Quakerism and Society," in J. F. McGregor and B. Reay, eds., *Radical Religion in the English Revolution* (New York: Oxford University Press, 1984), 148–49, 158–59; Michael R. Watts, *The Dissenters: From the Reformation to the French Revolution* (New York: Oxford University Press, 1978), 194, 210–11.

103. Hening, *Statutes at Large*, 2:198; Warren M. Billings, ed., "A Quaker in Seventeenth–Century Virginia: Four Remonstrances by George Wilson," *William and Mary Quarterly* 3d ser. 33 (1976): 130.

104. Quakers saw the parish levy differently and considered it a great and unfair burden. Sometimes they accused parish ministers of using the parish levy to devour widows' houses. Virginia Quakers, however, were not always consistent in their opposition to the parish levy and military service. While Quakers did not believe that they should be forced to pay tithes to the local parish on behalf of themselves, some Virginia Quakers thought they legitimately owed these dues to the parish on behalf of any of their slaves who received religious instruction from the parish minister. The Chuckatuck Meeting thought this issue so important that its members wrote to the London meeting for advice. They were instructed to pay no tithes at all. See Worrall, *Friendly Virginians*, 110–11, 117.

105. Brydon, *Virginia's Mother Church*, 1:248–50; Nelson, *Blessed Company*, 242.

106. H. R. McIlwaine, ed., *Executive Journals of the Council of Colonial Virginia*, 1:161, 167.

107. Hening, *Statutes at Large*, 3:298; Worrall, *Friendly Virginians*, 114–15.

108. "Religious Differences Between George Walker and His Wife," *Virginia Magazine of History and Biography* 16 (1908): 79–81; "Old Kecoughtan," *William and Mary Quarterly* 1st ser. 9 (1900): 127.

109. Worrall, *Friendly Virginians*, 113; H. R. McIlwaine, *Executive Journals of the Council of Colonial Virginia*, 3:469, 611. The 1663 statute is in Hening, *Statutes at Large*, 2:180–83. The course of the repeal may be followed in PRO CO 5/1318, 118–19, 153–60, 167–68.

110. Anthony Gavin to Bishop Edmund Gibson, 5 August 1738, Fulham Palace Papers, vol. 14, no. 51.

111. Robert Beverley, *The History and Present State of Virginia* (London, 1705), ed. Louis B. Wright, (Chapel Hill: University of North Carolina Press, 1947), 261; Butler, *Awash in a Sea of Faith*, 101.

112. Virginia Quakers did not always show a great deal of consistency regarding what constituted military service. In 1711, for example, when word reached Virginia that a French squadron was on the way to attack the colony, Governor Spotswood mobilized the militia to rebuild Fort Algernon. Spotswood tried to accommodate Quakers in the area by exempting them from bearing arms as long as they worked to rebuild the fort. Quakers on the lower James River refused, although Quakers further upriver at Curles agreed to repair a battery at Jamestown. The Curles group, however, later refused to sell the governor pork to provision the militia. See Worrall, *Friendly Virginians*, 111–12.

113. Bruce, *Institutional History of Virginia in the Seventeenth Century*, 1:262–63; Butler, *Awash in a Sea of Faith*, 49, 101; Morton, *Colonial Virginia*, 2:583–84; Brydon,

Virginia's Mother Church, 2:72–78; Painter, "The Anglican Vestry in Colonial America," 56. For Makemie, see Allen Johnson et al., *Dictionary of American Biography*, 20 Vols., 7 Supplements (New York: Charles Scribner's Sons, 1928–1981), 12:215–16. Makemie received a warmer welcome in Virginia than he did in New York where Lord Cornbury, the governor, had him arrested. Cornbury described Makemie as a "Jack of all Trades; he is a Preacher, a Doctor of Physick, a Merchant, an Attorney, or Counsellor of Law, and which is worse of all, a Disturber of Governments."

114. Butler, *Awash in a Sea of Faith*, 124–25.

115. Joan Rezner Gundersen, "The Huguenot Church at Manakin in Virginia, 1700–1750," *Goochland County Historical Society Magazine* 23 (1991): 19–40; Morton, *Colonial Virginia*, 1:367–68; Davies, *Intellectual Life in the Colonial South*, 2:696; Jon Butler, *The Huguenots in America* (Cambridge, Mass.: Harvard University Press, 1983), 220; Brydon, *Virginia's Mother Church*, 1:261–64. Gundersen's work offers the fullest treatment of the Huguenots in Virginia.

116. The discussion of German religious groups in Virginia comes from Brydon, *Virginia's Mother Church*, 2:83–93, 98–104; *Colonial Virginia*, 2:592; Rev. Patrick Henry to Rev. [John Peter] Stehelin, 4 September 1734, Certificate of Governor William Gooch, 18 September 1734, in John C. Van Horne, ed., *Religious Philanthropy and Colonial Slavery: The American Correspondence of the Associates of Dr. Bray, 1717–1777* (Urbana: University of Illinois Press, 1987), 79–81. For more on the Lutherans in Virginia, see William Edward Eisenberg, *The Lutheran Church in Virginia, 1717–1962, including an Account of the Lutheran Church in East Tennessee* (Roanoke, Va.: Trustees of the Virginia Synod, Lutheran Church in America, 1967). For more on the Mennonites in Virginia, see Harry Anthony Brunk, *History of Mennonites in Virginia, 1727–1900* (Staunton, Va.: McClure Printing Company, 1959). Jon F. Sensbach, *A Separate Canaan: The Making of an Afro-Moravian World in North Carolina, 1763–1840* (Chapel Hill: University of North Carolina Press, 1998) is essential for understanding the Moravians in America.

117. The term was first used in 1841 in Joseph Tracy, *The Great Awakening: A History of the Revival of Religion During the Time of Edwards & Whitefield* (n.p., 1841). See Butler, *Awash in a Sea of Faith*, 164.

118. George William Pilcher, *Samuel Davies: Apostle of Dissent in Colonial Virginia* (Knoxville: University of Tennessee Press, 1971), 21. For a scholarly treatment of Tennent see Milton J. Coalter, Jr., *Gilbert Tennent, Son of Thunder: A Case Study of Continental Pietism's Impact on the First Great Awakening in the Middle Colonies* (Westport, Conn.: Greenwood Press, 1986).

119. John Spurr, *The Restoration Church of England, 1646–1689* (New Haven, Conn.: Yale University Press, 1991), 334.

120. Spurr, *Restoration Church of England*, 108. See also "Draft Representation of the Society for Propagating the Gospel in Foreign Parts to King George I," 3 June 1715, Fulham Palace Papers, vol. 36: 42–43.

121. William Beveridge, *A Sermon concerning the Excellency and Usefulness of the Common Prayer . . .* (1682; London, 1779); Davies, *Worship and Theology in England*, 2:196; Blair, *Our Saviour's Divine Sermon on the Mount*, 4:9.

122. Beveridge, *Excellency and Usefulness of the Common Prayer*, 7–8. This passage is also quoted in Isaac, *Transformation of Virginia*, 64; and Davies, *Worship and Theology in England*, 3:26–27.

123. Beveridge, *Excellency and Usefulness of the Common Prayer*, 17, 21–23, 39.

124. Beveridge, *Excellency and Usefulness of the Common Prayer*, 11. Some Anglican apologists argued that brief collects or "arrow-like prayers" required less time than the long extemporaneous effusions of the dissenters and therefore ran less risk of losing the auditors' attention. See Davies, *Worship and Theology in England*, 2:212; and Blair, *Our Saviour's Divine Sermon on the Mount*, 4:9.

125. Pilcher, *Samuel Davies*, 23–25, 62. See also Philip N. Mulder, "Converting the New Light: Presbyterian Evangelicalism in Hanover, Virginia," *Journal of Presbyterian History* 75 (1997): 141–51.

126. Uncle of the patriot.

127. Samuel Davies, *The State of Religion among the Protestant Dissenters in Virginia; in a Letter to the Rev. Mr. Joseph Bellamy . . .* (Boston, 1751), in Alan Heimert and Perry Miller, eds., *The Great Awakening: Documents Illustrating the Crisis and its Consequences* (New York: Bobbs Merrill Company, 1967), 384–85.

128. Rhys Isaac, "Religion and Authority: Problems of the Anglican Establishment in Virginia in the Era of the Great Awakening and the Parsons' Cause," *William and Mary Quarterly* 3d ser. 30 (1973): 22–23; Pilcher, *Samuel Davies*, 27–29. For a more detailed account of Presbyterians in the South, see Ernest Trice Thompson, *The Presbyterians in the South*, 2 Vols. (Richmond: John Knox Press, 1963).

129. Isaac, "Religion and Authority," 24–25; Brydon, *Virginia's Mother Church*, 2:158–60; A Petition of Five Church of England Ministers to the General Assembly, n.d. [but after Samuel Davies' arrival in Virginia in 1747], Fulham Palace Papers, vol. 14, no. 26. This petition provides a good indication of many Anglican ministers' attitude toward the Great Awakening, especially in areas where the dissenters challenged the established church. Consider the petition's contemptuous opening and its underlying fear of disorder: "That there have been frequently held in the Counties of Hanover, Henrico, Goochland, & some others, for several Years past, numerous Assemblies, especially of the common People, upon a pretended religious Account; convened, sometimes by merely Lay-Enthusiasts, who, in those Meetings, read sundry fanatical Books, & used long extempore Prayers, and Discourses; sometimes by strolling pretended Ministers; and at present by one Mr. Samuel Davies, who has fixed himself in Hanover." Leaders' concern with itinerants predated the outbreak of the Great Awakening. As early as 1699 the Council sent a questionnaire to each county court which included, among other queries, "whither any wandering Strangers come into their Counties as Preachers or upon any other pretence of Religion whatsoever." See McIlwaine, *Executive Journals of the Council of Colonial Virginia*, 1:456.

130. Isaac, "Religion and Authority," 25.

131. Biographical material on Davies may be found in Pilcher, *Samuel Davies*, 3–19, 171–80, 186. For a study of his preaching, see Barbara Ann Larson, "Rhetorical Study of the Preaching of the Reverend Samuel Davies in the Colony of Virginia

from 1747–1759" (Ph.D. dissertation, University of Minnesota, 1969). Davies was also one of several ministers in colonial Virginia who wrote poetry. James Maury and Jonathan Boucher circulated copies of their verse privately. Davies and William Dawson both published collections of their poetry in Williamsburg. See Samuel Davies, *Miscellaneous Poems, Chiefly on Divine Subjects* (Williamsburg, 1752). There is a modern edition, which includes Davies' uncollected poems as well. See Samuel Davies, *Collected Poems*, ed. and introd. by Richard Beale Davis (Gainesville, Fla.: Scholars' Facsimiles & Reprints, 1968). [William Dawson], *Poems on Several Occasion, by a Gentleman of Virginia* (Williamsburg, 1736); modern editions are available in *Poems on Several Occasions, by a Gentleman of Virginia*, ed. Earl Gregg Swem (New York, 1920), and *Poems on Several Occasions, by a Gentleman of Virginia, Reproduced from the Edition of 1736 with a Biographical Note by Ralph K. Lusk* (New York: Facsimile Text Society, 1930).

132. Pilcher, *Samuel Davies*, 17–18, 34, 54; Brydon, *Virginia's Mother Church*, 2:161–62; Morton, *Colonial Virginia*, 2:592–94. Gooch issued his proclamation on 3 April 1747; Davies requested a license from the General Court in Williamsburg on 14 April 1747. Davies did not settle in Virginia permanently until 1748.

133. Isaac, "Religion and Authority," 26, n. 99.

134. Samuel Davies to William Dawson, 3 February 1749/50, Dawson Papers, 1:82–83, Library of Congress. In 1733, the Augusta County court had allowed an Old Side Presbyterian minister, the Reverend Alexander Craighead, to officiate at marriages. These were likely not isolated cases. See Brydon, *Virginia's Mother Church*, 2:76. A statute of 1748 set ministers' fees for performing a marriage at 20 shillings if the couple had secured a license from the governor and 5 shillings if the minister had published the banns, for which he also received one shilling and six pence. County courts issued the licenses. See Hening, *Statutes at Large*, 6:84. Earlier schedules of fees may be found in Hening, *Statutes at Large*, 1:160, 184; 2:55; 3:445. For the established clergy's view of Davies, see note 129 above.

135. Pilcher, *Samuel Davies*, 87–88; Thomas E. Buckley, S.J., *Church and State in Revolutionary Virginia, 1776–1787* (Charlottesville: University Press of Virginia, 1977), 13.

136. Isaac, "Religion and Authority," 27, 32; Pilcher, *Samuel Davies*, 14, 121–22; Bonomi, *Under the Cope of Heaven*, 181–82; Morton, *Colonial Virginia*, 2:594. In 1752 controversy over the degree of religious toleration extended to New Lights and other dissenting groups in the colony erupted in a series of letters published in the *Virginia Gazette*. An opponent of toleration wrote: "If we admit the *extensive* Toleration, I apprehend all our Preachers both of the *Church* and among the *Sectaries*, instead of recommending Virtue and Piety to their Hearers, will get to Daggers drawing among themselves, and mauling one another, while we stand by and cry, *Halloo!* to it Boys! by Way of being *edified* with Recreation. This I am informed is a Diversion weekly exhibited by the *dissenting* and *contending* orators of *Pennsylvania*, which does not seem calculated to diminish the *useless Lumber* among our Preachers, but I own may be agreeable to such, as go to Church or Meeting for Sport, and had rather be *entertained*

than *instructed.*" See *Virginia Gazette* (Hunter), 3 April 1752. The other letters may be found in *Virginia Gazette* (Hunter), 5 March 1752, 20 March 1752. Another newspaper dispute, this one between the Reverend Isaac Giberne of Lunenburg Parish and the Reverend James Waddell, a Presbyterian minister, may be traced in *Virginia Gazette* (Rind), 21 July 1768; 18 August 1768, supplement; 15 September 1768.

137. Small groups of Regular (Calvinist) Baptists had lived in the colony since at least the 1690s. They tended to concentrate in the Northern Neck, a peninsula between the Rappahannock and Potomac Rivers. After 1770, they spread across the Allegheny Mountains. Unlike the Separates, the Regulars tended to adhere to the laws of the state and usually sought licenses for preachers and meetinghouses. See Buckley, *Church and State in Revolutionary Virginia*, 13–14; Brydon, *Virginia's Mother Church*, 2:178–79; Garnett Ryland, *The Baptists of Virginia, 1699–1926* (Richmond: Virginia Baptist Board of Missions and Education, 1955), 1–39.

138. Christine Leigh Heyrman, *Southern Cross: The Beginnings of the Bible Belt* (New York: Alfred J. Knopf, 1997), 17.

139. Buckley, *Church and State in Revolutionary Virginia*, 14. For a denominational history of the Baptists, see David Benedict, *A General History of the Baptist Denomination in America, and Other Parts of the World*, 2 Vols. (Boston: Lincoln and Edmands, 1813). See also Janet Moore Lindman, "A World of Baptists: Gender, Race, and Religious Community in Pennsylvania and Virginia, 1689–1825" (Ph.D. dissertation, University of Minnesota, 1994.)

140. *Virginia Gazette* (Purdie and Dixon), 4 October 1770, 31 October 1771.

141. Heyrman, *Southern Cross*, 17–19. For additional examples of Baptist persecution see Ryland, *Baptists of Virginia*, 56–59. Anglican animosity to Baptist preachers can be overstated. Ministers sometimes acted to prevent their harassment. See Gundersen, *Anglican Ministry in Virginia*, 191–92; Brydon, *Virginia's Mother Church*, 2:185.

142. Gundersen, *Anglican Ministry in Virginia*, 190.

143. Isaac, *Transformation of Virginia, 1740–1790*, 173; Buckley, *Church and State in Revolutionary Virginia*, 13.

144. Arminianism is identified with the revolt against deterministic Calvinism associated with the Dutch Reformed theologian Jacobus Arminius (1560–1609). It challenged all the major points of Calvinism—man's total depravity, unconditional election, limited atonement, irresistible grace, and the perseverance of the saints. Arminians believed that man is not "wholly passive in the process of regeneration but actively chooses . . . or refuses, a preferred salvation." See Heimert and Miller, *Great Awakening*, xviii, n. 4. For an excellent study of Calvinism and Arminianism in Early Modern England, see Peter White, *Predestination, Policy, and Polemic: Conflict and Consensus in the English Church from the Reformation to the Civil War* (New York: Cambridge University Press, 1992).

145. Rhys Isaac, "Evangelical Revolt: The Nature of the Baptists' Challenge to the Traditional Order in Virginia, 1765–1775," *William and Mary Quarterly* 3d ser. 31 (1974): 358, 353; Heyrman, *Southern Cross*, 20–21. See also Janet Moore Lindman,

"Acting the Manly Christian: White Evangelical Masculinity in Revolutionary Virginia," *William and Mary Quarterly* 3d ser. 57 (2000): 393–416; and Jewel L. Spangler, "Becoming Baptists: Conversion in Colonial and Early National Virginia," *Journal of Southern History* 67 (2001): 243–86.

146. Pilcher, *Samuel Davies*, 89; Ryland, *Baptists of Virginia*, 41.

147. Isaac, "Evangelical Revolt," 360–61; Heyrman, *Southern Cross*, 16; Brydon, *Virginia's Mother Church*, 2:181–82; Morton, *Colonial Virginia*, 2:822.

148. Isaac, *Transformation of Virginia, 1740–1790*, 170–71.

149. Paul K. Longmore, "'All Matters and Things Relating to Religion and Morality': The Virginia Burgesses' Committee for Religion, 1769–1775," *Journal of Church and State* 38 (1996): 775–98; see also Daniel L. Dreisbach, "George Mason's Pursuit of Religious Liberty in Revolutionary Virginia," *Virginia Magazine of History and Biography* 108 (2000): 3–44.

150. Pronounced clark.

151. Buckley, *Church and State in Revolutionary Virginia*, 4.

152. Jon Butler, *Huguenots in America*, 220.

153. Hening, *Statutes at Large*, 2:511, 517.

154. Devereux Jarratt, *The Life of the Reverend Devereux Jarratt*, John Coleman, ed. (Baltimore, 1806; reprint, New York: Arno Press, Inc., 1969), 16, 20, 35.

155. Philip Ludwell to Philip Ludwell II, 20 December 1707, Lee Family Papers, Virginia Historical Society; John Page, *Deed of Gift to My Dear Son*, 216.

156. Marvin Yeoman Whitings, "Religious Literature in Virginia, 1685–1786: A Preface to a Study of the History of Ideas" (M.A. thesis: Emory University, 1975).

157. *Virginia Gazette*, 15–22 December 1738.

158. John Talbot to Richard Gillingham, 3 May 1703, SPG Archives, ser. A., vol. I, 120. Books were such an important means of spreading the Gospel that among the Bishop of London's queries sent to colonial clergy in 1724 was a question about parish libraries.

159. Worrall, *Friendly Virginians*, 98; [Charles Leslie], *The Snake in the Grass: or, Satan Transform'd into an Angel of Light. Discovering the Deep and Unsuspected Subtilty Which is Couched Under the Pretended Simplicity of Many of the Principal Leaders of Those People Call'd Quakers* (London, 1696); Joseph Wyath, *Anguis Flagellatus: or, A Switch for the Snake. Being an Answer to the Third and Last Edition of The Snake in the Grass. Wherein that Author's Injustice and Falshood, Both in Quotation and Story, are Discover'd and Obviated. And the Truth Doctrinally Deliver'd by Us, Stated and Maintained in Opposition to His Misrepresentation and Perversion* (London, 1699). Numerous references to Quaker books sent to Virginia may be found in the Library of the Society of Friends. See, for instance, Epistles Sent, vol. 1 (1683–1703), 245, 399; Epistles Sent, vol. 2 (1704–1726), 14; Meetings for Sufferings, vol. 2 (1680–1683), 164.

160. Richard Beeman, *The Evolution of the Southern Backcountry: A Case Study of Lunenburg County, Virginia, 1746–1832* (Philadelphia: University of Pennsylvania Press, 1984), 44–46, 52; James Craig to Thomas Dawson, 8 September 1759, Dawson Papers, 2:217–18, Library of Congress.

161. Pilcher, *Samuel Davies*, 105.

162. Paul E. Hoffman, *A New Andalucia and a Way to the Orient: The American Southeast During the Sixteenth Century* (Baton Rouge: Louisiana State University Press, 1990): 262–65; Charlotte M. Grady, "Spanish Jesuits in Virginia: The Mission that Failed," *Virginia Magazine of History and Biography* 96 (1988): 131–54. Many of the original documents pertaining to this mission may be consulted in Clifford M. Lewis, S.J., and Albert J. Loomie, S.J., *The Spanish Jesuit Mission in Virginia, 1570–1572* (Chapel Hill: University of North Carolina Press, 1953). For an account of Roman Catholicism in Virginia, see Gerald P. Fogarty, S.J., *Commonwealth Catholicism: A History of the Catholic Church in Virginia* (Notre Dame, Ind.: University of Notre Dame Press, 2001).

163. In the seventeenth century, the term "planter" referred to people who traveled to the New World and helped settle the continent. "Adventurers" were people who offered financial support to the colonization venture.

164. George Thorpe and John Pory to Edwin Sandys, 15 and 16 May 1621, Kingsbury, *Records of the Virginia Company of London*, 3:446.

165. Richard Ferrar to [George Thorpe], 13 December 1618, Ferrar Papers, 93.

166. Michael Anesko, "So Discreet a Zeal: Slavery and the Anglican Church in Virginia, 1680–1730," *Virginia Magazine of History and Biography* 93 (1985): 258–59, 268–69; W. Stitt Robinson, Jr., "Indian Education and Missions in Colonial Virginia," *Journal of Southern History* 18 (1952): 152–68, Andros quotation on 161.

167. Margaret Connell Szasz, *Indian Education in the American Colonies, 1607–1783* (Albuquerque: University of New Mexico Press, 1988), 69–74; Anesko, "So Discreet a Zeal," 273–76.

168. Szasz, *Indian Education in the American Colonies*, 74–77; Karen A. Stuart, "'So Good a Work': The Brafferton School, 1691–1777" (M.A. thesis: College of William and Mary, 1984), 70, 81.

169. Ira Berlin, *Many Thousands Gone: The First Two Centuries of Slavery in North America* (Cambridge, Mass.: Harvard University Press, 1998) 17–46, quotation on 29; Warren M. Billings, "The Cases of Fernando and Elizabeth Key: A Note on the Status of Blacks in Seventeenth-Century Virginia," *William and Mary Quarterly* 3d ser. 30 (1973): 469–71.

170. Hening, *Statutes at Large*, 2:260; Edmund Gibson, *Two Letters of the Lord Bishop of London . . .* (London, 1728; 2d. ed. London, 1729), 21–22. The best discussion of Gibson's letters may be found in Sylvia R. Frey and Betty Wood, *Come Shouting to Zion: African American Protestantism in the American South and British Caribbean to 1830* (Chapel Hill: University of North Carolina Press, 1998), 68–70. See also Thad W. Tate, *The Negro in Eighteenth-Century Williamsburg* (Williamsburg: Colonial Williamsburg, 1965), 65–90.

171. Woolverton, *Colonial Anglicanism in North America*, 72; Morgan Godwyn, *The Negro's and Indian's Advocate Suing for their Admission into the Church* (London, 1680), 36.

172. Berlin, *Many Thousands Gone*, 109–12.

173. Rev. James Marye, Jr., to Rev. John Waring, 25 September 1764, in Van Horne, *Religious Philanthropy and Colonial Slavery*, 219; Epistles Received, vol. 4 (1758–1778), Library of the Society of Friends, 56.

174. James Blair to Bishop Gibson, 20 July 1730, Fulham Palace Papers, vol. 13, no. 131; Gibson, *Two Letters of the Lord Bishop of London*, 14–15; Gundersen, *Anglican Ministry in Virginia*, 109; James Blair to Bishop Gibson, 28 June 1729, Fulham Palace Papers, vol. 15, no. 109; PRO CO 5/1322, Part I, 158.

175. Rev. Alexander Rhonnald to Rev. John Waring, 27 September 1762, in Van Horne, *Religious Philanthropy and Colonial Slavery*, 181.

176. Epistles Received, vol. 4 (1758–1778), 3, 26 (quotation), 56, 171.

177. Gundersen, *Anglican Ministry in Virginia*, 111–12.

178. Anesko, "So Discreet a Zeal," 252–53, 278.

179. Rev. Jonathan Boucher to Rev. John Waring, 9 March 1767, Van Horne, *Religious Philanthropy and Colonial Slavery*, 255; Pilcher, *Samuel Davies*, 105. See also Woolverton, *Colonial Anglicanism in North America*, 150–52.

180. William Dawson to Dr. Bearcroft, 12 July 1744, Dawson Papers, 1:22, Library of Congress.

181. Frey and Wood, *Come Shouting to Zion*, 96; Gundersen, *Anglican Ministry in Virginia*, 108–12.

182. Van Horne, *Religious Philanthropy and Colonial Slavery*, 6–7, 20–25; Gundersen, *Anglican Ministry in Virginia*, 114–15.

183. Thomas N. Ingersoll, "'Release us out of this Cruell Bondegg': An Appeal from Virginia in 1723," *William and Mary Quarterly* 3d ser. 51 (1994): 781–82.

184. Hunter Dickinson Farish, ed., *Journal & Letters of Philip Vickers Fithian, 1773–1774: A Planter Tutor of the Old Dominion* (Williamsburg: Colonial Williamsburg, 1965), 89.

185. Davis, *Intellectual Life in the Colonial South*, 2:682–83; Edward Miles Riley, ed., *The Journal of John Harrower, an Indentured Servant in the Colony of Virginia, 1773–1776* (Williamsburg: Colonial Williamsburg, 1963), xviii, 48, 124.

186. Nelson, *Blessed Company*, 264.

187. The Reverend Anthony Gavin provides a rare example of a colonial minister in Virginia who openly opposed the institution of slavery. See Anthony Gavin to Bishop Gibson, 5 August 1738, Fulham Palace Papers, vol. 14, no. 51: "it gives me great deal of uneasines to see the greatest Part of our Brethren taken up in farming and buying Slaves, which in my humble Opinion is unlawfull for any Christian, and particularly for a Clergyman, by this the Souls Committed to their Care must suffer." For more on Gavin, see Joan R. Gundersen, "Anthony Gavin's *A Master-key to Popery*: A Virginia Parson's Best Seller," *Virginia Magazine of History and Biography* 82 (1974): 39–46.

188. James Maury to Thomas Dawson, 6 October 1755, Dawson Papers, 2:237–38.

PART TWO

DOCUMENTS

~

CHAPTER TWO

John Page: A *Deed of Gift* to My *Dear Son*[1]

John Page's A *Deed of Gift to My Dear Son* ranks among the most significant sources for the study of religion in colonial Virginia, offering a rare extended account of the religious views of a colonial layperson. Colonel John Page (1627–1692), a royalist emigrant who came to Virginia in 1653 and a member of the governor's Council, wrote the book as a New Year's gift for his first son, Matthew. Part catechism, part devotional work, and part apology for the Church of England, A *Deed of Gift* contains a broad outline of the religious knowledge a father believed he should pass along to his son.

The volume emerged out of Page's own faith and experience. He was a man of faith deeply devoted to the Anglican Church. In 1678, he donated the land on which the first Bruton Parish Church building in Middle Plantation, later Williamsburg, was constructed. He wrote at least two devotional books reflecting his own piety for his son, Matthew—A *Deed of Gift* and a prior work on preparing to receive Holy Communion. The latter volume likely reveals Page's own devotion to the sacrament. These books also fulfilled a portion of what Page believed was the duty of a Christian father, to provide religious instruction and example for his children.

---

[1]John Page, A *Deed of Gift to My Dear Son, Captain Matt. Page* (n.p., 1687; reprint, Philadelphia: Henry S. Ashmead, 1856). Used courtesy of The Colonial Williamsburg Foundation.

Page gave each section in A *Deed of Gift* a title beginning with "Of," such as "Of Prayer" or "Of Marriage." In the following pages, sections beginning with "Of" indicate the use of Page's title and organization; sections beginning with "On," such as "On the Scriptures," indicate that I have reorganized Page's material under a different heading and have given the section a title denoting the topic.

Page's spiritual regimen included reading in the Bible and other Christian literature. He possessed a deep knowledge not only of the scriptures but also of the writings of the ancient church, the Protestant reformers, and more recent polemicists, all of whom he relied upon when he crafted A Deed of Gift. The number of Biblical proof texts Page relied upon easily reaches into the hundreds, and there are scores of quotations from the church fathers: Ambrose, Augustine, Chrysostom, Jerome, Oecumenious, and Basil. References to reformers such as John Calvin and Theodore Beza appear less frequently, although Page was obviously familiar with their works. He was conversant with Roman Catholic polemical literature as well, at one point attacking the views of Richard Bristow (1538–1581), an English Jesuit who wrote a treatise against the Church of England.

In many ways, Page acts less as the author than as the redactor of A Deed of Gift, combining passages from different authorities in support of his general positions. Sometimes he created memorable images in this manner. Elsewhere he simply borrowed entire sections from published English devotional books, most notably from Richard Allestree's The Whole Duty of Man, which he copied nearly verbatim in places.

Of Prayer[2]

The true worship of God, is for us to glorify God in our bodies and in our spirits, for they are God's.[3] And as we are Christians we are God's possession, the first-born which he hath redeemed by his first-born Christ. And being so, let us offer our first and best things to him. He hath deserved the priority of our

---

[2]This section offers a good example of Page's method. He "borrowed" much of the material from the chapter of Richard Allestree's The Whole Duty of Man devoted to "The Duty of Prayer." Page, however, modified portions of the original. See [Richard Allestree], The Whole Duty of Man (London, 1658; 1714), Sunday V., sections 1–25.

Page's practice of reworking religious materials from either the published works of English divines or from the Bible was popular in colonial Virginia. Colonists sought neither originality nor innovation in this practice. William Byrd II, for example, created a devotional reading to be used prior to receiving communion from portions of two penitential Psalms. And both Byrd and John Robinson wrote paraphrases of portions of the Old Testament, likely as devotional exercises. A more difficult work of this type may have been Philip Ludwell III's translation from the Greek of the Divine Liturgy of St. John Chrysostom. In his commonplace book, Ludwell appended to the liturgy a series of confessions of sin and a wide variety of prayers, many of them with a Greek Orthodox influence. See Philip Ludwell III, "The Divine & Holy Liturgy of St. John Chrysostom as it is performed without a Deacon," Archives of the Protestant Episcopal Church, Austin, Texas; microfilm, The Colonial Williamsburg Foundation.

Page's reliance on Allestree's popular devotional work also had parallels among Virginia's clergy. Numerous ministers when composing their own sermons either reworked or borrowed heavily from published discourses written by English ministers, especially the works of Archbishop of Canterbury John Tillotson. This indebtedness to the published works of English divines meant that theology in Virginia deviated little from that current in England, although the colony's circumstances made regular church attendance difficult for many colonists.

[3]I Corinthians 6:26.

service; therefore let our first study, in the morning, and our last at night be, to seek God by prayers with devout reverence. Let us worship, and fall down; and kneel before the Lord our Maker,[4] and make an humble confession of our sins to God, by enumerating the several sins we have committed, by aggravating them, together with the acts and circumstances of our sins: with shame, with grief, and hatred, acknowledging the guilt and desert of our sins, what we have done unjustly, and what we justly deserve to suffer. And this confession may be either general or particular. The general when we only confess in gross that we are sinners; the particular when we mention the divers sorts and acts of our sins. The former is most necessary always in our prayers, [211] whether public or private. The latter is proper for private prayer, and therein constantly to remember some of our greatest and foulest sins, though never so long since past; for such we should never think sufficiently confessed and bewailed.

The next part of prayer is to petition to God for what service we want, either for our souls or bodies. For our souls, we must first beg pardon for all our sins for Jesus Christ's sake, who shed his blood for the remission of sins. Then we must beg for the assistance of God's holy Spirit to enable us to forsake our sins, and to walk in obedience and newness of life in a godly conversation. We must also pray for the gifts and graces of his holy Spirit, the fruits thereof, as an irreprovable faith, unfeigned repentance, sincere love, and pure obedience and the like—especially those we most want; and if we find ourselves proud, to pray for humility; if impetuous, for patience; and so for all other graces we find needful. We must not only pray against sin and temptation, but we must watch and strive to overcome, resist and conquer sin in ourselves.

Secondly, we are to pray also for our bodies; [212] to ask of God such necessaries of life as are needful to us while in this world. But those to be conditional, if he please, and that his wisdom shall see it fit that it be good for us; we must not presume to be our own carvers, but refer our wills to his, in respect of outward things, as he sees most tend to the ends of our being here, the glory of God and the salvation of our own souls.

A third part of prayer is deprecation, to deliver us from all evil—either the evil of sin, or the evil of punishment. The evil of sin we are especially to pray against, most earnestly intreating that God will please by the power of his grace, to preserve us from falling into sin; especially those sins to which we find ourselves most inclined. This to be done daily, but chiefly when under any temptation and in danger of falling into sin: that we may cry out as St. Peter, when he found himself sinking, Lord save me![5] Humbly beseeching him

---

[4]Psalm 95:6; the "Venite" from The Order for Morning Prayer in the *Book of Common Prayer*.
[5]Matthew 14:30.

to withdraw the temptation, or strengthen us to withstand it, neither of which can we do of ourselves. We are likewise to pray against the evil of punishment; but principally against spiritual punishment, as the wrath of God, the [213] withholding of his grace, and eternal damnation. We may also pray against outward and temporal afflictions and punishments with submission to God's will, according to the example of our Saviour: Not as I will, but as thou wilt.[6]

A fourth part of prayer, is intercession—praying for others. In general, for all mankind—as well strangers as acquaintance. But more particularly, those to whom we have any special relation, either public as our governors in Church or State; and private as parents, husband, wife, children, friends, &c. We are also to pray for all the sons and daughters of sorrow—those especially that suffer for the testimony of a good conscience; yea, we are to pray for those that despitefully use and persecute us,[7] being the express command of Christ, and that highest example in praying for his very crucifiers, Father forgive them.[8] For all these persons we are to pray that God would give them the same good things. We beg for ourselves, and that God would give them in their several places and callings, all spiritual and temporal blessings. [214] Praying with the Church: Lord love the king; endue thy ministers with righteousness, and make thy chosen people joyful.[9]

The fifth part of the prayer, is thanksgiving; the praising and blessing of God for all his mercies, both spiritual and temporal to ourselves and others; but above all, for his inestimable love in the redemption of the world by our Lord Jesus Christ, for the means of grace, and for the hope of glory.[10] We pay to the king impost and subsidies. The Lord's subsidies and impost for all his blessings is our gratitude. What shall I render to the Lord for all his benefits towards me? I will take the cup of salvation, and bless the name of the Lord.[11] The king's impost or tribute is raised according to the goods of the people. God's tribute or subsidies from us, is according to our parts. The tribute of our eyes, are our tears; if we pay not this tribute of rain, we shall want the sunshine of mercy. The tribute of our mouths, are our praises. O Lord, open thou our lips, and our mouth shall show forth thy praise.[12] The tribute of our ears, are attention to his word. Mary sat at Jesus' [215] feet, and heard his word.[13]

[6]Matthew 26:39.
[7]Matthew 5:44; Luke 6:28.
[8]Luke 23:34.
[9]These petitions follow the Lord's Prayer and precede the second collect in both The Order for Morning Prayer and The Order for Evening Prayer in the Church of England's Book of Common Prayer.
[10]These petitions are taken from the General Thanksgiving in the Book of Common Prayer.
[11]Psalm 116:12.
[12]Psalm 51:15.
[13]Luke 10:39.

The tribute of our heads, are meditations of his power, justice, mercy, truth. The blessed man doth meditate in the law of the Lord day and night.[14] The tribute of our knees, are bending and bowing our joints. I bow my knees to the Father of our Lord Jesus Christ.[15] St. Stephen kneeled down and prayed,[16] &c. If our knees be too stout to pay this tribute, heaven's gate will be too low for our entrance. The tribute of our hands, are alms to the poor: the due payment of this interest, shall bless and increase the principal. Give and it shall be given to you.[17] These reduce Christianity to practice; it will be difficult to do good without it. We must praise God for the particular mercies we have received, both for our souls and bodies.

No employment, time or place can hinder our ejaculations to magnify and praise God, for his mercies towards us. These are the several sorts of prayer, and all of them to be used publicly and privately. The public use of them [216] is first, that in the church, where all meet to join in those prayers wherein they are in common concerned. And in these we should be very constant, there being a special blessing promised to the joint requests of the faithful.

A second sort of public prayer is that in a family, where all that are Christian members of it join in their common supplications; and this ought also to be very carefully attended to; first by the master of the family, who is to look that there be such prayers, it being as much his duty to provide for the souls of his wife, children and servants, as to provide food and raiment for their bodies. He cannot make a better choice than of the church prayers;[18] but what choice soever he make of prayers, let him be sure to have some. And let no Christian man (especially you my son) keep so heathenish a family as not to have God daily worshipped in it. Private prayer is that which is used by a man apart from all others, wherein we are to be more particular, according to our particular wants, than in public it is necessary to be. Private prayer is not to be excused by the performance of the public, being both required. Let us pray unto our Father in [217] secret, from whom we are to expect our reward, and not from the vain praises of men.[19]

This duty of prayer is to be often performed, by none, seldomer than morning and evening, it being most necessary that we should thus begin and end all our works with God, not only in respect of the duty we owe him, but

---

[14]Psalm 1:2.
[15]Ephesians 3:14.
[16]Acts 7:60.
[17]Luke 6:38.
[18]Page is referring to the Orders for Morning and Evening Prayer in the *Book of Common Prayer*.
[19]Matthew 6:6.

also in respect of ourselves, who can never be prosperous or safe but by committing ourselves to him, and therefore should tremble to venture on the perils either of day or night without his safeguard. And the more to stir us to this
duty, we are to consider the advantages and benefits of prayer. Every good
and perfect gift cometh from God, and the gift of God is eternal life.[20] Prayer
is the work of the soul, and not only of the tongue and lips, with zeal and purity. Let us be fervent, and lift up holy hands in prayer.[21] My son, let your
prayer to God be often and earnest, rather than long; and let thanksgiving be
ever a part of your prayer, for as God doth not usually bestow his blessings
without prayer, so neither doth he continue them without our thanks. Learn
so [218] to conform your will to God, that whatever by his providence may
happen to you, you may be ready to bid it welcome; and whatever shall be
taken from you, to bid it farewell; rather run than be drawn to devotion; but
neither run nor be drawn into sin. Be not persuaded to be evil, and be good
though none persuade you. You are bad enough by nature, do not make yourself worse by custom in sin. In all your approaches to God in prayer, consider
yourself a poor worm, and God's infinite power to bring you to acknowledge
your vile misery, and his glorious Majesty, that will hear in heaven the prayer
of his poor creatures on earth.

I beseech God give the spirit of grace, supplication and thankfulness to
you, and accept them from you, for Jesus Christ's sake. Amen.

On the Scriptures

First, I commend to your study the excellency of Scripture learning, which
[12] comprehends the soul of true divinity. Because the inspired oracles of
God contain in them the infallible rule of faith, the steadfast ground of hope,
the perfect guide of life, the sacred fount of devotion, the heavenly subject of
contemplation, and the everlasting spring of celestial bliss.

The canonical books of the Old and New Testament are exact maps of the
heavenly Canaan, drawn by the pen of the Holy Ghost, the authentic record
of the Church, the deeds of Almighty God, and evidences of man's salvation.
In the perusal whereof you will find exceeding great delight and comfort, not
to forego your hope of heaven for all that the earth can afford, there being in
them bequeathed to the children of promise[22] by their Heavenly Father,
treasures of grace here and crowns of glory hereafter.[23] In which respect, holy

---

[20]James 1:17; Romans 6:23.
[21]I Timothy 2:8.
[22]Galatians 4:28; Romans 9:8.
[23]I Peter 5:4.

David claimed them as his heritage forever;[24] and esteemed them above gold, yea much fine gold; sweeter than the honey and the honey-comb.[25] Let those jewels be worn about your neck and at your ears. Keep them always as tablets on your heart.[26] [13] With knowledge of those alone, you may, and, by ordering your life accordingly, shall go to heaven: but with all other learning you may, and without this, shall certainly go to perdition without the mercy of God in Jesus Christ.

All Scripture is given by inspiration of God, and is profitable for doctrine, for reproof, for correction, for instruction in righteousness.[27] We ought to adore and admire the fullness of holy Scripture, wherein every verse is, as it were, a chapter, and every chapter an epistle, and every epistle a volume, for the abundance of precious truths contained in them.

These holy writings (to use David's expression) are right, rejoicing the heart.[28] Plutarch's Morals,[29] Seneca's Epistles,[30] and such like books, in these moral writings there are excellent truths, but they are far short of those sacred books. Those may comfort against outward trouble, but not inward fears; they may rejoice the mind, but cannot quiet the conscience. They may kindle some flashy sparks of joy, but they cannot warm the soul with a lasting fire of solid consolation. Those writings of [14] heathen orators, and philosophers, &c., which formerly were so pleasing, are now dull and harsh in comparison of the comfort of the Scriptures. Therefore so diligently read, steadfastly believe, and obediently conform to these writings, that your joy may be full by them. Observe what the Prophet Jeremy saith of himself: "Thy words were found, and I did eat them; and thy word was to me the joy and rejoicing of mine heart."[31] The word caused in Jeremy joy and rejoicing, but by what means? It was by eating it. So must you get comfort in the Scriptures by eating, that is, reading, meditating, and applying them to yourself.

Let, then, that counsel which St. Ambrose giveth, be acceptable to you. Eat, and eat daily of this heavenly manna, that your hunger may be satisfied,

---

[24]Psalm 119:111.

[25]Psalm 19:10.

[26]This may be a reference to Deuteronomy 11:18.

[27]II Timothy 3:16.

[28]Psalm 19:8.

[29]Plutarch (b. before 50–d. after 120), Greek historian and philosopher; his Morals consists of seventy-eight essays on science, religion, philosophy, and morality.

[30]Lucius Annaeus Seneca (4 BC–AD 65), Roman moralist; his Epistles consist of over one hundred essays on morality.

[31]Jeremiah 15:16.

and your soul nourished to eternal life.[32] Remember the advice which St. Jerome[33] gives, whatever joys and pleasures others may take, let your delight be in the law of the Lord. Hearken to this exhortation also. Let not the law depart from your heart.[34] Read and ponder again and again, that you [15] may find the savor of this manna, and, with the bee, suck the sweetness of those heavenly flowers. And yet, more particularly, when you are in any danger, labor under any affliction, make use of these writings for your comfort, which are the only refuge in all temptations. Do you labor with ignorance? These writings are a light to your feet, a lantern to your paths.[35] Do you weep in the valley of tears? Here you may find that which will dry your eyes, and revive your spirit. Do you thirst after righteousness?[36] Here is a fountain of pure water.[37] Are you spiritually hungry? Here is the bread which came down from heaven;[38] indeed there is no condition that can befall you to which these holy writings afford not a suitable consolation. With joy shall ye draw water out of the wells of salvation.[39]

---

[32]Ambrose (ca. 339–397) was the Roman governor of Aemilia-Liguria. Although unbaptized and a Christian only by belief, Ambrose was the choice of the laity in 374 to succeed the recently deceased bishop of Milan. Ambrose reluctantly accepted the position, was baptized, and ordained. He then devoted himself to the study of theology. His major writings include a treatise on Christian ethics and sermons delivered to candidates for baptism. The reference is to *Expositio psalmi cxviii* 14.2. See also *Death as a Good*, 5.20; and Letter #77, Ambrose to Irenaeus.

From *Death as a Good*: "Moreover, some wounds of sinners are moistened with the ointments of Scripture and the stronger food of the word as with bread, and are treated with the sweeter word like honey. Elsewhere, too, Solomon teaches that there is food in words, when he says: 'Good words are a honeycomb.'

"And so in that garden there are good words, one to check fault, another to reprove iniquity, another to bring on the death of insolence and to bury it, when someone has been reproved for his errors and renounces them. There is also a stronger word, that strengthens the heart of man with the more powerful nourishment of heavenly Scripture. There is as well a word of persuasion, sweet like honey and still afflicting the conscience of the sinner in its very sweetness. There is also a word or more ardent spirit, that inebriates like wine and gladdens the heart of man, and also a word like milk, that is pure and clear. The bridegroom is saying to His friends that they should feast on these foods, these sweet and useful words."

From Letter #77: "But there is also spiritual manna, the dew of spiritual wisdom, which is shed from heaven upon those who are resourceful and in search of it. This waters the minds of the pious and puts sweetness into their mouths. Whoever experiences this downpour of divine Wisdom is delighted, and needing no other food, lives not on bread alone but on every word of God."

Letter #77 may be found in *The Fathers of the Church: A New Translation; Saint Ambrose: Letters Volume 26; Sister Mary Melchior Beyenka, O.P., trans. (New York: Fathers of the Church, Inc., 1954), 432–35.

[33]Jerome (ca. 342–420) was the greatest Biblical scholar of the early Church, famous for his translation of the Bible into Latin—the Vulgate version. In addition, he wrote numerous Biblical commentaries and devoted himself to a life of asceticism.

[34]Psalm 40:8.

[35]Psalm 119:105.

[36]Matthew 5:6.

[37]Revelation 22:1.

[38]A possible reference to John 6:31–58.

[39]Isaiah 12:3.

These wells of salvation are evangelical truths, spiritual sayings; therefore, by the bucket of faith, draw the water of comfortable doctrine out of those wells, to the joy and solace of your heart.

In those holy writings you may behold [16] yourself as in a looking-glass, and learn to know yourself as a man, a sinful man; descended by succession from the first man Adam, by whom sin entered into the world, and death by sin; and so death passed upon all men, for that all have sinned.[40]

On Christ as the Propitiation for the Sins of the World

The more generally received, and most genuine exposition of those words,[41] is by way of inclusion, according to which the sense is, that Christ is a propitiation not only for some but all, even the whole world.

To understand this aright, know that this phrase, the whole world, may be taken more strictly or largely, according to a double consideration of this proposition, either in respect of its actual efficiency, or virtual sufficiency.

These words, he is the propitiation, may be construed, he is actually and effectually the [138] propitiation; inasmuch as it is joined with his advocateship, it is very probable this is the Apostle's meaning, since Christ is effectually a propitiation to them, for whom he is an advocate. The sense of this Scripture will be best explained by paralleling it with those two texts in the Gospel. The one concerning Caiaphas,[42] who prophesied that Jesus should die for that nation; and not for that only, but that also he should gather into one the children of God that were scattered abroad. The other, Christ's own words in that excellent prayer, wherein he saith, Neither pray I for those alone; but for them also which shall believe on me through their word.[43]

Thus Christ is the propitiation for all that did, do, or shall hereafter believe in him. And however the number of them that believe and hold Christ effectually a propitiation to them, is still but small comparatively; in which respect it may seem strange they should be called the whole world; yet considering that before Christ came the believers of the old Testament were only to be found in Jewry, (some few proselytes of the Gentiles excepted,) now, since [139] Christ's death, the believers of the New Testament are to be found among all sorts of persons, in all nations, at some time or other, and so disposed through the

---

[40]Romans 5:12.
[41]This is a portion of a much longer discussion by Page of I John 2.2.
[42]John 6:51–52.
[43]John 17:20.

whole world; as they are fitly called in our creed, the Catholic Church, so here, by St. John, the whole world; to which purpose is that notable speech of St. Ambrose.[44] The people of God hath its fullness, and there is, as it were, a particular generality, whilst all men are taken out of all men, and a whole world is taken, chosen, and saved out of the whole world.

This exposition of these words, as it appeareth not to be irrational, so it wants not the consent of many interpreters, not only modern but ancient. The design of St. John, (saith Calvin,) in these words, is no other than to assert this benefit of propitiation common to the whole church.[45] Lest he should be thought by saying our, to restrain Christ's propitiation only to the Jews, he addeth the whole world, so Beza.[46] Besides these, this is St. Austin's[47] interpretation, speaking occasionally upon this text. As (saith he) the whole world is said to lie in wickedness, because of the laws, so Christ is said to be the propitiation for the [140] sins of the whole world, because of the wheat which groweth throughout the whole world.[48] Yea, the Greek fathers render this very sense of these words upon the text itself.[49] This, he saith, either because he wrote to the Jews, that he might extend this benefit to the Gentiles, or because the promise was not only made to those in that time, but all that shall come after them. So St. Cyril, comparing this Scripture with that of Christ's

---

[44]Page's reference is likely to either Prosper of Aquitaine, *The Call of All Nations*, book II, chs. 1–3, a tract sometimes erroneously attributed to Ambrose, or to Ambrose, *On Cain and Abel*, book II, ch. 3, par. 11.

[45]John Calvin, *Commentary on I John*. The reference is to Calvin's commentary on I John 2.2: "And not for ours *only*. He added this for the sake of amplifying, in order that the faithful might be assured that the expiation made by Christ, extends to all who by faith embrace the gospel. Here a question may be raised, how have the sins of the whole world been expiated? I pass by the dotages of the fanatics, who under this pretense extend salvation to all the reprobate, and therefore to Satan himself. Such a monstrous thing deserves no refutation. They who seek to avoid this absurdity, have said that Christ suffered sufficiently for the whole world, but efficiently only for the elect. This solution has commonly prevailed in the schools. Though then I allow that what has been said is true, yet I deny that it is suitable to this passage; for the design of John was no other than to make this benefit common to the whole Church. Then under the word *all* or whole, he does not include the reprobate, but designates those who should believe as well as those who were then scattered through various parts of the world. For there is really made evident, as it is meet, the grace of Christ, when it is declared to be the only true salvation of the world."
See also John Calvin, *The Institutes of the Christian Religion*, book III, ch. 4, par. 26.

[46]Theodore Beza (1519–1605) was born into a Roman Catholic family in Burgundy. He later converted to Calvinist Protestantism, formally renouncing his Catholic faith in 1548. Ten years later, John Calvin offered him a professorship at the academy in Geneva. His most important writings include *Confessio Christianae Fidei* (1562), a Greek text of the New Testament, *Vita Calvini* (1564), and *Tractationes Theologicae* (1570–1582). His writings are embued with a rigid Calvinism. See Theodore Beza, *A Little Book of Christian Questions and Responses in which the Principal Headings of the Christian Religion are Briefly Set Forth* (1570), esp. questions 198–200.

[47]Austin was an early English corruption of Augustine. Page's references to St. Austin are to St. Augustine of Hippo.

[48]Augustine, Epistle XCIII, ch. 9, par. 32; Augustine to Vincentius, 408.

[49]Page's note is to Oecumenius, 6th century Greek author of a treatise on the Revelation of John.

in the gospel: I pray not for the world, reconcileth them, by affirming that where St. John saith the whole world, he meaneth them that should be called of all nations, through faith, to righteousness and holiness.[50]

That which, according to this construction, we are to take no notice of, is the largeness of God's grace to the times of the New, above that to those of the Old Testament. They who, since the coming of Christ, partake effectually of his propitiation, are of all sorts and ages of the world; to which purpose is that acknowledgment which the four-and-twenty elders in the Revelation make to Christ. Thou wast slain and hast redeemed us to God by thy blood, out of every kindred, and tongue, and [141] people, and nation.[51] Among other resemblances, Christ is compared by the prophet Malachi to the sun,[52] because, like the sun, he communicates light, heat, life to all parts of the world, and therefore he saith of himself, I am the light of the world,[53] and again, I give light to the world.[54]

It is well observed, that the first promise of Christ, the seed of the woman, was not made to Abraham the father of the Jews, but to Adam, the father of the whole world; and whereas, the Jews called Christ the son of Abraham, and the son of David, who were Jews, Christ usually calleth himself the Son of man, which taketh in Gentiles as well as Jews. In this respect it is well taken notice of, that the place of Christ's birth was not a private house, but an inn, which is open for all passengers, and that not in a chamber, but the stable, which is the commonest place of the inn; to mind us that He who was born, should be a common Saviour to high and low, noble and base, rich and poor: besides the superscription on his cross was written, not only in Hebrew, the language of the Jews, but [142] in Greek and Latin, the languages of the Gentiles;[55] and the Cross was erected, not within the city, but without the gate, to intimate that it was not an Altar of the Temple, but the world. Indeed, what part of the world is it that Christ's propitiation reacheth not to? St. Basil putting the question, why the world was redeemed by a Cross,[56]

---

[50]Cyril (ca. 315–386) served as the bishop of Jerusalem from around 349. His most important work is a series of twenty-four "Catacheses," or lectures, delivered during Lent and Eastertide to candidates baptized on Holy Saturday. The source for Page's assertion is likely *The Catachetical Lectures*, Lecture XII, ch. 8.

[51]Revelation 5:9.

[52]Malachi 4:2.

[53]John 6:33.

[54]John 8:12.

[55]John 19:19.

[56]After an education at the best pagan and Christian centers of learning in the world, Basil the Great (ca. 330–379) undertook a monastic life. In 370 he succeeded Eusebius as bishop of Caesarea. He was renowned for his personal holiness. Basil's major writings include a treatise *On the Holy Spirit*, a large collection of letters, and a series of three *Books Against Eunomius*. Although Page's reference is to "Basil, in Essay, 11, 12," he seems to have been referring to Basil's *Commentary on Isaiah* i.249, a work many modern scholars believe is spurious.

makes this answer, that a Cross hath four distinct parts, which represent the four parts of the world; to all which the efficacy of the Cross reacheth. An emblem of this truth St. Cyprian[57] hath found in the four letters of the Greek word αδαμ, which is given to Christ, which letters are the first of those Greek words which signify the four corners of the world; and St. Austin in Christ's garment, of which St. John saith the soldiers made four parts, to each soldier a part,[58] which he conceiveth to figure the Church, gathered out of the four parts of the world.[59] This was God's promise to Christ, Ask of me, and I will give thee the utmost parts of the world for thy possession;[60] and to his Church, I will bring thy seed from the east, and gather those from the west, I will [143] say to the north, Give up, and to the south, Keep not back.[61]

From this assertion it appeareth that the Church (in itself considered) is a great multitude, and especially the Christian, in comparison of the Jewish Church. We read of Noah, that he blessed his two sons, Shem and Japheth,[62] the former a type of the Jews, the latter a type of the Gentiles: concerning Japheth, he saith, God shall enlarge him, and he shall dwell in the tents of Shem; to intimate, saith St. Jerome, the enlarged multitude of the Gentile believers; and the same Father, upon those words of the prophet, Enlarge the place of thy tent, and let them stretch forth the curtains of thy habitations, spare not, lengthen thy cords, strengthen thy stakes,[63] saith, this is to be un-derstood of the greatness and multitude of the Church, by reason of its spreading over all the world.

And surely, it concerns us much to meditate on this truth, whereby as the pride of the Jews is humbled, so the hope of the Gentiles is erected. And since it belongs to the whole world, it may well be matter of great joy, and [144] that such a joy as may put us upon thankfulness for this grace of God which hath appeared to all men, and bringeth salvation.[64]

---

[57]A former pagan rhetorician, Cyprian (d. 258) was converted to Christianity in ca. 246 and was soon elevated to the see of Carthage. He was martyred on September 14, 258, during the persecution of Christians under the Emperor Valerian. His major writings include *De Habitu Virginum*, *De Lapsis*, *De Catholicae Ecclesiae Unitate*, and *De Opere et Eleemosynis*.

[58]John 19:23.

[59]Augustine, *On the Gospel of John*, Tractate 118, par. 4: "Someone, perhaps, may inquire what is signified by the division that was made of His garments into so many parts, and of the casting of lots for the coat. The raiment of the Lord Jesus Christ parted into four, symbolized His quadripartite Church, as spread abroad over the whole world, which consists of four quarters, and equally, that is to say, harmoniously, distributed over all these quarters. On which account He elsewhere says, that He will send His angels to gather His elect from the four winds: and what is that, but from the four quarters of the world, east, west, north, and south?"

[60]Psalm 2:8.

[61]Isaiah 43:5–6.

[62]Genesis 9:27.

[63]Isaiah 54:2.

[64]Titus 2:11.

Christ is as well a light to lighten us Gentiles, as the glory of his people Israel, nor is he a propitiation for the Jews only, but for the whole world of them that believe in Him.[65]

My son, I hope you are (by what I have written) fully convinced of the odious nature of sin, by nature born and bred in you, and by addition of your probity by actual transgressions have provoked God to anger; which showeth the miserable state of a sinner to be under the wrath of God. Which, being seriously weighed by you, should put you on a diligent resolution not to sin hereafter; and if at any time you do sin, humble yourself before God, and make a true confession of all your sins, with an utter abhorrence and detestation of them, always considering that without confession and contrition, there is no remission: not that confession can be a meritorious cause of forgiveness; for it is satisfaction which merits remission. Therefore, apply yourself to Jesus Christ the righteous, who is an Advocate with [145] the Father, and is the propitiation for your sins, and not for yours only, but also for the whole world, that is, the world of believers.[66]

View, oh son! the heinous nature of your sins, from which nothing but Christ's blood can cleanse you. Behold, oh son! the exceeding love of your Saviour to you a miserable sinner, who, that he might cleanse you when polluted in your blood, was pleased to shed his own blood. A super-excellent work of charity. When the Scripture speaks of Christ's love, it presently annexeth his sufferings. So St. Paul, Gal. ii. 20, Who loved me, and gave himself for me; so St. John, Rev. i. 5, Who loved us, and washed us from our sins in his blood; so St. John in his Epistle, chap. i. verse 7, The blood of Jesus Christ cleanseth us from all sin. For which inflamed love of our blessed Lord and Saviour Jesus Christ, let us beholding magnify, magnifying admire, and admiring praise him for his inestimable goodness; saying with the holy Apostle, Unto him that hath loved us, and washed us from our sins in his own blood, be honor and glory for ever and ever. Amen.[67]

Of the Church

The Catholic or universal Church which is invisible, consists of the whole number of the elect, that have been, are, or shall be gathered into one under Christ. Ephes. i. 10. That in the dispensation of the fullness of time, he might gather together into one all things in Christ, both which are in heaven and which are on earth.

---

[65]Luke 2:32.
[66]I John 2:1. This verse would have been familiar to Anglicans from the "comfortable words" following the Confession of Sin in the Communion service in the Book of Common Prayer.
[67]Revelation 1:5.

The visible Church which is also Catholic, under the Gospel (not confined to one nation as before under the law) consists of all those throughout the world, that are sanctified in Christ Jesus, called to be saints, with all that in every place call upon the name of Jesus Christ our Lord.[68]

These two parts, triumphant and militant, make but one Church: My dove, my undefiled is but one, the only one of her mother.[69] The triumphant part is a company of justified spirits, triumphing over the world, the flesh, and the devil; rejoicing in the conquest over sin and death.[70] [147]

The militant part is a company of men living under the cross, and desiring to be with Christ. They suffer, and this is their way to glory: through much tribulation entering into the kingdom of God.[71]

That Jesus Christ is the alone or only head of his church, and can have no other partner to share with him in this dignity. And he is the head of the body, the church; who is the beginning, the first-born from the dead, that in all things he might have the pre-eminence.[72] Jesus Christ is the corner stone, in whom all the building fitly framed together, grows into an holy temple in the Lord.[73] He doth not only by his authority govern it, but also by his grace quicken it: so that we live not, but Christ liveth in us.[74] He requires no deputy, he needs none. For wheresoever you are gathered together in my name, I am in the midst of you.[75]

It is therefore a great arrogancy in the Pope to call himself head of the church. Christ is not so weak of himself, or so respectless of us, as to need any ministerial head. Call no man [148] your father upon the earth: for one is your Father which is in heaven.[76]

You must know that there is no salvation out of Christ's church; such as never become members of it, must eternally perish: they that are true members shall be saved. 1 John ii.19. If they had been of us, they would have continued with us: but they went out from us, that it might be manifest they were not of us. Without are dogs and sorcerers, &c.[77] All out of

---

[68]I Corinthians 1:2.
[69]Canticles 6:9.
[70]Hebrews 12:23.
[71]Acts 14:22.
[72]Colossians 1:18.
[73]Ephesians 2:21.
[74]Galatians 2:20.
[75]Matthew 18:20.
[76]Matthew 23:29.
[77]Revelation 22:15.

the ark perished in the waters.[78] The Lord added to the church daily such as should be saved.[79] Because there is no means of salvation out of it; no word to teach, no sacraments to confirm; and especially, because out of the church there is no Christ, and out of Christ no salvation.

St. Cyprian was a bishop of the true catholic church, who said, he cannot have God for his father, who will not have the church for his mother.[80] This teacheth us to honor our mother, and like children to hang at her breasts for sustenance.[81] That we suck and be satisfied with the breasts of her consolations, that we [149] may be delighted with her glory.[82] Like babes let us desire the sincere milk of the gospel, that we may grow thereby.[83]

The church is catholic in three respects: of time, of persons, of place. 1. Of time, because the church had a being in all ages ever since the promise was given to our first parents in Paradise. 2. Of persons, for it consists of all degrees and sorts of men, rich and poor, prince and subject, bond and free, every condition of believers. 3. Of place: it is gathered from all parts of the earth, especially under the New Testament, wheresoever this gospel shall be preached in the whole world.[84] When Christ gave his apostles

---

[78]See Cyprian, Epistle LXXIV, par. 15: "And as the ark of Noah was nothing else than the sacrament of the church of Christ, which then, when all without were perishing, kept those only safe who were within the ark, we are manifestly instructed to look to the unity of the Church. Even as also the Apostle Peter laid down, saying, 'Thus also shall baptism in like manner make you safe'; showing that as they who were not in the ark with Noah not only were not purged and saved by water, but at once perished in that deluge; so now also, whoever are not in the Church with Christ will perish outside, unless they are converted by penitence to the only and saving lava of the Church."

This paragraph seems to rely not only on Epistle LXXIV but also on Epistle LXXV, par. 2, and *On the Unity of the Church*, par. 6.

[79]Acts 2:37.

[80]The phrase appears in both Epistle LXXIII, par. 7, and in *On the Unity of the Church*, par. 6.

From Epistle LXXIII, par. 7: "But further, one is not born by the imposition of hands when he receives the Holy Ghost, but in baptism, that so, being already born, he may receive the Holy Spirit, even as it happened in the first man Adam. For first God formed him, and then breathed into his nostrils the breath of life. For the Spirit cannot be received, unless he who receives first have an existence. But as the birth of Christians is in baptism, while the generation and sanctification of baptism are with the spouse of Christ alone, who is able spiritually to conceive and to bear sons to God, where and of whom is he born, who is not a son of the Church, so that he should have God as his Father, before he has had the Church for his Mother?"

From *On the Unity of the Church*, par. 6: "The spouse of Christ cannot be adulterous; she is uncorrupted and pure. She knows one home; she guards with chaste modesty the sanctity of one couch. She keeps us for God. She appoints the sons whom she has born for the kingdom. Whoever is separated from the Church and is joined to an adulterous, is separated from the promises of the Church; nor can he who forsakes the Church of Christ attain to the rewards of Christ. He is a stranger; he is profane; he is an enemy. He can no longer have God for his Father, who has not the Church for his mother. If any one could escape who was outside the ark of Noah, then he also may escape who shall be outside of the Church."

[81]Isaiah 46:11.

[82]Isaiah 66:11.

[83]II Peter 2:2.

[84]Matthew 26:13.

their commission, he gave also the whole world for their parish. Go teach all nations and baptize, &c.[85]

The church of God is catholic, not Roman catholic: particular and universal are contradictories. A church lies hid through want of the word preached and public administration of the sacraments. So it was in the days of Elias, when he wished to die: I only am left; yet (verse 18) I have left seven thousand that [150] never bowed their knees to Baal.[86] The papists demand where our church was before the days of Luther. There was then an universal apostacy over the face of the world; the true church was not then visible, but the grain of truth lay hid under a great heap of popish chaff. But this invisibility doth not prove a nullity. The church of England holds no other doctrine than that the church of Rome primarily did hold; and that which St. Paul delivered to them in sacred writing: justification only by the blood of Christ.

On Respect for the Church

The Lord is present in his temple;[87] in vain shall we hope to find him elsewhere, if we do not seek him there. I will be in the midst of you gathered together in my name;[88] not any where, not everywhere, but in his house. Indeed, no place excludes him, but this is sure of him. He fills all places with his presence; he fills this with his glorious presence. Here he both hears us and is heard of us; he hears our prayers, and teacheth our lessons. No place sends up faithful prayers in vain; no place hath such a promise of hearing as the [167] temple. It is the Lord's court of audience—his Highness' court of requests.

There humble souls open their grievances, from thence they return laden with graces. Why are so many void of goodness, but because they are negligent of public devotions? Peter and John went up into the temple at the hour of prayer.[89]

Therefore, my dear son, seek the Lord in his house, the Church, where he may be found, and that with purpose of heart to serve the Lord, grounded on a voluntary devotion; saying with David, I will go into thy house, with burnt offerings I will pay thee my vows.[90]

---

[85]Matthew 28:19.
[86]I Kings 19:18.
[87]Psalm 11:4; Habakkuk 2:20.
[88]Matthew 18:20.
[89]Acts 3:1.
[90]Psalm 66:13.

When you go to the house of prayer, devoted to the service of God, enter it with reverence. Ye shall hallow my Sabbaths, and reverence my sanctuary: I am the Lord.[91] Look well to your feet before you enter these holy doors; there miss not the confession and absolution,[92] unless you think you have no sins to confess, or care not to be forgiven them; and be ready to join in the prayers of the Church, which are so excellent for matter and form that they well [168] deserve to be esteemed, as they are, the ancient and devout Liturgy of our English Church; which the first compilers extracted as a quintessence of the preceding liturgies of both of the Greek and Latin Churches. In God's house and business forget your own; be there as a member of the Church, not of the commonwealth. The Apostles gave themselves continually to prayer, and to the preaching of the word.[93] There prayer is put in the first place; yet many come to those holy places, and are so transported with a desire of hearing, that they forget the fervency of praying and praising God. The end is ever more noble than the means that conduce to it. Sin brought in ignorance, and ignorance takes away devotion. The word preached brings in knowledge, and knowledge rectifies devotion. So that preaching is but to beget your praying, to instruct you to praise and worship God. Knowledge is not an active quality, but only a means to direct a man in working.

God reckons not so much of our audience as of our obedience; not the hearers, but the doers are blessed in their deeds.[94] Indeed, Christ [169] saith, Blessed are they that hear the word of God; but with this condition, that they keep it.[95] Many men are content that God should speak earnestly to them, but they will not speak devoutly to him. As if it were only God's part to bless them, not theirs to bless God.

This is not written against frequent hearing of sermons, but to let you know that it is not the only exercise of a Christian to hear a sermon, nor is that Lord's-day well spent, that dispatcheth no other business for heaven. In heaven there will be no sermons, yet in heaven there will be hallelujahs. All God's service is not to be narrowed up in hearing; it hath greater latitude; there must be prayer, praise, adoration, and worship of God. To this end David came to God's house, and shall remain in glory, to praise the Lord. Neither is it the scope of Christianity to know, but the scope of knowledge is to be a good Christian. You are not an heathen, to ask what must I believe; nor a catechist to demand what must I do?[96] You know what to believe, you

---

[91]Leviticus 19:30.
[92]The confession and absolution were among the first acts of worship in the Orders for Morning and Evening Prayer. Page, in short, was instructing his son to make sure that he got to church on time.
[93]Acts 6:4.
[94]James 1:25.
[95]Luke 11:28.
[96]Luke 3:10.

know what to do, having given you a large information in my book delivered you concerning faith, and [170] preparation for receiving of the blessed sacrament of the Lord's Supper.[97] And the better to imprint those things in your mind, frequent the church, both to hear and to praise God. As David was not only a praiser but a preacher: Come and hear, all ye that fear God, and I will tell you what he hath done for my soul.[98]

Now every material temple, wherein the saints are assembled, the truth of the Gospel is preached and professed, the holy Sacrament duly administered, and the Lord's name is invoked and worshipped, is the temple of God.

As you are to preserve and sanctify your soul and body a temple consecrated to the Divine Majesty, for the habitation of the Holy Ghost;[99] so you ought to sanctify yourself and come with joy to the temple of God. No place of joy like the Church. I was glad when they said unto me, Let us go into the house of the Lord.[100] You cannot desire to receive more joy than that (Rom. xiv.17) peace of conscience and joy in the Holy Ghost; a joy that can neither be suppressed nor expressed. Or more joy to be communicated than (Col. iii.16) in psalms, hymns, and [171] spiritual songs, singing with grace in your hearts to the Lord. Come therefore with joy and delight into the house of God. Come also with holiness. It is holy ground; not by any inherent holiness, but in regard of the religious use. Put off thy shoes (your carnal affections,) the place where thou standest is holy ground.[101] Be the minister never so sinful; the word is holy, the action holy, the time holy, the place holy, ordained by the most Holy to make us holy.

My son, be not like some that when they come first into the church, sink down on their seats, clap their hats before their eyes, and scarce bow their knees: as if they come to bless God, not to intreat God to bless them. Be not you ashamed of God's service; but in his house of prayer and praise, let your carriage there be decent and devout, full of reverence, kneeling on your knees in the time of prayer. When the king gives a pardon for life, forfeited to the law, it is received on their knees; when he bestows favor or honor, men kneel for it. In that holy place, where men receive the forgiveness of sins, the honor of saints [172] —so gracious a pardon—so glorious a blessing—all persons

---

[97]Prior to writing *A Deed of Gift* for his son, Matthew, Page had already written him a book on how to prepare for receiving communion. If his method in *A Deed of Gift* is an indication of how he compiled the previous volume, Page probably based the first book on the enormously popular anonymous pamphlet *A Weeks Preparation Towards a Worthy Receiving of the Lords Supper* (London, 1681). There are no known extant copies.

[98]Psalm 64:16.

[99]I Corinthians 6:19.

[100]Psalm 122:1.

[101]Exodus 3:5.

should use this humble gesture of kneeling to the Lord; and be zealous to glorify God on earth, who we look should glorify us in heaven. O let us enter into his gates with thanksgiving, and into his Courts with praise: let us be thankful unto him, and bless his name.[102]

My son, what I have here laid before you concerning the Church and your duty, I charge you so to meditate and practise; that whether you eat or drink, work or walk, whatsoever you think, speak, or do; let all be to the glory of the Lord Jesus, who is ascended into heaven, humbly beseeching him to bring you to himself in heaven, through the exalting power of his own most blessed merits. Amen.[103]

On Other Denominations

You cannot be wholly ignorant of the damnable cruelty of the Papists in burning silly women for not understanding their inexplicable mystery of Transubstantiation,[104] and how those gunpowder divines[105] condemned others to the fire for not knowing that which they never knew themselves.

Having proved and approved the truth of our own Church; it is necessary to examine whether the Church of Rome be also a member of this Catholic Church. Errors that annihilate a church are of two sorts. Some weakening, others destroying the foundation, weakening error is the building of hay and stubble on the foundation: the stubble burnt, their souls may be saved.[106] Those which destroy the foundation, are the overthrowing errors; by them a Church ceaseth to be a Church. Yet if an error be against the foundation, we are to consider the persons; whether they err of malice or of weakness.

If of malice, like Jannes and Jambres, that withstood Moses resisting the truth;[107] it is no longer a Church. But if of weakness, we must not so peremptorily conclude: for Paul writes [155] to the Galatians as a Church of God, though they were perverted to another doctrine embracing a fundamental error of justification by works. The Church of Rome doth wilfully and obstinately

---

[102]Psalm 100:4.

[103]Compare this paragraph to the collects for Ascension Day and the Sunday After Ascension Day in the *Book of Common Prayer*.

[104]In Roman Catholic Eucharistic theology, the belief that the consecrated elements of bread and wine become the actual body and blood of Christ.

[105]The Roman Catholic conspirators who had plotted to blow up Parliament and King Charles I at the opening of Parliament in 1605. The plot was discovered on 5 November 1605, and the day was commemorated with bells and bonfires for much of the seventeenth century. A form of service to be used on Gunpowder Treason Day was added to the *Book of Common Prayer* in 1605. It remained in the prayer book until 1859 when its use was revoked.

[106]I Corinthians 3:12, 15.

[107]II Timothy 3:8.

destroy the foundation; therefore, may be concluded for no Church. If they will be justified by the works of the Law, they are fallen from grace.

Hear how they would quit themselves. They would do it by retorting all this back upon our Church: they tell us flatly that we are no Church. They say we have no Bishops, so no ministers, so no sacraments, therefore no Church. For answer, note what St. Paul saith to Titus: for this cause I left thee in Crete, that thou shouldst ordain Elders in every city.[108] Now we have true Bishops, therefore, true ministers; but they upbraid us and say, that we have all our Episcopal rites from them; if we have it from them, then we have it. They are Bristow's own words in his motives; the Protestants are apes of the Papists, the Communion Book is made altogether out of the Mass-book.[109] Why then do they not communicate with us? It is not for conscience, [156] but for malice. Let it be granted that we have this from them: but then they must grant withal, that Jacob, by God's disposing, hath gotten Esau's birth-right.[110] We abhor not Episcopal ordinations, but Papal. Our substance is from them, their circumstances remain to themselves.

But further, they object the continuance of their succession: it may be answered, the succession of person is nothing without the succession of doctrine; which they want. If it were by us granted, what shall never be by them proved, that Peter is succeeded by the Pope; yet as Matthias succeeded Judas,[111] and was never the worse, so the Pope succeeding Peter is never the better.

They further say, that in the Roman Church, Baptism for the substance of it is rightly administered: therefore it is a true Church. Indeed they have the outward washing, but quite overthrown the inward; which stands in justification by the imputed righteousness of Christ. The Lord, of his goodness, that hath given them the sign of the grace, give them also the grace of the sign, true washing away of their sins in the blood of Christ. All that can be [157] proved hereby is, that among the Papists there is a hidden church, in the midst whereof Antichrist domineereth, but hath no part of salvation in it. What cause then have we to bless our God, that hath brought us from Babylon to Jerusalem, out of darkness into His marvelous light, from the Romish Synagogue to the Church of the first-born, which is written in heaven? And the Lord of his mercy preserve us in it for ever and ever.

---

[108]Titus 1:5.

[109]Richard Bristow (1538–1581), Roman Catholic divine. The work Page refers to is Richard Bristow, *Motives Inducing to the Catholike Faith. Wherein are set down sundry plaine & sure Wayes to find out the Truth in the doubtfull & dangerous times of Heresy* (3d ed.; 1641). Page's references are to chapters 32 and 34, 230–49, 251–53. "Their own Communion-Booke to be made al-together out of our Masse-Booke, their owne *Puritans* will beare me witnesses, and so much have they already plainly opened up to the world," 253.

[110]Genesis 25:21–34 .

[111]Acts 1:26.

To conclude, there are divers censurers of the Roman Church. Some say it is no Church, but equivocally, as the picture of a man is called man; or a painted fire, a fire; others say it is not a sound member, but a member. It hath scriptures, but corrupted with traditions: but they have changed the native sense; and so are lanterns that show light to others, none to themselves. The Roman Church is truly a Church, but not a true Church. In popery is a Church, yet popery is not the Church. As a Church, it is of God; as Popish, of the devil. It is an incurable Church, that hates to be reformed; therefore no Church. She hath apostated into treason, clipped the great King of king's coin, the word of God; turned that pure [158] gold into sophisticated alchymy; prayer to Christ, into invocation of saints. They have damnable errors and heresies, that of free-will, merits, &c. It hath blended Judaism and Paganism together with Christianity, and so swelled up a superstitious worship of God: therefore no Church.

Mind what St. Paul saith to the Galatians, though we, or an angel from heaven, preach any other gospel to you, than that which we have preached unto you, let him be accursed.[112] Now, if neither St. Paul nor an angel from heaven, had any commission to preach any thing besides what is set down in the Scriptures, sure we may shut our ears to all the doctors that preach 'tis necessary to obey the Pope, esteem him infallible, to believe Purgatory or the like things, which are not expressed in Scripture, and conclude them accursed as St. Paul saith. And for you to believe in man, viz.: to believe any thing to be infallibly true because the Pope saith it, and to venture your salvation upon it, is direct idolatry, yea, though an angel said it, for in so believing in the Pope, you make him God, that is, [159] you worship him as God. Do not you take up any new doctrine not commanded by Christ, nor give any assured belief to any the most learned and most holy Fathers, further than they can prove their doctrine true by canonical Scriptures, that is, your complete rule of faith. Nor would I have you misconstrue one text the Papists so much make use of, for to hear the Church, saying what the Church believes we must believe, and if we will not hear the Church, we are heretics and heathens.[113] You must note the word Church never signifies the clergy, but the congregation of the people. What the Church was to determine in that place, was not matters of faith, but matters of fact, matters of trespass between neighbors. You can have no infallible assurance of your faith but the Scriptures, the word of God and not of man. Meddle not with the gross errors of Papists in matters of faith, nor with the foppish superstitions they practice, but mind what St. Paul saith, The word is nigh unto thee, even in

---

[112]Galatians 1:8.
[113]Matthew 18:17.

thy mouth, and in thy heart; that is the word of faith which we preach, that if thou shalt confess with thy mouth the Lord [160] Jesus, and shalt believe in thine heart, that God hath raised Him from the dead, thou shalt be saved.[114] Which, well considered, will prevail with you not to submit to novelties of the doctrines of men. Pin not your faith on the Pope's sleeve. Our Saviour said to one of the ten lepers that was cleansed, who returned to give thanks, Go thy way, thy faith hath saved thee.[115] Thy faith, not another's.

There is no salvation by a common faith; but as all true believers have one and the same faith, so every true believer hath a singular and individual faith of his own. The faith that believes your own soul redeemed, justified, saved by the merits of Jesus Christ—not without works answerable to this belief—is the faith and thy faith. A good life is inseparable from a good faith—yea, a good faith is a good life, which hath not appeared in many vile and wicked creatures that have been Popes. It will perplex you to find out where this infallibility lies, if we consider what strange, horrid, wicked creatures have been Popes. What possible assurance can be found sufficient to make us believe the infallible spirit of the Holy [161] Ghost inhabits in such dens of uncleanness and cruelty, as the breasts of such detestable monsters of iniquity? How can the Spirit of God and the spirit of the devil be united in the hearts of such abominable Popes? Besides, Alexander the Sixth,[116] guilty of rapine, murder, incest, &c., that wicked, blasphemous, devilish Pope, laughing, said, What mighty advantage hath that fable of Christ brought unto us! Blessed be God, who hath left us a short and safe way, his holy Scripture, in searching of which, with sincerity and humility, we shall be sure to find eternal life.

The images of God are idols, wherewith Popery abounds. An old man, sitting in a chair, with a triple crown on his head and pontifical robes on his back, a dove hanging at his beard, and a crucifix in his arms, is their image of the Trinity. This they seem to do, as if in some sort they would requite their Maker: because God made man according to his image, therefore they, by way of recompense, will make God according to man's image. But this certainly they durst not do, without putting the second commandment out of their Catechisms, and the whole Decalogue out of their [162] consciences.

---

[114]Romans 10:8–9.

[115]Luke 7:50 and 18:42.

[116]Alexander VI provided a convenient target for Protestants who wished to criticize the temporal abuses of the Roman Catholic Church. See Frances E. Dolan, *Whores of Babylon: Catholicism, Gender, and Seventeenth-Century Print Culture* (Ithaca, N.Y.: Cornell University Press, 1999), 56–57. For a tract on the subject popular in Page's day, see Barnabe Barnes, *The Diuils Charter: A Tragaedie Conteining the Life and Death of Pope Alexander the Sixt. . . .* (London, 1607); a modern edition is available in Barnabe Barnes, *The Devil's Charter*, ed. Jim C. Pogue (New York: Garland Press, 1980).

How is a body without a spirit, like to a spirit without a body? a visible picture, like an invisible nature? If they say that he appeared to Daniel in this form, because he is there called the ancient of days,[117] it is answered, that God's commandments, and not his apparitions, be rules to us: by the former we shall be judged, not by the latter. Certainly that should not be imaged, which cannot be imagined. The Lord hath forbidden the making of any image, whether of things in Heaven or things on earth, to worship them.[118] Now, till God revoke that precept, what can authorize this practice.

Their images of the saints, employed to such religious purposes, make them no less than idolaters. It is a silly shift to say, the honor done to the image, reflects upon the represented saints. When they clothe an image, is the saint ever the gayer or warmer? When they kneel to an image, the saint esteems himself no more worshipped, than the king holds himself honored when a man speaks to his picture, before his face. Could the saints in heaven be heard [to] speak upon earth, they would disclaim [163] that honor, which is prejudicial to their Maker. By nature we are all prone to idolatry: when little children, we loved babies; and being grown men, we are apt to love images: and as babies are children's idols, so idols and images are men's babies. It seems that idols are fittest for babes; therefore, so the Apostle fits his caution, Babes keep yourselves from idols.[119] As all our knowledge comes by sense, so we naturally desire a sensible object of devotion, finding it easier to see pictures than to comprehend doctrines. What agreement hath the temple of God with idols?[120]

If through simple ignorance the Church of Rome is misled, there is hope of return; but if affected, it is most wretched. Let us pray for them, as St. Paul for his Ephesians: That the eyes of their understanding being enlightened, they may know what is the hope of God's calling, and what the riches of the glory of his inheritance in the saints.[121]

[76] Solomon saith there is more hope of a fool, than of one wise in his own conceit.[122] Be not you a brain-sick novelist,[123] to like no speech or opinion but your own, nor stand high in your own imagination, to reform that man, that can better inform you; nor like the Quaker, who presumes so much of light, that if himself now set, our world would be without a sun.

---

[117]Daniel 7:9, 13, 22.
[118]Exodus 20:4–5.
[119]I John 5:21.
[120]II Corinthians 6:16.
[121]Ephesians 1:18.
[122]Proverbs 26:12.
[123]A person fascinated by innovation or novelty.

CHAPTER THREE

James Blair: *Our Saviour's Divine Sermon on the Mount*

James Blair's career as commissary, college president, and member of the governor's Council has led historians to consider him primarily as a politician or administrator rather than as a pastor. His faults in these positions of public trust are well known. Avarice, a degree of paranoia, and a jealous attachment to his own authority pervade Blair's public career. Yet Blair was also a parish minister whose 117 discourses on the Sermon on the Mount illuminate a less widely appreciated facet of his public life. And they reveal not the scheming Machiavel, quick to note and defend his own, the colony's, and the college's interests. Rather, these gentle—if not particularly stirring—discourses, reveal a man sensitive to human frailty, his condemnation falling upon the sin rather than upon the sinner.

Published in five volumes in 1722, Blair's sermons were written in response to Bishop Compton's charge in 1707 to the clergy of the Church of England urging them to interpret in their pulpit discourses the "whole mind of God so far as [it] relates to things necessary for salvation." His choice of the Sermon on the Mount as his topic discloses much about Blair's understanding of Christianity and the state of the Church in early eighteenth-century Virginia. In the preface to his sermons Blair noted that Virginia's clergy had little cause in their discourses "to enter the Lists with Atheists, Deists," or dissenters—since there were few in the colony—thus freeing them to preach on what he identified as the more serious threats to religion: "the usual Corruptions of Mankind, Ignorance, Inconsideration, Practical Unbelief, Impenitence, Impiety, Worldly-mindedness, and other Common Immoralities." Since the "Practical Part of

Religion" comprised the greatest part of Blair's pastoral charge, he believed that the Sermon on the Mount provided the best possible text for combating the deficiencies he had identified, "knowing that Christian Duties were there both very plainly Taught, and yet carried to a degree of Perfection beyond what the World ever knew before, or is perhaps as yet duly sensible of."[1]

Blair's emphasis on the practical part of religion and duties does not mean that his sermons are simply moral exhortations. When Blair wrote typical Anglican sentiments such as "Christ's Doctrine is a Practical Doctrine" or, in reference to the Sermon on the Mount, "Whosoever heareth these Sayings of mine, *and doeth them*," he indicated that faith was something believers lived, not merely a set of propositions. Faith without works was an incomplete faith.[2]

The greatest work or duty was repentance. Repentance was central to the spiritual pilgrimage of Anglicans, as important a part of their journey to God as conversion was to Nonconformists—a necessary part of the spiritual life without which all other religious exercises were of little value. Anglicans occasionally equated repentance and conversion, thereby suggesting that repentance marked the onset of an active spiritual life in which the individual consciously began moving toward heaven. Blair likened it to the "Pangs and Throws of the new Birth."[3] The intention to repent indicated a person's acceptance of God's offer of salvation, a decision to become a Christian by choice rather than by the accident of birth in a Christian nation.[4]

Yet Blair, whose sermons are typical of his Church, did not view repentance as a mechanical round of sin, sorrow, and brief amendment repeated

---

[1]Parke Rouse, Jr., *James Blair of Virginia* (Chapel Hill: University of North Carolina Press, 1971), 232; James Blair, *Our Saviour's Divine Sermon on the Mount . . . Explain'd; and the Practice of it Recommended in divers Sermons and Discourses*, 5 Vols. (London, 1722), 1:ii–iii. For a more detailed account of Anglican theology and practice in colonial Virginia, see Edward L. Bond, "Anglican Theology and Devotion in James Blair's Virginia: Private Piety in the Public Church," *Virginia Magazine of History and Biography* 104 (1996): 313–40. An analysis of the imagery in Blair's sermons may be found in Donna Joan Walter, "Imagery in the Sermons of James Blair" (M.A. thesis: University of Tennessee, 1967). See also Richard Beale Davis, *Intellectual Life in the Colonial South, 1585–1763*, 3 Vols. (Knoxville: University of Tennessee Press, 1978), 2:733–36; James A. Levernier and Douglas R. Wilmes, eds., *American Writers Before 1800: A Biographical and Critical Dictionary*, 3 Vols. (Westport, Conn.: Greenwood Press, 1983), 1:152–54.

Blair noted in the preface to the 1722 edition of his sermons that he completed the discourses before he had an opportunity to read those on the same subject by the late bishop of Exeter, Offspring Blackall. Blair, *Our Saviour's Divine Sermon*, 1:vii; Offspring Blackall, *Practical Discourses Upon Our Saviour's Sermon on the Mount. In Eight Volumes* (London, 1717–1718).

[2]Blair, *Our Saviour's Divine Sermon on the Mount*, 5:374. See also 2:199, 204.

[3]Blair, *Our Saviour's Divine Sermon on the Mount*, 1:104. A similar sentiment appears in Robert Paxton, sermon number 8, "On Repentance," 7, Robert Paxton Manuscript Sermon Book, Houghton Library, Harvard University.

[4]Deciding to define oneself as a Christian through choice rather than through the possession of an English surname is a major theme in James Blair's sermons. See *Our Saviour's Divine Sermon on the Mount*, 1:62; 2:14, 22, 31, 255; 3:186, 280; and 5:321. See also the influential works of John Tillotson, *The Works of the Most Reverend John Tillotson*, 3 Vols. (London, 1712), 1:151.

day after day, a cycle that reflected too closely what Protestants equated with the Roman Catholic sacrament of penance: brief contrition followed by the mumbled words of a priest, and penitents were free to sin again without formally amending their lives.[5] Nor did they believe repentance should be left to the deathbed. Delaying so long left no opportunity for the necessary amendment of life, and a sickbed repentance often proceeded from the wrong motives, fear of judgment rather than love of God.[6] Nor was the repentance God demanded accomplished at one time; it was a process that continued throughout a lifetime: "an habitual Temper of the Mind and Course of Life."[7]

Repentance represented the essential reorientation of an individual's life. Despite the necessity of an amended life as evidence and the emphasis ministers placed on outward behavior, the process of repentance more accurately described an internal change within the believer's heart or mind (Virginians did not present a consistent anthropology), which then resulted in a life that increasingly conformed to God's laws. "The inner Man of the Heart, is the chief Thing that God aims to govern," for "like the main spring in a clock, the heart animates and directs all a person's thoughts and motions. As this main Spring of the Heart goes, the Man thinks, contrives, speaks and acts."[8] Virginians often used the pilgrimage motif to express this shift in direction. Preaching on Christ's admonition in Matthew's Gospel, "where your treasure is, there will your heart be also," Blair suggested that the disposition of the heart determined the port toward which a person sailed.[9]

James Blair's 117 sermons remain the largest extant collection of pulpit oratory produced by an Anglican minister in colonial Virginia. They reveal the commissary as a systematic theologian, a man tolerant of other Christian denominations, and an advocate of contemplative prayer. His sermons have been criticized as "neither brilliant nor very readable,"[10] a fact which likely indicates their originality. Writing for publication, Blair could not afford the luxury of "borrowing" his sermons from the works of others.

---

[5]Blair, *Our Saviour's Divine Sermon on the Mount*, 2:167; 4:15.

[6]The theme appears in many colonial Virginia sermons. See Blair, *Our Saviour's Divine Sermon on the Mount*, 2:31, 167; 4:31; 5:357–58; Paxton, sermon number 8, "Of Repentance," 5. "It is a most desperate madness for Men to defer it till" they approached death, warned *The Whole Duty of Man*, a devotional volume popular among Virginians; see [Richard Allestree], *The Whole Duty of Man* (London, 1714 [orig. publ. 1658]), 121–22. This theme was extraordinarily common and appears regularly in Anglican devotional materials and published sermons from the seventeenth and eighteenth centuries.

[7]Blair, *Our Saviour's Divine Sermon on the Mount*, 1:96.

[8]Blair, *Our Saviour's Divine Sermon on the Mount*, 2:332. See also Page, *Deed of Gift to My Dear Son*, 40–55.

[9]Blair, *Our Saviour's Divine Sermon on the Mount*, 4:332.

[10]Rouse, *James Blair of Virginia*, 237.

The Peacemakers[11]

Mat[thew] V.9.
Blessed are the Peace-makers: for they shall be called the Children of God.

The Second Sermon on this Text.

Having in a former Discourse entred upon these Words, there were Three Things I proposed to do in the handling of them.

1. To give you a Description of the Duty of *Peace-making.*

2. To consider the Priviledge Annexed; what it is to be *called the Sons of God.* [226]

3. To shew how the Compliance with the Duty of *Peace-making* disposes and entitles us to this Priviledge.

As to the *first* of these, the Description of the Duty of *Peace-making*, after I had told you *Negatively* what it is not; and so cleared it from some wrong Notions Men might be apt to have of it; I proceeded to the Positive Rules and Exercises of it; and finding this a Subject of great Copiousness and Variety, I proposed

1. To consider the chief of the General Precepts belonging to it; directing our Practice of the Duty of *Peace-making* in general.

2. To consider some more particular Precepts relating to the Practice of this Duty under particular Circumstances; as we are Members of Ecclesiastical or Civil Society.

As to the General Precepts relating to the Duty of *Peace-making* in general, I then dispatched them; and shall proceed now to the more Particular ones, relating to the Practice of this Duty in particular Circumstances; as we are Members of Ecclesiastical or Civil Society.

I shall begin with the Duty of *Peaceableness* and *Peace-making* as we are Members of the Church or Ecclesiastical Society. Which Duty is but little understood in the Theory, and yet less regarded in the Practice. The chief Branches of it, I take to be these. [227]

1. That we carefully avoid all Errors and Heresies, by acquainting our selves with, and firmly believing, and adhering to the Doctrine of the Gospel as it is left us by *Christ* and his Apostles, and recorded in the Holy Scriptures.

2. That in the exercise of Church Government and Discipline, we submit our selves to such Rulers, Pastors and Teachers, as *Christ* has appointed in his Church.

---

[11]James Blair, *Our Saviour's Divine Sermon on the Mount . . . Explain'd; and the Practice of it Recommended in divers Sermons and Discourses,* 5 Vols. (London, 1722), 1:225–240. Used courtesy of The Colonial Williamsburg Foundation.

3. That we preserve Peace and Union with all Members of the Christian Church, unless sinful Terms of Communion are required.

4. That we exercise Brotherly Love so far as to allow Christian Liberty in Things indifferent to all other Churches; without condemning them for not complying exactly with our Model.

5. That there be a mutual Propensity and Inclination to Peace, by Sacrificing our private Opinions in lesser things, and yielding all we can for Peace's Sake.

There being Things of great Importance, and highly tending to the Peace of the Church, will require to be a little better explained, in order to their being rightly apprehended, and put in Practice.

1. The first thing then I recommend in order to the Peace of the Church, is a Knowledge and Belief, and firm Profession of the Doctrine of the Gospel, as delivered by *Christ* and his Apostles, and recorded in the Holy Scriptures. This Foundation, being [228] once well laid, would prevent a great many Schismatical Principles and Practices, which for want of a due regard to it, have been set up in the Church, and have there kindled the Fire of Contention. For 1. It is for want of Minding this Foundation, that the Church of *Rome* has taken upon her to impose so many other things as Doctrines, and to enjoin the Belief of them as necessary to Salvation. The Bishops and Pastors of the Church should always remember, that tho' they are *Christ's* Delegates, and have his Commission, it is not an Arbitrary Commission, to teach and enjoyn what they please; But a Commission directed and limited with Abundance of Instructions, which if they should take upon them to falsify or transgress, both they are Accountable to their great Master for the Highest Breach of Trust, and the People likewise are exempted from their Obedience to them in all such Particulars. *Though we, or an Angel from Heaven, Preach any other Gospel unto you than that which we have Preached unto you, let him be accursed;* saith St. *Paul,* Gal. i. 8. This I look upon as the greatest Infringement of the Peace of the Church, when any Particular Church takes upon them to Teach and impose for Doctrines the Commandments of Men. 2. All Enthusiasts, who leaving the Rule of the Holy Scriptures set up the private Spirit as the Guide, without any other Limitation or instruction, are bold Invaders of the Peace of the Church; For that is all one, as if in Temporals [229] we should lay aside all Laws, and leave every Man to do what seems good in his own Eyes. 3. All they who take upon them to impose forced and constrained Senses on the Holy Scripture, against the true literal Meaning of it, that they may bend it to their own Reason, being resolved to admit of nothing in Religion above what our weak Reason can comprehend, are highly culpable against this first Rule of the Churches Peace; for there is but little

difference between laying aside a Rule or Law altogether, and the detorting[12] it to a Sense, which we our Selves can't believe was ever intended.

But I confess I can't reckon in this Number of the Transgressors of the Churches Peace those who do their best, to find out the true Sense and Meaning of the Holy Scripture; when either through Weakness of Capacity, or for want of sufficient Helps to understand the Scriptures, or by reason of the Deepness of the Mystery, or the difficulty of the Scripture it self (for in all things it is not alike plain) they miss of the true Sense and Meaning of it, and purely upon that Account fall into any Error either of Judgment or Practice; provided they are not obstinate in it, but willing to hear Reason, and to yield to it, as far as they find themselves Convinced: For this is no more than what the sincerest Inquirers into Truth are subject to, in this imperfect State, where we see but in Part, and know but in Part; though, God be thanked, all that is necessary to Salvation, is so clearly [230] revealed in the Holy Scriptures, that he that studies it there with a sincere Mind may find it and put it in Practice.

2. A second Thing I mentioned as to the Peace of the Church, was that in the Exercise of Church Government and Discipline, we submit our selves to such Rulers, Pastors, and Teachers as *Christ* hath appointed in his Church. It is very plain in the *New Testament*, that our Saviour erected all Christian Believers into one Body or Society, called the Church; That out of them he chose some, with a Power of Teaching and Guiding Others in the way of Salvation, whom he called *Apostles*; that he likewise gave these Apostles Power of Ordaining others, both to take part of this Care in their Life time, and to succeed them in the whole after their Decease: Men set a part from the World, who should addict themselves to this great Work, the care of Souls: An Institution of absolute Use and Necessity to the end of [the] World; for what Confusion must it let in to any Society, where all are alike, none to Direct, none to Obey; where every one invades the Teachers Office at Pleasure, and this sacred Order of the Ministry is cast in common to every Bold Invader? Now this wholsom Institution has been many Ways neglected and overthrown, to the utter Destruction of Peace and good Order in the Church. For the *Quakers* and some other Enthusiasts have made an open Insurrection against the sacred Order of the Ministry, like *Corab* [231] *Dathan*, and *Abiram*,[13] who rose up against *Moses* and *Aaron*, and pretended that the whole Congregation was Holy. They have given

---

[12]To twist the meaning of a word or saying.

[13]Corab, Dathan, and Abiram all conspired against the leadership of Moses and Aaron during the Israelites' period of wandering in the wilderness. Blair refers to Moses and Aaron to symbolize the leaders of church and state. See Numbers 16, 26, and 27. The punishments of these three can be found in Deuteronomy 11:6 and Psalm 106:17.

Leave to Men without any External Call from the Church, if they have but Confidence enough to pretend to an Inward Call of the Spirit, to invade these sacred Offices; and not only so, but to deliver what Doctrine they themselves please, without giving any Account to the Rulers of the Church. And the Church of *Rome* has taken another way to invade the Peace of the Church in this particular; for the Ministry which by *Christ* was left in common to all the Apostles, and their Successors, they have by an unheard of Piece of Tyranny limited to one Man, whom they set up with an uncontroulable Power to Trample upon all the other Bishops and Pastors, and to countenance an infinite Number of Abuses and Corruptions, chiefly brought into the Church, to support his Worldly Pomp and Grandeur. These are the two chief Invasions, which have been made on the Order of Pastors in the Christian Church, by the Enthusiasts on the one Hand, and the *Papists* on the other; though it can't be denied that other very considerable Encroachments have been made on the Peace of [the] Church in this particular, by some who have overthrown the ancient Order of Episcopacy, to set up a Parity in the stead of it, which is always the Mother of Confusion; and by others, who have so encroached upon the Ecclesiastical Discipline in the Hands of the [232] Bishops and Pastors of the Church, that they have confounded the Spiritual with the secular Sword; and by the New Doctrine of Erastianism have destroyed the Discipline and Government of the Church: To that degree that there is a New Heresie sprung up in our Days, which destroys the very Being of the Church as a Society; and makes it a mere Creature of the State. So many ways has Satan with his Instruments endeavoured to over-turn this wholsom Order, at first appointed by *Christ* for so many good Ends and Purposes in his Church, particularly for the Preservation of Peace, Discipline, and good Government.

3. But though our great Care ought to be first for the Purity of Doctrine and Worship; next for such Pastours and Government as *Christ* hath set up in his Church; yet there is another Rule of Church-Peace as necessary as any of these: And that is, that we preserve Peace and Union with all the Parts and Members of the Christian Church, unless sinful Terms of Communion with them are required. The zealous Gentlemen that insist so earnestly for the good Government and Discipline of the Ancient Church, as if it were absolutely necessary to Salvation, put me in Mind of a just Complaint of *Tullie's* against *Cato;* that he gave his Opinion always in the *Senate,* as if he had been living in *Plato's* Common-wealth, and not among the Dregs of *Romulus.*[14] It is a

---

[14]Cicero, *Letters to Atticus,* II.1 par. 8. "For our friend Cato is not more to you than to me: but still with the best of intentions and unimpeachable honesty at times he does harm to the country: for the opinions he delivers would be more in place in Plato's Republic than among the dregs of humanity collected by Romulus."

much more proper Inquiry for us, what we may and ought to comply with for Peace's Sake, [233] in this corrupt State of the Church, than what those Noble Primitive Christians arrived at. We must not for every thing that is amiss break away, and make a Rent and Schism from the Body of the Church; If we do, I know not where we shall find a Church in the World at this Day so perfect, in which there are not many Things amiss; and which a good Man would not wish to be otherwise. The Question is which Way we may best contribute our Pains towards the Amendment or Reformation of them, whether by Continuing in the Church, or by Abandoning it? Which seems to me much such a Dispute, as if some more Angry than Skilful Men at Sea in a Leaky Ship, which yet by Working duly at the Pump, and Caulking, and Stopping the Leaks, would make very good Way, and at last carry the Passengers safe to their intended Port; as if, I say, these angry Men in such a Vessel should be for making a Mutiny among the Seamen and Passengers on this Account; and propose the leaving the Ship, and betaking themselves, some to the Long Boat, and some to the Pinnace for their Safety, and better dispatch of their Voyage. So I think the true Question should not be whether the Church we are in, is without Fault or Blemish, or whether She is to be compared, especially for Exactness of Discipline, with the Pure Primitive Church; Such a one as is not now to be found upon Earth; no more than perhaps there is any Civil Government equal to *Plato's* Common-wealth; but [234] whether it is not a Church, in which we may very well make a good Voyage to Heaven? And whether the Faults that are in it may not be better mended by our Staying in it, than by our Forsaking it, and betaking our selves to the Meeting or Conventicle?[15] I confess if there is any such great Leak as can not be stopt; and which if it be not stopt will sink the Ship, and drown the Passengers; such a Ship is at last to be abandoned; that is, if there is any one sinful Condition of Communion required of us, such as will endanger our Salvation, then after all other Endeavours to amend it, let us leave such a Church in God's Name; And this was our Case with the Church of *Rome*, which would not permit us to continue in her Communion, without professing several erroneous Doctrines, and Joining in several Parts of Idolatrous Worship; But if there is no sinful Condition of Communion required of us in the Reformed Churches, though there are some Things amiss in them all, let us so far study Peace, as to make no Separation from such Churches, but quietly work out our Salvation in them, striving in our several Stations to reform and improve them to the best Advantage.

---

[15]A religious meeting, often held in secret or by those who dissented from the established church.

4. It is a good Rule of Peace in the Church, to remember that the Points of mere Order and Decency are for the most part wisely left by our Saviour and his *Apostles* under General Rules, and the particular Rites and Ceremonies which may be constituted in Consequence of those General Rules, are [235] various and alterable; and therefore great Grains of Allowance should be made to particular Churches, to settle or vary them according to the different Circumstances of Time and Place, and the various Dispositions of the Persons, of whom that particular Church doth consist. We ought then to endeavour to lay no greater Stress on these Matters, than according to the Importance of them; and to comply with such innocent Customs, as are established in the particular Church where we reside; but at the same Time to have a Care, that we condemn not other Churches, which have judged quite different Rites more decent and proper. And though we our selves should happen to differ in our private Judgment, as to the Conveniency or Inconveniency of any of those Rites; while our Scruples are not about the Lawfulness or Unlawfulness, but only the Expediency of such Things, it is very fit for Peace's Sake, that we sacrifice all such Scruples to the Order and Authority of the Government in Church or State, under which we live.

5. Lastly there is another Rule of Peace recommended by St. *Paul*; that in the use of Christian Liberty great Regard is to be had to the Infirmities of our weak Brethren; lest they should be offended by our otherwise just Use of it.[16] That great Controversy which broke out so early in the Church between the Judaizing, and not the Judaizing Christians, with the many Rules for Peace and Christian Condescension laid down by St. *Paul* in the [236] managing of it,[17] should be a lasting Lesson to us for Moderation, in treating one another in our far less considerable Differences; which for want of the like Christian Spirit we have carried to such Unreasonable Heats and Divisions.

Thus much I thought proper to offer with Relation to our Duty of *Peaceableness* and *Peace-making,* as we are Members of the Church, or of an Ecclesiastical Society. The neglect of such Useful Rules has filled the Church with so many Schisms and Divisions, as rend it in sunder at this Day.

II. But as we are Members of the Church, we must remember that we are likewise Members of the State, and that there is a great Part of the Duty of *Peace-making* relates to our quiet Deportment under the several Civil Governments, we are Subjects of in the World. It is therefore a thing of great Consequence that we have right Notions of our Duty in this Respect. I shall as briefly as I can, guard you against some Principles, which have been advanced

---

[16]See I Corinthians 8:1–13.
[17]See Acts 11:1–18, 15:1–35, 21:17–26, and Galatians.

very destructive of the Civil Peace; and at the same Time endeavour to principle you with true Christian Notions in those Matters, and so to have done; for I perceive I shall get not further at this Time than the Description of the Duty of *Peace-making*.

1. *First* then, One False Notion in this Matter is that a great many Men have thought it was every ones Business to reform Abuses and Corruptions, not [237] only in their own Station (which would have been right) but by invading the Stations of Others, Magistrates, Legislators, Princes and Governours; which is the high Way, instead of Peace, to drive all Things to Anarchy and Confusion. Now as God is a God of Order, our Religion requires that every Man keep within his Own Sphere, and be not a Busy Body in other Men's Matter. If Grievances in any State can not be remedied upon our Humble Petition, Private Men must wait patiently, and neither stir up Discontents against the Government, nor flee to Arms, or any other irregular Methods of Redress.

2. Some have had so wrong Notions of Gospel Liberty, as if it exempted them from the Civil Duties they owe to their Superiors; nay some have been carried to that degree of Fanatical Delusion, as to believe that Dominion is founded in Grace; and that this World with the Possession and Government of it, belongs to the Saints, which Saints they take to be Themselves.[18] A Principle which would set all immediately in a Flame, and turn the Kingdom of *Christ* into one of the worst Worldly Kingdoms.

3. There are some who have so wrong Notions of the Power of Human Governments, especially in the Externals and Ceremonials of Religion, that they think They can enjoyn nothing, but what is already enjoined by the Laws of God: Whereas it is sufficient to recommend to us any Human Laws in these things, that [238] they be not contrary or disagreeable to God's Laws; between which two Notions there is a very wide Difference.

4. There is both an Active, and a Passive Obedience due to Civil Governments; but the Rules and Measures of both have been very much mistaken and misrepresented; which has occasioned that the Doctrines themselves have been ridiculed in Theory, and utterly neglected in Practice, to the total Overthrow of all the Principles upon which the Peace of Civil Governments doth subsist. The short of the Matter is, that whatever Form of Civil Government is by Law established in any Country, the Christian Religion requires us to submit our selves to it, not only for Wrath but for Conscience Sake. And therefore They who have pretended to flatter

---

[18]Blair is no doubt referring to the Puritans.

Princes, and to enslave Subjects, by endeavouring to prove from *Scripture*, that it countenances no Government but that of Absolute Monarchy;[19] that is, Monarchy unlimited by any Laws; and that all People were obliged either Actively or Passively to obey not only the Legal, but the Arbitrary and Illegal Commands of their Princes, have dangerously mistaken and misrepresented the Christian Doctrine, and brought a Scandal on our Religion, as if it enjoined the Doctrines of Tyranny and Slavery, and tended to the utter Overthrow of Liberty and Property among Men: Whereas it is the Established Laws and Constitution of every Country, which is the Rule both of our Active and [239] Passive Obedience in that Country; and it is a great Mistake to think that the Christian Religion encroaches on any Man's or any Country's Liberty or Property, further than the Laws and Constitution of the several Christian Countreys think fit to prescribe and direct. Christianity does indeed require our Obedience upon better Principles, I mean the Principles of Conscience; and upon a better Sanction, namely that of Eternal Rewards and Punishments; but still it is the same Legal Obedience, which is enjoined by the Laws and Constitution, and no other. And certainly Passive Obedience and Non-resistance, in this Sense, are so far from being Formidable or Enslaving Doctrines, that they are no more in effect, than if we should exhort Subjects to obey the Laws of their Country, in so far as they are not contrary to the Laws of God; and if they are contrary to any of God's Laws, or if they in their conscience think them so; that then they should submit to the Penalty, and not rise in Rebellion against the Government. A Doctrine so necessary for the Support of all Governments, that it is not easy to conceive how they can subsist without it.

Perhaps it would not have been improper upon this Subject, to have considered not only, as I have now done, the Principles of *Peaceableness*, as we are Members of the Church, and Subjects of the State, to avoid Schism in the one, and Sedition in the other; but likewise the Peace of Families, Neighbourhoods, and lesser Corporations and Societies; [240] together with the Common Differences, Controversies and Law Suits, which are incident to disturb it; But besides that Time will not permit, I think it needless to enter further into these Things, seeing for the clear understanding our Duty in all the various Cases which may happen, we want only a discreet Application of the General Rules of Peace; of which I discoursed at the last Occasion.

---

[19]Blair could have been writing against Robert Filmer, *Patriarcha: or, The Natural Power of Kings* (1680); Thomas Hobbes, *Leviathan* (1651); or, possibly, Charles Leslie, *A Short Account of the Original of Government*, in *The New Association* (London, 1703), part III.

And therefore referring only the Promise here annexed to the *Peace-makers*, to another Opportunity, I shall now make an End of my Description of the Duty of *Peaceableness;* which I pray God, so to engraft in all our Hearts, that we may not only live quiet and peaceable Lives in all Godliness and Honesty here upon Earth: but at last may attain to everlasting Peace and Rest with him in the Kingdom of Heaven, through the Mediation of our Blessed Lord and Saviour *Christ Jesus.* To *whom*, &c.

The Exemplariness of Our Good Works[20]

Mat[thew] V. 16.
Let your Light so shine before Men, that they may see your good Works, and glorifie your Father which is in Heaven.

The Seventh Sermon on this Text.

In a former Discourse on these Words, after I had explained the Terms, there were *Three* Things I proposed to consider from them, as being the Scope and Design of our Saviour, in this Passage of his Sermon on the Mount.

I. That [104] it is the Duty of us Christians to live exemplary Lives, eminent for all manner of good Works.

II. That in so doing we ought not only to have Regard to God, so as to keep a good Conscience toward him; but to have Regard likewise to Men, that they may be made better by our good Example.

III. That as to the Praise and Honour of this good Example, we are to have a special Care both to design and contrive it so, that it may not terminate in our selves, but in God our Heavenly Father.

Now having at the last Occasion spoke to the *First* of these, (at least as far as Time would permit) that it is the Duty of Christians to live Exemplary Lives, eminent for all manner of good Works; I proceed now to the *Second,* which is, That in doing our good Works, we ought not only to have Regard to God, so as to keep a good Conscience toward him; but to have Regard likewise to Men, that they may be made better by our good Example. *Let your Light so shine before Men, that they may see your good Works, and glorifie your Father which is in Heaven.* Where it is plain, the Good Works are to be contrived to be Publick and Exemplary, on Purpose that Men may see them, and take notice [105] of them; and be excited by them to glorify God. The Glory

---

[20]James Blair, *Our Saviour's Divine Sermon on the Mount . . . Explain'd; and the Practice of it Recommended in divers Sermons and Discourses*, 5 Vols. (London, 1722), 2:103–21. Used courtesy of The Colonial Williamsburg Foundation.

of God indeed is the ultimate End we ought to propose to our selves in our good Actions; but the Edification of Men is a subordinate End; and likewise has a direct Tendency to the Glory of God, which is the ultimate End. Now that I may handle this Part of our Duty more distinctly, I shall comprehend it in these Two. 1. I will a little further consider the Act of being Exemplary in Good Works. And 2. the View or Aim we are to have in this Act, namely, the Good of Others, that they may be duly affected with this good Example, so as to be excited to glorify God thereby.

(1) I will a little further consider the Act of being Exemplary in Good Works. And *First* as to Good Works.

That there is a Natural Distinction between Good and Evil; and that the very Heathen World understood what was meant by Good Works, is plain from all their Writings; and our Lord's Discourse here doth suppose it. And indeed I believe there is scarce any People to be found so Barbarous, but what in their own Minds set a Value on Truth and Honesty, on Mercy and Charity, on Kindness and Humanity, on Temperance and Diligence, and the like, before the contrary Vices of Falshood, Knavery, Cruelty, Hardheartedness, Pride and Passion, [106] Slothfulness and Drunkenness. It's true indeed this Distinction between Good and Evil, is both scanty and obscure by the Light of Nature, to what it is by the Laws of the Gospel. But this is to be said further in Commendation of the Light of Nature upon this Subject of Good Works, that tho' there are many excellent Things, which it could not find out of it self, yet when found out to its Hand, it can't help seeing the Beauty of them, and admiring the Persons who practise them, and the Institution which gives so good Precepts and Directions; and of this Nature are most of the Duties of the Christian Religion; such good Things as the World had either no Notion, or very imperfect Notions of before, which yet when they come to be understood, and put in Practice, and especially in that most perfect Manner Christ has enjoined, do wonderfully recommend themselves to the Approbation, Love and Esteem of Mankind. For, tho' there always were, and always will be such Men in the World, as do not approve of good Works by their own Practice and Example; there are scarce any Men so much depraved in their Judgments, but that they know in general that a Virtuous is far beyond a Vitious Practice; as appears by this, that if they are never so knavish themselves, they would have their Factors and Correspondents, and all others that [107] deal with them, to be just and honest; and if they are never so lewd and vitious themselves, they would be glad to have their Wives and Children and best Friends virtuous. We can't then be much to seek, what our Saviour meant by good Works; for no doubt he meant in general all such Works, as Men upon a good Use of their Faculties are apt to Esteem and

Love. And if I were to condescend upon particulars, I know not where I could find a better Collection of them, than in this same excellent Sermon on the Mount; where our Saviour beginning with removing the false Notions they had of the Messiah, and the wrong Dispositions of Mind and Practices of Life growing therefrom, lays the Foundation of the Opposite Graces and Virtues in the eight Beatitudes;[21] then clears the Moral Law from all the wrong Interpretations [that] had been put on it, and sets it off in its due Latitude and Extent of Duty; and especially shews how it was designed to govern the inner as well as the outward Man, and to be a Rule for our Thoughts as well as our Words and Actions. Then lastly superadds several more special Gospel Duties, such as Love of Enemies, Humility, Devotion, Fasting, Heavenly-mindedness, Charity, Candour in censuring, Importunity in Prayer, Strictness of Life and Conversation, and living up to the Laws of the Christian Profession. Here we have good Works enough [108] taught by the best Master, and illustrated by the best Pattern.

Let us next inquire what is meant by being exemplary in good Works; for it is not a bare Glimmering of Light which is here recommended, but such a bright Sunshine of it as may excite the Attention and Admiration, and make deep Impressions in the Hearts of the Heathen World, in Favour of the Christian Religion. But having said a good Deal of this Exemplariness from the first Point I handled from this Text at the last Occasion, I shall not now repeat, but add something of such Observations as may help further to illustrate this Matter.

1. *First* then, whereas other Religions were made up of a vast deal of Ceremony, and but a little of substantial Duty; the Christian Religion has this Advantage as to Good Works, that it consists wholly of Substantial Duty, and little or no Ceremony. This Observation is so true of the Pagan Religions, that I shall not need to prove it; they turned all Religion into Pomp and Gaudiness, neglecting both the inward Purity of the Heart, and the external good Examples of Life. This *Persius*, one of their own Poets, complains of; and advises that instead of the Trinkets they offered to their Gods, they would offer a well composed, just, honest Mind, and a good Life.[22] The *Jewish* Religion [109] indeed was made up of both; there was a great Deal of good Morality in their Moral and Judicial Law, mixed with a great Heap of Ceremonies, which, for the Hardness of their Hearts, and to keep them from Idolatry, had been enjoined them. But they quickly found a Way to make the Ceremonial Part eat out the Moral; and instead of the Examples of good Life, to be a little more costly in the Num-

---

[21]Matthew 5:3–11.
[22]Persius (34–62), Roman satirist and Stoic. Blair's reference is to Satire II, especially lines 61–75.

ber of their Sacrifices, which they thought would make up the Business. This God by his Prophets often found fault with, Shewing them that he valued the Example of a Good Life far before the Numbers and Costliness of their Sacrifices. *To what Purpose is the Multitude of your Sacrifices unto me? saith the Lord; I am full of the burnt Offerings of Rams, and the Fat of fed Beasts, and I delight not in the Blood of Bullocks, or of Lambs, or of He-goats:* Nay, he calls these Things *vain Oblations,* and *Incense an Abomination,* Isa. i. 13. And then at the 16th ver. directs them to the proper Method, which was truly acceptable to him, *Wash ye, make you clean, put away the Evil of your Doings from before mine Eyes, cease to do Evil, learn to do well, seek Judgment, relieve the Oppressed, judge the Fatherless, plead for the Widow.* And then it follows immediately; *Come now and let us reason together, saith the Lord: tho' your Sins be as Scarlet, they shall be as white as Snow; tho' they be red like Crimson,* [110] *they shall be as Wool.*[23] Now can any one think otherwise, than that a Religion, which doth not give any Evasion to the Understanding, nor divert the Attention by Ceremonies, but directly requires the Substantials of Good Life and Practice, is more likely to abound in Examples of good Life, than a Religion which evaporates in Ceremonies, and consumes its Zeal in what has not the least Tendency to a good Life?

2. Especially, if we add in the next Place, that the Christian Religion not only gathers in our Zeal to the Substantials of Duty, but requires very High Measures of Care and Concernedness in all these Things; for it is not the little Matters of the Law, *the Tything of Mint, Anise and Cummin;* but the great Concerns of it, *Justice, Mercy, and Fidelity,*[24] it chiefly insists upon; nor is it *the outside of the Cup and Platter,*[25] but much more the *inside,* it requires to be kept clean; not but that it calls for an Outward Decency and Decorum as much as any Religion in the World; but this outward good Behaviour it requires to come from the Heart, and that there be nothing hypocritical or counterfeit in it, but all sincere and Genuine. It requires a constant Eye to God and another World. It is not for compounding for a neglect of some Duties by an over-Zeal in others; but requires a steady Regard to all God's [111] Commandments; and that not in a low Degree, but with the most intent and diligent Care, that we should love God with our whole Heart, and our Neighbour as our selves; that we should in the *First* and principal Place *seek the Kingdom of God and the Righteousness thereof,*[26] and other Things but as Accessories; that we should mind Religion as the *one Thing necessary,*[27] and

---

[23]Isaiah 1:18.
[24]Matthew 23:23.
[25]Matthew 23:25.
[26]Matthew 6:33.
[27]Luke 10:31.

spend our Skill and Pains about it; like St. *Paul*, who exercised and trained himself in *this* as his main Business, *to keep a Conscience void of Offence, both towards God and Men.*[28]

3. This was to be a very Bright Example, because the Light of it was to shine all over the World at once, and was not to be confined to one Corner of it, as the Light of the Law of *Moses* was. The Illumination was great, both in Regard of the vast Number of Lights, Burning and Shining Lights that were set up; and in Regard of the advantagious placing them in the most eminent Cities of the civilized World; and in Regard of the wonderful Success they had in illuminating the dark Corners of the Earth, and in banishing the Darkness of Superstition and Vice.

So much for the Act of being exemplary in good Works.

(2) Let us next inquire into the View or Aim we are to have in this Act, namely, the Good of others, that they may be duly affected [112] with this good Example, so as to be excited to glorifie God thereby; *That they may see your good Works, and glorifie your Father which is in Heaven.* The Christian Institution doth not rest in the regulating of our External Actions; but proceeds to the directing of our Intentions aright in all those our Exemplary Actions. And two noble Intentions we are directed to here in the Text in all our good Examples. One is, the Good of our Neighbour; the other, the Glory of God. Instead of those worthless or base Motives Men commonly act by, Humour, Self-Interest, Hypocrisie, Vanity, Force of Education, Fear of Parents, Masters, or Magistrates, Fashion, Party, Imitation of others, the Importunity of Friends, the Emulation of Enemies, and many other Intrigues and Designs, which are not easy to be all observed or enumerated: Our Saviour directs us only to these two, the Good of our Neighbour, and the Glory of God. The Good of our Neighbour is what we are now upon under this Head. And it is a Thing which ought to be well considered. The World is full of Designs which Men carry on against one another; commonly to supplant their Neighbour, and to serve their own selfish and carnal Ends out of him. They have their Traps and Snares, and Arts and Instruments for that End; and most of their Wit and [113] Parts, nay, most of their Learning and Skill in their several Arts, and Sciences, and Callings, is imployed to this End. The Attacks and Defences of this Nature are the chief Employment of Mankind. Under all the Pretences of Friendships and Civilities, they are spreading their Nets for one another, and are sure to embrace every Advantage that presents. But how then! are we Christians to be void of all Aim and Design in our Actions? Are we to be so thoughtless and simple, as to act without any Intention? No,

---

[28]Acts 24:16.

not so neither; we are to have Designs upon our Neighbour, but contrary to those of the World; Designs to do him Good, to bring him to the Love of Virtue and Hatred of Vice; we are to consider his Circumstances as carefully as the worldly Man doth, and to contrive how, by our selves or others, we may do him the most Good; and are to lay such Traps in his Way, whereby he may be most gained to the Love of God and his Duty. These are the innocent Designs we are to have upon him; if ye ask me, what way all this is to be done? I answer, that it is a Work of that vast Extent, and takes in such a great Compass of Means; and these diversified according to the various Circumstances of our Neighbour, and of our own Talents, that it is no easie Matter to reduce them within any certain Rules; Strategems here [114] altering, as in War, upon the various Accidents of Time and Place, and our own, and the Enemies Circumstances. But apprehending, notwithstanding, that it may be a Thing of good Use to give some general good Directions, as to our Conduct in this Affair, how to carry on our Designs upon our Neighbour to the best Advantage of his Soul; I shall adventure upon some of the plainest, and most general, and inoffensive to this Purpose.

1. *First* then, Let us endeavour to be always possessed with a sincere, good Intention, to do all the Good we can to our Neighbour. We find that whatever Intention or Desire is uppermost, or most prevalent in Men, the very Eagerness of the Intention makes them ingenious to find out Ways and Means to compass it. The Covetous Man, for Example, how fruitful in Invention has he in contriving several Ways and Arts of getting and saving? And if he happens to hear or read of any Project, or Method, that tends to the carrying on of his Purposes, with what diligent Attention does he observe it? And with how faithful a Memory does he remember it? And how careful is he at last to try the Experiment, and put it in Practice? So if once we resolve with our selves to carry on these Designs on Men for their Good, the very Strength and Eagerness of that Design will put us upon a thousand Inventions, to [115] gain their Affections, and to find out the most commodious Times of Access, and to choose the most winning Language and Behaviour, and to put them into the best Methods for Books, and Company, and Business, to carry on the Design, that can be.

2. Next to a good Intention, I know nothing more apt to gain upon Men, than that Spirit of Love and Charity, which is so much recommended in the Gospel. This puts us upon all those innocent Arts of gaining upon their Affections, and obliging them, which of all Things makes them the most apt to open their Hearts to us, and receive Benefit by our Advices and good Examples. And here I can't but observe a singular Piece of good Providence of God to prepare the Way for the Reception of the Gospel; in that he gave a Power

to the first Preachers and Propagators of it, to work a great many beneficial and obliging Miracles, by which the Hearts of People were first gained; and then their Understandings came to be enlightened. But it was not by their Miracles alone they gained so upon Mankind; we find a very obliging conde-scending Behavior joined with their other Gifts, carefully avoiding the giving Offence either to the *Jews* or *Gentiles*, or to weak Christians. And this oblig-ing Practice St. *Paul* frequently recommends to others, and tells us, that he followed it himself, *Rom.* [116] xv. 2. *Let every one of us please his Neighbour for his good to Edification.* And xiv. 19. *Let us therefore follow after the Things which make for Peace, and Things wherewith one may edify another.* And there is a very notable Passage to this Purpose, I *Cor.* x. 31. From whence it appears, that this was the chief Rule St. *Paul* walked by in his Eating and Drinking, and all other indifferent Matters. *Whether therefore ye eat or drink,* says he, *or whatsoever ye do, do all to the Glory of God: give no Offence neither to the Jews, nor to the Gen-tiles, nor to the Church of God: even as I please all Men in all Things, not seeking mine own Profit, but the Profit of many that they may be saved.*

3. One of the surest, and most inoffensive Ways of gaining upon Mankind, is that of good Example. It is one of the readiest Ways both to inform the Judgment, and to please the Fancy, and to convince the Understanding, and to make Impression on the Memory, and to excite our Zeal, and to provoke our Emulation, and to remove the Difficulties, by Demonstration that good Things are feasible and practicable; it is one of the most real Ways of Argu-mentation, least Subject to Delusion; and likewise one of the most silent and modest, and consequently the most taking; as Men are more taken with a modest, than with a talkative Beauty. And in short this seems to be the Method chiefly recommended in my Text, [117] that Men should be edified by *the Sight of our good Works.* But there is another Thing commonly goes along with this Sight, which usually makes a greater Impression; and that is, the Observing, and perhaps the real Feeling the good Effects of them, at least the feeling of them by Sympathy in the Refreshments of others, if we have had no Occasion or Opportunity to be refreshed by them our selves. Now this of Sense and Experience is a feeling Argument indeed; and enters deep, and makes very lasting Impressions.

4. If we would have our Aims to answer well to make Impression upon our Neighbour for his Edification, we must consider his particular Circum-stances, that so we may find out which way he is best to be managed, and to be wrought upon to do good. *Let us consider one another to provoke unto Love, and to good Works*; says the Apostle, *Heb.* x. 24. All Men are not to be man-aged the same Way; therefore let us consider one another's particular Cir-cumstances, and make use of them *to provoke unto Love and good Works.*

Sometimes the Dangers and Temptations the Person is immediately under, call for our Help, and direct us to that sort of good Works, which is most proper to be used to one in his Circumstances, and then the Seasonableness of the Kindness makes a wonderful Impression. Sometimes we must [118] mind the Person's Humour and Temper, the *mollia Tempora fandi*,[29] the Times when he is most accessible, and fittest to receive good Impressions; sometimes we must mind his outward Circumstances, when God has blest him best in his Affairs, and then move him to Charity and good Works; Some Men are hard to be moved to do much of that Nature alone, who yet will act handsomely in Conjunction with others; and as some are easiest to be wrought upon in a Day of rejoicing, so others in a Day of Grief and Affliction; then their Hearts have the tenderest sense of Religion, and are most capable of Charitable Impressions. These few Instances are sufficient to convince us, that he who has Designs upon his Neighbour for his good, must acquaint himself with his Heart and Life, and outward Circumstances, if he intends to make such Advantageous Impressions upon him, as are necessary to stir him up to do much good.

5. There are many Means which God has left in his Church and in the World for promoting good Works; all which Means we should contrive, by our Example and Authority, in our several Stations, to countenance and encourage, and to discourage all the contrary Attempts: e.g. Are we convinced that a settled Ministry is a good Means, by the Blessing of God, to carry on the great Ends of the [119] Gospel? Then let us countenance it where it is, and endeavour to set it up where it is wanting. Are we sensible that Separations, Schisms, and Divisions, have a bad Influence upon Religion, and are a great Hindrance of our Progress in Christian Virtue? Then, according to the Apostle's Advice, *Heb.* x. 25. *Let us not forsake the Assembling of our selves together, as the manner of some is.* Are we sensible that the careful Institution of Children in the Fear of God is a great Help to their good Behaviour all their Life afterwards? Then let us encourage Schools, and the Fear of God in Families, and do what we can towards the good Education of all over whom we have any Power, Interest, or Authority.

Lastly, Are we sensible that the Vigilance of Rulers and Magistrates, and a careful Execution of Laws, a Discouragement of Vice, and Encouragement of virtuous Persons, have a mighty Influence on the good Government of Mankind? Then let Magistrates learn to be diligent in the Execution of their Function, and to employ it to those good Ends; and let all People learn to

---

[29]See Virgil, *Aeneid*, book 4, line 293. The phrase roughly translates as "the happiest season for speech" or "the easiest time to speak."

honour and countenance Rulers and Magistrates for their Office Sake; to pray to God for them, and to yield them all due Obedience, and to have a Care how they join in with such disorderly People, as would bring in Anarchy and Confusion in Church or State.

6. *Lastly*, [120] Towards the carrying on any good Design upon others, it is necessary that we take Care to preserve our own Minds in a good Frame and Temper; and likewise our Lives clear from all Blot and Scandal; there being nothing that will either more dispirit us in administring to others, or more hinder those others from receiving any Benefit from our Endeavours, than our own contradicting them in our Lives. And therefore let us count it one of the best Undertakings, to try the Force of our Advices and Admonitions upon our selves, before we can expect they will have much Influence upon others. And to all our other Endeavours, let us not fail to join that of our hearty and importunate Prayers at the Throne of Grace; a Means, than which there is none better, either for drawing down a due Measure of Grace upon our selves, or others to whom we administer the same.

I have been all this while discovering to you a great Secret of Christian Practice; namely, what Aims and Intentions we ought to have in the good Examples we set before one another; and I have been exhorting to Duties very much neglected, namely, instead of carrying on Designs to our Neighbour's Prejudice, to lay out our whole Skill in contriving his Edification, and thereby the Glory of God. And this would have led me to the *last* Thing I proposed to speak [121] to from the Text; namely, that as to the Praise and Honour of our good Works, we are to have a special Care to design and contrive it so, that it may not terminate in our selves, but in God our Heavenly Father: But this, for want of Time, I must leave to another Opportunity.

God give us Grace to consider one another, that by all good Examples in Word and in Deed, we may *provoke unto Love and to good Works*. Now to this great God, &c.

General Observations on the Lord's Prayer[30]

Mat[thew] VI.9

After this Manner therefore pray ye: Our Father which art in Heaven, hallowed be thy Name.

V.10. Thy Kingdom come. Thy Will be done in Earth, as it is in Heaven.

---

[30]James Blair, *Our Saviour's Divine Sermon on the Mount . . . Explain'd; and the Practice of it Recommended in divers Sermons and Discourses*, 5 Vols. (London, 1722), 4:1–18. Used courtesy of The Colonial Williamsburg Foundation.

V.11. *Give us this Day our Daily Bread.*
V.12. *And forgive us our Debts, as we forgive our Debtors.*
V.13. *And lead us not into Temptation, but deliver us from Evil; for thine*
is the Kingdom, and the Power and the Glory, for ever. Amen.

The First Sermon on this text.

This excellent Form of Prayer being composed and dictated by our Lord himself to his Disciples, deserves, on that Account, a very particular Regard, and therefore I shall apply my self to as diligent an Explication of it as I can.

But [2] before I come to speak of the particular Petitions, there are several good Things we may observe from it in general, which because I think they will not so properly fall in from any one of the Parts, as from the whole, I shall therefore consider at this Time, before we enter on the Particulars.

I. The first Thing then I observe from this Prayer, is concerning the Lawfulness and Usefulness of Set Forms of Prayer.[31] For, taking this Institution of our Saviour's at the lowest, namely, that it was a proper Help for his weak Disciples, to assist them, till the Descent of the Holy Ghost, when it is to be supposed they would learn to walk alone, without Leading-strings, and to frame Prayers of their own, fitted for all Occasions; taking it, I say, at present for no more but this, as a seasonable Supply to the Infirmities of his Disciples, I argue from thence for the Use and Conveniency of Set Forms of Devotion at this Day. For

(1.) If we consider the Circumstances of the Church, and what the Generality of Christians is, we must confess they want as much Assistance in their Devotions now, as our Saviour's Disciples did then. If there are any endowed with larger Measures of the Spirit, we must be sensible that there are but very few such, in comparison of the far greater Number of weak Christians, who want the Help [3] of better Composures for Devotion, than they themselves can frame.

(2.) If we consider the Difficulty of forming and framing our Devotions aright, we shall be convinced that well composed Forms of Devotion are very useful. There is nothing perhaps we are more ignorant of, than the Nature of God, and the right Manner of addressing him. It was an old Observation and Complaint of some wise Heathens, that Men mixed their own corrupt Sentiments and Desires in their Prayers to their Gods; nay, that they would put up such Prayers to their Gods, as they would be ashamed to speak out, and to own to Men: Prayers, dishonourable to God, and hurtful to the Persons that present them, and to all their Neighbours, who would have been very much

---

[31]This was an important theme in the sermons of many Anglican ministers after the Restoration.

injured by the Grant of such uncharitable Petitions, as Men, when left to themselves; would be apt to present to God Almighty. And it was not only the Heathens were guilty of this, but the *Scribes* and *Pharisees*, the best of the *Jewish* Doctors, who made such long Prayers, as if they understood not that *Our heavenly Father knows what Things we have need of, before we ask him.*[32]

(3.) Let us consider that the Jewish Church, in our Saviour's Days, used several Set Forms of Devotion, which our Saviour was so far from reproving, that he himself imitated them, taking most of this excellent Form of Prayer out of the *Jewish* Lyturgies, as has been observed by several, who are [4] well acquainted with that Sort of Learning. *John* the Baptist too taught his Disciples Set Forms of Prayer, as we may gather from that Desire of our Lord's Disciples, *Luk.* xi. 1. *Lord teach us to pray, as* John *also taught his Disciples.* Upon which Request our Saviour taught them this same Prayer. The Primitive Church used always Lyturgies, or Set Forms,[33] several of which are preserved to this Day: And not only the *Romish*, but the *Greek* and the Reformed Churches too, every one of them have their Set Forms. Which makes it so much the stranger, that the Presbyterians, Independents, Anabaptists, and Quakers, those late Sects among us, should muster up This as an Objection against the Church of *England*, that she has prescribed a Form of Common-Prayer.

(4.) But as to the Presbyterians, it is very observable, that after they had preached and wrote a great deal against Set Forms, they found it necessary at last, (to prevent the Nonsense, Rashness, and other Inconveniencies of extemporary Effusions) to prescribe Forms of their own, by the Name of a *Directory*[34] for the publick Worship of God.

So much for the first Observation I made, that Set Forms of Prayer are neither useless nor unlawful.

As this first Observation is made from our Saviour's composing a Form for the Use of his Disciples, the next three general Observations I shall make, shall be from the Connexion of this Prayer with [5] what went before. Our Saviour had in the Context reprehended three Errors in the Devotions of those Times. One was a pharisaical Ostentation; the other the spending Devotion in Words, without minding the Sincerity and Intenseness of Affections; the third was a prescribing to God, in many Particulars which he knew better than we, and before we ask him. Now in opposition to these Errors, and with a direct Design to amend them, as appears by the Particle, Therefore, *After this Manner therefore pray ye*; in opposition to these Errors, I say, there are three Things we may observe,

---

[32]Matthew 6:8.
[33]Some colonial Virginians translated ancient liturgies from the original languages as a form of devotional exercise. See page 76, footnote 2.
[34]*The Directory of Worship*, 1645.

1. In opposition to Ostentation, that our Saviour calls us away from the Eyes of Men, to mind *Our Father which is in Heaven.*

2. That in opposition to vain Repetitions, and a great Luxuriancy of Words, he has set us a Model of a very short compendious Prayer.

3. That in opposition to our prescribing to God in a great many minute Particulars, we are taught here to propose our Wants and Requests in general Terms, leaving the Particulars to Almighty God, to answer those Wants in which particular Manner he pleases. Now then,

II. The second general Observation I make from this Prayer, is, that we are called off from minding the Eyes of Men, to mind only *Our Father which is in Heaven.* In our Prayers our Business [6] is solely with God; and therefore, laying aside Pride, and Vanity, and Affectation to be thought pious and devout; and laying aside all worldly Designs, of which the *Pharisees* were full, who *for a Pretence made long Prayers that they might devour Widows Houses;*[35] let us open our Hearts to God, who is infinitely wise to know all our Wants, infinitely powerful, and infinitely good and willing to relieve them. And the Consideration, that it is to him, and to him only, that we speak, will be a good Direction as to all the other Rules we are to observe in our Devotions.

III. The third general Observation I would make, relates to the Shortness of our Prayers: *After this Manner therefore pray ye;* q. d. Seeing therefore ye have, or ought to have better Notions of God than that he wants to be either informed, or persuaded by us; or that he is delighted with a Fluency of Words and Rhetorick, as Men are; let us address ourselves to him accordingly, more with Vehemency and Ardency of Affections, than with many Words: And accordingly I give you an Example here of a Prayer very short and substantial.

Before I leave this Observation, the Usefulness of this Prayer, from its Brevity, is to be considered; notwithstanding something I said formerly on this Head. And here I can easily discern a threefold Use of Brevity.

(1) That [7] it suits better with the Conceptions we ought to have of Almighty God.

(2) That it consults better our own Weakness and Infirmities.

(3) That it gives us a truer Notion of Prayer and Devotion

(1) First, Few Words in Prayer suit better with the Conceptions we ought to have of Almighty God. If he were a Being that did not concern himself with Human Affairs, but as he is appealed to, and solicited to consider our Business; or if, like some of the Princes of the World, he were so taken up in minding the great and weighty Affairs of State, that he had no Leisure to attend to our little Concerns; or if he were a Being drowsy or sleepy, or diverted with other

---

[35]Matthew 23:14; Mark 12:4; Luke 20:47.

Things, than the Addresses of his Creatures; (which seems to be the Notion the Priests of *Baal* had of him, and which *Elijah* mocked them for: (a) *Cry aloud, says he, for he is a God; either he is talking, or he is pursuing, or he is in a Journey, or peradventure he sleepeth, and must be awaked.*)^A Or if God were a Being, like some Men, dull of Apprehension, that did not understand a Thing, unless it were inculcated over and over again, and explained with Abundance of Care to their weak Apprehensions. Or if he were a Being hard to be moved, as some Men are, to [8] come to Account, and to pay their Debts, except they are wearied out with Abundance of Dunning and Importunity. Or if he were to be cajoled and flattered, as several inferiour Beings are with fair Words, and a smooth Tongue: Then indeed there might be some good Ground for a great many Words in our Addresses to Almighty God. But all these are very unworthy Notions of God, and we are taught to have quite other Conceptions of him, namely, that (a) *His Eyes are upon the Ways of Men, and that he seeth all his Goings;*^B Nay, that (b) *the Eyes of the Lord are in every Place, beholding the Evil and the Good.*^C And therefore there is no Occasion of Words to stir up his Attention. That the smallest and most minute Things, as well as the greatest, fall under the Care of his Providence. (c) *Not so much as a Sparrow falls to the Ground without him*; and that *the very Hairs of our Head are all numbred:*^D And therefore there is no fear that the minding of greater Affairs will so employ him, as to make him forgetful of our lesser ones. He is *The Searcher of Hearts, and Trier of the Reins.*[36] (d) *He knows our Down-sitting, and Up-rising, and understands our very Thoughts afar off.*^E So that there is no Occasion to explain Matters minutely to him. (e) He runs out and embraces his returning Prodigals, and even prevents their fine Speeches:^F He is [9] more ready to hear than we to pray; and to grant more than we either desire or deserve. So that there is no Occasion of either Dunning, or long Arguments with him. And therefore all this Prolixity, and many Words in Prayer is unsuitable to those reverent Thoughts and Apprehensions we should have of Almighty God.

(2.) Few Words in Prayer doth likewise suit better with our own Weakness and Infirmities. Not many know what to say to God, he is so infinitely above our weak Apprehensions. (a) *He is in Heaven and we upon Earth, therefore let our Words be few.*^G The Memories too of the greater Part of Mankind are but

---

^AI Kings 28:27.
^BJob 34:21.
^CProverbs 15:3.
^DMatthew 10:29.
[36]See Revelation 2:23.
^EPsalm 139:1–2.
^FLuke 15:20.
^GEcclesiastes 5:2.

weak, and therefore short Prayers for them are best. And above all, our Affections are so wandering that we can't easily fix them long on so glorious an Object. And such is the Nature of Speech, that as it tires and flags the Spirit, so it dissipates a Spirit of Devotion, which as it is fed by Meditation, so it is spent by many Words and Talking.

(3.) Brevity in Words gives us a truer Notion of the Nature of Devotion. For Prayer is the Language of the Heart to God; and great Care is to be taken that it be not turned to *A drawing near to God with the Lips, while the Heart is far from him;*[37] that is, to an outward Formality, [10] instead of an inward Devotion. For avoiding of which some have recommended in our secret Devotions the Abstaining from Words altogether, and the Betaking our selves to mental Prayer.[38] And indeed the Use of Words in secret Prayer can't be to express our Minds to God, who understands the Language of our Hearts; but only to affect ourselves, and to kindle our Devotion to a greater Height; which Aim it misses of, when it runs out in too great a Length of Words.

IV. The fourth general Observation I would make, and which our Saviour seems to deduce from the Doctrine he had formerly laid down, relates chiefly to the avoiding too great a Minuteness or Particularizing in Prayer, as a Thing not so proper for us, who should come to God like children to a Father, exposing in general our Nakedness and Wants, but leaving it to him to supply them in such a Manner as he thinks most convenient for us. This seems to be very fairly deducible from the foregoing Words, applied to this Prayer with a *Therefore.* The foregoing Words were, *Your Father knoweth what Things ye have need of before ye ask him;* then follows, *After this Manner therefore pray ye.* And the Prayer we find consists all of general Petitions, leaving the particulars to God himself to bestow, as he in his Wisdom and Goodness should think fit. In the *first* Petition we pray that his Glory may be advanced, which [11] is the main End of all, to which all our other Ends and Designs ought to be subordinate. But we leave it to himself to contrive the infinite Ways and Means how to promote his own Glory. Only in the *second* Petition we pray for the Advancement of his Kingdom, that is, the Propagation and flourishing State of the Gospel; That being the chief Means whereby his Glory is to be promoted; leaving still the particular Ways and Means how This is to be carried on to himself. In the *third* Petition we pray that he may be obeyed, and his Blessed Will better complied with here upon Earth, in imitation of

---

[37]See Matthew 15:8; Mark 7:6.
[38]Blair seems to be advocating the practice of contemplative prayer, a practice with a long history in England. See James Walsh, S.J., ed., preface by Simon Tugwell, O.P., *The Cloud of Unknowing* (Ramsey, N.J.: Paulist Press, 1981), 1–50 of the Introduction, chapter 39 of the text.

the cheerful Service, that is performed to him in Heaven. But as to the innumerable Particulars of this Petition, and the infinite Ways and Means how it is to be effected, we leave all That to himself. In the *fourth* Petition instead of prescribing to God what Portion of worldly good Things we would have him to bestow upon us, all is summed up in a Petition for our daily Bread. Then for our Souls, all our Petitions are comprehended in these numberless Particulars of these Things to God himself; how, and when, and how much he thinks fit to bestow. This is a thing we ought to learn, either not to enlarge upon Particulars of Things not absolutely necessary, or at least to submit them to God's wiser Choice, whether, and when, and [12] how, and in what Measure he thinks fit to grant them.

V. A fifth general Observation we may make from this Prayer, is, concerning the right Preparations and Dispositions with which we ought to draw near to God. And of these we may easily observe a great many noble ones pointed at in this very Prayer. I shall instance in the following Graces. Faith; the Love of God; the Love of our Neighbour; Humility and Resignation; Watchfulness against Temptations, and a Readiness to join Obedience with Prayer; All, noble Dispositions for the Duty.

1. I begin with Faith, which is a fundamental Grace, necessary in all our Addresses to God, as the Apostle says. (a) *He that cometh to God, must believe that he is, and that he is a Rewarder of them that diligently seek him.*[H] Now this Disposition of Faith appears in the very first Words of this Prayer, *Our Father.* As Children come to a Father, believing him both ready and willing to relieve them, and with an implicit Faith in his Goodness, leaving it to himself to supply them in what Manner he thinks most fit and expedient; so should we go to God, with an holy Confidence presenting our Requests; but withal leaving it [13] entirely with him in what Manner he will be pleased to relieve us.

2. Another good Disposition with which we are to address ourselves to Prayer, is the Love of God; and this is very visible in this Prayer, both in that we are supposed to come to God as Children to a Father; and in that we pray in the first and chief Place for the Advancement of his Honour and Glory; and what we pray for ourselves is only to fit us the better for his Service and Obedience.

3. A third good Disposition for Prayer, and very observable here, is Charity, or the Love of our Neighbour. For all the good Things which we pray for ourselves, we pray likewise for our Neighbour. We say, *Our Father*, not my Father; we pray for his daily Bread, and for the Pardon of his Sins, and that he may avoid the Snares of Temptation, as well as we pray for these Blessings to

---

[H]Hebrews 6:6.

ourselves. Nay, which is very remarkable, we pray for the Pardon of our own Sin, only upon the Condition, and with such Limitation, as we forgive them that have injured us. So that we put their Souls and ours in the same Bottom, and even in our secretest Prayers exercise that great Law of Charity of loving our Neighbour as our selves.

4. A fourth good Disposition for Prayer, and very observable in this Form of our Saviour's is Humility and Resignation. The whole of it savours of [14] this Grace. By coming in the Quality of Children, we acknowledge our own Ignorance and Want of Discretion to carve for ourselves, and submit ourselves to the wiser Will of our Father. By confessing him to be in Heaven and ourselves upon Earth, we own our own Infirmities and his Perfections, and so do implicitly submit all our imperfect Desires to his allsufficient Wisdom and Goodness. By preferring the Petitions for his Glory before those which are for ourselves, we shew that it is our Meaning and Desire that all these should be regulated by those. By saying, *Thy will be done*, we submit all our Desires to his. By praying for but a bare Competency of worldly Blessings, we shew that we are far from desiring great Things for our selves. By begging Forgiveness of our Sins, we shew that we are far from pleading Merit, but that in all Humility we implore Mercy. And lastly, by praying against Temptations we acknowledge our own Insufficiency to take the Conduct and Management of our selves, and that we are undone without the continual Assistance of the Grace of God.

5. A fifth good Disposition for Prayer, or at least Concomitant of it, is a Watchfulness against Temptations. Our Saviour joined these two together, *Watch and pray that ye enter not into Temptation*. And the bare Praying for Pardon of Sin, without great Vigilance and Care to guard against it for the future is but a Mocking of God, and a Deceiving [15] of our own Souls. The making of this then one Part of the Prayer, *Not to lead us into Temptation, but to deliver us from Evil*; shews us how we ought to have an Heart well fortified against all manner of Temptations, and ready to do our utmost Endeavour to shake off all evil Habits. For that Circle of confessing our Sins, and begging God's Pardon for them, and committing them quickly again is a great Sign of Unsincerity, and must needs put a Stop to the Pardon we sue out at the same Time.

6. I observe this Prayer is so framed that all along it supposes an Heart ready to yield Obedience to God's Commandments. By addressing to God as *Our Father which is in Heaven*, we own his Authority to command, and our Duty to obey. By praying that his Name may be hallowed, that is, that he may be duly honoured, we shew and profess ourselves disposed to pay him all Honour, which can't be done but by paying a Respect to all his holy Laws. By praying for the Advancement of his Kingdom, we own ourselves his faithful

and obedient Subjects. By praying that *his Will may be done in Earth, as it is in Heaven*, we pray for Grace to enable us cheerfully and readily to execute all his Precepts. By begging of him our daily Bread, we both shew our Dependance on his Providence, and that we are resolved to endeavour after a Livelihood in an honest and lawful Way, such as we may look up to him for his [16] Blessing upon it. By praying for the Forgiveness of our Sins, we profess ourselves to repent of them in good earnest: And when we add, *As we forgive them that trespass against us*, we shew our actual Compliance with one of the difficultest Duties, *the Love of Enemies*. And when we pray *Not to be led into Temptation, but to be delivered from Evil*, we deprecate all those Things, which may lead us aside from our Duty.

VI. Lastly, there is but one general Observation more I shall make from this Prayer; namely, that it is both to be a Form and Model, upon which to frame all our other Prayers; and likewise as a Prayer itself. This I gather both from the two Accounts of St. *Matthew*[39] and St. *Luke*[40] have given us of this Prayer, and from the Practice of the Church. St. *Matthew* says here, *After this Manner therefore pray ye*, intimating that our Saviour brought in this Form as a Model to shew us how we were to avoid several Errors in the Prayers both of the *Jews* and *Heathen*; and what good Rules we should observe in our Devotions, the chief of which I have already mentioned. Then St. *Luke* gives us an Account, *Luk.* xi. 2. how in answer of some of the Disciples Desire that he would teach them to pray, *as John* taught his Disciples; he taught them this Prayer, saying, *when ye pray say, Our Father which art in Heaven*, &c.

These [17] are the Observations I made from this excellent Prayer in general. I need not tell you how useful they would be in our Life and Conversation, if we would duly form our Devotion and our Practice by these Rules.

For by taking help from this, and some other well composed Forms, we should both shew more Reverence to God, and keep ourselves from several Indiscretions, which the trusting to an extemporary Way occasions.

And by contracting the Length of our Words, and employing that Zeal in the Intenseness of Affections, we should make our Prayers more hearty, and should find greater Life and Warmth in them.

And by contenting ourselves modestly with a general exposing of our Wants, without setting our Hearts too much on any one particular Manner of supplying them, and especially without prescribing it to God Almighty, we should both better consult his Honour, and much more surely obtain what we want.

---

[39]Matthew 6:9–13.
[40]Luke 11:2–4.

And if we draw near to God with those right Preparations and Dispositions of Faith, and Love and Charity, of Resignation, Watchfulness and Resolution of Obedience, Devotion would be a great Pleasure; and we should be sure of many gracious Returns of our Prayers, which now for Want of those good Dispositions we go without.

And [18] lastly, if we formed our Devotions by this Model, we should have God's Glory continually in our Eye, before the Thought of any Things for ourselves; we should be as glad of our Neighbour's Benefit as of our own; and we should have the Satisfaction in this difficult Part of Religion to follow the best Guide, and to steer by the Direction of so skillful a Pilot, till we arrived at the blessed End of our Voyage, and the Salvation of our Souls, by the Merits and Mediation of the same *Jesus Christ*; who when we pray taught us, how we should address ourselves to God.

Now to him with the Father, and the Holy Ghost, be all Praise, Honour and Glory, for ever and ever. Amen.

~

CHAPTER FOUR

James Maury

The son of Huguenot refugees who immigrated to Virginia in 1719, James Maury (1718–1769) became one of the most highly respected ministers in eighteenth-century Virginia. By the time of his death in 1769, Maury had gained a reputation as an essayist, teacher, and dedicated minister. He had authored a fine epistolary discourse on education and an unpublished tract on the Baptists. Thomas Jefferson thought highly enough of his former teacher to commend him as a "correct classical scholar." An obituary in the *Virginia Gazette* praised Maury and recommended that clergy who sought "the notice, the esteem, and the affection of your parishioners" would do well to be "taught by his example."[1]

Maury was typical of many eighteenth-century clergy, different from his colleagues in degree rather than in kind. Not every minister, to be sure, received a eulogy in the colony's newspaper, but despite criticism levied at Church of England ministers by a half century of monographs written by historians sympathetic to the evangelicals of the Great Awakening, most Anglican clergymen

---

[1]Joan R. Gundersen, *The Anglican Ministry in Virginia, 1723–1776: A Study of a Social Class* (New York: Garland Publishing, Inc., 1989), 123; James A. Levernier and Douglas R. Wilmes, eds., *American Writers Before 1800: A Biographical and Critical Dictionary* (Westport, Conn.: Greenwood Press, 1983), 2:989–91.

were held in high regard by their parishioners.[2] The author of Maury's obituary, in fact, was forced to amend his praise of the deceased minister after several people took offense at the obituary's implication that Maury alone among the colony's established clergy was worthy of emulation. An apology soon appeared in the *Virginia Gazette* noting the colony's good fortune in having "so many amiable and *exemplary parsons.*"[3] Virginia's Anglican ministers did not come from the dregs of England's clerical community; nor were those parsons educated at the College of William and Mary second-class men inferior to graduates of Oxford or Cambridge. Like several other ministers either before they sought orders or to supplement their incomes after beginning a career in the Church, Maury operated a school—only his students included a few men who later gained great fame: Thomas Jefferson, James Monroe, and James Madison,[4] later president of William and Mary and the first Episcopal bishop of Virginia. Like many other colonial ministers, Maury wrangled with his vestry over his salary—only Maury happened to be the primary plaintiff in the "Parson's Cause," one of the most famous litigations in colonial Virginia. And the attorney for the defense happened to be a young man who hoped to use the case to advance his own chances for election to the House of Burgesses, Patrick Henry. What makes James Maury unique among the Anglican clergy of colonial Virginia is neither the public praise he received nor his prominence as a public figure. What makes Maury unique is that historians know so much about him. His extant letters, sermons, and the one tract surely authored by him provide an unparalleled collection of sources detailing the ideas and activities of a colonial Virginia minister.

One of the first graduates of Virginia's College of William and Mary to serve the colony's established church, Maury sailed to England in 1742 to seek ordination from Edmund Gibson, the bishop of London. Maury returned to Virginia later in the year and took charge of St. John's Parish in King William County. In 1751, he moved on to Fredericksville Parish in Louisa (later Albemarle) County, where he spent the remainder of his career.[5]

---

[2]For a good overview of the historiography and an evenhanded defense of the Anglican clergy, see Gundersen, *Anglican Ministry in Virginia,* 119–42. See also Carl Bridenbaugh, *Myths and Realities: Societies of the Colonial South* (New York: Athaneum Books, 1968); Wesley Gewehr, *The Great Awakening in Virginia, 1740–1790* (Durham, N.C.: Duke University Press, 1930); William Meade, *Old Houses, Ministers and Families of Virginia,* 2 Vols. (1857; 1910; 1966); Rhys Isaac, *The Transformation of Virginia* (Chapel Hill: University of North Carolina Press, 1982). For another example of the high regard with which many ministers were held in colonial Virginia, see the Reverend William Dawson's praise of the Reverend Bartholomew Yates, Sr., in William Dawson to Bishop Edmund Gibson, 8 November 1734, Fulham Palace Papers, vol. 12, 211–12, Lambeth Palace Library, and a testimonial by members of Yates' congregation in The Vestry of Christ Church to Bishop Gibson, 12 April 1726, Fulham Palace Papers, vol. 12, 101–2.

[3]Gundersen, *Anglican Ministry in Virginia,* 121–22.

[4]Cousin of James Madison the president of the United States.

[5]Gundersen, *Anglican Ministry in Virginia,* 269.

Maury's writings reveal a man dedicated to the church and to education. Whether in the pulpit or the schoolroom, we might do best to consider James Maury first and foremost as a teacher. From the pulpit he espoused the truths of Christianity. In the classroom he shared his love of the classics and inspired in many of his students a lifelong commitment to learning. He loved books and the ideas they contained. He had read deeply in the ancients, in theology, and in contemporary literature. In 1768 he asked his friend Jonathan Boucher of St. Mary's Parish in Caroline County to "send to Glasgow for" over 40 books, including a History of Africa and Spain, a Sermon on Female Character and Education, a volume on "Moses & Bolingbroke," several collections of sermons, and The Vicar of Wakefield, the last a book that placed Maury in the small group of Virginians who owned novels. At his death, Maury's library numbered nearly 500 volumes, making it one of the larger collections in colonial North America. Like John Clayton and Nicholas Moreau, he too found time to indulge a passion for science and corresponded with friends about the discoveries he made in the Blue Ridge Mountains. He fancied himself a poet as well and graced some correspondents with copies of his "performances." At least some of Maury's poetic compositions had religious themes, such as the spiritual meditation on illness that he sent to Mary Grymes in hopes that it might serve her as a devotional aid in time of sickness.[6] What was once said of medieval monks might also be said of Maury: he possessed a love of learning and a desire for God.

As an educator, Maury was willing to adapt the traditional classical curriculum to American necessities. Although he enjoyed the classics himself and taught them to many of his own students, Maury nonetheless questioned whether the classics offered the best course of study for colonial students. A classical education, of course, provided the necessary preparation for those young men who wished to enter law, medicine, or divinity. Few colonials, however, entered the clergy or aspired to become doctors since these professions offered only modest financial rewards. Nor did Virginians' style of life suit them for the classics. Most colonists earned their living in trade or "by the Culture of our Staple," tobacco, pursuits that left colonists

---

[6]James Maury to Jonathan Boucher, 19 December 1768, Jonathan Boucher Papers, Box 2, folder 3, Special Collections, Earl Gregg Swem Library, College of William and Mary, Williamsburg, Virginia; David D. Hall, "Books and Reading in Eighteenth-Century America," in Cary Carson, Ronald Hoffman, and Peter J. Albert, eds., Of Consuming Interest: The Style of Life in the Eighteenth Century (Charlottesville: University Press of Virginia, 1994), 363–64; Levernier and Wilmes, American Writers Before 1800, 2:989–91; James Maury to Mrs. Mary Grymes, 16 January 1768, James Maury Letterbook, 1763–1768, Sol Fienstone Collection, David Library of the American Revolution, on deposit at the American Philosophical Society.

little leisure time with which to indulge a passion for Greek or Latin. Virginians also married young, and the care of families thus intruded upon the leisure time that could have been devoted to the study of ancient history and literature. Virginians, Maury believed, required an education grounded upon "useful, practical Knowledge," by which he meant reading, writing, arithmetic, rhetoric, grammar, contemporary literature, and history. Preparation in these fields would provide a Virginia gentleman with the tools necessary to enjoy learning in his private life and to serve the public as an elected official.

Despite his own broad background in the classics, Maury tried to shape his sermons for the rural parishioners who would have comprised the largest portion of his congregations. Many of his plain style discourses are filled with proof texts taken from the Bible, passages likely familiar to most of those who heard his preaching. For the most part, he avoided allusions to the ancients in his pulpit oratory, confining such references to his correspondence or classes, although there were rare occasions when he probably lost many in the congregation because he chose to argue a point by tracing the etymology of a Greek word.

Nonetheless, Maury's extant sermons—based as they are on reason, revelation, and tradition—provide good examples of both occasional sermons and the typical discourses delivered at an Anglican parish on an average Sunday. Practical piety and clear, straightforward discussions of theology dominate his sermons. Like other Anglicans, Maury stressed the centrality of repentance in the Christian's pilgrimage to Heaven. Like Samuel Davies and James Blair, who authored a paraphrase of the Sermon on the Mount for children, Maury too emphasized the importance of religion to children and of an early piety.

Maury believed Christianity was a rational religion and often blended literal and allegorical interpretations of the scriptures, as he did in a sermon first delivered on Whitsunday 1746. In a discussion of Christ's Ascension into heaven, he argued that Christ's sitting at the right hand of God had been "prophetically foretold" in Psalm 110, yet urged his parishioners to understand the action figuratively, "For God is a Spirit & consequently has no bodily Parts or material Members." An allegorical interpretation was necessary, Maury explained, because the human mind failed when confronted with the immensity of God. The deity had therefore condescended to "speak after the manner of Men" in order to assist their understanding. Thus, by Christ's sitting at God's right hand, the scriptures meant to signify Christ's "perpetual Residence" in heaven, his "sovereign Authority & Dominion," and his role as "Judge of the World."

As Maury grew older, his religious writings began more and more to show the influence of the Enlightenment's appeal to reason. He turned a 1761 sermon on John 3:2—"Rabbi, we know that you are a teacher come from

God"—into a discourse on the reasonableness of Christianity, even buttress-
ing his opinions with arguments taken from Lord Bolingbroke, whose works
he quoted at length. And his tract against the Baptists began with a state-
ment defending Christianity as a rational religion:

> Christianity, my brethren, by all its friends and many of its enemies, is allowed
> to be, what the religion of such a creature as man ought to be, agreeable to
> reason. Its moral precepts, and the motives enforcing them, are in the high-
> est degree rational. So also, if we may abide by the testimony of one of its
> keenest adversaries, are even the two positive ordinances in its system; Bap-
> tism and the Supper of the Lord. Such, moreover, is the tendency, and such
> the evidence of its doctrines, even of those that are most sublime and myste-
> rious, that to believe them and be influenced by them is highly rational. Some
> of them indeed transcend all human comprehension. What then? we, in per-
> fect consistency with reason, firmly believe, and are actuated by what we do
> not comprehend, in many instances, on the credible testimony of others. The
> incomprehensibility therefore of some of these cannot render our belief of
> them irrational. The christian's faith and practice are equally free from that
> imputation. He is not required to believe an article, or perform a precept, till
> he hath received rational satisfaction of the credibility of the one and the
> obligatory force of the other. His religion then may justly be termed an address
> to his reason.[7]

Yet he did not wish to belittle the importance of revelation and admitted later in the tract that reason alone, even "in her highest state of culti-
vation and improvement," provided an incomplete understanding of ultimate reality.[8] Revelation, as Maury proclaimed in a Whitsunday sermon,
remained primary; reason guided the application and interpretation of the
Bible.

Sermon Number 90

Mark the perfect Man, and behold the upright: for the End of that Man
is Peace.[9] Psalm 37:37

---

[7]James Maury, *To Christians of Every Denomination Among Us, Especially those of the Established Church, An Address Enforcing an Inquiry into the Grounds of the Pretensions of the Preachers, Called Anabaptists, to an Extraordinary Mission from Heaven to Preach the Gospel* . . . (Annapolis, 1771), 3, Mary-land Historical Society.

[8]Maury, *To Christians of Every Denomination Among Us*, 8.

[9]In the lectionary of the 1662 *Book of Common Prayer*, Psalm 37 was appointed to be read at Evening Prayer on the seventh of each month. Portions of this sermon are based on "Of the Inward Peace and Pleasure Which Attends Religion," in *The Works of the Most Reverend Dr. John Tillotson, Late Lord Archbishop of Canterbury: Containing Fifty Four Sermons and Discourses* . . . (3d edition, London, 1701), 130–39.

The second Sermon on this Text.

[These words have already been taken into Consideration in a former Discourse; wherein, after a brief [E]xplanation of these [page ripped] & Substance [page ripped]; That the Practice of Religion affords the greatest Satisfaction & Peace of Mind. The Truth of this we then endeavoured to establish by an Argument founded upon express Testimonies of divine Revelation. And in order to make the Matter still more evident, another Argument was produced in it's Defense, drawn from the necessary Tendency & natural Aptitude that are in Religion to produce those happy Effects. And that this Argument might not suffer for want of [I]llustration, we discovered in what Manner Religion brings about this happy Work of establishing Peace & Concord in the human Breast. From all which [2] it manifestly appeared, that Religion clears the Mind of all those Doubts & Anxieties concerning our future Condition with which it is clouded by Vice & Impiety; & frees it from the Stings of Guilt, which wicked Actions leave behind them; & consequently removes the principal Causes of Trouble & Uneasiness. Nay more, it was then plainly made out, that Religion lays the best Foundation for Equanimity & Peace of Mind, by rendring a Man's Actions capable of being justified by the Sentence of his own Reason, & by securing to him the Favour of God, & thereby most effectually promoting his present & future Happiness & Interest. There still remains another Branch of this Argument untouched][10] which was postponed for Want of Time to handle it fully: & that is

Thirdly this, That Religion is productive of inward Tranquility & Peace, as it administers the homefelt Satisfactions, which always result from reflecting upon a well-spent Life. The perfect & upright Man, as oft as he takes a View of his past Life, enjoys a great Degree of Pleasure & Comfort. It is not more natural for the Body to be followed by it's Shadow in a shining Day, than it is for [3] the Remembrance of generous & worthy Actions to be attended with Content & Delight. The upright Man, tho thro' the Infirmities of Nature he may find some Difficulty in the due & regular Discharge of his Duty[,] yet when it is done, he is sure of enjoying the greatest Satisfaction, as often as he looks back upon it. Nothing there will give him any Ground for Displeasure against himself. For no Man's Conscience ever yet upbraided him for running the Way of God's Commands. The human Mind was never yet haunted with Disquietude or Remorse upon the Consideration of having acted in Conformity with the Dictates of Nature & the Precepts of Revelation. The Man, whose Life has

---

[10]Maury added the brackets to his text, likely to indicate introductory material that could be deleted from the sermon.

been in the general Course of it a Series of Soberness, Righteousness & Godliness, never can be sensible of Regret & Dissatisfaction, when he reflects either upon the Days that are past, or those to come. [On the contrary, [whenever his Memory renews in his Mind the Performance of any laudable & virtuous Action; as oft as his Conscience assures him he has discharged his Duty; as oft as he reflects that he has lived righteously & godly in this [4] present World: his Soul is refreshed with Pleasures that cannot be uttered, with Joys that cannot be described. And indeed there cannot be a surer Basis of mental Tranquility & spiritual Rejoicing than the Testimony of our Conscience, that in Simplicity & godly Sincerity we have had our Conversation in the World.^A On the other Hand, none can be guilty of any Act of Impiety to God, or of any Violation of Duty to Man, or of any Breach of the Rules of Moderation & Temperance with Regard to himself; but Conscience will straitway sting & torment him. A free Gratification of Desires & an unrestrained Indulgence of inordinate Affections, may at present afford a momentary Satisfaction. But that will soon be forgotten & totally blotted out of the Memory by that lasting & exquisite Torture of Mind that will succeed.][11] Reflections upon what they have done are Occasions of such Anguish & Throes to the wicked; that they make Use of every Method that can be invented, & every Artifice that can be thought on, to prevent themselves from falling into such Reflections. A thorough View of himself is the most grievous, & melancholy Prospect, that can be presented to a Sinner. Nothing can dispirit or displease, disquiet [5] or chagrine him so much, as the Memory of his own Irregularities & Misdemeanours. Good God, how great the Dissimilitude, how wide the Difference, between the Condition of the Sinner and that of the perfect and upright Man! The former from the Commission of a sinful Deed may tis possible reap a Pleasure, which, at longest, is extreamly short & transient. For it will speedily be interrupted by Stings of Conscience, by an Anguish & Vexation of Spirit that will long remain. Whereas the latter in the Performance of a virtuous Action, it is possible, may find some Difficulty & Trouble; but then they can be but short. And besides the Pleasures that succeed are the most sublime & refined, perfect & satisfactory. Nay more, they are permanent also, & will be an unexhausted & neverfailing Spring of Peace & Consolation to the righteous Man as long as he lives, & be his greatest Comfort & Support when he comes to die. And this is a very considerable Enhansement & Recommendation of a religious Course of Action. If it is most liberal of it's Consolations in Times of the greatest Calamity & Distress; surely every prudent Man will be desirous of

---

^A II Corinthians 1:12.

[11] Maury added the brackets to his text, likely to indicate portions of the sermon that were optional.

laying up a plentiful Stock against a gloomy [6] & unfortunate Hour. When in Health & Prosperity, there are a thousand Methods to rejoice, to divert & amuse us. But most of them are so imperfect in themselves & so unable fully to satisfy our enlarged Capacities; that where they find a Man empty of the solid Blessings of Health & Competence, they afford but little Joy[,] Delight or Amusement. So that a Man must already be in a great Measure happy; or else he can have but little Relish, & reap but little Satisfaction, in the Enjoyment of them. That therefore, which can cheer our drooping Spirits when sinking under a Load of Adversity & destitute of temporal Advantages & finally when nothing else can afford Comfort & Delight; that, I say, must be the most valu-able & excellent Enjoyment of all: & that is the Pleasure resulting from Re-flections on a well-spent Life. And what besides this can dart the reviving Beams of Comfort into the Mind, when under the Pressure of heavy Afflic-tions? What besides this can render the Breast undaunted & composed, upon the near Approach of the King of Terrors? [7] What besides this can poise the Mind in so even a State, so to be calm & undisturbed in the midst of outward Storms & Perturbations? What is it in short that can mitigate the Pains of Dis-ease, alleviate the Burden of the Infirmities of old Age, & preserve the Soul vigorous & hale, notwithstanding it's intimate Union with a feeble & languid Body; but a Consciousness of having lived soberly & righteously & godly in this present World? When nothing is to be seen without but Commotions & Clouds & thick Darkness; a clear Conscience it is that renders all within the perfect Man peaceful, & composed. And this is doubtless the Meaning of those various Observations made upon the good Man by the inspired Penmen; that he shall shine forth out of Obscurity & be as the Morning;[B] that to the upright there ariseth Light even in Darkness;[C] & that Light is sown for the righteous & Gladness for the upright in Heart.[D] The pious Actions of the upright Man are so many fruitful Seeds, which produce him a plentiful Harvest of Joy & Contentment, & enable him to lay up a plentiful Stock of [8] Spiritual Re-freshments within his Mind, from whence he may draw Succors in the Day of Need. And such Seeds they are, as will spring & flourish & be productive of Fruit, not only when cherished by the Sunshine of Fortune & the Showers of Prosperity, but even in Times of Dearth & Distress. A Retrospect upon a re-ligious Life is at all Times comfortable and satisfactory; but, when all the other Pleasures & Enjoyments of Life desert & abandon us, when the Pangs of Death are ready to seize us, & when all Kinds of Evils approach to invade us, it is then

---

[B]Job 11:17.
[C]Psalm 112:4.
[D]Psalm 97:11.

most eminently serviceable & furnishes the Mind with a Most seasonable Re-
freshment. A good Conscience is a faithful & constant Friend, that will never
desert us. Tis a Friend indeed; because it will stand by us in Times of Necessity,
when the greatest Supports & Consolations are required. The Days wherein a
Man suffers Adversity are those, wherein the spiritual Comforts of the upright
Man abound & overflow. Then it is that these Reflections create a Kind of
Heaven in his Mind; & not only inspire him with Hopes of the Glory that shall
be revealed, but also give him some ravishing Foretastes of those Felicities
upon Earth, which he one Day hopes to enjoy in Heaven. So true it is, that the
righteous Man hath [9] Hopes even in Death; & that they who submit to the
Difficulties of Religion & sow the Seeds of virtuous Actions in Tears shall reap
in Joy![12] [For he that now goeth on his Way weeping & beareth forth good
Seed shall doubtless come again with Joy & bring his Sheaves of Comfort &
Satisfaction with him at the last.][13] But as for the ungodly, it is not so with
them. When they are in the greatest Distress, their Guilt rages with the greatest Fierceness. As outward Troubles encrease, their inward Pangs are multiplied. When they are sinking under Misfortune, instead of lifting them up, they
sink them deeper. When they are in greatest Need of Comfort, then they find
the least Alleviation, nay rather the most exquisite Misery. The wicked, when
confined to the Bed of Languishing, instead of the grateful Cordial & kindly
Lenitive,[14] taste nothing but Wormwood, Gall & Bitterness.[15] When setting
out on their Journey for the other World, instead of the cheerful & pleasant
Companions[,] Innocence & Virtue, they are accompanied with Horrors &
Apprehensions, Fiends & Furies. When the Sinner's Mind is filled with Confusion & Amaze;[16] his Guilt, instead of calming all within, sets all in Uproar &
Tumult, & renders him an Image of a troubled & tempestuous Sea which cannot Rest.[17] [Then he bitterly reflects upon all his Miscarriages with Remorse &
Reared with Rage [10] & Indignation against himself. Then his Conscience
upbraids him for having been so foolish as to omit the Discharge of those Duties of Religion, in Times of Health; which in his present Circumstances would
have yielded him unspeakable Pleasure & Delight. Then in a Word he con-
demns himself for having neglected the Things which belonged to his temporal Peace & eternal Welfare, while he had so many gracious Opportunities of

---

[12]Psalm 126:5.
[13]Maury deleted this material from the text of his sermon.
[14]A mild laxative.
[15]Compare Lamentations 3:19.
[16]Bewilderment.
[17]This imagery would have held special meaning for any Virginians who had survived an Atlantic crossing. James Blair made frequent use of nautical imagery in his sermons. See Joanne Donna Wal-ter, "Imagery in the Sermons of James Blair" (M.A. thesis: University of Tennessee, 1967).

knowing them; which, by Way of Punishment for that Neglect, are now for ever hid from his Eyes.][18] And this I think is pretty evident, that Vice & Impiety subvert the whole State of the Mind, throw every Thing there into Disorder & Confusion, & produce nothing but Misery & Discontent: & on the other Hand, That the Practice of Religion affords the greatest Satisfaction: & consequently that the Proposition is true which is contained in these Words— Mark the perfect Man & behold the upright; for the End of that Man is Peace.

Now if this cannot be a sufficient Recommendation of Religion; if this Argument cannot prevail upon all prudent & considerate Men to walk in the Paths of Righteousness & to run the [11] Ways of God's Commandments; 'tis not easie to conjecture what will. Were the Intent of this Discourse, to persuade you to enter upon some fruitless & hazardous Enterprize; to do something that would oppose your Interest, endanger your Life, or be destructive of your Happiness; or to undertake a Business attended with insuperable Difficulties: Reason would dictate, that Success must be despaired of. But when you are persuaded to be religious, you are not persuaded to any Thing of that Sort. For to enter upon a Course of Religion is far from being a fruitless Enterprize: because you may be assured, that, if you be zealous, immoveable & abundant in that good Work, your Labour shall not be in vain in the Lord.[E] Neither is it an hazardous Undertaking, for the Lord is the Defender of the righteous & shall deliver him from Evil: for thou, Lord, will give thy Blessing unto the righteous; & with thy favourable Kindness will thou defend him as with a Shield.[F] Neither is Religion inconsistent with your Happiness; because we are informed by divine Revelation, that it's constant Effects are Quietness & Peace & Assurance for ever;[G] which are the surest Foundations of human Felicity. Neither is it inconsistent with your Interest to be religious; because your short [12] Labours here will be rewarded with Treasures that are laid up in Heaven, where neither Moth nor Rust doth corrupt & where Thieves do not break through & steel;[H] & because an Inheritance incorruptible, & undefiled, is reserved in Heaven for those who love the Lord & do his Commandments.[I] Neither is it in general a Matter, the Execution of which will endanger either your Fortunes or your Lives: because the religious Man is like a Tree planted by the Water-side, that will bring forth his Fruit in due Season: his Leaf shall not whither; & look, whatsoever he doth, it

---

[18]Again, Maury's brackets apparently indicate portions of the sermon that were optional.
[E]I Corinthians 15:58.
[F]Psalm 5:12.
[G]Isaiah 32:17.
[H]Matthew 6:20.
[I]I Peter 1:4.

shall prosper:[J] & also because, as the Apostle asks, who is he, that shall harm you, if ye be Doers of that which is good?[K] Neither, in the last Place, is it an impracticable Undertaking, or an Undertaking attended with Difficulties insuperable: because we see many, who partake of the same frail & mortal Nature in common with ourselves, have been able to atchieve it: because the just & good God, who has prescribed us our Duty, never fails to enable us to perform it: because whenever any uncommon Difficulties are to be encountered in the Way of Duty he inspires us, upon due Application, with an uncommon Degree of spiritual Might in the inner [13] Man: because the Scriptures assure us, that God's Commandments are not grievous:[L] & finally, because the divine Founder of our Religion, altho' he stiles it a Yoke & a Burden, comforts his Followers with this Assurance, that the Yoke is easy & the Burden light.[M]

For all which Reasons I cannot help renewing my Instances, that you will vigorously endeavour, & peremptorily resolve, with the divine Assistance, henceforth to be religious; for that is the only way to acquire, to enjoy & to secure both your present Peace & future Happiness. Man, ever since his Forfeiture of true Felicity, has been rambling over all the Regions of Nature in Search after Happiness. So keen is his Appetite, so violent his Thirst, for this sovereign Good, that the visible World has not been able to bound his Pursuits. And notwithstanding, you may think it strange, that this same Happiness, which hath been sought with so much Study[,] Thought & Time, is the Thing itself, which I have been recommending; namely to be religious. This is the summum Bonum,[19] the supreme Happiness of human Nature. Let me but prevail upon you to be religious; & if you are not happy, then may I meet with the [14] Fate of Cassandra, never to be believed more.[20] You will find yourselves under a great Mistake, & perhaps when it cannot be rectified, if you expect to find it in Heaps of Gold, or pompous Titles; in the Enjoyment of extensive Possessions, or in the Gratifications of Sense. Here is her Seat, this is her Habitation. In holy Retirements, in the Closet devoted to secret Prayer, & in the Temple of the Lord of Hosts, she frequently resorts & may be found. As 'tis both my Duty & Interest, & also my Desire to promote your present Peace & future Happiness; you are here directed to the most certain

---

[J]Psalm 1:3–4.
[K]I Peter 3:13.
[L]I John 5:3.
[M]Matthew 11:24–30.
[19]The highest or greatest good.
[20]According to Greek mythology, Apollo gave Cassandra prophetic powers in an attempt to win her love. Cassandra turned down Apollo's advances and Apollo, in turn, decreed that none of her prophecies would ever be believed.

& effectual Means of promoting & securing both. Your past Errors & Wan-derings & Searches after these to no Purpose are Matters both of Wonder & Compassion. The Ways of Peace & the Paths of Happiness are so accurately laid down in the Gospel; that one is justly amazed how Mankind can be guilty of such Deviations & Mistakes. And the Consequences of these are so fatal & destructive; that it must be an Heart of Stone, that can consider these unhappy Wanderers without compassionating their Misery. Tis therefore but acting the christian & charitable Part to tell you; that tho' Happiness has been your End, yet you have been widely mistaken as to the Means proper to conduct you to it. For that [15] which hath been here recommended & pointed out, is the only Way to it; & that is, to be perfect & upright; to lead an holy & a virtuous Life; to live soberly, righteously, & godly in this present World;[21] or to sum up the Whole in one Word, to be religious. For mark the perfect Man & behold the upright; for the End of that Man is Peace. To be religious, is to be free; & that is an Happiness. Tis to be exempt from Anxiety & Doubt about our future Condition & final Doom; & that is an Happiness. It is to act consistently with the Principles of Wisdom & the Dictates of Rea-son; & that also is an Happiness. It is to be a Stranger to Self-Condemnation; & that is an Happiness. It is to be peaceable & quiet; & that is an Happiness. It is to be contented; & Contentment is an Happiness. It is to be innocent; & Innocence is an Happiness. To be religious is, to subdue our Lusts & conquer our Passions; & Victory is both Pleasure & Happiness. It is to rule & com-mand our Affections & Desires, without Limit & without Controul; & Mankind esteem Dominion & Empire an Happiness. But he is the most ab-solute Prince and uncontrollable Monarch, who commands himself. And none but the religious Man is really invested with this sovereign Power. In short, to be religious is to possess & enjoy every Thing, that can render us easy & [16] quiet & contented here, & blessed & happy hereafter. And if we imi-tate the perfect & upright Man; if we follow the wise Directions & observe the salutary Precepts of Religion; we shall be all that: that is, we shall obtain Ease & Quietness, Satisfaction & Contentment in this World; &, thro' the Merits of Christ, in the World to come Life everlasting. Amen.

Preached at my Lower Church June 29, 1746.[22]

Preached at my upper Church July 6, 1746.[23]

L.C. Jan. 10, 1747/8.[24]

---

[21]Titus 2:12.
[22]The Fifth Sunday after Trinity.
[23]The Sixth Sunday after Trinity.
[24]The First Sunday after the Epiphany.

L.C. Fred. Sept. 22, 1751.[25]
U.C. Fred. Sept. 27, 1751.[26]
M.C. Fred. Sept. 29, 1751.[27]
M.C. Fred. Mar. 9, 1755.[28]

Sermon Number 130

Remember now thy Creator in the Days of thy Youth, while the evil Days come not, nor the Years draw nigh, when thou shalt say, I have no Pleasure in them.[29] Ecclesiastes 12:1

[2] In discoursing upon which it is proposed—To explain the Duty of remembring God, To inquire, what obligations to do so flow from considering him as our Creator, And to consider the Reasons why Men ought to remember him, in the Days of Youth, rather than at any other Time.

I. In order then to explain the Duty of remembring God, it will be proper to consider the Meaning of remem[bring][30]. . . . [3] Violation of them. So that the Duty here recommended, is to take God into frequent Consideration, & enter upon a Course of Action, conformable with his holy Laws, as soon as we come to Years of Understanding & Discretion; to devote the Prime of Life to his Service; to imprint religious Notions & reverent Sentiments of him on the Mind, while it is yet tender & most susceptible of good Impressions; to have an Eye to his Glory in all we do & in all we design; to pay him Honour & Fear, Love & Obedience; & in short to act consistently with the Character of Persons who are always mindful [of] God & continually set him before their Eyes. This I take to be the Meaning of the Precept in the Text, to remember God.

II. What obligations thus to remember him flow from considering him as our Creator is next to be inquired into. To think upon the Supreme Being, under this Notion, evidently tends to create the greatest Respect & Reverence in the Mind, both for himself, & for whatever he shall declare to be his Will;

---

[25]The Sixteenth Sunday after Trinity.
[26]The Friday before the Seventeenth Sunday after Trinity.
[27]The Seventeenth Sunday after Trinity; also the Feast of St. Michael and All Angels.
[28]The Fourth Sunday in Lent.
[29]This sermon is incomplete. A portion of the first page containing Maury's introductory remarks has been torn away. The discourse also relies heavily upon a published sermon by Archbishop John Tillotson (1630–1694) devoted to the same text, "Of the Advantages of an Early Piety." Although Maury has reworked Tillotson's material substantially and composed part of the sermon himself, the reliance on Tillotson is unmistakeable. See John Tillotson, *The Works of the Most Reverend Dr. John Tillotson, Late Lord Archbishop of Canterbury*. . . (7th. ed; London, 1714), 637–38.
[30]The remainder of this page is missing.

inasmuch as Creation is the strongest Argument of his Being, of his Power, & of his Goodness. For, of all others, this is the most obvious [4] & sensible Argument of the Being of God. For every Object, which your Eyes encounter, is a new Demonstration, that there is one Supreme, by whom both we & all Things exist. Tis the Doctrine of the Psalmist, That the Heavens declare the Glory of God & that the Firmament sheweth his handy Works;[31] & of Saint Paul, that the Creator's eternal Power & Godhead, which he calls the invisible Things of him, are clearly seen from the Creation of the World, being understood by the Things which are made.[32] And this must needs be an Obligation to perform the Duty in the Text. Creation is further an Evidence of unbounded Power: an Attribute, which works most effectually upon our Fear, the most wakeful & suspicious Passion of the Soul. This is so confessedly true, that the Atheist imputes the original Belief of a God to the natural Apprehensions & Fears of Men. But this is a gross Mistake: because Religion stands on a very different Foundation. For, if there be a God who made us, & we remember or consider him; reasonable it is to the last Degree, that we reverence & obey, serve & adore, think upon & contemplate, fear & endeavour to please him: from an Apprehension, in Part, lest that same unlimited Power, which made us, [5] be provoked by a contrary Conduct to render our Condition miserable. Which is another Motive & Obligation to practice the Duty we are now recommending. But further, this same Remembrance of God as our Creator naturally reminds us of his Goodness in communicating a Being to us. For of his Goodness we were created. His end in creating us was, not to advance his own Happiness, that being already so compleat, as to be capable of no Augmentation; but to communicate Part of his own Happiness to us. Nay not only created were we by Him, but by him we also are preserved & continued in Being. Which are some of the highest Instances of a pure & disinterested Goodness. Now, when young Persons are capable of exercising their Reason, & discover God to be the beneficent Author of their Beings & Preserver of their Lives; how can they avoid being mindful of him? How can they refrain breaking out in the grateful Raptures of David; O come let us worship & fall down & kneel before the Lord our Maker: for he is the Lord our God, it is he that hath made us & not we ourselves, we are his People & the Sheep of his [6] Pasture![33] Which is another very powerful Incentive to a dutiful Regard & religious Remembrance of God; and naturally flows from considering

---

[31]Psalm 19:1.

[32]Romans 1:20.

[33]Psalm 95:6–7. This verse would have been familiar to most Anglicans from the "Venite" in the Order for Morning Prayer in the *Book of Common Prayer*.

him under the venerable & majestic & amiable Notion of an eternal, almighty & benevolent Creator.

III. So that I now proceed to consider the Reasons, why Men ought to begin this Study in the Days of our Youth, rather than at any other Time. For that the Preacher meant this, when he advises you to remember your Creator in the Days of your Youth, before the evil Days come, & the Years draw nigh, in which you shall say, I have no Pleasure in them, is too plain to need Illustration. And that he advises us so to do with the greatest Wisdom & Reason, I hope to convince you by a few Considerations. In the first Place then, let it be considered, that Youth either is that Age, wherein there is Reason we should be most sensible of our Obligations to remember our Creator. For then the Blessing of Life is new, & the Benefit still fresh & recent on the Mind. When we are just grown up to the Use of our Reason; tis but natural to think we must be apt to inquire, to whom [7] are we indebted for Life & all its concomitant Blessings? And when we have either discovered, or been informed, that God is both the original Giver & continual Preserver of that & More; our Minds, if influenced in the least by Reason, must needs be filled with a religious Surprize & pious Wonder, not only at the Bounty & Benevolence of the Donor, but also at the Novelty & Greatness of the Benefit. Again, when young People begin to consider themselves, & the World of irrational & inanimate Creatures around them; to reflect upon the many excellent Endowments & noble Faculties, with which they are adorned, & which a wise Creator hath thought fit to refuse to so many of his Creatures; & to observe, that themselves are made but one Degree lower than Angels,[34] &, like to many Lords & Sovereign[s] of the Earth, invested with an extensive Dominion over the brute Creation:[35] must not their Hearts be apt to overflow with an holy Joy & pious Gratitude to their great Benefactor? Must they not be prompted to make the Enquiry of Elishu in Job; Where is God, my Maker, who teacheth me more than the Beasts of the Earth, & maketh me wiser than the Fowls of Heaven?[36] So that on our first [8] Arrival at the Knowledge of our Creator, when the Sense of his Bounty is fresh on our Memories, when the Blessing of Life is in its Verdure & Bloom, when the Constitution is in its' Vigor & Perfection, & when the Enjoiments of Life are most palatable & grateful; then most especially there is abundant Reason, that we should be mindful of our Creator. Be it further considered, that, without this, those very Things, which constitute your greatest Happiness now, your Youth &

---

[34]Psalm 8:5.
[35]Genesis 1:26–31.
[36]Job 35:10–11.

Health & Strength, I mean, must at last prove your Bane & Destruction. Another Reason, why your Creator ought to be remembred in the Days of your
Youth. For you are now most exposed to Temptations; &, consequently, in
greatest Need of Preservatives against them. Now you are most addicted to
Pleasures; & therefore in greatest Need of such religious Reflections, as tend
to restrain you from Voluptuousness & Debauchery. Now your Passions are
most fierce & violent, ungovernable & headstrong; & therefore a Curb is
now most eminently needful. Now you are most apt to be giddy & thoughtless, rash & precipitate; & therefore now your volatile Spirits stand most in
Need of Wisdom & religious Reflections to steddy [9] & ballast them. And
nothing but the Remembrance of your Creator can conduct you safe thro'
the Perils & Dangers of that slippery Age; as appears from the Psalmist's Resolution of that important Enquiry—Wherewith shall a young Man cleanse
his Way? By taking Heed thereto according to thy Word.[37] Besides, be it ever
remembred, that Youth is the fittest Age to begin the Study, the fittest Age
to enter upon the Practice, of Religion. For, altho' it must be granted, that
young People are remarkably prone to be forgetful of God; yet they are as remarkably fit to imbibe worthy and reverent Conceptions of him. Your present Age, to the Young I speak, is an Age of Discipline. Tis submissive & com-
pliant, 'tis docile & manageable, & therefore excellently calculated to
imbibe Instruction. Your Tempers are now tractable & obsequious, flexible &
pliant; apt to receive any Mould, capable of any Tincture, most susceptible of
any Impressions. Now you resemble tender Slips, which may easily be bent
to any Shape; like Wax, you are then fittest to receive any Characters; like
Mettals, softened in the Furnace, you are malleable & ductile. Now then is
the [10] golden Opportunity for stamping on the Mind Impressions of Religion. Now [is] the happiest Season for sowing the Seeds of Virtue, in a Soil
newly broken up & freshly prepared, & not yet overgrown with noxious
Plants & poisonous Weeds. And therefore the Work of Religion may now
most successfully be begun. Be it now then your Care timely to habituate
your Minds to Virtue, before they be strongly prepossessed with Vice. For if
Religion be not cultivated there; Vice will inevitably spring up, flourish &
take Root in so fruitful a Mould. But if you tincture your tender Minds with
the Knowledge of God & the Remembrance of your Creator; they will probably retain the Tincture to the last. Moreover, as a Religious Course is a State
of Combat & Warfare against the Enemies of Salvation, the World, the Flesh
& the Devil; Youth is most capable to enter the Lists against such formidable Opponents. In the Days of their Youth Men are most proper for Conflict

---

[37]Psalm 119:9.

& Labour. For then they are mettalsome, enterprizing & adventurous. Tho' Youth is not the most expert at Counsel, yet it can achieve Wonders in [11] acting. For it is warmed with a generous Sense of Honour & Merit; tis sensibly affected with Censure or Applause; incessantly spurred on by Ardor & Emulation; eagerly Thirsts, nay burns, for Fame; & is exquisitely fond of Reputation & Glory: &, upon all these Accounts, is admirably calculated for enterprizing, carrying on & bringing to Perfection, the noble & difficult & glorious Work of Religion & Virtue. But this is not all; for Youth is moreover the most acceptable Season for the Remembrance of our Creator. Under the Law God claimed the first Fruits & the first Born as his peculiar Prerogative.[38] Which clearly intimates, that the most excellent of Beings is best pleased, when we sacrifice to him the Prime of Life, the Vigor of our Age, & the Excellency of our Strength. For this is an evident Proof of our Love; in that we think nothing too good to be devoted to him. Tis a Proof of our Gratitude; in that we esteem no Acknowledgments too great to be made to his Bounty, whence all our Blessings plentifully flow. Tis likewise a Proof of our Sincerity; in that the Oblation is cordial & voluntary, not forced & extorted: which last is too often the Case of those, who remember not their Creator, til [12] the evil Days come & the Years draw nigh, when they must own they have no Pleasure in them. If there be Joy in Heaven at the Repentance even of an enfeebled & worn out Sinner;[39] how much more delightful a Spectacle must it be to God & Angels, to behold a Youth, in the Flower of Age, tho solicited by the Seducer & tempted by the Vanities of the World & Allurements of Vice, tho courted by Honours & soothed by Pleasures, & caressed by the fascinating Bewitcheries of temporal Enjoiments, yet with Scorn & Indignation look down upon & reject them all, & inviolably cleave to his great Creator! Upon which & many other Accounts Youth is certainly the most acceptable Season, wherein to devote yourselves to the Service of God. Finally, there is another Reason, why you should remember your Creator in the Days of your Youth; & that a very alarming one too; because it may perhaps be the only Season of Life allowed you, wherein to perform that most needful Task. If you defer it, on a Presumption of discharging it in a Maturer Age, 'tis possible, that Life may come to an End, before the Arrival of the destined Time. And then what must be your Doom? What milder Sentence can you expect, than to be turned [13] into the Place of Weeping & Wailing & Gnashing of Teeth with all the People, who are forgetful of God?[40] To be

---

[38]Exodus 13:1–16.
[39]Luke 15:7.
[40]Matthew 8:12; 13:42,50; 22:13; 24:51; 25:30; Luke 13:28.

religious & mindful of your Creator, is the most indispensably needful of all Things. It must be done, or else you are inevitably ruined, eternally lost. You cannot therefore begin it too early in the Morning of Life; but you may easily refer it too late. And if you do, your Misery is reverseless. So that if you will not venture your All upon the greatest Hazard, you must make Religion the first Business of Life, & remember your Creator in the Days of Youth.

Betimes then, for these & various other Reasons that might be urged, ingage in a Course of Piety & Virtue. Permit not the Gratifications of Sense to cheat you, nor a Flow of Prosperity & Health to delude you, nor your present State of Pleasure & Delight to dissolve & unman your Spirits. Your Youth and Health, on which all these Enjoiments depend & whence your Power of Fruition flows, tho' firm & perfect now, may soon decay. The Warmth of your Blood may shortly be chilled, the Fire of your Spirits be quickly extinguished, the Blossom of [14] Youth speedily blasted. Tis true, you are now at your best Estate, but Man even then is no better than Vanity.[41] Tho' you are young, yet you are mortal. [And altho you never considered this before, yet doubtless you can't help making the Observation now; while a moving Spectacle of the Mortality of Youth is before your Eyes. For Behold our Sister, a tender Flower, untimely cropped in it's Prime & vernal Bloom. But happy were it for all young Persons, were they as well provided for the fatal Stroke, as our departed Sister, to whose Remains we now are paying our last Respects. Happy were it, if all were adorned with her meek & gentle Spirit, with her humble & modest & peaceful Temper, with her thoughtful & sedate Disposure of Mind, with her dutiful Deportment to her Superiors, with her industrious Application to all the Emploiments suitable to her Sex & Age, & in short with many other good Qualities, which rendred her beloved while living, & regretted now dead. But, rather than launch out in Encomiums on the dead, let me inculcate to the living the Doctrine of my Text, & urge you hence to remember your Creator in the Days of your Youth, before your Sun be [15] set, before the evil Days approach, & before the Candle of the Lord which now sheds so beautiful a Lustre on your Heads be quite extinguished.][42] Be it thoughtfully considered, that all Flesh is Grass,[43] & the Glory of Man as the Flower of the Field,[44] easily nipt by any rude & sudden Blast, short-lived & fading, tender & apt to wither & languish. Since then such is the Frailty of Nature, you ought to make Use of this most happy Season for the Plantation

---

[41]Psalm 144:1.
[42]The brackets are Maury's. He used this sermon several times, only the first of which was obviously at a funeral. The bracketed portions include material peculiar to the sermon's first delivery.
[43]Isaiah 40:6–7; I Peter 1:24.
[44]Psalm 103:15.

& Culture of Virtue. It will besides be much easier to do this now, than any Time hereafter. For you are yet in some Measure innocent & unspotted, at least not greatly inslaved to vicious Habits, but still capable of the best Impressions. The work you have to do is great, & the Time to do it in not only short, but uncertain. It cannot be begun & compleated in a Day. Defer it then not one Moment. With the utmost Assiduity apply yourselves to it before the Night comes, when none can Work.[45] Remember not to swim with the Tide of Corruption, which overflows the present Age. Suffer not the Contagion, which surrounds you, to deprave your Principles, to debauch your Morals, to vitiate your Hearts, or taint your Innocence[.] [16] Consume not those precious Moments, in Risks & Debauchery, Idleness & Vice, which, prudently managed, will purchase Heaven. Devote yourselves to the Study of Virtue, to the Practice of Piety, to the Consideration of God & Religion. Provide a plentiful Fund of Consolations against a Time of Need, which may cheer & revive your Spirits under the Infirmities, which will accompany those Years, in which you will say you can find no Pleasure. This, let me tell you, is your bounden Duty; &, to recommend it to your Practice, I do assure you, tis your true & real Interest. Slight not then such wholesome Advice. Depend upon it, if you spend your Youth in Sin, your old Age (should you live to be old) will be quite overwhelmed with Remorse & Discomfort, and your Lot after Death an unchangeable Scene of Misery & Horror. However you may flatter yourselves now, however slightly you may think of it, however you may make a Mock of Sin & a Jest of Religion; yet one Day you will surely find your dreadful & deplorable Mistake. Applicable hereto is that bitter Sarcasm of the Author of Ecclesiastes, rejoice, O young Man, in thy Youth; & let thy Heart cheer thee in the Days of thy Youth; & walk in the ways of thine [17] Heart & in the Sight of thine Eyes: but know thou, that for all these Things, God will bring thee into Judgment![46] In which should it be your Fate to be condemned, which God forbid[,] think before hand what a cutting Reflection it must be to consider, that once Time was when thro God's Grace you might have escaped that Place of Torture. It must needs be a stinging Aggravation of the Miseries of the Damned to reflect, that 'tis their own Fault they are not amongst the Number of the saved[.] Altho' then you are now young & robust & hale, yet seriously consider the Imbecillity of Youth, the Precariousness of Health, the Instability of Life, the Certainty of Death & future Retribution. Be instructed now so to number your Days, as to apply your Hearts to Wisdom. Thoughtfully now in this your D[ay] reflect

---

[45]John 9:4.
[46]Ecclesiastes 11:9.

upon such Things & take Measures, as will effectually secure your future Peace. Altho' you now be youthful & strong, altho' you should live many Years & rejoice in them all; yet wisely remember the succeeding Days of Darkness, for they shall be many.[47] Finally, Remember now thy Creator in the Days of thy Youth, when the evil Days come not, nor the Years draw nigh, when thou shall [say] I Have no Pleasure in them. To observe which saving Advice may God vouchsafe you all the Grace, thro' Christ our Lord. Amen.

Preached at the funeral of a young woman on Xber. 23, 1748.

—— at Mr Dunbar's Lower Church Feb. 5, 1748/9[48]

U.C. Feb. 12, 1748/9[49]

L.C. April 2, 1749.[50]

L.C. Fred. Aug. 26, 1753.[51]

U.C. Fred. Oct. 27, 1754[52]

M.C. Fred. Nov. 3, 1754.[53]

M.C. Fred. Sept. 2, 1759.[54]

L.C. Fred. Sept. 9, 1759.[55]

Sermon Number 177

Rabbi, we know, that you are a Teacher come from God.[56] John 3:2

The First [Sermon] on this Text.

This is Part of the Address of a sincere but timorous Disciple to Christ. Among others, whom Jesus's Doctrine & Miracles had convinced of his divine Mission, Nicodemus, a Pharisee & Member of the grand Jewish Council, was one. As these Miracles were extraordinary and apt to gain Mens Attention, he was desirous to be more particularly instructed in the Doctrine they were wrought to confirm, [2] & with that Intent paid Jesus the Visit mentioned in the Chapter of my Text. But for Fear of disgusting his Countrymen & Brother-counsellors by an open Profession of Christianity, he

---

[47]Ecclesiastes 11:8.
[48]Quinquagesima Sunday, or the Sunday before Lent.
[49]The First Sunday in Lent.
[50]The Second Sunday of Easter.
[51]The Tenth Sunday after Trinity.
[52]The Twentieth Sunday after Trinity.
[53]The Twenty-first Sunday after Trinity.
[54]The Twelfth Sunday after Trinity.
[55]The Thirteenth Sunday after Trinity.
[56]The lectionary in the 1662 *Book of Common Prayer* appoints this text as the Gospel lesson for Holy Communion on Trinity Sunday.

chose to wait on him by Night. When admitted to his Presence, he accosts him with that express Acknowledgment of the Divinity of his Mission in my Text; Rabbi, we know, that thou art a Teacher come from God.

This is what all true Christians stedfastly believe, but what the Enemies of revealed Religion affect to disbelieve. The Unreasonableness of the Infidelity of these may appear from taking a cursory View of some of the Reasons, on which the Belief of [3] those is founded; such as the Character & Behaviour of the Teacher himself; the Nature & Tendency of the Doctrine he taught; the Credentials he brought to prove his divine Commission to teach it; & the Success & Effects of it, where it has been taught and received.

I. The Character & Behaviour of our blessed Lord shall first be considered. That he was a Person of the strictest Integrity & Honor, Truth & Honesty, appears from the whole Tenor of his Actions, as they stand recorded by the Evangelists; whose Veracity as Historians shall at present be only supposed, tho' hereafter, God willing, [4] it shall be supported & proved. And from the Accounts, which these Authors have handed down to us, we must judge him incapable of Fraud or Imposture. There he appears honest & sincere, just & upright; a fond Admirer of Simplicity & Plainness, Truth & Candor; remarkably averse to Fraud & Deceit & Double-dealing; artless & free from selfish Designs & sinister Views; contented with his low Condition, resigned to all the Disposals of Providence, & influenced neither by Vain-glory, Avarice nor Ambition. In the History of his Life we see eminently exemplified in his Conduct every one of those moral & religious Precepts, which he so warmly recommended & so powerfully enforced in his Doctrine. Besides, his whole Life was spent in [5] doing Good to Mankind, in instructing them in the Principles of their Duty, & urging them to the faithful Discharge of it in all it's Branches. The miraculous Powers, with which he was invested, were exerted not for Ostentation & aggrandizing his Reputation, but for the Relief of Mens bodily & spiritual Distempers & Needs. All the Honors, were those of Roialty, which the rest of Mankind so eagerly desire, when proffered by admiring & applauding Multitudes, were modestly refused & industriously declined. His Contempt of worldly Grandeur & Pomp is evident from the whole Course of his Behaviour. The Kindness & Generosity of his Temper, the [6] Meekness & Humility of his Spirit, the Openness & Affability of his whole Deportment, were as conspicuous, as they were amiable. Besides all this we can't help observing, how fervently he prayed, even in the Article of Death, for the Pardon of his Persecutors & Slanderers & Murderers. In Fine, with a Degree of Charity & Benevolence, til then unheard of, he laid down his Life to purchase the Redemption & Salvation even of his most bitter & rancorous Enemies. This is a very imperfect Sketch of the Character &

Behaviour of the blessed Jesus; as all must be sensible, who are acquainted with the Gospels, where the interesting Transactions of his Life are recorded. But, imperfect as it is, it may induce us to look upon it [7] as utterly incredible, that a Person of this Character should falsely pretend to be commissioned from Heaven to teach the Will of God, if in Truth he had received no such Commission. The Character then given of our Redeemer by the Evangelists, whose Veracity & Credit are equal at least to those of any other antient Historians, must go a great Way in determining the rational & unprejudiced to subscribe to Nicodemus's Assertion in the Text, that he was a Teacher come from God.

II. But of this we shall, perhaps, be further convinced, if we examine into the Nature & Tendency of the Doctrine he taught: which is another good Rule, whereby [8] to judge, whether that high Claim of his be just or not. For if our Enquiries into this Matter shall satisfy us, that Christ Jesus delivered a Body of the strictest Morality & purest Religion, that ever the world has been acquainted with, it will be but reasonable to think favorably of his claim to a divine Commission. For, on Supposition, that the theological Truths, which he has revealed & taught, & that the moral Precepts, which he has delivered, were the pure Product of natural Reason & human Wisdom; it will not be easy to account, how it has happened, that the moral & religious Systems of all others, who were endowed with the same Reason & [9] had greater Opportunities of acquiring Wisdom in the ordinary & usual Way, are yet confessedly so vastly deficient & imperfect in Comparison with his. If the Gospel was of Man, whence is it, that all the Legislators & Philosophers & Moralists, who had ever appeared before, with all their Learning & all their Reason, have never been able to produce any Thing of this Sort, that is worthy to be named with the christian Scheme? On that Supposition, tis utterly unaccountable, that a Person, educated in the Manner our blessed Instructor was, should in this Point so far excel the Lycurguses,[57] Numas,[58] Platos[59] & Aristotles[60] of Antiquity. The transcendent [10] Excellency then of the Doctrine of Christ above that of all other Teachers must be accounted for on some other Foot. And no other can be devised, that will so satisfactorily remove the Difficulty, as saying, that it undoubtedly came from Heaven. Other Teachers had been left to make the best Use they could of that natural Fund of Reason & Wisdom, which Providence had given them the Means of at-

---

[57]Spartan legislator, traditionally credited with founding Sparta's "good order."
[58]Pompilius Numa (715–673), second king of Rome, credited with establishing the Roman religion.
[59]Plato (ca. 428–347), Athenian philosopher.
[60]Aristotle (384–322), Athenian philosopher.

taining to. But as to the great Author & Finisher of our Faith, he was super-naturally & divinely assisted. And this points out the true Reason, why he has so far excelled all others. Tis manifest from his History, that his Parent-age was obscure. He was born in a Country, where the liberal Arts & Sci-ences had scarce [11] ever been so much as heard of; & usually resided in one of the rudest & most unpolite Parts of it. That Season of Life too, which is the properest for Study & the Acquisition of human Knowledge, was chiefly spent in mechanical Labour. So that he was destitute of every Advantage, that a learned Education can give. But this was not the Case with the Philosophers & Sages, who had before been the Instructors of Mankind. To many of them Nature had no doubt been as liberal as to any of her Children. Their Fund of Genius & natural Abilities had also been carefully cultivated & improved by Study & Education. They likewise had the additional [12] Advantage of conversing with the most eminent Proficients in every Branch of Literature whether in Agypt, Athens or Rome, those celebrated Nurseries of Science & Seminaries of Wisdom. Now, if it shall appear, that the great Author of Christianity, tho destitute of all these Advantages, which the Philosophers & Moralists before him enjoyed, yet formed a more perfect & compleat System of Religion, than any of them all, the superior Excellence of the christian System can then rationally be ascribed to nothing else, but the Assistance & Cooperation of Heaven. This Consequence unavoidably flows from those Premisses. And, in Order to shew, that the Premisses are true, let us take a short Survey of some both of the speculative & practical [13] Parts of Christianity, that we may be satisfied whether it is as compleat & excellent as it is pretended.

1. In its speculative Parts, it soars far above the highest Flights of human Wisdom & Philosophy. The christian System in the old & new Testaments gives us a satisfactory Account of the Origine of the Universe, which it cannot be said any other has done. It acquaints us, that the material World was not produced by Chance or Fate, as the Philosophers absurdly taught, but by an in-finitely powerful & intelligent Being. It informs us of one great Catastrophe, the Deluge, which has already befallen it, & predicts it's final Dissolution by another, [14] the general Conflagration. Instead of the Philosophers absurd Ac-counts of the Formation & original of the human Race, it acquaints us, that the primitive Pair, from whom the rest of Mankind have descended, were the immediate Production of the great Creator's forming Hand. It clearly asserts, & as clearly proves, the Superintendency of the supreme Being over all his Works; & that he governs the World by exercising a particular, as well as a general, Providence: which is much more rational, as well as much more con-sistent with our Notions of God, than setting at the Helm of the Universe an

indolent & sleepy Deity, quite regardless of the Happiness or Misery of his Creatures, [15] or subjecting the whole Machine to the Directions either of blind Chance or of a rigid Fatality. While the Doctors of Paganism taught the worship of a Multitude of Gods & paid that Honor to the Creature, nay to the vilest of Creatures[,] which is the incommunicable Right of the Creator; our divine Instructor asserts, that there is but one true & supreme God only, who has a Right to divine Honors exclusively of all others. The Omnipotence & Immensity, the Justice & Mercy, the Purity & Holiness, the Wisdom & Goodness, & other adorable Perfections of the Deity, are all much more consistently taught in the christian, than in [16] any other religious, Institution. There too we find the Depravity & Corruption of our Nature & the origine of Evil satisfactorily accounted for, which yet had so long & to so little Purpose perplexed the Wits & racked the Inventions of those boasted Oracles of human Wisdom to discover & solve. Herein too is shewn, what the Pride of Philosophy scarce ever dreamt of, the absolute Need of a Redeemer to ransome Men from the Captivity of Sin & Death & from the Miseries of Guilt unattoned. The Gospel-plan of Redemption, by Means of an all-sufficient Attonement & Satisfaction, is so consistent & so rational, as to leave the divine Attributes intire & unhurt & in a perfect Harmony, & to prevent the gracious Propensions[61] of God's Mercy from clashing with [17] the righteous Determinations of his Justice. So that here in the Psalmist's significant Language Mercy & Truth have met together, Righteousness & Peace have kissed each other.[62] These alone, without particularizing many other Doctrines of the Gospel, either not at all or very imperfectly known & taught by the Heathen Sages, are abundantly sufficient to shew the just Preeminence of Christianity in speculative Matters above any other religious System. Had such momentous Truths been established & such important Discoveries been made by any of the Pagan Moralists, we should no Doubt justly admire him as a Prodigy of Wisdom; & might [18] impute his so far surpassing all other Men in Knowledge & Wisdom to the Superiority of his Genius & Attainments. But, when it is remembred, that these sublime Truths & mysterious Doctrines were disclosed & delivered by so obscure a Person, as Jesus Christ appeared to be in his State of Humiliation; & that they were afterwards propagated & taught almost in every Part of the then known World by a few poor illiterate Fishermen, whom he instructed to qualify them for the Instruction of the rest of Mankind: to what can we impute all this? It can't be rationally ascribed to the Efficiency of human Means; nor to any extraordinary Efforts of human Reason, Wisdom or

---

[61]Inclinations or leanings.
[62]Psalm 85:10.

Learning. There were none of all these in the Case. And [19] if there had been, they yet are Causes quite unequal to such stupendous Effects; which must therefore be allowed to have been produced, not by any Exertions of human Reason or Philosophy, but by the Inspiration of the blessed Spirit, & by Exertions of the Divinity, which dwelt & resided in this divine Teacher, whom Nicodemus in my Text declares he knew came forth from God.

2. But no less wonderful & perfect above all others are the practical Rules of Christ's Religion. However obscure in his Birth, however destitute of [20] the Advantages of a learned Education, yet so it is, that Jesus has published a System of Morality, which far surpasses all other Systems. Tis he alone, who has instructed Mankind in the true Nature of God and in the true Method of approaching him thro' a divine & coeternal Mediator, & that this God alone tis to be worshipped in Spirit & Truth.[63] He it is, who has recommended that amiable Virtue Humility, which the Pride of Philosophy had before condemned, as a Mark of a mean & dastard Spirit. Tis he, who has prescribed the most effectual Methods for acquiring & maintaining that Peace & Serenity of Mind, without which Life is nought but a Scene of Wretchedness. Tis he, who has taught us patiently to bear with each others Foibles & Infirmities, generously to pass by Injuries & Wrongs, & not only to [21] pardon but pray for Enemies.[64] He has established on its true Principles & enforced that one Precept, which alone is of more avail in our Dealings & Intercourse one with another, than whole Volumes of pagan Ethics; whatsoever ye would, that Men should do to you, do ye even so to them.[65] It is from the Philosophy of the Gospel you must learn the best Rules for the Government of the Passions; the important Lessons of Patience & Resignation & Contentment; the cardinal Precepts of Temperance & Justice & Prudence & Fortitude; a Contempt of the World, whenever it interferes with the Discharge of Duty, and a becoming Disregard of every terrifying or alluring Object, that would either deter or seduce us from a steady Pursuit [22] of Heaven & Happiness. In a Word, the blessed Jesus by the Precepts he has delivered in the Gospel, by the Manner in which he has accomplished them in his own Conduct, & by the Perspicuity with which they are expressed, has done more, than the Platos & Plutarchs[66] & Ciceros[67] & all the other pagan Doctors of Morality together, towards the Reformation of Mens Manners, weakening the Forces of Sin & Satan, & reinstating Reason in her rightful Throne;

---

[63]John 4:23–24.
[64]Matthew 5:44.
[65]Matthew 7:12.
[66]Plutarch (b. before 50–d. after 120), Roman philosopher.
[67]Marcus Tullius Cicero (106–43), Roman orator and philosopher.

towards inspiring the human Mind with noble & heroic Sentiments of Virtue; towards securing the Happiness & Quiet of Mankind both in their individual & social Capacities; towards giving them the Mastery over their unruly Appetites & Inclinations, & strengthening and [23] inlarging their intellectual Powers; towards restoring the will to it's native Rectitude & Freedom, & in short towards repairing in Man the defaced Image of God, which consists in Righteousness & true Holiness. Christ has moreover inforced the Observance of these wise & useful Precepts by such Motives, as the Doctors of natural Religion were either totally unaquainted with themselves, or had no sufficient Authority to propound to others: such as, Proffers of supernatural Aids to assist human Frailty & Impotence; Engagements thro Christ to pardon our Deviations from Duty on Repentance & Amendment, in order to prevent Offenders from sinking into Despair; [24] the most terrifying Denunciations of eternal Punishment against the incorrigibly perverse & rebellious, in order to deter them from Presumption; & Promises of everlasting Glory and Bliss to the obedient, with a View of rendring us stedfast & unmovable & abounding in the Work of the Lord, forasmuch as we may thence be assured, our Labour shall not be in vain in the Lord.[68] So that Christianity, whether you consider it's doctrinal Points, or it's moral Precepts, so far transcends every other Religion in these Respects, as leads us to acknowledge, with Nicodemus in my Text, that it's illustrious Author was undoubtedly a Teacher sent from God. All this amounts to so forcible a Proof of the Divinity of the Gospel, that even some of it's most virulent [25] Enemies have been carried against the Torrent of their Prejudices & Wishes to make the same honorable Acknowledgments in it's Favour. And as the favorable Testimony of Enemies has ever been deemed of great Weight in other Causes, & may be reasonably deemed so in this; I shall here subjoin some Concessions made to Christianity by a late noble Author, the general Drift of whose Writings has been to subvert the Authority of the Gospel, & who therefore is considered by our modern Deists as the Goliah of their Cause & the grand Apostle of Infidelity; by which I suppose you'll very easily [26] discover I mean the late Lord Bolingbroke.[69] This noble Writer, as an attentive Reader must observe, in sundry Passages of his works in general, but particularly between Page 281 & 433 of his fourth Volume,[70] makes such Acknowl-

---

[68]I Corinthians 15:58.

[69]Henry Saint-John Viscount Bolingbroke (1678–1751), British statesman and prominent deist.

[70]Maury is referring to Essay IV of Bolingbroke's *Essays or Letters Addressed to Alexander Pope, Esq* or, as the work is better known, *Essays on Human Understanding.* The page and volume numbers below refer to the following edition: *The Works of Lord Bolingbroke in Four Volumes,* Reprints of Economic Classics (London: 1844; reprint, New York: 1967). Essay IV may be found in Vol. 3; *Fragments or Minutes of Essays,* which Maury also cites, may be found in Vol. 4.

edgments in Favor of Christ & his Religion, even while he is attempting to blast the Credit of both, as are really amazing, & can be ascribed to nothing else, than to the prevailing Force of Truth, which, at some Seasons, as it were, irresistibly guides his Hand to assert the Justice of that very Cause, which the Prejudices & Corruptions of his Heart determined him to combat in opposition to the Dictates of his Conscience. His Lordship acknowledges in express Terms, "That no Religion ever appeared in [27] the World, whose natural Tendency was so much directed to promote the Peace & Happiness of Mankind as Christianity;"[71] that "no System can be more simple & plain than that of natural Religion, as it stands in the Gospel;"[72] & that "both the Duties, required to be practiced, & the Propositions, required to be believed, are concisely and plainly enough expressed in the original Gospel, properly so called, which Christ taught, & which his four Evangelists recorded."[73] He further owns, That "no Institutions can be imagined more simple, or more void of all those pompous Rites & theatrical Representations, that abounded in the religious Worship of [28] the Heathens & Jews, than these two" (that in the Sacraments of Baptism & the Lord's Supper) "were in their Origin"; and that "they are, not only innocent, but profitable Ceremonies, because they were extremely proper, to keep up the Spirit of true natural Religion by keeping up that of Christianity, & to promote the Observation of moral Duties by maintaining a Respect for the Revelation, which confirmed them."[74] His Lordship moreover allows, That "the System of Religion, which Christ published & his Evangelists recorded, is a compleat System to all the Purposes of Religion natural & revealed;" & that "it contains all the Duties of the former; enforces them by asserting the divine Mission of the Publisher, who proved his [29] Assertions at the same Time by his Miracles; & enforces the whole Law of Faith by promising Rewards & threatening Punishments, which he declares he will distribute, when he comes to judge the World."[75] This noble Author further confesses, That "Christianity, as it stands in the Gospel, contains not only a compleat but a very plain System of Religion"; and that "it is, in Truth, the System of natural Religion, & such it might have continued to the unspeakable Advantage of Mankind, if it had been propagated with the same Simplicity, with which it was originally taught by Christ himself."[76] He even grants, that, "supposing Christianity to have been a [30] human Invention, it had been the most amiable & useful Invention, that was

---

[71]*Essays on Human Understanding*, Essay IV, section IV, 396.
[72]Essay IV, section VI, 403.
[73]Essay IV, section VII, 404.
[74]Essay IV, section VII, 410.
[75]Essay IV, section VIII, 418.
[76]Essay IV, section VIII, 420.

ever imposed on Mankind for their Good"; that, "as it came out of the Hands of God, it was a most simple & intelligible Rule of Belief, Worship & Manners, which is the true Notion of a Religion";[77] & that "the Gospel is, in all Cases, one continued Lesson of the strictest Morality, of Justice, of Benevolence & of universal Charity."[78] Lord Bolingbroke furthermore declares, That "the Theology, contained in the Gospel, lies in a narrow Compass, is marvellous indeed but plain, & employed throughout to enforce natural Religion";[79] that "the Charge, which the Enemies of Religion bring against Christianity on this Account" (that is Persecution) "is unjustly brought;" & [31] that "these Effects" (that is Disputes, Heats, Quarrels & Persecutions) "have not been caused by the Gospel, but by the System raised upon it, not by the Revelations of God, but by the Inventions of Men."[80] The last Concession of this noble Author, which shall at present be cited; is, That "genuine Christianity was taught by God;"[81] That, "the christian System of faith & Practice being revealed by God himself, it is absurd & impious to assert, that the divine Logos revealed it incompletely or imperfectly"; & that "it's Simplicity & Plainness shewed, that it was designed to be the Religion of Mankind, & manifested likewise the Divinity of it's Original."[82] [32]

These Declarations of Lord Bolingbroke, so advantageous to Christianity, have been thus collected & brought together in one View, in order to satisfy you, that the Evidence, resulting from the Character of it's divine Founder & from the Nature & Tendency of its Doctrines & Precepts, is sufficiently weighty to convince, not only the candid & impartial Enquirer, but even the captious & prejudiced Caviller. Of this, perhaps, there is no stronger Instance, than his Lordship. For tho' the formal Design of his Essays & Fragments from which these Passages have been extracted was, to destroy the Credit & Authority of the Gospel, & weaken it's Influence on the Minds of Men; yet, by some powerful Impulse or other, he has [33] been determined to make such Declarations in it's Favor, as manifest, that, notwithstanding his Enmity & Prejudices against it, his own Conscience convinced him, its Excellence is unequalled & its origin divine. Therefore we may join, not only the teachable Nicodemus, but the partial & uncandid Adversaries of the Gospel, in the Address in my Text to the Author of our Faith; Rabbi, we know, that thou art a Teacher come from God.

---

[77]Essay IV, section XVIII, 474.
[78]*Fragments or Minutes of Essays*, chapter 20, 237.
[79]*Fragments*, chapter 33, 286.
[80]Essay IV, section VIII, 417–18.
[81]Essay IV, section XIII, 442.
[82]Essay IV, section XXVI, 512–13.

As there is not Time to do Justice to the other two Criteria, or Rules for forming a Judgment of the Truth & Divinity of the christian Revelation; our Examination of them must be postponed to some future opportunity. [34]

In the mean Time I must remind you, how much it imports you, who profess the most perfect Religion, & have been instructed by the completest Master, to become the best & most excellent of Men. And I know of no happier Method for making such a Proficiency, than that, which the great Apostle of us gentiles recommends to the Practice of his favorite Philippians. Finally, my Brethren, whatsoever Things are true, whatsoever Things are honest, whatsoever Things are just, whatsoever Things are pure, whatsoever Things are lovely, whatsoever Things are of good Report, if there be any Virtue, if there be any [35] Praise, think on these Things.[83] For these are the Things, whereby the Gospel is most honorably distinguished above all other religious Institutions, & whereby the Christian should as honorably distinguish himself above the Heathen, the Mahometan or Jew. Therefore those Things, which you have both learned & received & heard from Christ & his Apostles & succeeding Pastors & Teachers, take care to practice. And, upon these Conditions, you have the word of the same inspired Apostle, that the God of Peace shall be with you throughout the whole of your Existence both in this world & in the other. Amen![84]

U.C. Fred. Feb. 8, 1761.[85]

L.C. Fred. Feb. 22, 1761.[86]

Chap. Fred. March 1, 1761.[87]

M.C. Fred. Mar. 15, 1761.[88]

L.C. Fred. Jul. 15, 1764.[89]

U.C. Fred.—22, 1764.[90]

---

[83]Philippians 4:8.
[84]Romans 15:33.
[85]The First Sunday in Lent.
[86]The Third Sunday in Lent.
[87]The Fourth Sunday in Lent.
[88]Palm Sunday.
[89]The Fourth Sunday after Trinity.
[90]The Fifth Sunday after Trinity; also the Feast of St. Mary Magdalene.

CHAPTER FIVE

~

Samuel Davies

A Christmas-Day Sermon, 1758[1]

And suddenly there was with the angel a multitude of the heavenly host,[A]
praising God and saying; Glory to God in the highest! and on earth, peace!
good-will towards men. Luke 2:13, 14

This is the day which the church of Rome, and some other churches that
deserve to be placed in better company, have agreed to celebrate in memory
of the birth of the Prince of peace, the Saviour of men, the incarnate God,
Immanuel. And I doubt not, but many convert superstition into rational and
scriptural devotion, and religiously employ themselves in a manner acceptable to God, though they want the sanction of divine authority for appropri-
ating this day to a sacred use. But, alas! it is generally a season of sinning, sensuality, luxury, and various forms of extravagance; as though men were not
celebrating the birth of the holy Jesus, but of Venus,[2] or Bacchus,[3] whose
most sacred rites were mysteries of iniquity and debauchery. The birth of Jesus was solemnized by armies of angels: they had their music and their songs

---

[1]Davies originally delivered this discourse on 25 December 1758 in New Kent County, Virginia. It
appears in *Sermons on Important Subjects, By the Late Reverend and Pious Samuel Davies, A.M. Some
Time President of the College in New Jersey*, 3 Vols. (Boston, 1811), 3:386–404. Used courtesy of the
Virginia Historical Society. For biographical material on Samuel Davies, see pages 35–40.
[A]The soldiery of heaven.
Davies' Greek reproduced in his note does not match that in the text. Luke's Greek is πληθος
στρατιας ουρανιου.
[2]Roman goddess, known as the patron of seduction and, like Bacchus, linked with wine.
[3]God of wine and intoxication.

on this occasion. But how different from those usually used among mortals! "Glory to God in the highest! on earth, peace! good-will to men!" This was their song. But is the music and dancing, the feasting and rioting, the idle songs and extravagant mirth of mortals at this season, a proper echo or response to this angelic song?[4] I leave you to your own reflections upon this subject, after I have given the hint; and I am sure, if they be natural and pertinent, and have a proper influence upon you, they will restrain you from running into the fashionable excesses of riot on this occasion.

To remember and religiously improve the incarnation of our divine Redeemer, to join the concert of angels, and dwell in extatic meditation upon their song: this is lawful, this is a seasonable duty every day; and consequently upon this day. And as [387] Jesus improved the feast of dedication,[B] though not of divine institution, as a proper opportunity to exercise his ministry, when crowds of the Jews were gathered from all parts; so I would improve this day for your instruction, since it is the custom of our country to spend it religiously, or idly, or wickedly, as different persons are differently disposed.

But as the seeds of superstition, which have sometimes grown up to a prodigious height, have been frequently sown and cherished by very inconsiderable incidents, I think it proper to inform you, that I may guard against this danger, that I do not set apart this day for public worship, as though it had any peculiar sanctity, or we are under any obligations to keep it religiously. I know no human authority, that has power to make one day more holy than another, or that can bind the conscience in such cases. And as for divine authority, to which alone the sanctifying of days and things belongs, it has thought it sufficient to consecrate one day in seven to a religious use, for the commemoration both of the birth of this world, and the resurrection of its great Author, or of the works of creation and redemption. This I would religiously observe; and inculcate the religious observance of it upon all. But as to other days, consecrated by the mistaken piety or superstition of men, and conveyed down to us as holy, through the corrupt medium of human tra-

---

[4]For an example of the type of Christmas celebrations deplored by both Davies and the Reverend William Dawson see the account of a Christmas celebration at the home of William Fitzhugh in 1686, in Gilbert Chinard, ed., *A Huguenot Exile in Virginia or Voyages of a Frenchman exiled for his Religion with a Description of Virginia & Maryland* (The Hague, 1687; reprint, New York, The Press of the Pioneers, Inc., 1934), 158.

"He (Fitzhugh) treated us royally, there was good wine & all kinds of beverages, so there was a great deal of carousing. He had sent for three fiddlers, a jester, a tight-rope dancer, an acrobat who tumbled around, & they gave us all the entertainment one could wish for."

[B]John x.22. This festival was instituted by Judas Macabaeus, in memory of the restoration of the temple and the altar, after they had been profaned by their heathen enemies; the original account of which we have, I Mac. iv. 56, &c. Where what is called τα εγκαινια by the evangelist, is called τον εγκαινισμου (v.56.).—See also Joseph. Antiq. I. xii. C. 11.

dition, I think myself free to observe them or not, according to conveniency, and the prospect of usefulness; like other common days, on which I may lawfully carry on public worship or not, as circumstances require. And since I have so fair an opportunity, and it seems necessary in order to prevent my conduct from being a confirmation of present superstition, or a temptation to future, I shall, once for all, declare my sentiments more fully upon this head.

But I must premise, that it is far from my design, to widen the differences subsisting among christians, to embitter their hearts against each other, or to awaken dormant controversies concerning the extra-essentials of religion. And if this use should be made of what I shall say, it will be an unnatural perversion of my design. I would make every candid concession in [388] favour of those who observe days of human institution, that can consist with truth, and my own liberty. I grant, that so many plausible things may be offered for the practice, as may have the appearance of solid argument, even to honest inquirers after truth. I grant, that I doubt not but many are offering up acceptable devotion to God on this day; devotion proceeding from honest believing hearts, and therefore acceptable to him on any day—acceptable to him, notwithstanding their little mistake in this affair. I grant, we should, in this case, imitate the generous candour and forbearance of St. Paul, in a similar case. The converts to christianity from among the Jews, long retained the prejudices of their education, and thought they were still obliged, even under the gospel dispensation, to observe the rites and ceremonies of the law of Moses, to which they had been accustomed, and particularly those days which were appointed by God to be religiously kept under the Jewish dispensation. The Gentile converts, on the other hand, who were free from these early prejudices of education and custom, and had imbibed more just notions of christian liberty, looked upon these Jewish holy-days as common days, and no longer to be observed. This occasioned a warm dispute between these two classes of converts, and St. Paul interposes, not so properly to determine which party was right, (that was comparatively a small matter) as to bring both parties to exercise moderation and forbearance towards each other, and to put a charitable construction upon their different practices in these little articles; and particularly to believe concerning each other, that though their practices were different, yet the principle from which they acted was the same, namely, a sincere desire to glorify and please God, and a conscientious regard to what they apprehended was his will. "Him that is weak in the faith, receive ye, but not to doubtful disputations—one man esteemeth one day above another: another esteemeth every day alike. He that regardeth the day, regardeth it unto the Lord: and he that regardeth not the day, to the Lord he doth not regard it;"[C] that is, it is a conscientious *regard to the Lord*, that is the principle upon which both parties act, though they act differently in this matter. Therefore, says the apostle, "Why dost thou judge thy brother"? why dost thou severely censure him for practising differently in this little affair?—"hast thou faith?" says he, hast thou a full persuasion of what is right in these punctilios and ceremonials? Then "have it to thyself before God;"[D] keep it to [389] thyself as a rule for thy own practice, but do not impose it upon others, nor disturb the church of Christ about it. It becomes us, my brethren, to imitate this catholicism and charity of the apostle, in these little differences: and God forbid I should tempt any of you to forsake so noble an example. But then the example of the same apostle will authorize us, modestly to propose our own sentiments and the reasons of our practice, and to warn people from laying a great stress upon ceremonials and superstitious observances. This he does particularly to the Galatians, who not only kept the Jewish holy-days, but placed a great part of their religion in the observance of them. "Ye observe days, and months, and times, and years;" therefore, says he, "I am afraid of you, lest I have bestowed upon you labour in vain."[E] The commandments of God have often been made void by the traditions of men; and human inventions more religiously observed than divine institutions: and when this was the case, St. Paul was warm in opposing even ceremonial mistakes.

Having premised this, which I look upon as much more important than the decision of the question, I proceed to shew you the reasons why I would not religiously observe days of human appointment, in commemoration of Christ or the saints. What I have to say shall be particularly pointed at what is called *Christmas-day*; but may easily be applied to all other holy-days instituted by men.

The first reason I shall offer is, that I would take my religion just as I find it in my Bible, without any imaginary improvements or supplements of human invention. All the ordinances which God has been pleased to appoint, and particularly that one day in seven, which he has set apart for his own immediate service, and the commemoration of the works of creation and redemption, I would honestly endeavour to observe in the most sacred manner. But when ignorant presuming mortals take upon them to refine upon divine institutions, to make that a part of religion, which God has left indifferent, and consecrate more days than he has thought necessary; in short, when they would mingle something of their own with the pure religion of the Bible: then I must be ex-

---

[C]Romans 14:1, 5, 6.
[D]Romans 14:22.
[E]Galatians 4:10, 11.

cused from obedience, and beg leave to content myself with the old, plain, simple religion of the Bible. Now that there is not the least appearance in all the Bible of the divine appointment of Christmas, to celebrate the birth of Christ, is granted by all [390] parties; and the divine authority is not so much as pretended for it. Therefore a Bible-christian is not at all bound to observe it.

Secondly, the Christian church, for at least three hundred years, did not observe any day in commemoration of the birth of Christ. For this we have the testimony of the primitive fathers themselves. Thus Clemens Alexandrinus,[5] who lived about the year one hundred and ninety-four, "We are commanded to worship and honour him, who, we are persuaded, is the Word, and our Saviour and ruler, and, through him, the Father; *not upon* certain particular or *select days*, as some others do, but constantly practising this all our life, and in every proper way."[6] Chrysostom,[7] who lived in the fourth century, has these words, "It is not yet ten years, since this day, that is, Christmas, was plainly known to us;" and he observes, the custom was brought to Constantinople from Rome.[8] Now since this day was not religiously observed in the church in the first and purest ages, but was introduced as superstitions increased, and Christianity began to degenerate very fast into popery; ought not we to imitate the purity of these primitive times, and retain none of the superstitious observances of more corrupt ages?

Thirdly, if a day should be religiously observed in memory of the birth of Christ, it ought to be that day on which he was born. But that day, and even the month and the year, are altogether uncertain. The Scriptures do not determine this point of chronology. And perhaps they are silent on purpose, to prevent all temptation to the superstitious observance of it; just as the body of Moses was secretly buried, and his grave concealed,[9] to guard the Israelites from the danger of idolizing it. Chronologers are also divided upon the point: and even the ancients are not agreed.[F] The learned generally suppose that Christ

---

[5]Clement of Alexandria (ca. 150–ca. 215), theologian.
[6]See *The Stromata, or Miscellanies*, book VII, ch. 7, par. 35.
[7]John Chrysostom (ca. 347–407), Bishop of Constantinople.
[8]See Chrysostom's homily, *In diem natelem Domine*.
[9]Deuteronomy 34:6.
[F]Clemens Alexandrinus mentions the different opinions about it in his time, especially among the heretics; for as to the catholics, they pretended to determine nothing about it in his day. "There are some," he says, "who very curiously determine not only the year, but also the day of our Saviour's birth, which they say is the 28th year of Augustus, and the 25th of the month of Pachon. The followers of Basiledes [Alexandrian Gnostic, fl. 120–140] celebrate also the day of his baptism, and say, that it is the 15th year of Tiberius, and the 15th of the month Tabi. But others say, it is the 11th of the same month. Some of them also say, that he was born on the 24th or 25th of Pharmouthi." But none of these computations fix it on the 25th of December.
Davies' source is Clement's *Stromata*, book I, ch. 21.

was born two or three years before the vulgar reckoning. And as to the month, some suppose it was in September, and some in June. And they imagine it was very unlikely, that he was born in the cold wintry month December, because we read, that at the [391] time of his birth, shepherds were out in the field, watching their flocks by night;[10] which is not probable at that season of the year. The Christian epocha, or reckoning time from the birth of Christ, was not introduced till about the year five hundred; and it was not generally used till the reign of Charles the Great,[11] about the year eight hundred, or a little above nine hundred years ago. And this must occasion a great uncertainty, both as to the year, month and day. But why do I dwell so long upon this? It must be universally confessed, that the day of his birth is quite uncertain: nay, it is certain that it is not that which has been kept in commemoration of it. To convince you of this, I need only put you in mind of the late parliamentary correction of our computation of time by introducing the new-style;[12] by which Christmas is eleven days sooner than it was wont to be. And yet this chronological blunder still continues in the public prayers of some, who give thanks to God, that Christ was born *as upon this day*. And while this prayer was offered up in England and Virginia on the twenty-fifth of December old-style, other countries that followed the new-style, were solemnly declaring in their thanksgivings to God, that Christ was born eleven days sooner; that is, on the fourteenth of December. I therefore conclude, that neither this day nor any other was ever intended to be observed for this purpose.

Finally, superstition is a very growing evil; and therefore the first beginnings of it ought to be prevented. Many things that were at first introduced with a pious design, have grown up gradually into the most enormous superstition and idolatry in after ages. The ancient christians, for example, had such a veneration for the pious martyrs, that they preserved a lock of hair, or some little memorial of them; and this laid the foundation for the expensive sale and stupid idolizing of the relics of the saints in popish countries. They also celebrated their memory by observing the days of their martyrdom. But as the number of the martyrs and saints real or imaginary, increased, the saints' days also multiplied to an extravagant degree, and hardly left any days in the year for any other purpose. And as they had more saints than days in the year, they dedicated the first of November for them all, under the title of *All-saints-day*. But if the saints must be thus honoured, then certainly much more ought Jesus Christ. This seemed a natural inference: and accordingly, these superstitious devotees appointed one

---

[10]Luke 2:8.
[11]Charlemagne (742–814), Holy Roman Emperor.
[12]Great Britain adopted the Gregorian Calendar in 1752.

day to [392] celebrate his birth, another his baptism, another his death, another the day of Pentecost, and an endless list that I have not time now to mention. The apostles must also be put into the Kalender; and thus almost all the days in the year were consecrated by superstition, and hardly any left for the ordinary labours of life. Thus the people are taught to be idle the greatest part of their time, and so indisposed to labour on the few days that are still allowed them for that purpose. This has almost ruined some popish countries, particularly the pope's dominions in the fine country of Italy, once the richest and best improved in the world. Mr. Addison,[13] bishop Burnet,[14] and other travellers, inform us, that every thing bears the appearance of poverty, notwithstanding all the advantages of soil and climate: and that this is chiefly owing to the superstition of the people, who spend the most of their time as holy-days. And if you look over the Kalender of the church of England, you will find that the *festivals* in one year, amount to thirty-one—The *fasts* to no less than 95, to which add the fifty-two Sundays in every year, and the whole will make one hundred and seventy-eight: so that only one hundred and eighty-seven days will be left in the whole year, for the common purposes of life. And whether the poor could procure a subsistence for themselves and their families by the labour of so few days, and whether it be not a yoke that neither we nor our fathers are able to bear, I leave you to judge. It is true, that but very few of these feasts and fasts are now observed, even by the members of the established church. But then they are still in their Kalender and Canons, and binding upon them by the authority of the church; and as far as they do not comply with them, so far they are *dissenters*: and in this, and many other respects, they are *generally dissenters*, though they do not share with us in the infamy of the name. Now, since the beginnings of superstitious inventions in the worship of God are so dangerous in their issue, and may grow up into such enormous extravagance, we ought to shun the danger, by adhering to the simplicity of the Bible-religion, and not presume to make more days or things holy, than the all wise God has been pleased to sanctify. He will be satisfied with the religious observance of his own institutions; and why should not we? It is certainly enough, that we be as religious as he requires us. And all our will-worship is liable to that confounding rejection, "Who hath required this at your hands?"[G] [393]

---

[13]Joseph Addison (1672–1719), statesman and essayist, contributed essays to both *The Tatler* and *The Spectator*. Davies' allusion is to Addison's *Remarks on Several Parts of Italy* (1705).

[14]Gilbert Burnet (1643–1715), chaplain of the Rolls, bishop of Salisbury. There are several versions of Burnet's work. See Gilbert Burnet, *Some Letters Containing an Account of What Seemed Most Remarkable in Travelling Through Switzerland, Italy, Some Parts of Germany, &c in the Years 1685 and 1686* (London, 1689).

[G]Isaiah 1:12.

I now proceed to what is more delightful and profitable, the sublime anthem of the angels: "Glory to God in the highest! on earth, peace! good-will to men!"

What a happy night was this to the poor shepherds, though exposed to the damps and darkness of midnight, and keeping their painful watches in the open field![H] An illustrious angel, clothed in light which kindled midnight into noon, came upon them, or suddenly hovered over them in the air, and the glory of the Lord, that is, a bright refulgent light, the usual emblem of his presence, shone round about them. No wonder the poor shepherds were struck with horror, and overwhelmed at the sight of so glorious a phenomenon. But when God strikes his people with terror, it is often an introduction to some signal blessing. And they are sometimes made sore afraid, like the shepherds, even with the displays of his glories. The first appearance even of the great deliverer, may seem like that of a great destroyer. But he will at length make himself known as he is, and allay the fears of his people. So the gentle angel cheers and supports the trembling shepherds: "Fear not," says he, you need not tremble, but rejoice at my appearance; "for *behold*," observe and wonder, "*I bring you*," from heaven, by order from its Sovereign, "*good tidings of great joy*,"[1] the best that was ever published in mortal ears, not only to you, not only to a few private persons or families, not only to the Jewish nation; but good tidings of great joy, "*which shall be to all people*," to Gentiles as well as Jews, to all nations, tribes, and languages—to all the various ranks of men—to kings and subjects—to rich and poor; to free and bond: therefore let it circulate through the world, and resound from shore to shore. And what is this news that is introduced with so sublime and transporting a preface? It is this: "For unto you is born this day in the city of David, a Saviour, which is Christ the Lord."[15] Unto *you* mortals—unto you miserable sinners, is born a *Saviour*—a Saviour from sin and ruin; a Saviour of no mean or common character, but *Christ*, the [394] promised Messiah, anointed with the Holy Spirit, and invested with the high office of Mediator; Christ the *Lord*, the Lord and Ruler of heaven and earth, and universal nature. He is *born*—no longer represented by dark types and prophecies, but actually entered in the

---

[H]"In midnight shades, on frosty ground,/They could attend the pleasing sound,/Nor could they feel December cold, nor think the darkness long." Dr. Watts.

The verse is from "Converse with Christ," lines 10–12, Isaac Watts, *Horea Lyricae: Poems, Chiefly of the Lyric Kind, in Three Books, Sacred: I. To Devotion and Piety, II. To Virtue, Honour and Friendship, III. To the Memory of the Dead* (London, 1706), book I. Watts wrote the original in first person singular.

[1]The original has a force in it, which I cannot convey into a translation: but one that understands Greek, is struck with it at first sight—ευαγγελιξομαι υμιν χαραν μεγαλην. Luke 2:10.

[15]Luke 2:11.

world—born *this* day—the long expected day is at length arrived; the prophecies are accomplished, and the fulness of time is come: born *in the city of David*, in Bethlehem, and therefore of the seed and lineage of David, according to the prophecies: though he be a person of such eminence, *Christ the Lord* is now a feeble infant, just born. The Son born and the Child given, he is the mighty God, the everlasting Father, the Prince of Peace.[J]

The condescension of the angel, and the joyful tidings he brought, no doubt recovered the shepherds from their consternation, and emboldened them to lift up their faces. And how was their joy heightened, that they were chosen and appointed by Heaven, to be the first visitants to this new-born Prince? "This shall be a sign to you," said the angel, by which you may know this divine Infant from others—What shall be the sign? shall it be, that they will find him in a palace, surrounded with all the grandeur and majesty of courts, and attended by the emperors, kings and nobles of the earth; lying in a bed of down, and dressed in silks and gold and jewels? This might be expected, if we consider the dignity of his person. It would be infinite condescension for him to be born even in such circumstances as these. But these are not the characteristics of the incarnate God: no, says the angel, "This shall be a sign to you, *ye shall find the babe wrapped in swaddling clothes, lying in a manger.*" LYING IN A MANGER![K] Astonishing! who could expect the new-born Son of God to be there?—there, lying in straw, surrounded only with oxen and horses, and waited upon only by a feeble, solitary mother, far from home, among unkind, regardless strangers, who would not allow her room in the inn, even in her painful hour. Perhaps her poverty disabled her from bearing her expenses in the ordinary way; and therefore she must take up her lodging in a stable. In such circumstances of abasement did the Lord of glory enter our world. In these circumstances, he was *"seen of angels,"*[L] who were wont to behold him in another form, in all the glories of the heavenly world. And [395] how strange a sight must this be! How bright a display of his love to the guilty sons of men!

The angel, that was the willing messenger of these glad tidings, did not descend from heaven alone. He appears to have been the hierarch, or commandant of an army of angels, that attended him on this grand occasion. For suddenly there was with him a *multitude* of the heavenly host, or, as it might be rendered, of *the militia*, or *soldiery of heaven*.[M] The angels are not a confused

---

[J]Isaiah 9:6.
[K]Luke 2:12.
[L]I Timothy 3:16.
[M]Davies' note referred to the Greek text, but his Greek does not match that in the New Testament.

irregular body, or unconnected independent individuals; but a well-disposed system of beings, with proper subordinations; all marshalled into ranks under proper commanders. Hence they are called "thrones, and dominions, and principalities, and powers;["]^N and we read of angels and arch-angels^O—of Michael and his angels.^{P} They are all called in the military style, the Lord's *hosts*, and the *army* of heaven,^{Q} to signify the order established among them, and also their strength and unanimity to execute the commands of their sovereign, to repel the dragon and his angels, and defend the feeble heirs of salvation, on whom they condescend to wait. Order and subordination is still retained even among the fallen angels in the kingdom of darkness. Hence we read of the prince of the devils,^{R} the dragon and his angels,^{S} legions of devils,^{T} which was a division of the Roman army, something like that of a regiment among us.

Now a regiment of the heavenly militia descended with their officer, to solemnize and publish the birth of their Lord, when he took upon him our nature. And no sooner had their commander delivered his message, than they immediately join with one voice, filling all the air with their heavenly music; "praising God, and saying, glory to God in the highest! on earth, peace! goodwill to men!" The language is abrupt, like that of a full heart: the sentences short, unconnected, and rapid; expressive of the extacy of their minds.

"*Glory to God in the highest!*" This deservedly leads the song. It is of more importance in itself, in the estimate of angels, and of all competent judges, than even the salvation of men. And the first and chief cause of joy and praise from the birth of a [396] Saviour is, that he shall bring glory to God. Through him, as a proper medium, the divine perfections shall shine forth with new, augmented splendour. Through him, sinners shall be saved in a way that will advance the honour of the divine perfections and government; or if any of them perish, their punishment will more illustriously display the glory of their offended Sovereign. The *wisdom*, *grace* and *mercy* of God, are glorified in the contrivance of this scheme of redemption, and making millions of miserable creatures happy forever. His *power* is glorified, in carrying this scheme into execution, in spite of all opposition. His *justice* is glorified, in the atonement and satisfaction made for the sins of men by an incarnate Deity, and in the right-

---

^{N}Colossians 1:16.
^{O}I Thessalonians 4:16.
^{P}Psalm 103:21; Psalm 118:2.
^{Q}Daniel 4:35; Revelation 19:14.
^{R}Matthew 9:34.
^{S}Revelation 12:7.
^{T}Mark 5:9.

eous and aggravated punishment executed upon those that obstinately reject this divine Saviour, and who therefore perish without the least umbrage of excuse. Oh! what wonders does Jehovah perform, in prosecution of this method of salvation! What wonders of pardoning mercy and sanctifying grace! What miracles of glory and blessedness does he form out of the dust, and the polluted fragments of human nature! What monuments of his own glorious perfections does he erect, through all the extensive regions of heaven! From these wonderful works of his, the glory of his own name breaks forth upon the worlds of angels and men, in one bright unclouded day, which shall never be obscured in night, but grow more and more illustrious through the endless ages of eternity! Of this, the choir of angels were sensible at the birth of Christ; and therefore they shout aloud in ascriptions of glory to God. It was especially on this account they rejoiced in this great event. And all believers rejoice in it principally on this account too. "Glory to God," is the first note in the song of angels: and "hallowed be thy name;"[16] that is, let thy name be sanctified, or glorified, is the first petition in the prayer of men. The glory of God should always be nearest our hearts: to this every thing should give way; and we should rejoice in other things, and even in our own salvation, as they tend to promote this. Such is the temper of every good man: his heart is enlarged, and extended beyond the narrow limits of self: he has a generous tender regard for the glory of the great God; and rejoices in the way of salvation through Christ, not merely as it makes him happy, but especially as it advances and displays the divine honour. This is his temper, at least in some hours of refined, exalted devotion. Self is, as it were, swallowed up in God. And, brethren, is this your temper? [397]

"Glory to God *in the highest!*"—In the *highest*; that is, in the *highest strains*. Let the songs of men and angels be raised to a higher key, on this great occasion. The usual strains of praise are low and languid, to celebrate the birth of this illustrious prince. This is a more glorious event than ever has yet happened in heaven or earth; and therefore demands a new song, more exalted and divine than has ever yet employed even the voices of angels. At the birth of nature, the sons of God, the angels, sang together, and shouted for joy: but when the Author and Lord of nature is born, let them raise a loftier and a more extatic anthem of praise.

Or, "Glory to God *in the highest*," may signify, let glory be given to God in the *highest heaven* by all the choirs of *angels*. This celestial squadron call upon their fellow-angels, whom they left behind them in their native heaven, to echo to their song, and fill those blessed regions with the melody of new ascriptions of

---

[16]Matthew 6:9; Luke 11:2.

praise, as if they had said—though men receive the benefit, let all the angels of heaven join in the song of gratitude. Though men be silent, and refuse to celebrate the birth of their Saviour and Lord; though earth does not echo with his praise, though more intimately concerned; let the heavenly inhabitants sound aloud their ascriptions of glory, and supply the guilty defect of ungrateful mortals.

Or finally, "Glory to God *in the highest*," may mean, glory to God who *dwells* in the *highest heavens*: glory to the high and lofty One, that inhabiteth eternity, and dwelleth in the high and holy place;[U] and yet condescends to regard man that is a worm,[V] and sends his Son to assume his humble nature, to lie in a manger, and die upon a cross for him. Glory to God for this astonishing condescension and grace!

The next article of this angelic song is, "Peace on earth!" Peace to rebel man with his offended Sovereign; peace with angels; peace with conscience; peace between man and man; universal peace on earth, that region of discord and war.

Peace *with God to rebel man*. The illustrious Prince now born comes to make up the difference, and reconcile the world to their offended Sovereign. He is the great Peace-maker, who shall subdue the enmity of the carnal mind, and reduce the revolted sons of Adam to a willing subjection to their rightful Lord. He [398] will bring thousands of disloyal hearts to love God above all, which were wont to love almost every thing more than Him. He will reconcile them to the laws of his government, and the practice of universal obedience and holiness. He will set on foot a treaty of *peace* in the *ministry* of the gospel, and send out his ambassadors, to beseech the rebels in his stead, to be reconciled to God. He will also reconcile God to man, by answering all the demands of his law and justice, paying the debts of insolvent sinners, and making amends for all their offences. He will appear as an all-prevailing advocate with his Father, in favour of a rebel world, and turn his heart to them again. So that this revolted province of his dominions, shall again become the object of his love, and he will look down and smile upon the obnoxious sons of men. O happy peace! Oh blessed peace-maker! that puts an end to so fatal and unnatural a war, and brings the Creator and his creatures, the offended Sovereign and his rebellious subjects, into mutual friendship again, after the grand breach, that seemed likely never to be made up, and indeed never could be made up but by so great and powerful a Mediator; a mediator of infinite dignity, merit and authority, able to remove all obstructions in the way of both parties.

[U]Isaiah 57:15.
[V]Job 25:6.

The Peace proclaimed on this grand occasion may also imply, *Peace with angels*; peace between the inhabitants of heaven and earth. The angelic armies, the militia of heaven, are always upon the side of their Sovereign; always at war with his enemies, and ready to fight his battles. And upon the apostacy of our world they were ready to take up arms against the rebels. But now, when their Sovereign proclaims peace, they lay down their arms, they acquiesce in the peace, and receive the penitent, returning rebels with open arms. These benevolent beings rejoice in the restoration of their fellow-creature man to the divine favour, and shout forth their songs of praise upon the publication of the news.

Again; this proclamation of peace may include *peace with conscience*. When man commenced an enemy to his Maker, he became an enemy to himself: his own conscience took up arms against him, and is perpetually fighting the cause of its Lord. But now the guilt of past sin may be washed away from the conscience with the pacific blood of Jesus, and all its clamours silenced by his all-satisfying righteousness. And now the peace will be preserved, and the contracting of new guilt prevented, by [399] the sanctifying influence of the grace of this new-born Prince. His grace shall change disloyal hearts, and reform rebellious lives; and those shall enjoy the approbation of their conscience, who were wont to sweat and agonize under its tormenting accusations. Thus, self-tormenting sinners shall be reconciled to themselves; and peace in their own breasts shall be a perennial source of happiness: a happiness

"Which nothing earthly gives, nor can destroy,
The soul's calm sun-shine, and the heartfelt joy."[17]

Farther; peace on earth includes peace between man and man. Now the Prince of peace is born; and upon his appearance let animosity and discord, contentions and wars cease; and let universal harmony and benevolence prevail through the world. Let the bonds of love unite all sons of Adam together in the closest friendship. It was love that constrained him to put on the nature of man, and to change his throne in heaven for a manger: love is the ruling passion of his soul: love is the doctrine he shall preach: love is the disposition he shall inspire; and love is the first principle of his religion. Therefore, let all the world be melted and moulded into love. Let the wolf and the lion put on the nature of the lamb; and let nothing hurt or destroy through all the earth. "Let nation no more lift up sword against nation: let them beat their swords into ploughshares, and their spears into pruning-hooks; and let them learn war no more."[W] For of him

---

[17]Alexander Pope, *Essay on Man* (1733–1734), Epistle iv, lines 167–68.
[W]Isaiah 11:6–9.

it is foretold, that in his "days abundance of peace shall flourish, so long as the moon endureth."[X] This, my brethren, has already been accomplished in part: for peace and benevolence is the genius of christianity; and wherever it has prevailed, it has introduced peace and harmony in families, in neighbourhoods, and among nations: nor can the present disturbed state of things, the animosities, quarrels and wars, that are in the world, disprove what I say: for these prevail only so far as the christian spirit does not prevail. Just as much as there *is* of these among men, just so much of christianity is *wanting*; just so far the genuine tendency of the birth of Jesus fails of its efficacy. However, we rejoice in the hope, that our world shall yet see better times, and experience the full effects of this illustrious birth: when the kingdom of the Prince of peace shall become universal, and diffuse peace among all nations. Oh! when shall that glorious revolution commence! [400]

The next article in the song of angels is, "Good-will towards men.["] That is, the good-will and grace of God is now illustriously displayed towards men, sinful and unworthy as they are. And may they dutifully receive it, and enjoy all the happy effects of it!

Thus the angels *declared*, *foretold*, and *wished*. They *declared*, that even then glory would redound to God, peace be established on earth, and the good-will and favour of God enjoyed by guilty men. And they *foretold*, that thus it would be more and more to the end of time, and even through all eternity. And they also *wished* these glorious effects might follow, as agreeable to the high regard they had for the divine honour, and their generous benevolence to their unworthy fellow-creature, men.

This suggests a question, and also an answer to it. The question is, since the angels were not redeemed by Jesus Christ, and do not share in the benefits of redemption, as man does, why did they thus rejoice and sing at his birth? This we can account for from their regard to the glory of God, and their good-will to men.

Their happiness consists in the knowledge and love of God: and the more he displays his perfections in his works, the more they know of him, and consequently the more they love him. Now the redemption of sinners through Jesus Christ gives the most bright and amiable view of the divine perfections: and on this account the inhabitants of heaven rejoice in it. They know more of God from this great event, than from all his other works of creation and providence. Hence St. Peter represents them as

---

[X]Psalm 72:7.

bending, and looking with eager eyes, to pry into this mystery.[Y] St. Paul also intimates, that the founding of a church in our guilty world, and particularly the gathering of the poor outcast Gentiles into it, was a secret even to the angels, till revealed by the event; and that the revelation of it discovered to them more of the wisdom of God, than they ever knew before. "This," says he, "was a mystery, which from the beginning of the world was hid in God:" but it is now revealed, "to the intent that unto principalities and powers,"—to the various ranks of angels, [401] "might be known by the church the *manifold wisdom* of God."[Z] This cleared up many of the dark events of providence, which they could not before account for; and enabled them to see farther into the designs of divine wisdom. Methinks when Abel, or the first saint from our world, arrived in heaven, the glorious natives of that country were struck with agreeable surprise, and wondered how he came there. They were ready to give up the whole race for lost, like their kindred angels that fell; and could contrive no possible method for their recovery. And how then are these earth-born strangers admitted into heaven? And when they found, by the proceedings of divine Providence, that God had gracious designs towards our world, and that these designs were to be accomplished by his Son, must they not be agreeably perplexed and bewildered to find out the manner in which he would accomplish them? In what way could he satisfy divine justice, who was himself the judge? How could he die for sin, who was all-immortal? These and the like difficulties must perplex the inquiries even of angels. But now, all is made plain; now the grand secret is disclosed. The Son of God must become the Son of man, must obey the law, and die upon a cross; and thus he was to accomplish the great design, and restore guilty man to the favour of God.[AA] Angels must rejoice at this discovery, as advancing the glory of God, and increasing their own happiness.

Again; the angels are benevolent beings, and therefore rejoice at the birth of Christ, as tending to the salvation of poor sinners of the race of

---

[Y]εις α επιθυμουσιν αλλελοι παρακυψαι. I Peter 1:12.
See how they bend! see how they look!
Long had they read th' eternal book,
And studied dark decrees in vain;
The cross and Calvary makes them plain. WATTS' LYR.
The verse is from "Jesus the Only Saviour," lines 29–32, in Watts, *Horea Lyricae*, book I.
[Z]Ephesians 3:9, 16.
[AA]"Now they are struck with deep amaze,
Each with his wings conceals his face:
Now clap their sounding plumes and cry,
The wisdom of a Deity!" WATTS
"Jesus the Only Saviour," lines 33–36.

man. The Lord of angels tells us, "there is joy among the angels of God over one sinner that repenteth."[BB] And how much more must they rejoice to see the grand scheme disclosed, by which numerous colonies were to be transplanted from our guilty world to people the heavenly regions, and perhaps fill the vacant seats of the fallen angels?

I may add, it is not unlikely that the angels may receive some great advantages, to us unknown, by the mediation of Christ; [402] though they do not need a mediator in the same sense that we do. But I have not time to enlarge upon this.

You now see the reasons of the joy of angels on this occasion: and it is no wonder they sung, "Glory to God in the highest, for peace proclaimed on earth, and good-will towards men."

But how ought we to improve this subject more immediately for our own advantage? This is our great concern; for we are personally interested in it, which the angels were not; at least, not in the same degree. Hence then,

We may learn how we ought to celebrate the birth of Christ—celebrate it like angels, not with balls and assemblies—not with revelling and carousing, and all the extravagancies that are usual at this season; as if you were celebrating the birth of Venus or Bacchus, or some patron of iniquity; not with the sound of bells, muskets and cannons, and the other demonstrations of joy, upon occasions of a civil nature. Some of these are not innocent upon any occasion, and have a direct tendency to make men still more thoughtless, and giddy, and to prevent the blessed effects of this illustrious birth. Others of them, though lawful upon seasons of public national joy, for temporal blessings or deliverances, yet are impious and profane, when practised in honor of the incarnation of the holy Jesus. You will all grant, no doubt, that religious joy ought to be expressed in a religious manner; that the usual mirth, festivity, and gaiety of a birth-night, in honour of our earthly sovereign, are not proper expressions of joy for the birth of a spiritual Saviour—a Saviour from this vain world—from sin and hell. Therefore, I say, celebrate it as the angels did; giving glory to God in the highest, in your songs of praise; giving him glory by dwelling upon the wonders of redemption, in delightful meditation; by giving him your thoughts and affections; and by a life of devotion and universal obedience. Celebrate the birth of this great Prince of peace, by accepting that peace which angels proclaimed. Give a welcome reception to this glorious stranger. Do not turn him out of doors, as the Bethlemites did; but entertain him in your hearts. Let every faculty of your souls open to receive him. "Lift up your heads, O ye gates: and be ye lifted up, ye

---

[BB]Luke 15:10.

everlasting doors, that the king of glory may come in."[CC] O let every heart cry, "Come in, thou blessed of the Lord: [403] wherefore standest thou without?"[DD] He came to procure and restore peace between God and man; therefore I, his poor ambassador, "pray you in his stead, be ye reconciled to God."[EE] No longer continue in arms, rejecting his authority, trampling upon his laws, and refusing the offers of his grace: otherwise, this peace will not extend to you; but war, eternal war, will continue between you and the Lord God omnipotent. But if the boldest rebel among you this day submit to his government, you shall enjoy the blessed peace, which angels proclaimed at his entrance into the world, and which he left as a legacy to his friends, when he was about to leave it.[FF] Make peace also with your own conscience; and scorn to live at variance with yourselves. How ill do you take it, when others condemn you? and can you be easy, while perpetually condemning yourselves? Let conscience have full liberty to exercise its authority upon you, as Jehovah's deputy, and dare not to disobey its orders. Live in peace also with one another. Silence; ye noisy brawlers: the Prince of Peace is born. Peace! be still! ye contentious, angry passions: the Prince of Peace is born. Away slander, backbiting, quarrelling, envy, malice, revenge—away to your native hell: for know ye not, that the Prince of peace has entered into this world, and forbid you to appear upon it? Thus, brethren, celebrate the birth of the Saviour, and that not only upon this day, but every day through all your lives: and thus you may have a *merry Christmas* all the year round.

To conclude. What encouragement may this angelic proclamation afford to trembling desponding penitents? Fear not; for behold I bring you good tidings of great joy; for to you is born a Saviour, Christ the Lord. Oh! do not your hearts spring within you at the news? I have somewhere heard of a crowd of criminals under condemnation, confined in one dungeon: and upon a messenger's arriving from their king, and proclaiming a pardon, they all rushed out so eagerly to receive the pardon, and see the publisher of the joyful news, that they trod and crushed one another to death. And shall there be no such pressing and crowding to Jesus Christ in this assembly to-day? Shall there be no such eagerness among us to receive a pardon from his hands? Alas! will any of you turn this greatest blessing of heaven into a curse? Was it your destroyer that was born, when the angels [404] sung the birth of a Saviour? Indeed, if you continue to neglect him, you will find him such to you; and it would have been better for you, that neither you nor HE had ever

---

[CC]Psalm 24:7.
[DD]Genesis 24:31.
[EE]II Corinthians 5:20.
[FF]John 14:27.

been born. Even the birth of the Prince of peace proclaims eternal war against *you*. I therefore now pray you in his stead to be reconciled to him. *Amen*.

The Duty of Christians to Propagate Their Religion among Heathens[18]

For I know him, that he will command his Children and his Houshold after him, and they shall keep the Way of the LORD, to do Justice and Judgment. Genesis 18:19

A Creature formed for *Immortality*, and that must be happy or miserable through an *everlasting* Duration, is certainly a Being of vast Importance, however mean and insignificant he may be in other Respects. His Immortality gives him a Kind of *infinite* Value. Let him be white or black, bond or free, a Native or a Foreigner, it is of no Moment in this View: [8] he is to live *for ever!* to be for ever *happy*, or for ever *miserable!* happy or miserable in the *highest Degree!* This places him upon a Kind of Equality with Kings and Princes; nay, with Angels and Arch-angels: for it is this that adds Importance and Dignity to the most exalted Parts of the human, and even of the angelic Nature.

In this View, the Crowds of neglected Negroe Slaves among us, have often appeared to me as Creatures of the utmost Importance. The *same* Immortality is entailed upon them, as upon us. They are Candidates for the *same* eternal State with us, and bound for the *same* Heaven or Hell. How awful and important a Trust, then, is *the Care of a Soul!* the Soul even of a poor *Negroe* slave! To be entrusted with the Care of forming and educating an *Immortal* for his everlasting State! to be instrumental in preparing him for eternal Joys, or eternal Torments! to be accountable for our Management in this Trust, to the supreme Judge of the Universe, with whom there is no Respect of Persons! to be rewarded for our Faithfulness; or punished for our Negligence, as having promoted the Happiness or been accessory to the Ruin of an immortal Soul! Pause, and think of these Things, and they will certainly appear very solemn and weighty.

This solemn and important Trust, I must tell you, Brethren, is committed, not only to Parents, with regard to their Children, those dear other Selves; but to *Masters*, with regard to their Servants and Slaves, of whatever Coun-

---

[18]Samuel Davies, *The Duty of Christians to Propagate Their Religion among Heathens, Earnestly recommended to the Masters of Negroe Slaves in VIRGINIA. A Sermon Preached in Hanover, January 8, 1757* (London, 1758). Used courtesy of the Virginia Historical Society.

try or Colour they are. And as this Duty is most scandalously neglected in this Christian Country; and the Neglect is likely to be followed with the most dangerous [9] and ruinous Consequences to Thousands, both Masters and Slaves; permit me to address you upon this Head, with the utmost Plainness and Solemnity. You are my Witnesses, that I have looked upon the poor Negroes as a Part of my ministerial Charge; and used various Endeavours to bring them to the Faith and Practice of Christianity, not without promising Appearances of Success, in sundry Instances. It affords me no small Pleasure to reflect, and I mention it with Gratitude to God and Man, that my Endeavours of this Kind have, of late, met with no Opposition from the Masters, of whatever Denomination, in any one Instance that I can recollect. And it affords me a still greater Pleasure to reflect, that sundry of you not only consent that your Negroes should receive Instruction from me, but also zealously concur with me, and make Conscience of your own Duty to them, in this Respect. But alas! are there not some among you, and are there not Thousands in our Country, who must be conscious of their wilful Negligence; nay, who, perhaps, are rather instrumental in hardening their Slaves in Sin, and confirming their Prejudices against our holy Religion, than in promoting their Conversion to God? Were your Negroes but so many *Brutes*, you might treat them as you do your Horses, fodder them, and make them work for you, without once endeavouring to make them Sharers with you in the glorious Privileges of Religion, the distinguishing Prerogative of human Nature. But I hope you have Divinity and Philosophy enough to know, this is not the Case. Let me therefore plainly lay your Duty before you, with regard [10] to them, in order to engage you to the Practice of it. For sure, you are not hardy enough to neglect the Practice, in spite of Conviction. Sure, you dare not sin on still, and continue your Career to Ruin with your Eyes open.

Abraham is often proposed as a Pattern to Believers in general; and I may particularly recommend his Example to your Imitation, in your Conduct towards your Domestics. Here you have his Character drawn by the all-knowing God Himself. "I know him, that he will command his Children, and his Houshold after him, and they shall keep the Way of the Lord." He not only instructed, advised, persuaded, entreated; but he used his *Authority*; he COMMANDED—not only his Children, but his HOUSHOLD; which included his Servants, *Slaves*, and all his Domestics of every Order. *Abraham's* Family was like the Generality of ours, in this, that he had hereditary *Slaves* in it, who were his Property during Life. We repeatedly read of his "Servants *born in his House*, and *bought with Money* of Strangers:"[A] both which were

---

[A]Genesis 17:12, 13, 23, 27.

probably *Slaves*. And he had so numerous a Family of them, that, when he went upon an Expedition to rescue *Lot* from Captivity, we are told, "he armed his trained Servants, *born in his own House*, Three hundred and Eighteen."[B] Where, by the By, it is remarkable, and the Remark is very pertinent to the present State of our Country, that by instilling good Principles into them, and by humane Treatment, this numerous Crowd of Slaves were become so faithful to their Master, [11] that he could safely confide in them, without Fear of their deserting him in the Engagement, and going over to the Enemy, in Hopes to recover their Liberty. All these, as well as *Ishmael*, and his Favourite *Isaac*, he had instructed in the true Religion. He had laid his *Commands* upon them to serve the Lord, not only during his Life, but *"after him,"* i.e. after his Decease. Though he was mortal, he endeavoured to make Religion immortal in his Family. He was solicitous to leave the World with the joyful Hope, that his Domestics would retain and observe his pious Instructions, when he should be no more their Head.

It is sufficient to recommend this Example to our Imitation, that it is the Example of *faithful Abraham*. But it is still more strongly enforced by the express Approbation of God Himself. "The Lord said, shall I hide from Abraham the Thing that I do?"[19] No, I may trust him even with my Secrets: "For I know him;" I approve of him; I have full Proof of him, and therefore may safely trust him; *"because*[C] he will command his Children and Houshold, and they shall keep the Way of the Lord:"[20] being once entered in the Way of the Lord by his Instructions, they will keep it. "Train up a Child [12] in the Way in which he should go, and when he is old, he will *not depart* from it."[D]

It is not my present Design to consider the general Duty of Family-Religion and good Education, though my Text is a very proper Foundation for it. But I intend only to inculcate *the particular Duty of instructing Slaves* in the true Religion, and using all proper Means to enter them in the Way of the Lord. To give you Directions how to perform it, before you are convinced it is your Duty, would be useless and preposterous. And therefore,

My first and principal Business shall be, *To convince you, that this is really your Duty, and that it is a Duty of the utmost Importance and Necessity.*

[B]Genesis 14:14.

[19]Genesis 18:17.

[C]The original [Hebrew] may be rendered *eo quod, because, forasmuch as*. And thus it points out the Ground of the divine Approbation and Confidence in Abraham, and the Way in which he shewed himself worthy of it, *viz.*. his faithful Care to propagate the Knowledge and Service of God among his Domestics.

[20]Genesis 18:17–19.

[D]Proverbs 22:6.

Here, I take it for granted, you are, at least, professed *Christians* yourselves, *i.e.* you profess to believe that the Christian Religion is divine, and to embrace it as *your* Religion. Otherwise, instead of persuading you to endeavour to Christianize your Negroes, I would first persuade you to become Christians yourselves. I would then deal with you, as with your Heathen Negroes, and labour to convince you of the Truth and Divinity of the Religion of Jesus, from those numerous Topics of Argument, by which so clear and important a Truth may be demonstrated. But you are fond of wearing the Christian Name; you present your Children to be initiated into the Christian [13] Church by Baptism; you acknowledge the Truth of the Scriptures, by complying with the usual Ceremony of kissing the Bible in taking an Oath; you attend upon the Forms of Worship in the Christian Church, and externally conform to them. These Things you do; and these Things are certainly a strong Profession, that you are Christians. And none of you, I presume, will dare to renounce it, rather than admit the Conviction that I would now force upon your Minds from this Consideration.

Therefore, taking this for granted, I need no other Principle to convince you of the Duty I am now recommending. And I shall reason from the Nature and Design of Christianity—from the Example of Christ and his Apostles—from the Worth and Importance of the Souls of your poor Slaves—from the happy Influence Christianity would have upon them, even for your own Interest—from the Zeal and Generosity of others in this Affair—and from your Relation to them as their Masters.

1. If you Consider the *Nature* and *Design* of Christianity, you cannot but be convinced of this Duty.

Christianity, in its own Nature, is calculated to be a *catholic*, or *universal* Religion, and is equally the Concern of *all* the Sons of Men. It proposes *one* God, as the Object of *universal* Adoration to White and Black, Bond and Free: *one* Lord Jesus Christ, as a *common* Saviour for Britons, Africans, and Americans: *one* Holy Spirit, by whom alone Sinners of *all* Nations, Colours [14] and Characters, can be sanctified: *one* Faith to be embraced, *one* Rule of Morality to be observed, by Masters and Servants, Rich and Poor: *one* Heaven and *one* Hell, as the last Mansions of *all* the Millions of Mankind; to which they shall be adjudged according to their moral Character, and, if they have heard the Gospel, according to their Acceptance or Non-Acceptance of it; and not according to the trifling Distinctions of Country, Colour, Liberty or Slavery. Christianity is a *Religion for Sinners*; for Sinners of *all* Kindreds, and Nations, and Languages. They *all* need those Instructions, which its heavenly Light sheds upon a benighted World. They *all* need that Pardon, which it offers; that Grace, which it communicates; and that Salvation, which it ensures. In short, *all* its Doctrines intimately concern them: *all* its Precepts are binding upon them: *all* its Blessings are needed by them: *all* its Promises and Threatenings shall be accomplished upon them, according to their Character. And must it not then be the grand Concern of *all?* Yes; as there is but one Air for Whites and Blacks, Masters and Servants to breathe in; one Earth for them to walk upon; so there is but *one common* Christian Religion for them *all*, by which they can please God, and obtain Salvation. To be a sinful Creature of the Race of Man, under the Gospel, is sufficient alone to render it his greatest Concern, and a Matter of absolute Necessity, to be a Christian. And to be entrusted with the Care of such a Creature, is alone a sufficient Foundation for the Duty I am recommending; and strongly [15] binds it upon every one of us, to whom that Trust is committed.

And as Christianity is, in its own Nature, the common Concern of all, and calculated to be the universal Religion of Mankind; so it is *designed* by its great Author to be propagated among all. No Corner of our World was left out in the Commission, which the gracious Founder of our Religion gave to the Teachers of it. "Go ye into *all* the World, says he, and preach the Gospel to *every* Creature; *i.e.* to every Creature of the human Race." (*Mark* xvi. 15) The great God "now commandeth *all* Men *every* where to repent." (*Acts* xvii. 30) And when the Apostles went out to discharge their extensive Commission, the Holy Spirit concurred with them, and rendered their Labours successful in Asia, Europe and Africa, without Distinction. He put no Difference between Jews and Gentiles, but purified the Hearts of both by the same Faith![E] The Doors of the Church were thrown wide open, for the Admission of all, that would come in upon the Terms of the Gospel. The Roman Centurion, the AEthiopian Eunuch, Onesimus, a run-away Slave, were as welcome, as the Jews in Jerusalem. "All were one in Christ Jesus; in whom there is neither Greek nor Jew, Barbarian, Scythian, Bond or Free." (*Colos.* iii. 11) A black Skin, African Birth or Extract, or a State of Slavery, does not disqualify a Man for the Blessings of the Gospel; does not exclude him from its Invitations, nor cast him out of the Charge of its Ministers. If History [16] may be credited, the Gospel did once flourish in Africa, and penetrated far into those inhospitable Desarts, which are now the Regions of Mahometism, or Heathen Idolatry. And we have all the Certainty which the *sure Word of Prophecy* can afford, that it will yet visit that miserable Country. Yes, Brethren, "the Earth shall be full of the Knowledge of the Lord, as the Waters cover the Sea." (*Isai.* xi. 9) "The Kingdoms of this World shall yet become the Kingdoms of our Lord, and of his Christ." (*Rev.* xi. 15) And "from

---

[E]Acts 15:9.

the rising of the Sun unto the going down of the same, his Name shall be great among the Gentiles; and in *every* Place Incense shall be offered to his Name." (*Mal.* i. 2) "AEthiopia," Guinea and Negroe-land, "shall yet stretch out their Hands unto God." (*Psal.* lxviii. 31) Negroes and Slaves are included in that "*Fulness* of the Gentiles," which, St. Paul tells us, "shall come in." (*Rom.* xi. 25) And may the happy Few, who in this Land of their Bondage, have been made Partakers of "the glorious Liberty of the Sons of God," be the First-fruits of this blessed Harvest to Christ in Africa!

And now, Brethren, do you not begin to feel this Argument conclude? Is Christianity adapted and intended to be the *universal* Religion of Mankind? And must it not then be the Duty of Christians, to do their utmost to spread it through the World? Is it the Design of Heaven, that it shall be propagated among all Nations? And is it not the Duty of Christians, especially of Masters, who have a Command over others, to concur in this gracious Design, and do all in their Power to [17] hasten that blessed Period, which has been so long the eager Wish and Hope of Believers? The Man that can be inactive and indifferent in such an Affair as this, must have a Temper directly contrary to that Religion which he professes; must be entirely careless about the Glory of God and the Redeemer, and the Happiness of his Fellow-Creatures, and disaffected to the gracious Designs of Providence towards them. Has he imbibed the Spirit of the Christian Religion, who can keep, perhaps, half a Score of Heathens under his Roof, and oblige them to drudge and toil for him all their Lives; and yet never labours to gain them to the Faith of Christ? Alas! how can he keep his Conscience easy in such a Course? But,

2. The Example of Christ and his Apostles obliges you to this Duty.

The Example of Christ must certainly be a Law to his Followers; and in vain do they pretend to that Character, unless they conform themselves to it. And what did Christ do in this Case? Why, he left all the Glories of his native Heaven; he assumed human Nature with all its common Infirmities, and, in Circumstances of uncommon Abasement, he spent Three and Thirty tedious and painful Years in this wretched World, and passed through an uninterrupted Series of Poverty, Fatigue, Ill-Treatment and Persecution; he at length died in Ignominy and Torture upon a Cross. And what was all this for? It was for *Africans*, as well as Britons: it was for the contemptible *Negroes*, as well as Whites: [18] it was for poor *Slaves*, as well as for their Masters. Yes, for poor *Negroes* and *Slaves*, he thought it worth his while to shed the Blood of his Heart. As "God would have *all* Men to be saved, and to come to the Knowledge of the Truth," so Christ "gave himself a Ransom for *all*;"[F] i.e. for

---

[F] I Timothy 2:4, 6.

some of *all Ranks* and *all Nations*. In this Extent, at least, the Words must be taken. This we may learn also from the Songs of Heaven, which run in this Strain, "Thou art worthy—for thou wast slain, and hast redeemed us unto God by thy Blood, out of *every* Kindred, and Tongue, and People, and Nation."[G] You see, Brethren, some of *every* Kindred, and Tongue, and People, and Nation, share in the Benefits of this Redemption, and therefore join in the Song of Praise. Africans and Americans, as well as Europeans and Asiatics, bear their Part in this celestial Concert. And oh! that the poor Negroes among us, who have so peculiar an Ear for Music and Psalmody, may be admitted to join in it, with still superior Extasy and Harmony!

I am sure, such of you as are Lovers of Christ, begin already to feel the Force of this Argument. Did he live and die, to save poor Negroes? And shall not we use all the Means in our Power, to make them Partakers of this Salvation? Did he pour out the Blood of his Heart for them? And shall we begrudge a little Labour and Pains to instruct them? We are not called to agonize and die upon a Cross for them: but Jesus was; and he did not refuse. And shall we refuse those easier [19] Endeavours for their Salvation, which are required on our Part? If we are capable of such a Conduct, it is high Time for us to renounce all Pretensions of Regard to him, and his Example.

The Example of the Apostles also, and the primitive Ministers of the Gospel, binds us to the same Duty. When they received their extensive Commission, the Love of Christ carried them through the World, to discharge it, among Jews and Gentiles, among Masters and Servants. Wherever they found a Sinner, they preached to him "Repentance towards God, and Faith towards the Lord Jesus Christ,"[21] without regard to the cutaneous Distinction of Colour, or the humble State of a Servant, or a Slave. "The *Poor* had the Gospel preached unto them;"[22] and among such it was most successful. "Not many mighty, not many noble after the Flesh, were called: but God chose the weak, the foolish, the base and despised Things of the World—that no Flesh should glory in his Presence." (*I Cor.* i. 26–29) St. Paul, in particular, the Chief of the Apostles, and who was eminently the Apostle of the *Gentiles*, shunned no Fatigues or Dangers, to carry this joyful News to the remotest and most barbarous Parts of the World. For this End, he became a wandering Pilgrim from Country to Country: he braved the Dangers of Sea and Land, and all the Terrors of Persecution; and at last gloriously died in the Attempt. Servants and Slaves were not beneath his Care. Many Parts of his Writings are addressed to them; from whence we learn, that

---

[G]Revelation 5:9.
[21]Acts 20:21.
[22]Matthew 11:5; Luke 7:22.

many of them had embraced [20] the Gospel, which he had published in their Ears. He thought it an Object worthy of his apostolic Office, to give them Directions for their Behaviour, and to exhort them to be chearfully contented with their mortifying Condition in Life. "Let every Man, says he, abide in that Calling, wherein he was called." Christianity makes no Alterations in Matters of Property, in civil Distinctions or Employments. "Art thou called, being a *Servant?* Care not for it—for he that is called, being a Servant, is the Lord's Freeman."[H] The Servants he here speaks to, were probably not indented Servants or Hirelings, but what we call *Slaves*.[I] And in those Times it was a much more common Practice, than it is now among the civilized Nations of Europe, to make *Slaves* of the Prisoners taken in War. But even to these, St. Paul says, "If thou art called, being a Servant, or a Slave, *care not* for it:" a Christian may be happy, even in a State of Slavery. Liberty, the sweetest and most valuable of all Blessings, is not essential to his Happiness: for if he is destitute of civil Liberty, he enjoys a Liberty still more noble and divine: "He is the Lord's free Man." The Son hath made him free from the Tyranny of Sin and Satan; and therefore he is free indeed. What a striking Instance is this, both of apostolic Zeal for poor Slaves, and of the invaluable Advantages of being a Christian, which can [21] render the lowest and most laborious Station in Life so insignificant, that a Man need *not care* for it, but continue in it with a generous Indifferency! I shall only add one Instance more, and that is the Case of Onesimus, Philemon's Servant. He had been once unprofitable to his Master, and run away from him, as some of your Negroes do now. But in his Ramblings, he happened to come in St. Paul's Way, while a Prisoner in Rome. The Apostle did not despise the unhappy *Runagade*, but esteemed his Conversion to Christianity a Prize worth labouring for. He therefore communicated the Gospel to him; and it pleased God to open his Heart to receive it, and he became a sincere Convert. Upon this, the Apostle wrote a Letter to his Master in his Favour, which is still preserved, among his immortal Epistles, for the Benefit of the Church in all Ages. He shews all the Affection and Concern of a Father for him, and does not disdain to call him *his Son*, dear to him as *his own Bowels*. "I beseech thee," says he to his Master, "for *my Son* Onesimus, whom I have begotten in my Bonds: who in Time past was unprofitable, but now is profitable to thee, and me: whom I have sent again: thou therefore receive him that is *mine own Bowels*—for perhaps he therefore

---

[H]I Corinthians 7:20–22.

[I]So the original Word δουλος often signifies: and so it is rendered by Dr. Doddridge. *Fam. Exp. In loc.*
Philip Doddridge (1702–1751) was a nonconformist minister. In addition to sermons and commentaries on the Scriptures, Doddridge wrote a great many hymns, often patterning them on the model of Isaac Watts. The book Davies refers to is Philip Doddridge, *The Family Expositor, or a Paraphrase and Version of the New Testament*, 6 Vols. (London, 1739–1756).

departed for a Season, that thou shouldst receive him for ever; not now as a Servant, but above a Servant, a *Brother beloved*, especially to me; but how much more to thee, both in the Flesh and in the Lord? If thou count me therefore a Partner, receive him *as myself*. If he hath wronged thee, or oweth thee ought, put that on mine Account. I Paul have written [22] it with my own Hand, I will repay it. Yea, Brother, let me have Joy of thee in the Lord: refresh my Bowels in the Lord, by thy Compliance."[J] What fatherly Affection and Solicitude, what ardent Zeal is here, for a poor run-away Slave! How different is this from the prevailing Spirit of the Christians of our Age? Had the Apostles and their Fellow-Labourers been as careless about propagating the Gospel among Heathens, as the Generality among us are, Christianity would have soon died in that Corner of the World, where it had its Birth; and we and the rest of Mankind would now have been as much Heathens, as the African Negroes?

But do these Examples lay no Obligation upon us to follow them? Did the Apostles discover such an ardent Zeal for the Salvation even of Servants and Slaves; and shall we be quite negligent and careless about it? Did they take so much Pains, pass through such severe Sufferings, risk their Lives, and even lose them, in the generous Attempt? And shall not we take the easier Measures required of us for their Conversion? Alas! Is the Spirit of primitive Christianity entirely lost upon Earth? Or is Christianity declined with Age, and become an insignificant Thing, unworthy of zealous Propagation? Or have the Souls of Slaves lost their Value, so that it is no Matter what becomes of them? How can you pretend to learn your Religion from the Apostles; and yet have Crowds of Negroes in your Houses or Quarters, as ignorant Heathens, as when they left the Wilds of Africa, [23] without using any Means for their Conversion? Will ye not endeavour to be Followers of the Apostles in this Respect, as they also were of Christ? If their Example has no Weight, methinks the Conduct of Jews, Heathens, and Mahometans may shame you. They are all zealous to gain Proselytes to their Religion, though antiquated, or false. And will not you labour to proselyte your Domestics to the divine Religion of Jesus? Certainly, if you do not, even Jews, Heathens and Mahometans may rise up in Judgment against you. But,

3. Your Duty in this Respect will appear, from the Worth and Importance of the Souls of your poor Slaves—This I have hinted at already; but it deserves a more full Illustration.

The Appointments of Providence, and the Order of the World, not only admit, but require, that there should be civil Distinctions among Mankind; that some should rule, and some be subject; that some should be Masters, and some

---

[J]Epistle to Philemon.

Servants. And Christianity does not blend or destroy these Distinctions, but establishes and regulates them, and enjoins every Man to conduct himself according to them. In this Respect, there are many Distinctions in the World. But these Distinctions are confined to this World, and do not reach beyond the Grave. As to the Affairs of Religion and Eternity, all Men stand upon the same Footing. The meanest Slave is as immortal as his Master; as capable of Happiness or Misery, in the highest Degree, and of eternal Duration; as much a Candidate for Heaven or Hell. Now it is this that gives Importance [24] to a Being. An Angel, or the most exalted Creature, if the Being of a Day, or a thousand Years, would be but a Trifle, a Shadow. When his Day, or his thousand Years are past, he is as much nothing, as if he had never been. It is little Matter what becomes of him; let him stand, or fall; let him be happy, or miserable; it is all one in a little Time. But Immortality is so important an Attribute, that it adds a Kind of infinite Value to every Being to which it belongs, however mean and insignificant in other Respects. An IMMORTAL! a Being that shall never cease to be! a Being whose Existence runs on for ever in parallel Lines, with that of the eternal Father of Spirits! a Being whose Powers of Action, and whose Capacities for Pleasure or Pain, shall never become decrepit or contracted, but ripen, improve and enlarge, thro' the Revolutions of eternal Ages! a Being, that shall perpetually ascend, in an endless Gradation, from Glory to Glory, from Perfection to Perfection, in the Scale of Blessedness; or that shall sink for ever, from Deep to Deep, from Gulph to Gulph, in Hell! What an awful important Being is this! a Sharer with Angels, in their highest Prerogative and Dignity! a black Skin, or a State of Slavery for sixty or seventy Years, is no Consideration at all, in our Estimate of such a Being.[K] To be entrusted with the [25] Care of such a Being, in its State of Trial, to form it for its everlasting State! How vast, how awful the Trust! To be instrumental to render such a Being happy, through

---

[K]*"Immortal!* Ages past, yet nothing gone!
Morn without Eve! a Race without a Goal!
Unshortened by Progression infinite!
Futurity for ever future! Life
Beginning still, where Computation ends!
'Tis the Description of a Deity!
'Tis the Description of the meanest *Slave!*
The meanest *Slave,* dares then Lorenzo scorn?
The meanest *Slave* thy sovereign Glory shares—
Man's *lawful* Pride includes Humility;
Stoops to the lowest; is too *great* to find
Inferiors; all *immortal!* Brothers all!
Proprietors *eternal* of thy Love.["]
        Night Thoughts, Number 6
  The reference is to Edward Young, *The Complaint; Or, Night Thoughts,* Night VI (The Infidel Reclaimed), lines 542–55.

its immortal Duration! to "SAVE A SOUL FROM DEATH!" to save that precious immortal Thing, the *Soul!* to save it from *Death!* from that *dreadful* Kind of Death, which a *Soul* can die.[L] How benevolent an Act, how noble an Exploit, how glorious a Salvation is this! more benevolent, more noble, more glorious, than to deliver Nations from Slavery, or Famine, or the severest *temporal* Distress. But to be accessary by Negligence, or more *direct* Means, to the Ruin, the eternal Ruin, of such a Being! to render its Immortality its Curse, a meer Capacity of immortal [26] Pain! how horrid the Crime! how deep the Guilt! how shocking the Thought! To be accessary to the Murder of the Body, to lay Countries waste, and turn Cities into ruinous Heaps, were nothing, in Comparison of this: for what are mortal Bodies, perishable Countries and Cities, when compared to an immortal Soul? Well, *such* a Soul, such a *precious immortal* Soul, has the meanest *Slave.* Yes, those stupid despised black Creatures, that many treat as if they were Brutes, are, in this important Respect, upon an Equality with their haughty Masters. And can you think it is no Concern of yours, to endeavour to bring these Immortals into the Way of Salvation, and save them from an endless Duration of exquisite Misery? God has communicated to you the *grand Secret* of obtaining his Favour, and eternal Life; I mean the Revelation of Jesus Christ, which you have in your Bibles: "a Mystery, which was hid from Ages and Generations."[23] And he has communicated it to *you,* that you may communicate it to *others,* particularly to your Domestics, who are your immediate Care. And will you still reserve it to yourselves, when immortal Souls under your Roof, are perishing for Want of the Knowledge of it? Is it nothing to you, that their Blood should be upon your Heads; or that the supreme Judge should condemn you, as accessary to their eternal Destruction? What do you think of being shut up with them, in the same infernal Prison, without any Distinction or Superiority; unless it be *distinguished* and *superior* Misery, as having sinned in spite of clearer Conviction, and stronger Obligations? Are you Proof [27] against the Terrors of such a Thought? Or are you insensible to the generous Pleasure of being instrumental in rendering those happy for ever, in the World to come, who have done you so much Service in this; and in peopling the heavenly Regions with Inhabitants transplanted from the barbarous Wilds of Africa? I beseech you, have Pity upon these miserable Immortals. For God's Sake, for their Sakes, and for your own, do not let them sink into Hell from between your

---

[L]This Paraphrase seems to me to point out the striking Emphasis of the Apostle's short Expression. (*James* v. 19, 20) "Brethren, if any of you err from the Truth, and one convert him; let him know" this for his Encouragement, and he neither needs, nor can have a stronger "that he which converteth the Sinner from the Error of his Way, SHALL SAVE A SOUL FROM DEATH." An illustrious self-rewarding Exploit! a glorious Salvation indeed!

[23]Colossians 1:26.

Hands, for want of a little Pains to instruct them. I hope you would by no Means exercise Barbarities upon their Bodies; and will you be so barbarous, as to suffer their precious never-dying Souls to perish for ever; when, thro' the divine Blessing, you might be the Means of saving them? Sure you are not capable of such inhuman Cruelty.

4. The Duty I am urging will appear, if you consider the happy Influence your religious Instructions might have upon your Negroes, even for your *own Interest*.

Your own Interest inclines you to wish, they would become good Servants; faithful, honest, diligent and laborious. Now there is no Expedient in the World, that can so effectually render them such, as to make them *real Christians*. You cannot but own, that the *Precepts* of Christianity, are a compleat Directory for the Behaviour of Servants, and enjoin upon them every Duty, that a Master can reasonably require of them: and that the *Temper* and *Spirit* of Christianity, [28] is the most excellent and amiable, that can adorn human Nature, in any Station of Life. There never was a good Christian yet, who was a bad Servant. To be a Christian, as it refers to Man, is to be obedient to Superiors, kind and benevolent to all, faithful in every Trust, diligent in every Calling. And is not this the very Character you wish your Servants to deserve? Well, endeavour to make them true Christians; and if God bless your Endeavours, such they will be. Indeed, they may be baptized, and be Christians in *Name*, and yet be as bad Servants, and as bad Men, as if they were Heathens. But this is not the Thing I am urging. Endeavour to make them Christians *indeed*; and then you will find, they will deserve the Character I have described. This will make them better Servants, than the Terror of the Lash, and all the servile and mercenary Measures you can use with them. Then they will be governed by a *Principle of Conscience* towards God: a Principle, which will make them as honest and diligent in your Absence, as while under your Eye. Then, according to St. Paul's Injunctions, they will "be obedient to their Masters in all *lawful* Things; not with Eye-service, as Men-pleasers, but in Singleness of Heart, fearing God;" whose Eye, they will be sensible, is always upon them. Then, "whatsoever they do, they will do it *heartily*, as to the Lord, and not to Men: knowing, that of the Lord they shall receive the Reward" of their Fidelity; "for they serve the Lord Christ," even in serving their earthly Masters; and he will reward the Service, as [29] done to himself.[M] You see, therefore, that your *own Interest* would be promoted by this Means: In other Cases, you are not insensible of the powerful Influence of Interest. And shall it not prevail upon you, to use proper Endeavours for

---

[M]Colossians 3:22–24.

the Conversion of your poor Negroes? Did some spend that Time in the Use of such Endeavours, which they spend in tying them up, and whipping them, they would probably receive more Advantage from it. Resolve, at least, to make Trial of this Expedient; and pray for a divine Blessing upon it: and you will probably see the happy Effects of it.

5. The Zeal and Generosity of others may stir you up to the Discharge of this Duty.

Sundry good People in *England,* at the Distance of near Four thousand Miles, who have no Connection with your Slaves, but what they have with human Nature in general, are much more zealous and active for their Conversion, than, alas! Thousands of their Masters among us. As Reading is one important Mean of acquiring religious Knowledge, they are very solicitous the Negroes should learn to read; and that such of them as have learned, should be furnished with good Books. For this Purpose, they have been at the Expence of Two hundred Pounds Sterling in Books, which they have, at different Times, sent over to be distributed among them. A most seasonable, pious and disinterested Charity! And may the God of all [30] Grace crown it with Success! I solicit your Prayers with my own, for this Blessing; that our generous Benefactors, though they should not receive the Intelligence sooner, may meet in Heaven with many from Virginia, both Whites and Blacks, who were brought thither by Means of this Charity. And I cannot but hope, and even believe, that this, in some Instances, will be the happy Consequence. Such Assistance from so remote a Quarter is a new Spring to my Endeavours among you; and gives me some Encouragement, that God has remarkably gracious Designs towards this guilty Land. It sometimes seems to me, as if the strong Holds of Sin and Satan among us were attacked from all Quarters; and therefore, that it is determined in Heaven, they shall fall. Oh! let your Prayers contribute to the Accomplishment of my Hope.

Now, my Brethren, I may leave yourselves to judge, whether the religious Instruction of your Negroes, be not a Duty incumbent upon *you.* Is this the Concern of Christians on the other Side of the vast Ocean? And is it not much more yours, for whom these poor Creatures labour and toil all their Lives, and who receive the Benefit of their Labours? No Creatures in the British Dominions stand in greater Need of such a Charity from our British Friends, than the poor Negroes among us. But yet, I must say, this Necessity proceeds rather from the Want of pious Zeal and Generosity in their Masters, than from the Want of Ability. Certainly, he that can lay out Forty or Fifty Pounds to purchase a Slave, is able to spare a few Shillings to furnish him with a few Books for his Instruction. This [31] is undoubtedly the Case in general, though there are some Exceptions. And who so strongly obliged to furnish your Slaves with these, as yourselves, who reap the Benefit of their Labours? Methinks you might blush to receive Assistance in this Case. But waving this Point at present, what I would inculcate upon you is, that you would, at *least*, concur with the Endeavours of the noble-spirited Benefactors, to christianize your own Domestics. Let their Example fire you with Emulation, and engage you in this apostolic Work. Some of you, I doubt not, will honestly make the Attempt. But alas! I am afraid, others will continue negligent, even after these Helps are put into their Hands. If so, I warn you beforehand, that you must give an Account to the great God for your criminal Omission; and it is Time for you to bethink yourselves, what Defence or Excuse you shall be able to make. To enforce this Argument the more, let me add,

6. The Relation you bear to your Negroes as their *Masters*, obliges you to instruct them in the Christian Religion.

Indeed, this Duty is not yours *alone:* it is the Duty of *every* Christian, according to his Station, to do all in his Power for the Conversion of others: and there is no Person so insignificant, but he may contribute something, through divine Grace, to this benevolent Design. The meanest Member in a Family may drop a Word, or at least lead a Life, that may tend to give favourable Impressions of Christianity to those around [32] him. The Instruction of Negroes is particularly the Duty of *Overseers*, who have the immediate Care of them; and they will find it impossible to excuse themselves, by flinging the Fault upon the Owners; especially if they are removed beyond the Reach of the Owner's Inspection. Their Souls will be required of the Overseer's Hand. And I tremble to think, what a terrible Account many of them must give. But after all, the Care originally and principally lies upon the Masters and Proprietors. It is as much their Duty to feed their Minds with sacred Knowledge, as to feed and clothe their Bodies. All the numerous and strong Arguments for Family-Religion in general, are equally conclusive in Favour of this particular Branch of it. But I cannot now take Time to mention them. Will the Example of *Abraham* in my Text, have no Weight with you? Are not you under the same Obligations with *Joshua*, to resolve, that, let others do what they please, "as for you and your *House*, you will serve the Lord?"[N] It is mentioned to the Honour of the Roman Centurion, that he feared God *with all his House*; and some of his *houshold Servants* or Slaves, and the Soldiers under him, were devout Men.[O] And why should not you endeavour to render your Slaves such? But I need not enlarge upon so plain a

---

[N]Joshua 24:15.
[O]Acts 10:1, 7.

Point. I will venture to leave it to your own Consciences, to determine, whether God would place immortal Souls under your Care, without obliging you to endeavour to educate them for a happy Eternity? Shall they work and [33] drudge for you all their Lives? And are not you bound, in Justice and Gratitude, to retaliate them, by endeavouring to make them Partakers of the rich Blessings of the Gospel? Will you not labour to make this Land of their Slavery, a Land of spiritual Liberty to them; and to bring them to share in the heavenly Inheritance, in Exchange for their Liberty, and as a Reward for the Fruits of their Labours, which you enjoy?

And now, upon a Review of all these Arguments together, I would have you come to some Conclusion what you intend to do with regard to this Duty, of which, I presume, you are now convinced. Brethren, what do you determine to do? I am sure, if you have any Regard to the Religion you profess, or the divine Author of it; if you have any Regard to the Salvation of an immortal Soul, or to the Laws of Justice and Gratitude; if you have the least Spark of sincere Piety towards God, or true Benevolence to Men; you will honestly begin the Attempt, and will not dare to live one Week more, in the Neglect of so plain and important a Duty. But I know, those that are disaffected to the Duty, will try to ward off the Conviction, by various Pleas and Excuses. And were you now to speak your Minds, I should probably hear you start a thousand Objections.

Some of you, perhaps, would object, "That your Negroes are such sullen perverse Creatures, or stupid Dunces, that it is impossible to teach them any Thing that is good." This is undoubtedly the true Character of some of them; and it must afford a great deal of Grief to [34] such of you, as are really concerned for their everlasting Happiness. All you can do, in such a discouraging Case, is, to continue your Endeavours; and earnestly pray for a Blessing upon them, from that God, who alone can render them efficacious. And who knows what may be the Issue? Do you wait patiently; and you may yet reap the Fruits of your pious Labours. Sullen, and perverse, and stupid as they are, divine Grace can render them gentle, pliable, and teachable, as a little Child. But should your Endeavours always continue unsuccessful, as you may expect they will with regard to sundry; yet you have this solid Consolation left you, that you are clear of their Blood, and have delivered your own Soul, and your Reward is with the Lord. He will accept and reward even *unsuccessful* Fidelity. But I am apprehensive this Objection, in many Cases, is but an idle Pretence. Your Negroes may be ignorant and stupid as to divine Things, not for want of Capacity, but for want of Instruction; not through their Perverseness, but through your Negligence. From the many Trials I have made, I have Reason to conclude, that making Allowance for their low and barbarous Education, their imperfect Acquaintance with our Language, their having no Opportunity for intellectual Improvements, and the like, they are generally as capable of Instruction, as the white People. Besides, Christianity, as far as it is essential to Salvation, is not a difficult Science; and if they do not learn it, the Fault lies in the Heart, rather than in the Head. Some of them shew, that they have Sense enough to love God, and hate Sin, though they are very ignorant [35] in other Respects. But to be short—Be sure you make a thorough Trial, before you start this Objection. Take all proper Means to teach them, before you conclude they are unteachable. And bear upon your Minds a deep Sense of the Vanity of all human Endeavours, without the Concurrence of the Holy Spirit; for which, pray without ceasing.[24]

Some of you, perhaps, will object, "That you can find no Time to instruct your Negroes; nor can you allow them Time to attend to Instruction." I grant, that Religion should by no Means be made a Pretence for Idleness in Masters or Servants; and that moderate Industry in your lawful Callings, is as much your Duty, in its Place, as the religious Instruction of your Domestics. But granting this, there is no plausible Ground for the Objection after all. For are not the Affairs of Eternity of infinitely greater Importance to you, than those of Time? Should you not be much more solicitous how you and yours shall subsist through eternal Ages, than how you shall subsist for a few Years in this vanishing World? If a proper Care of the one, be inconsistent with the other, to which should you give the Preference? If you have not Time enough to lay out upon both, which, do you think, should be neglected? Time or Eternity? Earth or Heaven? your perishing Bodies, or your immortal Spirits? Can you hesitate a Moment in so plain a Case? Whatever become of yourselves or your Families in this World, by no means neglect to provide for your and their Happiness in the eternal World, which is just before you. Whatever be undone, let not the Work [36] of Salvation be undone. Rather be poor, yea, rather perish through Hunger and Nakedness in this World, than let your Souls and Bodies, and those of your Slaves, perish for ever in the World to come. This is a sufficient Answer to your Objection, upon the worst Supposition you can possibly make, *viz.* that the religious Instruction of your Negroes is inconsistent with your temporal Interest, and would render them useless, or a Burden to you. But this Supposition is wholly groundless: for the Discharge of your Duty to them, would not take up so much Time, as that the Loss would be perceivable at a Year's End. Let this Duty take up your Sunday Evenings, and other leisure Hours, which both you and your Slaves now spend in trifling or sinning. And if you should set apart two or three stated

---

[24]I Thessalonians 5:17.

Hours in the Week for this Purpose, where would be the mighty Loss? Will you begrudge this short Space of Time for the Salvation of those poor Creatures, who spend their whole Lives in your Service? Besides, you may easily drop a Word of Instruction, while you are looking after them in the Field. Their Ears are open, and their Thoughts may be employed about divine Things, with an Ax or a Hoe in their Hands. In short, you will find, that this Duty may be so managed, as to be no Hindrance at all to your Business: and in the Issue, it may be a great Advantage to it. For if God should bless your pious Diligence, it will render them much better Servants to you, as well as to him. Therefore, no longer think to excuse yourself with this frivolous Pretence; but immediately attempt what is unquestionably your Duty.

Will [37] any of you farther object, "That christianizing the Negroes makes them proud and saucy, and tempts them to imagine themselves upon an Equality with white People?" But is this the *native Tendency* of real genuine Christianity? Is the true Christian Spirit haughty and insolent? Do the Doctrines or Precepts of Christianity tend to cherish Pride and Disobedience? If you think so, why do you not renounce it yourselves? Will you profess a Religion, which has a native Tendency to make Men worse, and cherishes and confirms their wicked Dispositions? Will you initiate your Children into such a diabolical Religion? If you have such Notions of Christianity, you are as rank Heathens at Heart, as the rudest African Negroe: and your Christian Profession is a most glaring Absurdity. But you cannot but know in your Consciences, that *true* Christianity is quite another Thing; that it tends to inspire its Subjects with Modesty, Humility, Meekness, Faithfulness, and every Grace and Virtue; and that a *good Christian* will always be a *good Servant*. Recollect what I have said on this Head already, and it will entirely remove your Objection. I grant indeed, that there is nothing so excellent, but the depraved Heart of Man may be capable of abusing it to the vilest Purposes. But this is no Objection against the *Thing*, but against the unnatural *Abuse* of it. A Man may be proud of his good Sense, Learning, Estate, or any real or imaginary Excellency. But will you hence infer, that you should keep yourselves or your Children ignorant, illiterate, poor, and destitute of every good Quality, in order to keep you humble and pliable, and to guard [38] against Pride and Insolence? Upon this Principle, you would leave human Nature naked of every Excellency, and, to prevent Pride, make it a meer Mass of Deformity. In like Manner, the holy Religion of Jesus may be abused as an Occasion of Vanity and Self-conceit, by those that usurp the Name and external Badges of it, without imbibing its Spirit. A Negroe may desire to be baptized, merely that he may be in the Fashion; and even from this base Principle he may be prompted to make such a Profession of his Faith and Repentance, as the Ministers of the Gospel, who cannot inspect the Heart, may judge sufficient for his Admission to the Privileges of the visible Church, though his Profession was but gross Hypocrisy in the Sight of God, and may afterwards appear such to them. Baptism and the Christian Name may indeed render such a wretched Creature worse. But that is not because he *is* a Christian, but because he is *not* a Christian, that is, a Christian *indeed*, while he vainly *imagines* himself such. Nothing can be inferred from hence, but that great Care should be taken in the Admission of Catechumens to Baptism: And it is your Duty to give all the Informations to Ministers on this Point, which may help to direct them in so difficult and important an Affair. I am sensible that the Ordinance of Baptism, learning the Creed, Ten Commandments and the Lord's Prayer, a confused Desire to be admitted to Church Privileges, and such superficial Qualifications, are far from rendering them *true* Christians; and if they are admitted upon no better Evidence, they, as it were, receive a deadly Blow [39] from the Hand that baptizes them; and the Christian Name will be of no Service to *them;* and they are likely to be a Scandal to *it.* Let them first see their Sins; let their Hearts be broken with penitential Sorrows for them; let them long and cry after Jesus as the only Saviour; and receive him with all their Hearts; let them, in short, give some hopeful Evidences, that they are Christians indeed; and then let them wear the Christian Name, and share in all the Privileges of the Children of God. Some such, blessed be God, are to be found among us; and to their Lives I may refer you for the most effectual Confutation of your Objection. Are not the Savages transformed into Lambs and Doves? They still have their Imperfections; and the best Christian among us cannot boast an entire Freedom from them in this Life: but are they not habitually humble and meek, dutiful, faithful, diligent, and the Reverse of what they once were? Such would all the Negroes be, were they all sincere Christians: and what can be a more striking Evidence of the happy Tendency and powerful Efficacy of our holy Religion, to make Men of all Nations, and in all Stations, truly good?

But you will perhaps say, "Some, who once made a great Profession of Religion, and were baptized, have apostatized, and become as bad as ever." This, alas! is true as to some: and the Lord have Mercy on the miserable Backsliders, whose last State is worse than their first! But you know, this is not the Case of all, nor, I hope, of the Generality: and to find even a few chosen, among the many that are [40] called, is an unspeakable Pleasure; and a sufficient Encouragement to the Duty I am recommending. But were the Ground of this Complaint more general than it is, what would you infer from it? that it is not the Duty of Christians to propagate their Religion, and particularly of Christian Masters to propagate it among their Domestics? This would be an extravagant Inference indeed; and upon this Principle, you would banish all Religion out of the World. Are there no Apostates among white People, among Britons and Virginians? Would to God there were not! but the melancholy Fact is too notorious to be denied. And shall all religious Instructions be given up on this Account; and the immortal Religion of Jesus suffered to die with the present Generation, without any farther Endeavours to preserve and spread it, lest some that have pretended to embrace it, should afterwards renounce it in Practice or Profession? The Truth is, Offences must come; Apostasies must happen, in the present State of Things. There have been Apostates from all the Religions that ever were in the World, whether true or false: Apostates from Judaism, Mahometism, Heathenism, (if I may call them Apostates) as well as from Christianity. And if we must give over our Attempts to propagate it on this Account, it is to consent to put an End to all Religion, whether Natural or Revealed, whether true or false. The best Remedy against this, is what I prescribed in Answer to the last Objection, *viz.* to take all possible Care, that none be admitted to Baptism, and into the Christian Church, but such as give hopeful Evidences of a thorough [41] Conversion. After all, it must, alas! be expected, that while Ministers can judge only by *external* Appearances, and some even of the unpolished Negroes are artful enough to deceive, many will unavoidably be admitted, who, like the Crowds of Christians among us of a *fairer* Colour, are but Hypocrites; and, notwithstanding all their Privileges, will be condemned at last as Workers of Iniquity; or may, perhaps, even in this Life, throw of the Mask, and render it necessary to exclude them from the Communion of Christians.

The dullest of Mankind have generally a very ready Invention to find out Objections against a Duty that is disagreeable to them: And it may be impossible for me to particularize them all. But I dare say, your Judgment is already convinced; and, however unwilling you may be to own it, your Conscience is on my Side. You may pretend this and that as the Reason of your Omission. But shall I tell you the plain Truth? The true Reason is, your stupid Carelessness about Religion, and about your own Souls, as well as those of your Slaves. Could this Objection, the Objection, not of your *Reason*, but of a *wicked Heart*, be once removed, we should hear no more of the rest. For this is a certain Truth, that he that loves Religion himself, will endeavour to bring others to love it; he that is concerned about his own Salvation, will be also concerned about that of others; and he, and only he, who is careless what becomes of his own Soul, can be careless about the Souls committed to his Charge. And are you fit for Heaven, or likely to be admitted thither, while this Temper [42] is predominant in you? Are you prepared for the Region of Holiness, while you are thus disaffected to it? Alas! no; in your present Condition, you are *fitted for Destruction*, and nothing else. And is it not Time for you to awake to the Care of your *own* immortal Souls? When once you begin to take Care of them, you will soon extend your Care to the Souls of your poor Negroes.

And now, Sirs, may I not hope, you are determined to live in the willful Neglect of this Duty no longer? If not, will you not be self-condemned? Will you not carry an uneasy Monitor in your own Breasts, that will be perpetually urging you to your Duty, and remonstrating against your Omissions of it? And oh! what Account will you give to the great God at last? Oh! that you may think of it in Time: for I can assure you, it deserves your most serious Thoughts.

What now remains is, to give you some Directions for the right Performance of this Duty. And these shall refer both to the *Qualifications* required in you as the Instructors of your Slaves, and the best *Manner* of instructing them. I shall not enlarge upon either: for, I know, if you are zealously set upon the Discharge of the Duty, a few short Hints as to the Manner, will be sufficient.

The Directions with regard to *yourselves* are such as these.

Endeavour to furnish your own Minds with religious Knowledge; otherwise, it is impossible [43] you should communicate religious Knowledge to your Domestics. For this Purpose, read, hear, pray, meditate, and diligently attend upon all Means of Instruction. In this Way, you may hope to remove an Objection, which, alas! has as much Truth in it, as any of those I have answered, *viz.* "That you are so ignorant yourselves, that you are not capable of teaching others." How scandalous and criminal is this, to be ignorant of the Religion you profess! to be ignorant of it, with Bibles in your Hands, and Means of Instruction all around you! How dangerous a State this is! Can you expect to *blunder* into Heaven at Random, without knowing the Way that leads to it? Alas! you may be destroyed for *lack of Knowledge*,[P] as well as by the grossest Vice. Therefore labour to furnish your Minds with useful Knowledge. Again;

Endeavour to maintain a deep Sense of eternal Things upon your Spirits. Or, labour to get your Hearts deeply impressed with the Things you know. This will at once excite you to use proper Means for the Conversion of those under your Care, and make you serious and solemn in the Use of them.

Let your Example enforce your Instructions, and exhibit to them a living Pattern of practical Religion. The dullest Negroe has Sense enough to see the Absurdity of a meer Profession of Religion, without a correspondent Practice.

[P]Hosea 4:6.

But if they see that your Religion makes you good Men, and [44] consequently good Masters, it will be a strong Presumption to them in its Favour.

In a Word, Endeavour to be true Christians yourselves, in Knowledge, in
Temper, and in Practice; and then you are qualified to instruct your Families.
But without these Qualifications, you will not either make the Attempt; or
are not likely to succeed in it.

Let me now add a few Directions as to the *Manner and Ways* of Instruction.

Encourage your Negroes to learn to read, and give them all the Assistance in your Power. Encourage your Children to teach them: or let one of
themselves be taught either at Home, or at School; and let him teach the
rest.Q There may be some of them so old, so stupid, or so ignorant of our
Language, that it may be almost impossible to teach them. But as to the
Young, especially those that are born in your Houses; and as to those that
are desirous to learn, though advanced in Age, I have found by Experience, this Direction is very practicable. Let us zealously [45] make the Attempt with the present Generation; and then they will be able to teach
their Children themselves; and thus this useful Branch of Learning will be
conveyed down to their Posterity, with little Trouble or Expence to their
Owners.

Frequently speak seriously to them upon the great Concerns of Religion.

Endeavour to teach them some short Summary of the Christian Religion.
And I know none so proper for them, because none so plain, as Dr. *Watts first
and second Setts of Catechisms:*[25] which, if you cannot, or will not provide for
them, I shall endeavour to furnish them with.

Maintain the daily Worship of God in your Families. And endeavour to
time it so, that your Slaves may have Opportunity of attending. What can
more familiarly teach them their Wants and Mercies, their Duties and Sins,
than to hear you solemnly mention them every Day in your Prayers to God?

Restrain them from rambling about on the Lord's Day, the most proper
Time for them to get Knowledge; and do not connive at their working upon
it for themselves; much less oblige them to it, in order to furnish themselves
with those Necessaries, which it is your Duty to provide for them. *Command
and oblige them* to spend those sacred Hours in public and private Atten-

---

QAs I would earnestly recommend reading the Scriptures and singing the Praises of God as Parts of
Family-Religion; so I would recommend it, as an easy and very useful Expedient to improve the Negroes in Reading, that, when they begin to read, they be ordered to bring their Bibles and Psalm Books
with them, when they attend upon Family-Worship, and to look over the Chapter or Psalm, as it is
read by the Master of the House. This I have found by Experience to be a very good Expedient.

[25]Isaac Watts, *The First Catechism of the Principles of Religion: or, The Catechism for a Young Child,
to be Begun at Three or Four Years Old* (London, 1730); and *The Second Sett of Catechisms and Prayers:
or, Some Helps to the Religion of Children . . . from Seven to Twelve Years of Age* (London, 1730).

dance upon divine Worship; and endeavour to make them sensible of the Ends and Designs of it.

Maintain [46] a proper Authority over them, and do not make yourselves contemptible to them, by excessive Familiarity and Indulgence. But, on the other Hand, do not treat them with Barbarity, as if they were Dogs, and had no Share in the same human Nature with yourselves.

Finally; be always sensible, that the Success of all your Endeavours depends upon the Concurrence of divine Grace; and earnestly pray to God for the Blessed Spirit to make them effectual.

These short Directions are easy to be understood by those that are disposed to practice them. And certainly, they are not impracticable, thro' the Grace of God, to a Christian. The Objections against them must arise not from Reason or Inability, but from a slothful disaffected Heart. The Omission will involve you in very dreadful Guilt, and it is likely to occasion the eternal Ruin of Thousands of immortal Souls. The Observance of them, through the divine Blessing, might contribute to your Satisfaction and Interest in Time and Eternity, and advance a very miserable Part of human Nature to all the Glory and Happiness of the heavenly World. If any of you are Proof against the Energy of such Considerations as these, I have none more weighty or affecting to propose to you. But some of you, I doubt not, have already felt their Force, and others will, I hope, submit to it for the future. Which may God grant for Jesus' Sake. *Amen.*

CHAPTER SIX

~

Thomas Bacon:
Second Sermon on Colossians 4:1[1]

Thomas Bacon (1700?–1768), poet, composer, wit, publisher, and minister, traveled to Maryland in 1745 where he soon took charge of St. Peter's in Talbot County. Bacon was also embarking on a new career when he set sail for Maryland. He had previously managed the coffeehouse owned by his wife, "a smart widow," and published two newspapers, the *Dublin Mercury*, one of the more literary of the town's papers, and later Ireland's official newspaper, the *Dublin Gazette*. In 1743 Bacon decided to give up his career in publishing and began to prepare for a vocation in the ministry, studying for his exams with Thomas Wilson, bishop of Sodor and Man.

Bacon prospered in Maryland. In 1747 one acquaintance wrote that he had already become "a very considerable Man here and in great Esteem with every Man from the Governor to the Parish Clarke." He composed minuets and performed concerts. He was elected an honorary member of the famous Tuesday Club and frequently delighted the members with his violin playing.

As a minister, Bacon was especially interested in educating poor children and spreading the Gospel to slaves. He started a charity school in 1752 and sometimes performed concerts to help raise funds for the institution. He also published numerous discourses on the duty of Christianizing slaves as well

---

[1]*Sermons Addressed to Masters and Servants, and Published in the Year 1743 [sic], by the Rev. Thomas Bacon, . . .*, ed. William Meade (Winchester, Va.: 1813 [?]), 23–40. Used courtesy of The Colonial Williamsburg Foundation. Bacon's sermon first appeared in Thomas Bacon, *Four Sermons, upon the great and indispensable Duty of Christian Masters and Mistresses to bring up their Negro Slaves in the Knowledge and Fear of God* (London, 1750).

as discourses preached to slaves "at their *Funerals* (several of which I attended)—and to such small Congregations as their *Marriages* have brought together, as well as at my own House, on Sunday, and other Evenings, when those in the neighbourhood come in." His published sermons on the duty of Christianizing slaves found a welcome audience among many Virginians. He visited Williamsburg and preached at Bruton Parish on several occasions during the 1750s.[2]

> *Masters give unto your Servants that which is just and equal, knowing that ye also have a Master in Heaven.* Colossians 4:1

In the former discourse upon these words, it was observed, how the great creator of heaven and earth, who is the common parent and protector of mankind, and consults the good of all his children in the course of his providential dealings towards them, hath been pleased to make all men, in some sort, dependent one upon another, and by a mutual exchange of service and assistance, to contribute to the comfort and support of each in particular, as well as the general benefit of the whole: And that upon this necessary intercourse of good offices are founded all the laws of society, the rules of equity, and those [24] particular *duties* which are called *relative*, and which make up the bulk of the moral obligations between man and man: every act of kindness or service, from one person to another, requiring its correspondent return. And that hence *servants*, have an undoubted right by the law of nature and reason, as well as by the revealed will of GOD, to have *what is just and equal* from their *masters*, in recompense of their labour.

Intending only to insist upon that principal branch of duty to our slaves which consist[s] in bringing them up in the knowledge and fear of almighty God, it was proposed to our consideration under the following heads:

I. The Nature of this great and indispensible Obligation.
II. The advantages attending a due compliance therewith.
III. The common objections and excuses which are made concerning it.
IV. In what manner this duty may best be performed, to the due discharge of our consciences, and with the greatest probability of success.

The first of these heads hath been already examined, and the nature and force of this obligation shewn, by various considerations drawn from—the nature of that service we receive from our Slaves, and the return we owe of

---

[2]J. A. Leo Lemay, *Men of Letters in Colonial Maryland* (Knoxville: University of Tennessee Press, 1972), 313–42; "Diary of John Blair," *William and Mary Quarterly* 1st ser. 7 (1899): 142–43, 147.

all necessaries suitable to the condition of men and women, the whole produce of whose lives and labours are bestowed upon us—the care and love of GOD towards all his creatures, and the apparent kind designs of his Providence, in sending them into a country where they may exchange the darkness [25] of paganism for the light of the gospel, and their temporal liberties here, for an eternal freedom in heaven hereafter; the positive command of GOD to the *Jews*, concerning the circumcision of their slaves, whether purchased when grown up, or born in their houses, with the penalty threatened in case of neglect: the great duties of mercy and charity, and endeavours to promote the kingdom of GOD upon earth, to which all christians are absolutely bound, as they have opportunity of putting them in practice; and especially heads of families, in the present case, from the near relation they bear to their slaves, as common parents: the vast authority and influence which GOD hath given us over them, and which we ought to make use of for the promoting of his glory, and the good of their souls: and the strict account we must one day give to our great master in heaven of the use we have made of all these talents and advantages, with which he hath been pleased to intrust us for our own benefit, and setting forward the salvation of his poor uninstructed children, and conveying those mercies to them, which he, in his goodness and mercy, hath been pleased to convey down to us, from our converted fathers, many ages ago.

We now come to examine,

II. The advantages arising from a due compliance with this great and indispensable obligation.

And as the consideration of the former head shewed this to be a duty owing to GOD and to our brethren, (as these poor creatures, notwithstanding the meanness and slavery of their condition, really are,) so the examination of this must needs convince us, that it is a duty we likewise owe to [26] ourselves, with respect to our earthly as well as eternal welfare.

We are all apt to complain of bad servants—and truly, so far as there is justice and reason in this complaint, I am of opinion the fault is, in a great measure, our own: we do not take the proper methods of making them good. For what, in the name of GOD, can we expect from poor ignorant creatures, who have little or no care taken of their principles; little or no notion of an all-seeing GOD, or a future judgment; nothing but sense and appetite to guide them; nothing but the present object to allure or terrify them? If we are, at any time, under a necessity of leaving our affairs to the management of others, we do not think it prudent to commit them to any but such as we have a good opinion of as honest, conscientious men, who would render us a faithful account of them to the best of their abilities. Our slaves are daily and hourly intrusted with our substance, and the sucess of our crops and dealings do often depend upon their diligence and fidelity: And how can we assure ourselves of these qualifications in them, otherwise than by taking care to instill good principles into their minds, by setting before them much greater rewards than our poor services, or even the whole world can afford; and awakening their consciences by the dread of much greater punishments, and pains far more intolerable than they could suffer by perishing of hunger, or cold, dying upon a rack, being cut to pieces, or whipped to death for their faults. The strongest tie upon the human mind is plainly that of conscience. All other restraints, of what sort soever, like *cords* and *withs* upon the *arms* of a *Sampson*,[3] are easily broke through; and when the [27] passions grow strong, dissolve before them *as flax burnt with fire*.[4] Where conscience is wanting, ways and means of eluding or escaping the penalties of human laws are seldom wanting: or, at least, the bold sinner, when the vice is inviting, will readily run the venture, as every day's experience may teach us. If he escapes, he reckons it as so much gain: and if discovered, will either make light of the punishment, or receive it as a caution to lay his scheme better the next piece of wickedness he attempts. How many unfortunate people do we hear of, whose crimes have brought them to untimely ends; who being hardened to infidelity, and having their consciences seared through a long course of wickedness and irreligion, have been quite regardless of the greatest of all human punishments; have faced a gibbet with intrepidity, and looked upon a most shameful death, as nothing more than the laying down of a wretched being, and stepping out of an ill-natured world, that for the preservation of society would not let them live in it as they thought proper? And can we, my brethren, hope for any better from our slaves, while they remain strangers to conscience and religion, and ignorant of the rewards and punishments of the life to come? Consider their state of labour and servitude: that the drudgery is theirs, and the profit entirely ours: that their senses are as perfect, and their passions and appetites equally strong with ours: and consequently their temptations to ease or idleness, to drinking or riot, to filching for the supply of their pleasures and extravagance, or to any present gratification, increase in force as the means of satisfying them are further removed from their reach, and seldomer fall in their way. And then, putting [28] religion out of the question, say what better security you have for their good behaviour than the dread of the lash, or a continual uneasy watch kept over them? Both these may find a way to disappoint: they may grow hardened under corrections, or at length disregard life itself, which affords them so little of their own ways

---

[3]Judges 15:13; 16:19.
[4]Judges 15:14.

and desires. Whereas, to convince them of the certainty of a future state, and that the eyes of Almighty GOD are continually upon them, who will reward them for their honest service, though no man was to take notice of it, and punish them for their idleness and dishonesty, though their owner or over-seers were never to come to the knowledge of it, must necessarily tend to make them as careful of our business and substance behind our backs as be-fore our faces, and as much afraid of doing an ill thing under covert of the greatest darkness and secrecy, as they would in the open day, before a thou-sand witnesses. If then it be so plain, that a religious conscience is the best security for any person's fidelity and honesty, we cannot but own that to *bring up our* SLAVES *in the knowledge and fear of* GOD,[5] must needs be of great ad-vantage to our temporal affairs: and that a little care and watchfulness be-stowed in this way, may save us a vast deal of time and trouble in another. For, to sum up this point in the words of a pious author. "He that hath con-science needs no spies; and he that hath none will outwit a hundred."

Our blessed saviour, speaking of all things necessary for the support and comfort of life, hath assured us that if we first *seek the kingdom of* GOD *and his righteousness, all these things shall be added unto us:*[6] which words, unless they contain an absolute promise of temporal blessings, [29] to such as make *the kingdom of* GOD *and his righteousness* their first and principal care, I must own have, to me, no meaning at all. But what right can any person claim to these advantages who neglects performing the conditions? Or how can any one be said to have a real concern for promoting the kingdom of GOD, and his righteousness, or to make that his first and principal care, who lays out his whole pains in making his *slaves* profitable to his worldly interest, with-out bestowing some time and labour upon making them servants of GOD? Or, is *the Lord's hand waxed short that we* question whether *his words shall come to pass unto us or not?*[A] They surely must have *little faith* in GOD who can pos-sibly *doubt* in such a case; and yet, *to our shame I speak it,* our sad negligence in this respect, and eager struggles for promoting our earthly advantages, make us look more like *unbelievers* than *christians*; more like people who de-pend absolutely on themselves, than such as own a divine Over-ruling Prov-idence, or put any trust & confidence in that GOD, whose laws and prom-ises we acknowledge are contained in the holy scriptures, wherein the above remarkable words are recorded for our encouragement in this duty.

But besides this, and many other passages to the like purpose, GOD has

---

[5]Ephesians 6:4.
[6]Matthew 6:33.
[A]Numbers 11:23.

thought fit to leave us examples, in those sacred writings, of masters who have received extraordinary blessings upon account of the piety and virtue of their servants: all of which *Jacob* and his son *Joseph* are instances worthy the strictest notice. *Laban* whom *Jacob* served, was an idolater, (as appears from his pursuit after him to demand *his gods* or images, which *Rachel had stolen* unknown to *Jacob*)[7] — [30] yet we find from his own confession, that he was thoroughly sensible of the reason of GOD'S extraordinary favours to him, and how great a loss it would be to part with such a servant, which put him upon so many contrivances to retain him in his house. For when *Jacob* desired leave to retire with his own family, *Laban said unto him, I pray thee, if I have found favour in thine eyes, tarry: For I have learned by experience, that the Lord hath blessed me for thy sake.*[B] *Joseph* also served an heathen master, *Potiphar*; who soon perceived the great value of his pious young slave: "For this master saw that the Lord was with him; and that the Lord made all that he did to prosper in his hand. And it came to pass, that from the time that he had made him overseer in his house, and over all that he had, that the Lord blessed the Egyptian's house for Joseph's sake; and the blessing of the Lord was upon all that he had in the house, and in the field."[C] And when, by the wicked accusation of his abandoned mistress, he was thrown into prison, the blessing of GOD followed him also into that dismal place; and the Gaoler now becoming his master, enjoyed the advantage of his fidelity, and that favour of heaven which went along with him: For *the keeper of the prison looked not to any thing that was under his hand because the Lord was with Joseph; and that which he did, the Lord made it to prosper.*[D]

We cannot but know, that the utmost human industry and care, can do no more than put our affairs under a prudent regulation: And when we have done all in our power, the success must be left to a divine, over-ruling Providence. *Except the LORD build the house* (or establish a [31] family in wealth, power, or reputation) *they labour in vain that build it.*[E] (That is, their struggles & contrivances are all ineffectual; and attempts for raising themselves and their families in the world, are all fruitless and insignificant[.]) *It is vain* therefore, for us *to rise up early, to sit up late and to eat the bread of* toil *and sorrow*, whilst GOD is against us.[F] "He disappointeth the devices of the most crafty, so that they cannot perform their enterprize."[G] "Both riches and honour

---

[7]Genesis 31:14–35.
[B]Genesis 30:27.
[C]Genesis 34:3, 5.
[D]Genesis 34:23.
[E]Psalm 127:1.
[F]Psalm 127:2.

come of him.[H] He putteth down one, and setteth up another."[I] And though *the lot* be *cast in the lap,* yet *the whole disposing thereof is of the LORD.*[J] Since, then, GOD hath not only the disposal of all earthly good things, but hath also positively promised a competent share of them to such as strive to promote his kingdom and his righteousness; and since his blessing doth so visibly follow the labours of *servants* who love and fear him, shall not these advantages prevail with us to bring up our *slaves* in his faith and fear? And may we not rationally expect a double blessing, in such a case, even in our worldly affairs; not only because we take the very method he hath pointed out to us, but also upon account of such of these poor creatures, as by our means are fitted to convey his mercies to us and our families, by their worshipping and serving of him?

If another *Joseph* were now to be sold, and his value known beforehand, there is no doubt but he would bear a very high price; and that no person, capable of purchasing such a one, would be sparing of his money, when he knew that he was at the same time buying a blessing from Heaven upon whatsoever that slave should take in hand. [32] We cannot indeed hope to purchase a *Joseph* among poor ignorant Heathens: But, as every good christian hath the same title to the favour of Almighty GOD, have we not the strongest reason to hope, that we shall find a *Joseph* in every *slave* who is reclaimed, by the Grace of GOD assisting our pious endeavours? And shall we then be so sparing of a little time and pains in securing that particular blessing, upon the labours of those *slaves* who are already in our possession, which we were taught to expect from making them servants of the most high GOD? Or if, from our neglect, they want those principles of conscience and fidelity without which it is impossible to have a good servant, and a curse should follow whatever they have a hand in, upon account of their wickedness or Idolatry, may we not justly blame ourselves, who have it so much in our power to make them beneficial to us, and acceptable to Almighty GOD?

The children of *Israel* had the highest veneration for the ark of the covenant, because GOD was pleased to manifest his divine presence in a more particular manner from the mercy-seat which crowned it: So that when it was *taken* by the *Philistines,* they considered themselves as lost and undone, the *glory* and protection of GOD being *departed from Israel.*[K] When it was af-

---

[G]Job 5:12.
[H]I Chronicles 29:12.
[I]Psalm 75:7.
[J]Proverbs 16:33.

terwards brought home, and at its second removal was lodged some time at the house of *Obed-Edom, the LORD blessed Obed-Edom, and all his household, and all that pertained to him, because of the ark of GOD.*[L] If, then, such blessings do follow the presence of the Almighty, and since our Saviour hath promised, that *where two or three are gathered together in his name, there will* [33] he be *in the midst of them:*[M] May not every christian family, wherein the worship of GOD is established, and the servants brought up in his faith and fear, be looked upon as having the Ark of GOD within their walls? And may they not expect an equal blessing with *Odeb-Edom*, from the happy influence of that divine presence, which is so positively *promised* by him that *is faithful,*[N] and in whom *all the promises of GOD are Yea and Amen,*[O] and which nothing but their own neglect and contempt can ever deprive them of? And doth not every person, who suffers his slaves to remain in ignorance and idolatry, so far deprive himself and his family of the comfort of that divine presence, which is accompanied with so many blessings: and provoke that GOD to hide his face from him, who *is of purer eyes than to behold evil, and cannot look upon iniquity?*[P]

He then covets good servants; He that is desirous of GOD'S *blessing* upon his *own* and *their* labours, and *upon all that he hath in the house, and in the field;*[8] He that would assure himself of the favor of heaven, and a comfortable enjoyment of earthly good things, let him strive to bring up his SLAVES and family in the knowledge and fear of GOD: And let him depend upon it, that he, who is truth itself and cannot lie, will be faithful and just[9] in performing his promises; will bestow upon him whatever advantages are suitable to his condition, and deny him nothing which is necessary for his comfort here, and is at the same time conducible to his eternal welfare hereafter.

But now a fresh scene of blessings opens itself to our view, and leads us to consider the [34] advantages which arise from *the instruction of our slaves in the knowledge and fear of GOD,* with respect to a *future state*: Wherein we shall find the motives grow stronger, and receive an additional force, in proportion as the *good things* of *another life* are more valuable and lasting than the *good things of this life.*

It is no small *advantage*, arising from the instruction of others, that *we our-*

[K]I Samuel 4:21.
[L]I Samuel 6:11, 12.
[M]Matthew 18:20.
[N]Hebrews 10:23.
[O]II Corinthians 1:20.
[P]Habakkuk 1:13.
[8]Genesis 39:5.
[9]I John 1:9.

selves grow more knowing in the things we strive to show them. Those who have taken the pains of catechising their children, (I do not mean such as barely teach them the questions and answers by rote, but such as also labour to make them apprehend the meaning and understanding of the principles of the christian religion), must needs have found by experience, how much themselves have increased in the knowledge of GOD, by endeavoring to impart it to their little ones. And, for myself I cannot but own, with unfeigned thanks to Almighty GOD, who has called me to be your Pastor, that the necessity I am under of providing instruction for my beloved flock, hath been the source of much comfortable spiritual knowledge to me: And that the consideration of every single subject, which I endeavour to explain in this place, discovers more and more to me of my own ignorance in things, which I thought myself sufficiently master of, till that attempt hath shewn my mistake, and convinced me of my great deficiency. If we would but duly consider the inestimable value of this knowledge, and the great danger of neglecting it: that *Solomon* pronounceth *the man* to be *happy* who *findeth wisdom*, and *getteth understanding*; and *the merchandize of it* to be *better than the merchandize of silver, and the gain thereof than fine* [35] *Gold.*Q And our blessed Saviour hath declared *this* to be *life eternal, that we may know the only true GOD, and Jesus Christ whom he hath sent.*R If we would but call to mind, that the *Jews* (who were the chosen of GOD) were sent into captivity, because they had no *knowledge;*S and because they were a people *of no understanding: therefore he that made them* would *have no mercy on them:*T If we would but reflect that these punishments, and this loss of GOD'S favour and mercy, was not owing to their want of sense, or of human learning and cunning, but to their neglect of applying themselves to the study of the laws of GOD; as appears from his description of them, by the mouth of the Prophet *Jeremiah*: *My people is foolish, they have not known me; they are sottish children and they have no understanding; they are wise to do evil, but to do good they have no knowledge;*U And that they were destroyed for lack of this heavenly knowledge; which they having *rejected,* GOD did also *reject* them:V Whereas, on the other hand, *Daniel* assures us, that the *people who know their GOD, shall be strong, and do exploits: and they that understand among the people shall instruct many.*W If we I say, would thus consider, and moreover, that St. *Paul,* though he *bare record of* the *Jews* in his

---

QProverbs 3:13, 14.
RJohn 17:3.
SIsaiah 5:13.
TIsaiah 27:11.
UJeremiah 4:22.
VHosea 4:6.
WDaniel 11:32, 33.

days, that they had a commendable *zeal of GOD, yet* blames them that it was not according to knowledge,[X] we should, surely, with that blessed Apostle "count all things but loss for the excellency of the knowledge of Christ Jesus, that we might know him and the power of his resurrection."[Y] [36] And since the instruction of others is so effectual a means of obtaining it, we shall surely rejoice that GOD in his providential goodness, hath put such happy opportunities in our hands of propagating that knowledge in our slaves, and at the same time of improving it in ourselves, to their and our own unspeakable spiritual benefit. This will induce us to be careful and diligent, in searching and studying the holy Scriptures, those pure fountains of divine wisdom; "to lay up the word of GOD in our hearts, and in our souls; to bind them for a sign upon our hands, to be as frontlets between our eyes; to teach them to our children and *servants*; to speak of them when we sit in the house, and when we walk in the way[,] when we lie down, and when we rise up." And, strive to make them as plain, as intelligible, and as full to the view of ourselves and our households, as if they were *written upon the door-posts of our houses, and upon our gates.*[Z] And as a farther spur to our diligence herein, we may add the dread of that heavy *wo*, threatened by our saviour to the *Scribes and Pharisees*, who *shut up the kingdom of Heaven against men*, and *neither* went *in themselves*, nor would *suffer them that were entering to go in.*[AA]

If a plague or other mortal distemper were raging in our neighbourhood, we would, surely, make use of the best means in our power to keep it from our doors. Or if it had already seized any of the family, we would endeavour by wholesome remedies to cure the sick, and administer proper antidotes to such as had not yet caught the infection, to prevent it spreading farther. And if by such prudent means we succeeded in recovering the distempered, or preserving [37] the sound, we should in either case reckon it a great happiness, and sufficient recompence for the pains we had taken. Sin is a most dangerous and mortal disease of the soul, which having once got head is very difficult of cure, apt to spread fast, and often proves fatal to those who catch it. We all know and complain that vice abounds every where; and that no neighbourhood is free from wickedness of some sort or other. And as a set of religious principles is the only effectual remedy, under GOD, either for prevention or cure, is not this sufficient to awaken us to a timely care in the application of it? But if any member of a family hath got this terrible disor-

---

[X]Romans 2:10.
[Y]Philippians 3:9, 10.
[Z]Deuteronomy 11:18–20.
[AA]Matthew 23:13; Luke 11:52.

der, it is surely high time for the master to look about him, and provide against the malignity, lest the whole body should be endangered by the mortification of the limb. One wicked servant entices another; this carries the temptation still farther; And thus it proceeds from hand to hand, till it perhaps reaches the children of the house, and the master's own flesh and blood is often irrecoverably tainted. It is, indeed hard to conceive, what mischief one wicked servant is capable of doing in a family, and how daringly he will proceed in spreading it, while he is under no restraint from religion or conscience, and no pains are taken to set him right. This then may be reckoned among the great advantages of instructing our *slaves* in the knowledge and fear of GOD: We *cure them of the disorder of sin; or if they are so far gone, as we fail in that, we at least prevent its spreading farther, preserve the rest from taint and corruption,* and *deliver our own souls.*

We cannot but know, (if we are in the least acquainted with our own hearts) that we have many [38] sins to answer for, which should GOD *enter into strict judgment* with us, must needs condemn us, beyond all hope of *justification* or acquittal. If, then, any advantage in this respect be offered us, ought we not chearfully and thankfully to embrace the occasion, and lay hold of every opportunity given us, of lightening this burden, and staying the uplifted arm of divine justice? There are few of the common vices of mankind which do not affect more than one person, either by way of communication, example, or offence. This is plain in the case of riot, drunkenness, gaming, swearing, scoffing at religion and seriousness, lewdness in deed or word, and such like. And, surely, the least acknowledgement we can make to GOD and the world, for the corruptions or offences our persuasions or examples may have caused, is, after we have seen the error of our ways, and repented of our misdeeds, to strive to convert and reclaim others, who remain in sin and ignorance, and to bring them into the right way. To this purpose our blessed Saviour having fortold to *Peter* his repeated denials of him, exhorted him, when he should be *converted* to *strengthen his brethren.*[BB] And St. *James* expressly saith, *Brethren, if any of you do err from the truth, and one convert him, let him know that he which converteth the sinner from the error of his way, shall save a soul from death, and shall hide a multitude of sins.*[CC] Do we, then, my brethren, know ourselves to be sinners, and obnoxious to the just wrath of an Almighty, offended power? Do we know, that he expects we should strive to make some sort of amends for our own infirmities, by strengthening and confirming the minds of our weak brethren? [39] Do we know, that he hath promised by his

---

[BB]Luke 22:32.
[CC]James 5:19, 20.

holy apostle to *hide* or pass over a multitude of our sins, upon condition that we faithfully strive to convert other sinners? Hath GOD given us the means of performing this condition, by putting into our hands a number of poor, ignorant, unconverted souls? And shall we be so far wanting to ourselves and them, as to suffer them to perish, and thereby entail the punishment of a multitude of sins upon our own heads, which otherwise, through the merciful promise of GOD in Christ, would have been remitted to us?

But there is yet the *greatest* and most *glorious advantage* behind, which bringing up the rear, crowns and establishes all the rest: namely, *the glories of an happy eternity*. And these are expressly promised, to such as labour for the conversion of souls. *The fruit of the righteous is a tree of life*, saith Solomon, *and he that winneth souls is wise.*[DD] *They that be wise*, saith Daniel, *shall shine as the brightness of the firmament: and they that turn many to righteousness, as the stars for ever and ever.*[EE] This is a reward beyond the utmost stretch of human imagination; a happiness as impossible to be described by the tongue of man, as it is for him to comprehend, even in thought. *For eye hath not seen, nor ear heard[,] neither hath entered into the heart of man, the things which GOD hath prepared for them that love him.*[FF]

And are all these benefits, all these unspeakable glories laid before us my brethren? Are we pressed and invited to accept them upon the easiest terms, and shall we hesitate and turn our backs upon them? Shall we sit still and expect that all these blessings should be bestowed [40] upon us, without some care on our part in seeking for them? That GOD should do all for our glory, and we nothing for the advancement of his? Shall we vainly hope to rejoice for ever in the presence of Almighty GOD, while we use no endeavours for causing *joy in heaven over one sinner that repenteth*,[GG] and is converted by our means? Can we set up any rational claim to be *joint-heirs with Christ*, and to be *glorified together with him*, if we refuse to be *workers together with him*[HH] in promoting the salvation of men? Or what reasonable hope can we entertain of *shining forth as the sun* among the *righteous in the kingdom of their heavenly father*,[II] when we are so niggardly of the *light* of the gospel, which he hath so liberally and freely bestowed upon us; and instead of letting it shine in its full lustre *before* our poor, ignorant, benighted *slaves*, rather *hide it under a bushel*,[10] and ungratefully suffer them to remain in darkness? No my brethren, as the

---

[DD] Proverbs 11:30.
[EE] Daniel 12:3.
[FF] I Corinthians 2:9.
[GG] Luke 15:7.
[HH] Romans 8:17.
[II] Matthew 13:43.
[10] Matthew 5:15; Luke 11:33.

reward, so is the *labour of love* set before us, and the one is not to be expected, without the performance of the other: And if we will pretend any right to the wages of heaven, as *servants* and *stewards* of the most high GOD, who hath intrusted us with his *talents*,[11] we must, as *it is just and equal*, give a due proportion of christian instruction to our ignorant *slaves*; so that advancing his kingdom, by the addition of so many subjects to it here, we and they may be received into it hereafter.

Which may GOD of his infinite mercy grant, through our LORD and Saviour JESUS CHRIST, to whom, with the father and the holy spirit, be glory and honour, praise and dominion, now and for ever. *AMEN.*

---

[11]Matthew 25:14–30.

CHAPTER SEVEN

William Dawson: A Christmas Sermon[1]

The Reverend William Dawson (1705?–1752) was an important figure in mid-eighteenth-century Virginia: a scholar, poet,[2] minister, and church administrator. A graduate of Queen's College, Oxford, Dawson, who held a doctorate in divinity, immigrated to Virginia in 1728 or 1729 to take a position as a tutor at the College of William and Mary in Williamsburg. He soon became the college's professor of moral philosophy. In the early 1730s he began to assist James Blair at Bruton Parish by leading divine service and preaching sermons in place of the aging commissary. Sometime during the 1730s, but no later than 1737, Dawson was elected by the vestry of James City Parish to be their minister. He served the parish until his death in 1752. Following James Blair's death in 1743, Edmund Gibson, bishop of London, appointed Dawson the new commissary. A few months later he took a seat on the Governor's Council.[3]

Dawson first preached the sermon reproduced here on Christmas Day 1732 at Bruton Parish. Virginians' practice of observing Christ's birth with feasting, toasting, and a general series of convivial celebrations no doubt

---

[1]William Dawson, "A Christmas Sermon," Dawson Papers, 2:284–293. Used by permission of the Library of Congress. This discourse is incomplete. The material reproduced here represents a portion of a longer sermon, not all of which is extant.

[2]Dawson is generally thought to be the author of *Poems on Several Occasions, By a Gentleman of Virginia* (Williamsburg, 1736).

[3]George MacLaren Brydon, *Virginia's Mother Church and the Political Conditions Under Which It Grew*, 2 Vols. (Richmond: Virginia Historical Society, 1947–1952), 2:256.

inspired Dawson's sober-minded discourse. Dawson's sermon, like Samuel Davies' delivered in the 1750s[4] and Charles Clay's delivered even later in the century,[5] criticized the dominant culture's Christmas celebrations, warning that heterodox expressions of joy could easily degenerate into "Sin and Sensuality." Likewise, Dawson warned that Christmas festivities marked by "Luxury and Intemperance" ran the risk of casting scandal upon both Christ and Christianity. Dawson defined the joy of an orthodox Christian differently: "a sedate, rational, and manly Pleasure." Dawson's Christmas sermon sheds light on the Anglican clergy's understanding of this holy day, stands as a critique of popular culture, and hints of a struggle between ministers and laity in colonial Virginia to define the appropriate understanding of Christian culture.

> be of good Comfort: we our selves must live in Peace, in Peace with God, with our own Consciences, with all the World, and then the God of love and Peace will be with us. II Cor.13.11.

Without these good Dispositions, we have no Title to rejoyce in the Lord,[6] and are unqualified likewise for any true Joy in any Thing beside him. [The Joy of the Wicked is soon kindled, but it is quickly extinguish'd; it is glaring, but transient; it makes a Shew, but there is little Heat in it.][7] [As the crackling of Thorns under a Pot, so, says the wise Man, is the laughter of a Fool: Eccl. 7.6. such is the Joy of the wicked; it is soon kindled, but it is quickly extinguish'd; it is glaring, but transient; it makes a Shew, but there is little Heat in it. But the Joy of those who rejoyce in the Lord, is a sedate, rational, and manly Pleasure: their Delight is as much beyond that of the wicked, as the Enjoyment of our Health, and our Senses is more desirable, than those seeming Transports of Pleasure, w[hi]ch Men may sometimes fancy themselves to have in a Fever, or in a Frenzy. The Delights w[hi]ch some may hope to reap f[ro]m the Pleasures of Sin, are all empty and deceitful, stinted in their Measure, short in their Duration, bitter in the End, fatal in their Consequences, and unsatisfactory even in the very Enjoyment:][8] For, as the wise Man assures us, in the midst of all such Joy, the Heart is sorrowful, and the End of that Mirth is Heaviness. Pr. 14.13 [285] Such Joy as this is indeed for-

---

[4]See pages 159–76.

[5]Charles Clay, "For Christmas Day," 32, Clay Family Papers, 1769–1951, Sermons folder 6, section 2, items 46–47.

[6]Philippians 3:1; 4:4.

[7]Dawson deleted the material in brackets from the sermon's text.

[8]The material in brackets appears on page 292 of the manuscript. Dawson's notes indicate that he intended to insert it here.

bidden us; but it is because it robs us of truer and more valuable Joys: it cuts off our Title to much greater Pleasures in Reversion, and spoils the present Relish, w[hi]ch the Prospect of those Pleasures w[hi]ch even now afford us. We are to deny our selves in sensual, immoderate, excessive Joy, not because God hath forbidden us to rejoyce at all, but for this Reason, that <u>our Joy may be full</u>,^A and that we may rejoyce the more abundently. For as I propose'd to shew in the II^d Place, We lawfully may, and are in Duty bound, so to rejoyce.

Joy is a Passion w[hi]ch God himself hath implanted in our Natures; and it cannot be thought therefore that the Design of Religion is entirely to root it out: it is only to direct it to, and fix it upon, its best, most proper, and becoming Object. It is not only lawful, but necessary for us to desire Happiness, and to endeavour to attain, what we look upon to be good for us. But now there w[oul]d Be no Acc[oun]t to be given of these Desires; we sh[oul]d have no Inclination to choose and follow that, w[hi]ch we apprehend to be good, if it were not for that Complacency and Satisfaction, w[hi]ch we hope to take in it, [286] when we are posses'd of it. The Pleasure and Delight we promise our selves f[ro]m the Enjoym[en]t of any Object, is the Spring that sets all our Faculties on Work, and moves and quickens them in compassing the propos'd End. Whatever therefore we may lawfully desire to obtain, that, when obtain'd, we may lawfully delight in.

[Every good Christian,⁹ whatever his Condition and Circumstances are, hath always before him just Matter of Rejoycing. If the present Posture of his Affairs is not delightful and entertaining; He knows how to cast his Eyes forward, and place before his View such sure and lasting Materials of Joy and Comfort, as can never fail, as are never to be exhausted. He hath temporal, and he hath spiritual Joys; Joys common, and Joys peculiar; such as other Men may share with him, and such as the World hath no Part or Portion in: He is well pleas'd, when <u>He rejoyces with them that do rejoice</u>;¹⁰ and He can be content also, when his Rejoycing is in himself alone, and not in another. The Taste He hath of spiritual Pleasures, the Delight He takes in them, is no Way inconsistent with that Joy and Satisfaction, w[hi]ch temporal Blessings may afford him. [287] These are not the less, but the more agreeable to him, because He is sure of the other. He looks upon the temporal Felicity he possesses now, as a Pledge and Earnest of that far greater spiritual Happiness, He shall enjoy hereafter. He knows how to bring the Pleasure, w[hi]ch earthly Blessings yield him, within its proper Measure, Bounds, and Regulation; and

---

^AI John 1:4.
⁹Dawson's original uses the abbreviation "Xn."
¹⁰Romans 12:5.

being secure therefore of enjoying these Pleasures innocently, He must necessarily have a truer Taste of them, and a more just Satisfaction in them.][11]

Temporal Blessings, Health and Plenty, Pleasure and Prosperity, Honour and Reputation, are us'd frequently in Scripture, as Spurs to quicken, and Rewards to encourage, our Obedience. But these Motives w[oul]d be of no Weight with us, these Blessings would be of no Advantage to us, if it was not lawful to be pleas'd with them, and to rejoyce in them. The Delight and Comfort w[hi]ch they afford us, is the only valuable Thing in them; and they w[oul]d not therefore have been offer'd by God to us, if this Delight were any Way inconsistent with the Design and Scope of our [288] Religion; if it were any Bar to our Holiness here, or to our Happiness hereafter. We are taught to pray to God for the Comforts and Conveniences, as well as the Necessaries of Life; and what we may without Sin pray for, that we may, no doubt, innocently be pleas'd with.

They who place Religion in a morose Dislike, and pretended Detestation, of all the innocent unforbidden Pleasures of Life; and think that a sower,[12] melancholy, reserv'd and sullen Temper is the only true Sign of Grace, seem wholly to forget, that it is God alone who created these earthly Blessings; that it is He only who bestows them on us, and makes us capable of taking Pleasure in them. It is none of the smallest of those Privileges that are annex'd to <u>the Fear of the Lord</u>, that it <u>maketh a merry Heart</u>;[13] that it <u>giveth Joy and Gladness, and a Crown of Rejoycing</u>.[14] What mistaken Prejudices soever some Men may entertain ag[ain]st an easy, a chearful, and a sprightly Temper; how inconsistent soever they may think [289] it with that harsh, rigid, and severe Notion of Religion, w[hi]ch they have been taught to form; yet certain it is, that such a Frame and Temper of Soul, as this, is so far f[ro]m being a Proof, that a Man hath no Sense of God and Goodness upon his Mind, that it is rather an Arg[umen]t that He hath made great Advances in Religion, and render'd the harshest and most difficult Instances of his Duty habitual and familiar, and therefore easy and agreeable to him. Innocent and inoffensive Mirth and Cheerfulness sh[oul]d rather, one w[oul]d imagine, be inseparable f[ro]m Goodness, than inconsistent with it: and it seems contrary to the Reason of the Thing, that an ill Man sh[oul]d ever be of a cheerful, or a good one of a sad Countenance.

---

[11]The brackets are in Dawson's original text.
[12]Sour.
[13]See Proverbs 15:13–16.
[14]See Isaiah 35:10; 51:11; I Thessalonians 2:19.

True Joy, when it is founded upon a right Principle, directed to its proper Object, kept within its due Compass, and not suffer'd to exceed either in its Measure, or Duration, is not only lawful, but commendable; not only what [290] we may, without Sin, allow our selves in, but what we cannot, without Folly, abridge our selves of. Pleasure and Good, Pain and Evil, are but different Expressions for one and the same Thing. No Action is ever forbidden us, but what, upon the whole, brings more Pain than Pleasure; none is commanded us, but what, all Things consider'd, yields greater Degrees of Pleasure, than it does of Pain. And it can never therefore be an Objection ag[ain]st any Thing we undertake, that it will cause Joy; nor a Commendation of any Action, that it will produce Sorrow. True it is, the great Duty of Repentance does in the very Nature of it include Sorrow; but then the End of this Sorrow is, that we may be put into a Condition of rejoycing the more abundantly. The Sense of our Sins must make us <u>weep</u> and <u>lament</u>; but then <u>our Sorrow will</u> soon <u>be turn'd into Joy</u>. Tho' our Conversion hath its Pangs; yet we shall <u>no more remember the Anguish, for Joy that a new Man is born into the World</u>.^B [293]¹⁵

We have seen what it is to <u>rejoyce in the Lord</u>, and have been shewn, that we may, and that we must rejoyce in him. Let us therefore with an humble Confidence offer up our Prayers at the Throne of Grace, that God w[oul]d be pleased to <u>lift up the Light of his Countenance upon us</u>,¹⁶ that he w[oul]d <u>make us to hear of Joy and Gladness, that the Bones w[hi]ch he hath broken may rejoyce</u>;¹⁷ that he w[oul]d be pleas'd to establish his Kingdom in our Hearts, not <u>in Righteousness</u> only, but in <u>Peace and Joy in the Holy Ghost</u>;¹⁸ and that he w[oul]d teach, direct, and enable us <u>to rejoyce in the Lord</u>, yea, <u>to rejoyce in him always</u>. [291]

Whatever Reasons we may have for our Grief and Sorrow, they are mightily overbalanc'd by those Motives, that recommend Joy and Gladness. Christ's coming into the World was usher'd in with Joy; A Multitude of the Heavenly Host prais'd God, and sung Glory to Him, Peace on Earth, and Good Will towards Men.¹⁹ We must receive these glad Tidings with a religious Joy, and inflame and raise our Minds to the highest Pitch that we can. Let us therefore break forth into Joy, for unto us this Day is born a Saviour.²⁰

---

^BJohn 16:20–21.
¹⁵Dawson's sermon skips ahead several pages at this point.
¹⁶Psalm 4:6.
¹⁷Psalm 51:8.
¹⁸Romans 14:17.
¹⁹Luke 2:13–14.
²⁰Luke 2:11.

But let us take Care, that, during this Holy Season, our Joy does not degenerate into Sin and Sensuality; that we do not express it by Luxury and Intemperance, to the great Scandal of our Saviour and His holy [292] Religion. But let us so rejoyce, that we may at last be made meet to be Partakers of those Rivers of Pleasure, that are at God's right Hand for evermore. [293]

And may the God of Hope fill us with all Joy and Peace in believing, that we may abound in hope thro' the Power of the Holy Ghost,[21] that the Peace of God, w[hi]ch passeth all Understanding,[22] may rule in our Hearts, that we may rejoyce with Joy unspeakable and full of Glory,[23] and may at the last receive the End of our Faith, even the Salvation of our Souls.[24] W[hi]ch God of his infinite Mercy Grant, &c.

Williamsb.	Xtmas Day	1732
	Dec. 19	1736
	24	1738
	Augt. 17	1740

---

[21]Romans 15:13.
[22]Philippians 4:7.
[23]I Peter 1:8.
[24]I Peter 1:9.

CHAPTER EIGHT

~

William Stith: *The Nature and Extent of Christ's Redemption*[1]

William Stith (1707–1755), Anglican minister, historian, and president of the College of William and Mary, preached this discourse before Virginia's General Assembly in November 1753 as part of a public dispute with the Reverend Samuel Davies over the nature of salvation. He also published *History of the First Discovery and Settlement of Virginia* (Williamsburg, 1747) and two additional sermon discourses: *The Sinfulness and Pernicious Nature of Gaming: A Sermon Preached before the General Assembly of Virginia: At Williamsburg, March 1st 1752* (Williamsburg, 1752);[2] and *A Sermon Preached Before the General Assembly* (Williamsburg, 1745/46).

> *Enter ye in at the strait Gate, for wide is the Gate, and broad is the Way that leadeth to Destruction, and many there be which go in thereat: Because strait is the Gate, and narrow is the Way, which leadeth unto Life, and few there be, that find it.* Matthew 8:13–14

---

[1] William Stith, *The Nature and Extent of Christ's Redemption. A Sermon Preached before the General Assembly, of Virginia: At Williamsburg, November 11th, 1753* (Williamsburg, 1753). Courtesy of the Virginia Historical Society.

[2] *The Sinfulness and Pernicious Nature of Gaming* was one of the best-selling titles in Virginia during 1752; within a month and a half of its publication in March it had sold over 150 copies, an extraordinary figure. Two days after hearing the sermon, members of the General Assembly considered amending a 1748 Act for preventing excessive and deceitful Gaming, but soon tabled the measure. The best scholarly treatment of Stith, especially on his role as a historian, is Thad W. Tate, "William Stith and the Virginia Tradition," in Lawrence H. Leder, ed., *The Colonial Legacy*, Vol. III, *Historians of Nature and Man's Nature* (New York: Harper & Row, 1973), 121–45.

These Words, at first View, seem to carry a terrible Aspect, and to declare, that the greatest Part of Mankind will miss their Way to eternal Life, and perish everlastingly. And accordingly we find them so understood by some Persons; and particularly a late Author from our Press says: "Is it not certain, that the most of Mankind perish? And to hope the contrary, however natural it is to a generous Soul, is blasphemously to hope, that God will be a Liar."[A] This violent Denunciation against the greatest Part of Mankind is founded, I presume, upon this, and some other parallel Texts of Scripture. But however cautious I would be, of incurring the horrid Crime of Blasphemy, yet I must confess myself to be one of those [10] *generous Souls*, who not only *hope*, but firmly believe better things. And I have therefore chosen this Portion of Scripture, for the Subject of my present Discourse; in the Prosecution of which I shall endeavour

I. To settle and ascertain the Sense of these Words.

II. I shall consider some other Texts, which are thought to have the same Meaning, and to include the like dreadful Sentence against the greatest Part of Mankind.

III. And lastly, I shall shew the Universality of CHRIST'S Redemption; that *he is the Propitiation for our Sins, and not for our Sins only, but also for the Sins of the whole World.* I John ii.2.

I. I am to settle and ascertain the Sense of these Words. And to this Purpose it must be remembered, that but few of the Jews of that Age came in to Christ, and embraced the Gospel. And this was an Event, that was often

---

[A]This is said in a Pamphlet, intitled, *The impartial Trial, impartially tried, and convicted of Partiality*, 47.

Stith's discourse was part of a series of sermons and pamphlets written by ministers with Virginia connections that debated the merits of New Side Presbyterianism. The first tract was written in 1742 by John Caldwell, an Old Side Presbyterian, who spent a brief time in the colony: John Caldwell, *An Impartial Trial of the Spirit operating in this part of the world. . . .* (Boston, 1742). A reprint edition of 1747 contained a preface written by the Reverend Patrick Henry, one of the most outspoken Anglican opponents of the Great Awakening in Virginia.

Samuel Davies responded both to Caldwell and Henry in Samuel Davies, *The Impartial Trial, impartially Tried and convicted of Partiality. . . .* (Williamsburg, 1748).

Stith delivered *The Nature and Extent of Christ's Redemption* in 1753. Davies wrote a reply by July 1755. He decided, however, not to publish it, deferring publication first because word of a major English defeat in the French and Indian War—that of General Edward Braddock on the Monongahela River near Fort Duquesne—had recently arrived, and then because Stith died and Davies thought that publishing the pamphlet would insult the memory of an opponent whom he admired. See Samuel Davies, *Charity and Truth United. . . .*, ed., Thomas Clinton Pears, Jr. (Philadelphia: Department of History of the Office of the General Assembly of the Presbyterian Church in the U.S.A., 1941).

The course of the pamphlet debate may be traced in Richard Beale Davis, *Intellectual Life in the Colonial South, 1585–1763*, 3 Vols. (Knoxville: University of Tennessee Press, 1978), 2:739–40, 790–92.

foretold by the Prophets of the Old Testament, that only a *Remnant should be saved*. It is true indeed, that when the Prophets speak of this *Remnant*, their first and immediate Meaning respected the small Remainder of the Jewish Nation, which was to return from the Babylonian Captivity, and to settle in *Judea*, and again to become a Nation. But altho' this was their primary and immediate Meaning, yet we are not to restrain it wholly to this Sense. For with an Address, usual to the Prophecies of the Old Testament, it had a far-ther prophetical Glance at the Times of the Gospel; and signified, that a small Part only of the Jewish Nation should receive the MESSIAH, when he came, and accept those gracious Terms of Salvation, [11] which God, in his infinite Wisdom and Goodness, hath appointed.

I am sensible, how dangerous it is, to give into whimsical and distant In-terpretations of the Scriptures; yet think myself obliged to submit to any such Application of them, as is made or authorized by the inspired Writers. And I think, we are plainly led to this Allusion and Sense by St. *Paul*, in the xi Chapt[er] of his Epistle to the *Romans*. He is there treating of GOD'S Rejec-tion of the Jews, which he denies to be total, and instances in himself who was not only a Christian, but an Apostle. And then having alluded to *the seven thousand Men in Israel, in the Days of Elias, whom God had reserved to himself, and who had not bowed the Knee to* Baal, he adds: *Even so then, at this present Time also, there is a* REMNANT *according to the Election of Grace.* Rom. xi. 5 where the Apostle plainly refers to the *Remnant to be saved*, so of-ten mentioned by the Prophets of the Old Testament; as indeed Dr. *Ham-mond*,[3] and other Commentators, observe.

And now, since the Jews were such a perverse and stiff-necked Generation, and so obstinately set against Christ and the Gospel; and since this was so re-markable and eminent an Event, that it was often hinted, or even plainly fore-told, by their ancient Prophets; our Blessed SAVIOUR, in the Words of my Text, advises his Auditors to avoid the sinful and pernicious Conduct of the Generality of their Countrymen; *not to enter in at the wide Gate*, nor travel *in the broad Way* of their national Prejudices, in expecting worldly Advantages and a glorious temporal MESSIAH, and rejecting the lowly JESUS: *Because strait was the Gate* of the Gospel, *and* [12] *narrow the way* through the thorny Paths of Affliction and Persecution, *that led unto Life, and few* (Jews) *there were, that would find it.* So that (according to this Interpretation, and the Sense, which I have always had of these Words ever since my first studying or know-ing any thing of the Scriptures) they are to be understood of the Jews of that Age, and not to be extended to all Christians, or to Mankind in general.

---

[3]Henry Hammond (1605–1660), Anglican minister. The work Stith alludes to is likely Henry Hammond, *A Paraphrase and Annotations upon all the Books of the New Testament* (1653).

And this Sense and Interpretation will be still more evident, if we con-sider and collate with it the parallel Passage in St. *Luke*; where the Occasion is more particularly related, and the Application to the Jews more express and indubitable. The Words are: *Then said one unto him; Lord, are there few, that be saved? And he said unto them: Strive to enter in at the strait Gate; for many, I say unto you, will seek to enter in, and shall not be able. When once the Master of the House is risen up, and hath shut to the Door, and ye begin to stand without, and to knock at the Door, saying, Lord, Lord, open unto us; and he shall answer and say unto you, I know you not, whence you are: Then shall ye begin to say; we have eaten and drunk in thy Presence, and thou hast taught in our Streets.* (Which Circumstances did certainly only agree with the Jews of that Time, and can by no means be applied to all Christians throughout all Ages.) *But he shall say; I tell you, I know you not, whence you are; depart from me, all ye Workers of Iniquity. There shall be Weeping and Gnashing of Teeth, when ye shall see* Abraham *and* Isaac, *and* Jacob, (the grand Patriarchs of the *Jewish* Nation) *and all the Prophets,* [13] *in the Kingdom of God, and you yourselves thrust out. And they shall come from the East, and from the West, and from the North, and from the South,*[B] *and shall sit down in the Kingdom of God.* Luke xiii. 23–29. And now, in this parallel Passage, the Metaphor in my Text, *the entering in at the strait Gate, and that many should seek to enter in and should not be able,* is so clearly and so undeniably applyed to the Jewish Nation, that I shall not spend my Breath, or waste your Time and Patience, in proving so clear a Point; so clear indeed, that *Theophylact,*[4] *Grotius,*[5] and all the Commenta-tors, that I am acquainted with, are unanimously agreed in it.

Neither is it a sufficient Objection to this Interpretation, that the Words of my Text are found in our SAVIOUR'S Sermon on the Mount, which was designed to give a general Sketch of Christian Morals, for universal Instruc-tion and Improvement, and without Respect to the Jews or any other partic-ular Cases. For altho' such may be the general Nature and Tendency of that Divine Discourse, yet are we not wholly to exclude from it all Precepts adapted to particular Cases. For to instance only in that famous Precept in the foregoing Chapter of this Gospel: *I say unto you; Take no Thought for your Life, what ye shall eat, or what ye shall drink; nor yet for your Body, what ye shall put on.*[6] And so he goes on, proposing to Imitation the Thoughtlessness and

---

[B]I.e. The *Gentiles* shall come from all Parts of the Earth; and be gathered to the Gospel.

[4]A Byzantine exegete active in the eleventh century. He wrote several commentaries on books in the Old Testament as well as on the entire New Testament, with the exception of the Revelation to John.

[5]Hugo Grotius (1583–1645), Dutch theologian. The author of numerous works, Stith probably al-luded to his *Annotationes in Vetus et Novum Testamentum* (1642), one of Grotious's volumes of exegesis.

[6]Matthew 6:25.

Improvidence of the *Fowls of the Air, which neither sow, nor reap, nor gather into Barns,*[7] and yet are plentifully provided for and fed by our Heavenly Father. Nay, he even draws [14] an Example from senseless and inanimate Things, from *the Lilies of the Field, which neither toil, nor spin, and yet even Solomon in all his Glory was not arrayed like one of these.*[8] Even this famous Precept, I say, was particular, and peculiarly adapted to that Age and Time. For by the Apostles and first Propagators of the Christian Religion, it was to be taken in it's strictest and most literal Meaning. They were sent forth to preach the Gospel to all Nations, and were under a particular Providence of GOD, and the immediate Direction of his Holy Spirit; and therefore ought to be entirely free from all worldly Care and Solicitude, and wholly intent and taken up with the grand Business, they went upon. They ought not to have had any manner of Thought about *what they should eat, or what they should drink, or where-withal they should be cloathed;*[9] but to leave all such things to the Care of that Master, whose Errand they were upon; and who well knew, they had need of those things, and was well able to provide for them.

For them therefore, and for them only, for the Apostles and first Propagators of the Christian Doctrine, was this Precept immediately designed in it's strict and literal Meaning. But with Relation to Christians in general, it must of necessity be taken in a laxer and more extensive Sense; so as not to exclude a moderate Concern and Endeavour to provide for ourselves and Families, together with an honest Industry and prudent Management, and all the other ordinary Means of Living. For these are the Terms, upon which GOD hath granted us the Necessaries and Conveniences of Life; and to comply [15] with them is so far from being sinful, that it is in truth only to comply with the Dictate and Disposition of Divine Providence. But to make this Precept equally obligatory, in it's strict Signification, upon all Christians, and in all Ages, would be of very bad and ruinous Consequence to Mankind. There were indeed Men enough intent upon the Affairs of Life, to support the Apostles and first Propagators of Christianity; and their Labours were not missed in the general Provision of the World. But if this Precept was to be taken universally in it's literal Sense; what would become of Mankind? who would sow? who would reap? and who would gather into Barns the Staff of human Life, and make the necessary Provision for the World's Subsistance?

---

[7]Matthew 6:26.
[8]Matthew 6:28–29.
[9]Matthew 6:31.

As therefore this Precept is by the very Nature of the Thing limited, and adapted in its strict Meaning to the Apostles and first Preachers of the Gospel; so likewise have the Words of my Text their particular Sense, and are immediately designed for that perverse and murderous Race, the Jews of the Age. Altho' in a wider Signification, they may be understood excellently to express the Straitness and Difficulty of entering upon a Christian Course of Life; that it is very easy and natural for Men to fall into the broad Way of Vice; and that Multitudes, alas! but too many, travel down it into the very Gate of Hell and Destruction. But I now proceed

II. To consider some other Texts of Scripture, which are thought to have the same Meaning, and to include the like dreadful Sentence against the greatest Part of Mankind.

And [16] among these, there are none more eminent or more liable to be mistaken, than those Places, where it is said; *That many are called, but few are chosen.* Matt. xx.16; xxii 14. These Words some fiery Zealots eagerly lay hold of, and without Mercy, or the least Hesitation, condemn the Bulk of their Fellow-Christians to eternal Perdition. But this is a Point of much easier Discussion than the Words of my Text. For in expounding them I had no former human Guide, but was wholly led by the Light of Scripture and my own Reason; but here we have the plain Tract of the Commentators to follow, who all agree, that these Words relate to the Jews of that Age. But for the fuller Understanding of this Matter, it will be necessary to consider and explain the foregoing Parables to which these Words are a kind of Inference. I shall therefore endeavour to give an Exposition of the Parable of the Marriage-Feast, in the xxii. Chapt[er] of St. *Matthew's* Gospel;[10] in which I shall chiefly follow two excellent Interpreters of Scripture, *Theophylact* among the *Greeks*, and Dr. *Whitby*[11] of our Church.[C]

2. *The Kingdom of Heaven*, (i.e. the State and Success of the Gospel) *is like unto a certain King, which made a Marriage for his Son.* Where by the King is meant Almighty GOD; by the Son, CHRIST JESUS; and by the Marriage, the [17] Promulgation of the Gospel; or in Scripture Phrase, CHRIST'S Marriage with his Spouse the Church.

---

[10]Matthew 22:1–14.

[11]Daniel Whitby (1638–1726), English minister known for his provocative writings, his hostility toward Roman Catholicism, and his hope that the Church of England could reconcile with the Nonconformists. Stith was probably alluding to his *Paraphrase and Commentary on the New Testament*, 2 Vols. (1703).

[C]The same Sense of this Parable is likewise gathered from various Authors, by that diligent and laborious Compiler, Mr. *Poole, Synops. Critic. in loc.*

3. *And sent forth his*[D] *Servants* (i.e. he sent the Apostles and the Seventy, Chap. x.) *to call them that were bidden, to the Wedding,* (i.e. to call the Jews, who were instructed and invited to the Gospel, by the Prophecies and Scriptures of the Old Testament. Accordingly we find the Apostles and Seventy commanded by CHRIST, *not to go into the Way of the* Gentiles, *nor to any City of the* Samaritans, *but to the lost Sheep of the House of Israel.* Matt. x. 5. 6.) *and they would not come.*

4. *Again he sent forth other*[E] *Servants;* (meaning after his Ascension, he sent forth the Apostles and others, which were fitted by the Descent of the HOLY GHOST, Acts ii.) *saying tell them, which are bidden; Behold I have prepared my Dinner: my Oxen and my Fatlings are killed, come unto the Marriage.* For now it was high Time; the Lamb of GOD was slain, the Dinner was ready, and all things waited for the Jews to come to the Feast of the Gospel. [18]

5. *But they made light of it, and went their Ways, one to his Farm, another to his Merchandise.* (i.e.) Some of the Jews slighted the Gospel, and were drawn away by worldly Considerations, by the Pursuit of the various Interests and Pleasures of this Life.

6. *And the Remnant took his Servants and entreated them spitefully, and slew them.* But others acted more roundly and maliciously: They not only slighted GOD'S gracious Invitations to the Gospel, but despitefully used and slew his Apostles and Teachers.

7. *But when the King heard thereof, he was wroth; and sent forth his Armies* (the Roman Armies under *Vespasian*[12] and *Titus*[13]) *and destroyed those Murderers, and burnt up their City.*

8. *Then saith he to his Servants; the Wedding is ready* (i.e. the Times of the Gospel are come) *but they which were bidden* (the Jews) *were not worthy.*

9. *Go ye therefore into the Highways* (i.e. to the Gentiles) *and as many as ye shall find, bid to the Marriage;* Call all promiscuously into the Gospel, without Distinction of Persons or Nations.

10. *So those Servants went out into the Highways, and gathered together all, as many as they found, both* [19] *bad and good: and the Wedding was furnished with Guests.*

11. *And when the King came in to see the Guests* (at the last Day, when GOD shall make Enquiry into our Lives and Conversations) *he saw there a Man,*

[D]The Ancients, following *Origen,* interpret this of *Moses* and the Prophets. But *the Dinner's being prepared, and the Marriage's being now ready* (v. 4.8) will not permit us to understand these Servants to be the ancient Prophets; but the Vehemence and Urgency of the Invitation, as to a Thing now present, plainly point out and affix the Meaning to the Apostles, and first Preachers of the Gospel.

[E] These the Ancients interpret to be the Apostles, and first Propagators of the Gospel.

[12]Vespasian (9–79), Roman emperor (69–79).

[13]Titus (39–81), Roman emperor (79–81).

which had not on a Wedding Garment. (i.e.) whose Faith and Conversation were not such, as suited the Gospel.

12. *And he saith unto him; Friend, how camest thou in hither* (what Pretensions have you to a Place in Heaven?) *not having on a Wedding-Garment? And he was Speechless.*

13. *Then said the King to the Servants; Bind him hand and foot, and take him away, and cast him into outer Darkness* (i.e. into Hell) *There shall be Weeping and Gnashing of Teeth:* There shall they be in exquisite Torment, and in vain repent, and be vexed, and grieve, for their Folly and Ingratitude, in rejecting the Feast of the Gospel.

14. *For many* (Jews) *are called* (and invited to the Gospel) *but few* (of them) *are chosen* (and will accept GOD'S gracious Offer).

And now, according to this plain, and in my Opinion, this true and indisputable Sense of the Parable, it is evident, that these Words do no ways relate to Christians throughout all Ages, but were immediately aimed at the Jews, for their Wickedness [20] and Perverseness in rejecting Christ and the Gospel. And it would be very easy, to expound the other Parable, in the xx Chapt[er] of this Gospel, concerning the Housholder hiring Labourers into his Vineyard[14] in the same Sense and Manner; and to shew, that these Words, *(many are called, but few are chosen)* which are likewise used as an Inference to that Parable, are no ways designed against Christians or Mankind in general, but do solely respect the Jews of that Age. But this would perhaps be more tedious than necessary; and I hope, that what hath been said will be sufficient to vindicate these Texts from the Perversion of rash and violent Men, who are continually brandishing the Firebrands of Hell against all, they dislike; and who, if *they have a Zeal of God,* yet certainly *it is not according to Knowledge.*[15]

And as these Expressions were designed for the Jews, as Threats and Warnings to them, so we may observe, that they are only to be found in St. *Matthew's* Gospel; which was written for the Use of the Jews, and originally in Hebrew, altho' no authentic Copy of it is now extant in that Language. But it was translated very early into Greek (the Language at that Time universally used and understood through the Roman Empire) by some sure, if not inspired, Hand. For if we may credit the Tradition in[F] *Theophylact,* it was done by St. *John,* the Evangelist. And altho' there is one parallel Passage in St. *Luke* to the Words of my Text; yet there the Occasion and Application to the Jews is so plain, as not easily to be mistaken. [21]

---

[14]Matthew 20:1–16.
[15]Romans 10:2.
[F]Proem. in Evangel.

But it will perhaps be said, that this doth not yet salve the Matter, or clearly vindicate GOD'S Justice and Mercy. He hath created a Set of poor Creatures, to crawl upon the Face of this Earth, and continually to conflict with the Miseries and Troubles of this Life; and after that is ended, all of them, except a very few choice Saints, will be consigned to everlasting Torments in the Life to come. And all this, with GOD'S certain Foreknowledge, and premeditated Design; nay (to put the finishing Hand to the Horror of the Picture) by his own absolute and irreversible Decrees from all Eternity. Such is the amiable Light, in which some Men paint to us *the Father of Mercies and God of all Comfort.*[16] And this is the more confidently insisted upon, because the greatest Part and Bulk of Mankind, through all Ages, have been Heathens; and these they conclude to be all to a Man *turned into Hell,*[17] and damned without Dispute and without Reversion. Wherefore to clear up the Truth in this Matter, or at least to propose my honest and sincere, tho' perhaps simple, Opinion about it; I proceed,

III. And lastly to shew the Universality of CHRIST'S Redemption, that he is *the Propitiation for our Sins, and not for our Sins only, but also for the Sins of the whole World.* I John ii.2. And for the clearer and more distinct Explication of this Subject, I shall observe

1. That there is no Remission of Sin, or Salvation, but by the Merits and Sufferings of our Lord JESUS CHRIST. He is *the Lamb of God, which taketh away the Sin of the World;* (John i.29) who *not by the Blood of Goats and Calves, but by his own Blood, entered in once into the holy Place, having* [22] *obtained eternal Redemption for us.* Heb. ix.12. It is by his propitiatory Sacrifice, *offered once for all,*[18] and by the Satisfaction thereby made to GOD'S Justice (in a Manner, and upon Reasons, incomprehensible to our weak Sense and Understanding) that we can have any Access *to the Throne of Grace,*[19] or *Inheritance among the Saints in Light.*[20] He is therefore emphatically stiled by the Prophet, *The Lord, our Righteousness.* Jer. xxiii.6. *For with his Stripes we are healed,*[21] and by his imputed Righteousness we are justified and accepted in the Sight of GOD. *Neither is there Salvation in any other: For there is none other Name under Heaven, given among Men, whereby we must be saved.* Acts iv.12.

2. As we are thus, by CHRIST'S Merits and Satisfaction, put into a Capacity of Salvation, so is Faith required on our Part, as an indispensable Condition

---

[16]II Corinthians 1:3.
[17]Psalm 9:17.
[18]Hebrews 9:28.
[19]Hebrews 4:16.
[20]Colossians 1:12.
[21]Isaiah 53:5.

for entering into the Kingdom of Heaven; An indispensable Condition, I mean, to those, who have the Christian Faith offered unto them, or who have the Opportunity to know and embrace the Gospel. *For by Grace we are saved, through Faith.* Eph. ii.8. *So must the Son of Man be lifted up, that whosoever believeth in him, should not perish, but have eternal Life.* John iii.14,15. *He that believeth on the Son, hath everlasting Life: And he, that believeth not the Son, shall not see Life; but the Wrath of God abideth on him.* Ibid. v.36.

All therefore, to whom the Knowledge of the Gospel shall come, are obliged, at the Hazard of their eternal Salvation, to receive and believe it. However, GOD is not so rigorous, as to expect more from Men, than is given to them; and therefore,

3. From [23] those, who had only a confused Notion of the thing, and no distinct Perception of the Gospel Truths, and Terms of Salvation in CHRIST JESUS, there was not required a full and explicit Faith in all the Articles of the Christian Religion; but in them, a firm Trust in GOD'S Promises, and a general Belief in a MESSIAH to come, were sufficient to Salvation. And such was the Case of *Abel* and *Noah*, of *Abraham* and the *Patriarchs*, of *Moses* and the Prophets, and in short of all holy and pious Persons under the Jewish Dispensation. They were all certainly saved by the Death and Merit of JESUS CHRIST; and yet it is as certain, that they had very imperfect Ideas of that Death and Merit, and of the Nature of that Salvation. Their Eye never saw, neither did it enter into their Hearts to conceive, that the eternal Son of the Father, *who is over all God blessed for ever*, Rom. ix.5. should take upon himself our Nature, and therein *die for our Sins, and rise again for our Justification.*[22] Of these, I say, and other, the grand and constituent Truths of that great Mystery of Salvation, they had a very dark and imperfect Knowledge; or indeed, of the greatest Part, perhaps no Notion at all. And yet, I believe, it is universally allowed that these Men were saved; and saved by that very CHRIST, of whose Nature and Office they had so faint and glimmering an Idea. *Many Prophets and Kings* (saith our SAVIOUR) *desired to see the things, which ye see, and did not see them, and to hear the things, which ye hear, and did not hear them.* Luke x.24. For however *diligently the Prophets might enquire and search into* that mighty Salvation, which CHRIST hath wrought for us, *which things the* very *Angels desire* [24] *to look into* (I Pet. i.10,12) yet it is certain, that they only *had a Shadow of good things to come, and not the very Image of the things* (Heb. x.1)—only a Glimpse and imperfect Sketch of CHRIST'S Redemption, and not a full View and complete Knowledge of it. And ac-

---

[22]Romans 4:25.

cordingly GOD was content with their acting and believing according to that Proportion of Light, which he had vouchsafed to give them.

But as GOD was not severe, to require of the holy Men under the Old Testament a full and explicit Belief of all the Articles and Mysteries of the Christian Faith, so

4. Neither will he demand from the Poor and Ignorant under the Gospel, a particular and explicit Belief of all those Articles of Faith, whose Signification and Meaning it exceeds their Capacity to understand. As there are Different Degrees in Men's Opportunities and Understandings, so will there likewise be different Degrees in the things required of them; and in Acts of Faith, as well as in Works of Charity, *if there be first a willing Mind, it will be accepted according to that a Man hath, and not according to that he hath not.* 2 Cor. viii.12. And as these are plain Dictates of natural Justice, so

5. It seems equally unreasonable to think, that GOD will condemn to eternal Perdition, for the Want of Faith, those honest and virtuous Heathens, who, as far as human Frailty would permit, acted sincerely and conscientiously, according to the best of their Knowledge and Understanding, and whose Misfortune only it was to be ignorant of both the *Mosaical* and Christian Covenants.

It [25] is shocking to right Reason, and contradictory to the first Principles of common Sense, that Men should be held to Impossibilities. But as *to whomsoever much is given, of him shall much be required* (Luke xii.48) so is it equally a Dictate of natural Equity, that *to whomsoever little is given, of him can only little be required.* God is not so austere and cruel a *Task-master,* as to exact *the full Tale of Bricks*[23] without the proper Allowance of Straw: He will never condemn the Heathen for Want of Faith, in those things, which they neither knew, nor could know, without an express Revelation. On the contrary, he is a Being of infinite Truth and Justice, and will not damn any Man for what is not his own Fault. Nay, it is to be presumed, that whosoever hath the Unhappiness to be condemned at the last Day, their Guilt will be so clear and so undeniable, that they will not be able to open their Mouth against the Justice of the Sentence; *but God will be justified in his Saying; and clear, when he judgeth.* Ps. li.4.

And the Justness of this Reasoning seems plainly allowed by St. *Paul,* who says: *How shall they call on him, in whom they have not believed? and how shall they believe in him, of whom they have not heard? and how shall they hear without a Preacher? and how shall they preach, except they be sent?* Rom. x.14,15. Which was exactly the Case, I am now mentioning. No Prophet was sent to the

---

[23]Exodus 5.

Gentiles, *neither had the Heathen Knowledge of God's* revealed *Laws*; and consequently they could lye under no Obligation, arising solely from them. How could such a Man as *Socrates*,[24] or as *Confucius*,[25] the *Chinese* (who, by their Story, may be esteemed among the best [26] mere Men of unassisted Reason, that ever lived)—but how could they, I say, know (at least *without a Preacher*[26]) that Salvation was to be obtained only among the Jews, an obscure and despised Nation in their Days, and so remote, especially from *Confucius*, that it is not probable, that he ever so much as heard of them?

And agreeable to this is the express Doctrine of St. *Paul*, in the ii. Chapter of his Epistle to the *Romans*; where he clearly determines, that the Gentiles shall not be judged, at the last Day, by any revealed Law, but shall stand or fall, shall be received to eternal *Glory and Peace*, or delivered over to everlasting *Tribulation and Anguish*, according as they have acted up to the Law of Nature. But hear the Wisdom, Equity, and good Sense of the Divine Oracles themselves. *God will render to every Man according to his Deeds. v.6. Indignation and Wrath, Tribulation and Anguish, upon every Soul of Man, that doth Evil, of the Jew first, and also of the Gentile. But Glory, Honour, and Peace to every Man, that worketh Good, to the Jew first, and also to the Gentile. For there is no Respect of Persons with God. For as many, as have sinned without Law* (i.e. without the Knowledge of any revealed Law) *shall also perish without* (Respect to that) *Law: and as many as have sinned in the* (Light of the [27] revealed) *Law shall be judged by the* (revealed) *Law—In the Day, when God shall judge the Secrets of Men by* JESUS CHRIST, *according to my Gospel.* Rom. ii.9 &c. *For when the* Gentiles, *which have not the* (revealed) *Law, do by Nature the things contained in the* (written) *Law, these having not the* (revealed) *Law, are a Law unto themselves. Which shew the Work of the Law, written in their Hearts; their Conscience also bearing Witness, and their Thoughts the mean while accusing or else excusing one another.* ver. 15.

And here the Apostle's Doctrine is so clear and express, that we find the Generality of Expositors, ancient and modern, are agreed, that according to this, *Melchisedeck, Job, Jethro*, the Ninevites, and some other Heathens, were saved. But they seem very cautious, how they admit through this Gap the Rabble of *Greeks* and *Romans*, and other good and virtuous Heathens: As if they had a particular Pique and Exception against St. *Paul's* Word Ελληνος, used here ver. 9, 10; and because the *Greeks* are expressly mentioned for the *Gentiles* in general, they are therefore to be particularly excluded from the

---

[24]Socrates (470?–399 BC), Athenian philosopher and teacher.
[25]Confucius (551–479 BC), Chinese philosopher and teacher.
[26]Romans 10:14.

Terms of Salvation, here declared upon their acting up sincerely and conscientiously to the Law of Nature.

But if it be asked, how the *Gentiles* are saved? the Answer is only in general, that they are saved by the Death and Mediation of JESUS CHRIST. Neither [28] do I know a better Account of this Matter, than what is given by a very eminent, judicious, and learned Protestant Divine, *Philippus a Limborch*.[27] In a Letter to Mr. *Locke*, he says: "That the Fruit of CHRIST'S Sacerdotal Office is, that the World is reconciled to GOD; so that now, through CHRIST, all Men of all Kinds, Ages, and Nations (*omnibus omnino hominibus*) have a Remedy against that Misery into which they fell, by Occasion of *Adam's* Sin, and through their own actual Transgressions, and an Opportunity given them of attaining eternal Salvation. And from hence he thinks, a rational Account may be given, how those, who have never so much as heard of CHRIST, may yet be saved through CHRIST. If, by the Light of Nature they sincerely repent them of their Sins, and humbly ask Pardon of them, and fly to GOD'S Favour and [29] Mercy, that then GOD will apply to them the Grace obtained by CHRIST, for his Sake will impute Righteousness to them, and grant them Remission of Sins. And thus the Gentiles, by GOD'S gracious Imputation, and without a direct Faith in CHRIST, who was never preached to them, will obtain that Benefit, which cannot be obtained, where CHRIST hath been preached, otherwise than by a direct Faith in him. So that the Salvation of all Mankind is founded in CHRIST'S propitiatory Sacrifice. Neither is GOD limited in Points of Favour, but he may extend his Mercy and Benefits, beyond what the strict Words of his Promises may import."

And agreeable to this Opinion of Monsieur *Limborch* were the Sentiments of his Friend, that great Master of Reason, and diligent Searcher into Scripture, Mr. *Locke*. To this Question: "What shall become of all Mankind, who lived before our SAVIOUR'S Time; who never heard of his Name; and consequently could not believe in him? The Answer (says he) is so obvious and natural, that one would wonder, how any reasonable Man should think it worth the urging. No Body was, or can be required to believe, what was never proposed to him to believe."[28]

[27]Phillipus van Limborch (1633–1712), Dutch reformer. Limborch, a supporter of the anti-Calvinist doctrine known as Arminianism, carried on correspondence with several leading English thinkers and divines, including John Locke, John Tillotson, Gilbert Burnet, and Edward Stillingfleet. Stith's reference is to a volume I have been unable to locate: *Limborch apud Locke*, vol. 3, 621. Edit. Parker, 1727. Interested readers may wish to consult John Locke, *Twenty Years Literary Correspondence Between John Locke, Esq; Messieurs Limborch, Leibnitz, and the Reverend Mr. King of Exeter, from 1685 to 1705. . . .* (3d. edition, London, 1789).

[28]John Locke, *The Reasonableness of Christianity, as delivered in the Scriptures* (London, 1695). Stith cites vol. 2, pages 527, 529, &c of the 1727 edition.

And thus have I fairly and candidly delivered to you my Thoughts upon this Subject, without Disguise or Dissimulation, and I hope, without Offence. For as I am conscious to myself, that I had no other Motive to treat this nice Doctrine, but the Love of Truth and of the Gospel; so the same Affection [30] of Mind, and strict Attachment to *the Truth which is in Christ Jesus*, will make me always desirous of Information, and ready to correct any mistaken Notion, I may have formed. It is true, in explaining the various Scriptures, that have fallen under my Consideration in treating this Subject, I have often departed from the beaten Tract of the Commentators. I am sorry for it; and do profess a very high Regard and Veneration for these excellent Persons, who have spent their Time, their Parts, and their Labours, in opening and explaining to us those holy Volumes, which alone *have the Words of eternal Life.*[29] But however I may have varied from them, I hope, I have not departed from sacred Scripture and the Truth. Those are the grand Objects, which I have in View, and to which all other Regards shall for ever give place, and submit. To vindicate GOD'S Ways to Man, to clear up and explain to human Reason his righteous Methods of Grace and Salvation, and to reconcile the Gospel to the Dictates of natural Justice and Equity, was my sole Aim in undertaking this Subject. If I have any way succeeded in so noble an Attempt, it will be a sufficient Recompence, and my Pains are amply rewarded; but if I have not, yet the Consciousness of my Integrity will afford me abundant Comfort and Satisfaction, against any Growlings of Malice, or Flouts of Ignorance, that may be occasioned by it.

However, I would not be so far misunderstood, as if I meant to say, that Salvation is a trifling Affair, and easily obtained by any Body. I know, it requires a steady Course of holy Living—Piety and Obedience to GOD, Justice and Charity [31] to Mankind, and a regular Discharge of our Duty to ourselves and Families: which, in the present corrupt State of human Nature, cannot be deemed such a trifling and easy Matter. On the contrary, we are exhorted in Scripture, *to work out our own Salvation, with Fear and Trembling,* Phil. ii.12. and our State in this Life is expressed, by *running the Race, which is set before us,* Heb. xii.1. *by fighting the good Fight of Faith,* I Tim. vi.12. and by many other Contests of Difficulty and Danger. And in particular it is often compared to a Warfare, which is of all others the most hazardous Condition of Life.

Neither do I pretend to define, what Numbers shall be saved. The holy Scriptures have no where done it, that I know of; and I shall not interpose my weak Sense and Judgment in Points, where they have thought proper to

---

[29]John 6:68.

be silent. This perhaps is one of those secret Counsels, *which it is not for us to know, and which the Father hath put in his own Power*,[30] for very obvious Reasons. For had the Scriptures said, that many will be saved and few damned, it might have tended to make us remiss in our Christian Warfare, and negligent in the Way of GOD'S Commandments: Or had GOD acted by these Men's Advice, and declared with Vehemence and Passion, that the Kingdom of Heaven should be shut against all but a few choice Saints, it would have been apt to hurry Men into Despair, and to have made them give over a Pursuit, of so great Difficulty, and so little Chance of Success. My Design therefore, in this present Discourse, is only to explain the Sense of these Scriptures; and to shew, that they by no means contain a Denunciation of eternal [32] Perdition against *the most of Mankind*; but yet without presuming myself to determine, what Proportion will be saved. There is indeed great Room to hope well from that Judge, who is in his Nature infinitely kind and beneficent, *whose tender Mercy is over all his Works, and who in Wrath remembreth Mercy*; Habbakuk iii.2. and we may be assured, that nothing will be determined against us, that is hard or unjust, nothing but what is exceedingly tender, compassionate, and equitable.

Now unto him, that is able to do exceeding abundantly, above all that we ask or think, according to the Power, that worketh in us, Unto him be Glory in the Church by Christ Jesus, throughout all Ages, World without End, Amen. Ephes. iii.20, 21.

---

[30]Acts 1:7.

~

CHAPTER NINE

Charles Clay:
Sermon on Canticles 2:13[1]

Charles Clay was the minister of St. Anne's Parish in Albemarle County. Rather than attending the College of William and Mary, Clay studied for the ministry with the famous evangelical Anglican, Devereux Jarratt, and was likely one of the evangelicals within the Church of England himself. Between 1777 and 1785 he served the so-called Calvinistical Reformed Church in Charlottesville. In 1786 he left the ministry to take up a career in politics.[2]

Arise, my love, my Fair one, and Come away.

It is a Common practice with many to Redicule what they know nothing of. The Apostle describes such persons under the Character of those who, Speak evil of what they know not.[3] Whatever is beyond the Reach of their shallow Comprehensions they immediately determine to be absurd & Rediculous. This disposition has induced several to treat the Book of Jehovah himself, not only

---

[1]Charles Clay, Sermon on Canticles 2:13, in Clay Family Papers, 1769–1951, Sermons 40–41, sermon folder 5 (Mssl: c5795 a40–41). Used by permission of the Virginia Historical Society. I have silently expanded Clay's numerous abbreviations.
[2]Mark A. Beliles, "The Christian Communities, Religious Revivals, and Political Culture of the Central Virginia Piedmont, 1737–1813," in Garrett Ward Sheldon and Daniel L. Dreisbach, eds., *Religion and Political Culture in Jefferson's Virginia* (New York: Rowman & Littlefield, 2000), 8–12; Joan R. Gundersen, *The Anglican Ministry in Virginia, 1723–1766: A Study of a Social Class* (New York: Garland Publishing, Inc., 1989), 195, 197, 246.
[3]Jude 1:10; see also II Peter 2:12.

with indifference, but with the utmost Scorn & Contempt. Many there are who peruse the Sacred Scriptures meerly to find an opportunity of Cavilling at the great Truths Contained therein[.] To such as these till their hearts [2] are Renewed by the Spirit of God, the Scriptures will be only a Dead Letter; & the frequent perusal of them will but minister to their greater Condemnation[.] It has been the fate of this book of Canticles to meet with much of this treatment. Since it treats of the Love of Christ to his Church & faithful people the mere natural Man who has never experienced, nor desired to experience the power of this Love in his own heart, Cannot but pervert it to such Lewd purposes as his own filthy Imagination Suggests. [B]ut however the Devil & his agents may endeavour to turn the food of Gods people into poison, the delicious fare will always be welcome to those who are nourished & strengthened thereby. This Book of Canticles was dictated by the Holy Spirit of God, & describes the ex-cellency [3] of Our Redeemer, & his love to his people under such Images, em-blems, & Similituds, as are the best suited to Convey an Idea of it to them; In the words of the text, he invites us to leave our natural state of Guilt & Mis-ery, & to partake of those graces & blessings he purchased for Sinners by his own blood. The Chapter is introduced as giving an account of Our Lords invi-tation to her thus[,] My beloved Spake & Said unto me, Rise up my love, my fair one & Come away. for lo! the Winter is past, the Rain is over & gone. The flowers appear on the Earth, the time of the singing of birds is Come, & the Voice of the turtle is heard in Our Land; the fig tree putteth [forth] her green figs, & the Vines with the tender Grape[s] give a good Smell. Arise my love my fair One & Come away.[4]

These words may be Considered as [4] the language of Christ to his Church, or as his kind invitation to the Returning Sinner. It will furnish us I hope with great instruction to Consider them in both these lights; & may the good Spirit of God enable us to decern the beauty & propriety of them, while we Consider them in the first place as the language of Christ to his Church. You are sensible that the Church of God thro' out the Sacred pages is Com-pared to a Wife or Virgin. It would be endless & I presume needless to Remind you of the Several passages where this Comparison is made. Our blessed Re-deemer Speaks to his Church (& here by Church is not meant any particular Sect or party alone, but the whole Church of Christ wheresoever dispersed thro' out the whole World.) Our blessed Redeemer I say speaks to [5] his Church in the words of the text, under the Same tender & endearing Char-acter. I have often observd that Man, being Composed of a body as well as a Soul, Can Receive no Ideas but by the Mediation of his Senses. [F]or this Rea-

---

[4]Canticles 2:10–13.

son [?] the Sacred Writings, Ideas of Spiritual things are Conveyed to us under Sensible Images & illustrations. The emblems are taken from Nature in Order to acquaint us with the Spiritual truths of the Gospel, in the passage before us we have an instance of this Sort. Christ expresseth the love he bears the Church & his Readiness to be united to it, by the Image of most tender union, which does, or at least ought to, subsist between every Married pair. Arise My love my fair One & Come away. What endearing & engaging titles are these! How loving and Condescending is it in the Merciful Jesus to bestow Such [6] epithets on his Church! for lovely as she is in his Eyes, fair & beautiful as she appears before him, the Members that Compose her Body are Such miserable & ungreatful Sinners, as we are. How then can the Church of Christ (you'll say) being Composed of Such distorted limbs appear amiable & well proportioned in his Sight? Why not for any intrinsic worth or excellency in her: for She Considered in herself as Composed of Sinful Members is Really Vile. Mankind in themselves are sinful, helpless, & wretc[h]ed. What Could any in their unhappy Situation do to attract the Notice & observation of the blessed Jesus? Why My brethren, that very wretchedness & State of pollution excited the bowels of Compassion in him. Those whom the King delighteth to honor, had nothing to [7] Recommend them, nothing but his free Grace, & unmerited love, induced him to be favourable & propitious to them. The 16th of Ezekiel will Convince you of this (from the 1st to the 15th verses) & I would earnestly Recommend it to thy perusal. The Lord there addresses his Church, in that Chapter & Cuts off all Occasion of boasting on her behalf, by telling her, I Said unto thee when thou wast in thy blood[,] live; yea I Said unto thee when thou wast in thy blood[,] live. When She was polluted with Guilt, when no Eye pitied her, then the bowels of the blessed Jesus were moved with Compassion to her, & he Spake Comfortably unto her, & to Convince his People that he Really loved them, he divested him self of his Glory, was Cloathed with frail & feeble flesh, & at last Shed his blood to wash off all their impurities. Who then among you My [8] Sinful Seeking Brethren, who among you Can doubt the loving kindness of Jesus when he has done so much to Convince you of the love he bears his Church? But how Can this Church be Said to be lovely & amiable in the Eyes of her Lord & Husband when the Members of her body are defiled with Sin? We Read that God hateth Iniquity; & that no evil Can dwell with him.[5] [H]ow then Can Sinful Creatures laden with Iniquity be united to him by that Strong tie, of which the Matrimonial union is the known emblem? Why here My Brethren is the great mystery of Godliness. This is what the Angels desired to look into. & to Solve this

---

[5]Psalm 5:4.

difficulty, to unite these Contending parties (as a holy God, and Sinful Man must be allowed to be) he united their 2 Natures in himself, he bore the Sin & Guilt of his Church upon his Own Body [9] being Made Sin for it.[6] Christians how ever Sinful they are in themselves yet in Christ Jesus are Clean from their Iniquity & freed from Guilt. The Blood of Christ hath freed them & they are lovely in his Eyes. Lovely they most Certainly are, Since he laid down his Life for their Sakes. How should this tender Compassion of Christ excite the gratitude of his People, when merely for his Own unmerited Mercy, & on account of their wretchedness and Misery, he thus engagingly Stiles his Love? But our Redeemer Stops not at this title, but Calls the Church his fair One! This Seems more astonishing than the former appellation. [I]t was Mercy beyond expression to love a Set of beings who had So often provoked his Anger, & Rebelled against him. Yet the bowels of Jesus's Mercy might [10] indeed yearn over them & excite a pity which was Ripened into love. [B]ut to pronounce her fair, i.e. free and Clear from all defilements Seems a paradox indeed. The Church or Congregation of believers as Composed of Sinful members must of Consequence be Spotted & defiled with Sin; & then by the mystical union of the 2 Natures in the person of Christ her Sins were transferred to him[,] his Righteousness is imputed to her as in the afore Cited Chapter of Ezekiel. [T]he Lord Saies, & thou wast exceedingly beautiful, & thou didst prosper into a Kingdom, & thy Renown went forth among the heathen for thy Beauty: for it was perfect thro' my Comeliness which I had put upon thee, Saith the Lord God.[7] And how the opposers of imputed Righteousness Can otherwise account for this description of the Church in the text, I own is to me a Mystery, but in the [11] light the Riddle is expounded. The Church of Christ is lovely & fair in the Eyes of God, as being Cloathed with the wedding Garment of the Redeemers Righteousness. As this Glorious privilige will excite her gratitude, So will it always Make her humble, when She Recollects that, fair as She is yet like the moon She Shines with a borrowed lustre[,] that she is indebted for all her Splendor to the great Sun of Righteousness, who Rose upon her with healing under his wings. [T]his fair & lovely bride, whom he hath loved with an everlasting love, (admire O my Soul! this amazing mystery of Redeeming Grace) this Bride which is his Church, Resolves this Seeming Paradox, in her description of her Self. I am black but Comely[8] (O ye Daughters of Jerusalem.) I am black & defiled with Sin, Considered in myself, but I am Comely & fair, as being [12] invested with

---

[6]See II Corinthians 5:21.
[7]Ezekiel 16:13–14.
[8]Canticles 1:5.

the Righteousness of my Lord. [T]his Church (which Our Lord purchased with his Own blood) he Calls upon to arise from the Slumber her Enemies would betray her into, & to Come to him by prayer & faith. [H]e invites her to Come away from poverty & distress, from the power of her foes & to shelter herself in his beloved embraces. He invites her to Come away from her fears, to—from the Land of Scarcity into that delightful Garden, which his Right hand had planted. In the following Verses he gives her the Reason of this Invitation, & describes the blessings he had provided for her. For lo! the Winter is past, the Rain is over and gone. The Flowers appear on the earth; the time of the Singing of birds is come, and the Voice of the Turtle is heard in our land; the Fig tree putteth forth her green figs, and the Vines with the tender Grapes give a good Smell.[9] The blessed Jesus in the passage describes the Gifts & Graces [13] of his Church under the Emblem of Spring wherein Nature Rises from her gloomy Slumbers; & puts on her gayest livery. The Season of Spring is Nature's Resurrection, & Reminds us of the Resurrection of Our Redeemer, as also of the Christians Resurrection from Sin to Grace here; & from the dreary Regions of Death to the bright Mansions of Glory hereafter[.] It is impossible for any thing to be more eligantly descriptive than the Image of the Spring given in the Text. & had it been found in any Classic author, it would have been loaded with praises, & extolled to the Skies. But it is in the Book of God, & it is passed by unnoticed. Our blessed Redeemer, in Order to give us the highest Idea of the flourishing State of his Kingdom, paints it to our View under the pleasing Image of the Spring Season, & what the Sun does now in Nature [14] Jesus Christ the true light of Life Continues to do in Grace. [B]y taking a Short Survey of the delights of the Spring, you may be able to form a faint Idea of those delights attending a Spring time in the Soul. May the Spirit of God give you all to experience it for yourselves! [B]ut to observe the parallel: how delightful My Brethren is the Return of Spring to us all! [I]n winter we Saw Creation deprived of all its Ornaments, the trees & Plants were Striped of their Verdue, & the fertilizing Sap Retired to the lowest Roots. [T]he fruit of the Vines & fig tree failed, & the fields did yield no food, every thing had Retired to Silent Slumbers, & lay buried in the Grave of the Earth. But now blessed be God, (who Remembers us, how much Soever we forget him) how the Scene is Changed; all Nature [15] is Revealed & wears a Smiling Aspect. The Cold dark winter is past, the nipping frosts are Ceased, the Rain is over & gone, the Stormy winds & deluge of Waters & Snow are Stoped. & the Earth now Receives Such gentle drops, as enables it to Send forth it[s] fruits in due Season. The flowers appear on the Earth & perfume the

---

[9]Canticles 2:11–13.

Circumambient Air with their fragrant Sweets. The time of the Singing of birds has come & they delight the Ear with their melodious Notes; having at last found a place for the Soles of their feet upon the Slender twiggs, they tune their little throats, & upbraid their admiring hearers while they warble forth their gratitude in hymns of Praise to their God. The Voice of the turtle is heard in our land, which having been benumbed by the winter Cold, is now Revived, & by its Constancy to its mate [16] Reads the lawless libertine a lecture upon Chaste affection. The Fig Tree putteth forth her green figs, & yields a delicious Repast to the weary traveller. & the Vines with the tender grape give a good smell & dispense their pleasing Odours to all around them. The fig tree & the Vines where Solomon Reigned were Remarkable for their fragrancy & deliciousness. And in those Souls where a greater than Solomon Reigneth, the fruits of the Spring shall abound more & more. This is the Image Our Lord Makes use of, to Convey to his People an Idea of what he has done & now doth for his Church. Christ invites his Church to Come unto him with out any fears or doubts, for all dangers are Removed. You that are the happy Members of this Myst[i]cal body, Can give testimony to the truth of what I am about to deliver. And tho' my [17] Description falls Short, of what those have experienced, who have tasted the good word of God, & the powers of the world to Come, yet bear with Me while I attempt to give those unacquainted with the Comforts of Religion a faint View of what Our gracious Lord hath done for Sinners, that they also may be invited to Come in. Christ then invites his Church or faithful People, to arise & Come unto him. [H]ear this ye that have tasted of his Redeeming love. Arise and Call upon your God. Rouse your selves ye highly favoured of the Lord, from all Carnal fears. [A]re Ye in a gloomy disconsolate frame? Come away to Jesus whose arms are open to Shelter you from impending danger. [F]ear no evil for it is all Removed. [T]he winter is passed; this is the first blessing your Redeemer has purchased. You are by Nature the Children [18] of wrath even as others.[10] [Y]ou were born in Sin;[11] you Remember what it was to be in the Cold winter of Spiritual Death, & in the dark night of Guilt[. H]appy for you My Brethren this winter is past. The Sun of Righteousness arose & despersed the Clouds of Ignorance & unbelief, & a glorious [unclear abbreviation] has broken in upon your heart. [T]he Rain is over & gone; the Storms of Gods wrath Rained down Vengeance upon him, for your Sins & transgressions. Sin excited Gods anger & indignation; but to your unspeakable Comfort, the Storm is blown over. He Sustained the weight of his fathers wrath, that you might

---

[10]Ephesians 2:3.
[11]John 9:34.

have none of it to bear. [H]e has wrung out the dregs of that bitter Cup, & left the Sweet for you. [T]he flowers appear on the E[arth] even in the [illegible] Soil of your earthly Minds, have the Seeds of Grace been Sown; which [19] by the enlivening Rays of your Redeemers Righteousness, Spring up in so fair & pleasant flowers. The graces of the Holy Spirit evidence your profession & your good works are the fruit of your faith. & altho' till your Sun approaches Nearer to you, you will be exposed to many a Chilling blast, which may threaten the destruction of your flowers, yet being Rooted & grounded in your Masters love, ye need not feer, altho' a Cloud may hide his genial heat for a Season, altho the wind of temptation may Shake you for a time[,] yet a little while & the Cloud shall be dispersed; the Storm Shall cease when it has purged the Air of pestilential Vapours, & the glorious Sun of Righteousness Shall break thro' all opposition, Shall exhale the mists & damps of fears & doubts, & Shine [20] upon you with Redoubled Splendor. The time of [the] Singing of birds is come. [G]reatful hymns & Spiritual Songs are Sent up to your Redeemer by the faithful; prepare to Join in the Same delightful exercise: in your wintry State, indeed you had no Root, were made a prey by your Enimy, & fell into the Snare of the Cruel fowler; but now the Snare is broken, you are delivered; now you are Returned, with an Olive branch of peace in your Mouths plucked from the true Olive tree, which is for the healing of the Nations; in which you find a peaceful Shelter from the Storms that blow around you, & may Sit & Sing among the branches. [T]he Voice of the turtle is heard in your land. The heavenly mystic Dove, the Holy Spirit of God, applies many Comfortable promises to your Souls. [21] He has assured you of your peace & pardon, & he often breathes upon you, & brings a kind message from him whom your Soul loveth. [T]he Fig Tree putteth forth her green figs. [Y]ou are not barren fig Trees; you have not only the leaves of an outward profession, but are desirous of abounding in the fruit of all good works. Perhaps indeed Infirmities may Retard your growth, but your fruit is put forth, the Tree may be knows what it is, & in due time you Shall be transplanted into that happy Soil, where nothing Shall interrupt the Shining of your heavenly luminary upon you. [T]he Vines with the tender grape give a good smell. [W]ild & uncultivated as you were by Nature, being ingrafted into the true Vine you produce grapes, tho' as yet they are but tender; which nevertheless Send up a grateful Smell, a pleasing [22] Odour to the Almighty[,] its being the fruits of his Spirit.

Thus, My Brethren have I given you a faint Sketch of your glorious priviliges, not So much to inform you as to win the Careless & unawakened Sinner to an ardent longing after a Share in your happy Circumstances. Now the great alteration that is made in Nature in the Spring Season is Owing to the

Chearing influences & genial warmth of the Suns light. From hence all Vegitative life, & power Springs; it is impossible for the least shrub or meanest
plant to Spring from its grave of Dust into Vegitative life, without the Reviving influence of the Suns Rays, equally impossible would it have been for
you the Sons & Daughters of the Almighty, to Raise yourselves from the
grave of Sin & Death in which you were buried by Nature, had not Christ
the light of the World wrought upon your hearts, & given the glorious Order, [23] loose them & let them go.[12] It is observable that a Vine of it self will
Never grow upright, but Requires a wall, a Tree or Some prop to Support it,
other ways it Creeps upon the Ground; were you not Supported by Christ,
the well of Salvation which God hath appointed, you likewise would Still
Continue to Creep upon the Ground. [Y]our affections would be low & grov-
elling! & it is your happy union with Christ that hath Raised you up.

Christ having given you a description of your priviliges in the text, Renews his invitation to you to arise & Come away to him. Rise Men ye heaven
born Souls, Come away from all defences of your own devising: Come away
from fears, from doubts & disquietudes, & take your Sweet Repose under the
protection of the Mediator.

I Shall now give a Short view of the text as Relating to the Returning Sin-
ner, nor do I think the words the least forced while thus applied. [24] And
here perhaps, Some Seeking doubtful Soul will Start a difficulty at once, &
Say, I am Sure you will force the words if you apply them to me. How Can I
believe those endearing titles, my love[,] my fair One, belong to me? Indeed
My Brother they do belong to you. [Y]our Very Concern is a token of your
Redeemers Love. If you ask what there is in you to excite your Saviors Love:
I answer nothing; but Rather much to excite his anger. But tho' there is nothing in you, there is much in Jesus to induce him to extend his loving kindness to you. [H]is bowels yearn over the Returning Sinner, & he will most as-
suredly deliver him. Fear not then to apply this happy appellation to
yourselves. Altho' in yourselves you may be black & defiled with Sin, yet in
Christ Jesus you are fair & Comely in the Sight [25] of God. [Y]our Sins are
nailed to your Redeemers cross, & his Righteousness is imputed to you.[13] But
do not misunderstand me; I would not be thot to encourage any hardened
impenitent Sinners to hope for Mercy, & still live in Sin. I am not at present
speaking to them; & indeed they do not desire Comfort from Christ, they are
quite unconcerned about it; but I am now Speaking to encourage the Returning penitent, the Convicted Sinner: to those I Say there is mercy for the

---

[12]John 11:44.
[13]Romans 4.

Vilest Sinners, & those who are Concerned for their Sins, who desire to be freed from the power as well as the guilt of them, are intitled to the Redeemers mercy. To these I say & Repeat it again, your Sins are nailed to your Saviors cross. [F]ear not, nor write bitter things against yourselves. To prevent your doing this your blessed Lord gives you a most engaging Title, arise my Love my fair one; Rendered so by [26] My perfect Obedience & Death. [A]rise from unbelief, Come away from fears & distrust[.] Come to me; does the adversary pursue thee[,] dost thou fear, or wouldst thou avoid the wrath of an angry God? Come under the Shadow of my wings,[14] where thou shalt find a Shelter. [D]o the Enimies of your Soul perplex, & do your Corruptions bow you down? Come then to Jesus Christ by faith. Cast yourselves upon his Mercy, Rely upon him. [L]eave your whole Concerns with him, & you shall find him a Sincere & faithful Friend, fear not to Come to this Redeemer, for lo! the winter is past; the Cold winter of Sin is past, by the Rising of Christ the Sun of Righteousness in the flesh. The Rain is over & gone; Justice hath nothing to Require of you, for he has Sustained the Stormy wind & tempestuous Rain of his fathers wrath. The flowers appear on the earth; the Book of God like a watered Garden, abounds with pleasing flowers, with many Comfortable promises, [27] which you are invited to Come & gather. [T]he Time of the Singing of birds is come, the Sound of a Redeemer is now Sung in your Ears; the Ministers of Christ are no longer to you as Sounding brass or tinkling Symbals,[15] but sing sweetly in your Ears when ever they preach a Crucified Redeemer. The Voice of the turtle is heard in your Land, this is Supposed to be a prophecy of John the Baptist who was to prepare the way of the Lord, & may [?] with equal Justice with the former Clause be applied to the Ministers of Christ. [Christ is preached unto you with a Sure Mark of his love; for you may be assured that where ever Christ is openly & boldly preached he has Some Souls gathered unto him. God grant that it may be Verified in you this Day.][16] The Fig Tree putteth forth her green figs, here again will Some doubting Soul Say, now I am Sure the parallel will never hold good; for if by the green figs, are meant the fruits of Faith, I have none I am persuaded. [28] Well but they may be putting forth & your present fears, anxieties, & disquietudes, is a proof that you have begun to feel the enlivening Rays of Christ the Sun of Righteousness in your hearts which will Soon Cause the tender buds to Swell. The other encouragement given you to put your whole trust & Confidence in the Redeemer, is, that the Vines with the tender Grape give a good Smell. Ignorant as you may be of it, you are

---

[14]Psalm 17:8; 36:7; 57:1; 63:7.
[15]I Corinthians 13:1.
[16]Clay included the brackets in his manuscript.

ingrafted into Christ the true Vine, the Richness of this Vine are Communicating to you; & tho' your fruit may at present be but Small & tender, yet in Jesus you yield a greatful incense to the father of Spirits. My Brethren you may Venture to assure yourselves that the priviliges are yours. Refuse not the Repeated invitation of Christ your Lord & Spouse, arise My Love, my fair One; arise from the dark dungeon of legal [29] fears; Come away from the hold of unbelief & throw your Selves upon Christ, the great strong hold, ye prisoners of Hope; & may the Lord enable you to do So! I shall &c.

A word to the impenitent unconverted Sinners; you have heard (if you have bee[n] attentive) what great & glorious priviliges Christ has purchased for all those that believe, or desire to believe on his Name (viz.) pardon of Sin, power over it, & a Crown of Glory. But you're quite indefferent, & unconcerned whether you ever experience these blessings or not. To you, as yet a crucified Savior has no beauty that &c, be honest & Confess the truth. [H]ave you not been hitherto very little Solicitous whether you have an interest in Christ or no! And yet My Dear Brethren unless you have; good would it have been for you that you had never been born. [B]ut I will not threaten, nor [30] use terrifying words unto you but will address you in the language of the text, with the Voice of Love, will Solicit you with the endearments of affection, & intreat you with the tender expostulations of Friendship. [G]ive me your Serious attention I will not detain you long;

Convinced penitent Sinner whoever thou art, [I have a Comfortable Message this Day unto thy Soul. [P]erhaps you doubt it. You have been a profane wretch, a blashemious Swearer, a Sabbath breaker, a backbiter &c. Or at least, if you have been outwardly decent you have been quite indefferent about the Comforts of the Lord. Yet (Can you believe it? Stop & wonder at the news)][17] to you even to you does Jesus Speak in the words of the text. Spotted & defiled with Sin, as your Souls are, yet if you do but find it in your hearts [31] to be truly sorry for your transgressions, you are fair & lovely in his Eyes; he will Cast a Veil of oblivion over all your imperfections; O Sinner the Lord loves thee; he Came down from heaven for thee[;] he was despised for thee; he suffered & he bled for thee; he shed his blood to wash thy Soul from Sins defiling Stain. Hear him then, attend to his Call, [My dear unhappy because unconverted Brethren hear him][18] as he hangs upon the cross calling unto you; arise my love, my fair one and come away[. L]ittle dost thou think that the blood which you now behold with indefference, was Shed for thee. Arise from thy present lethargy, Arise from thy present Sinful

---

[17]Clay included the brackets in his manuscript.
[18]Clay included the brackets in his manuscript.

State & come away. Come away from Sin; Come away from all my former practices; Come away from Guilt, & let me embrace thee in the Arms of love. [T]his is my masters invitation; & in the Nature of that adorable Jesus, & by Vertue of the [32] Commission he has Given Me, I Call upon thee O Man; I Call upon thee O Woman to crucify My Lord no more. & I promise thee in the Name of the everlasting God; in the Name of the Sacred Trinity, that if thou art enabled to turn & Repent, & Come humbly to the Lord Jesus Christ that thy Sins & thy Iniquities Shall be Remembered no more. May the Son of God touch your hearts, & give you Cause to bless him for the words I have spoken in your Ears this Day. Amen.

1773

CHAPTER TEN

The Baptist Perspective

Massachusetts-born John Leland (1754–1841) was baptized into the Baptist faith in 1774 and licensed to preach the next year. Within months of receiving his license Leland set out on a preaching mission which took him from New England to Virginia. By 1778 he had settled in Virginia's Orange County and from there served a number of Baptist congregations in Orange, Spotsylvania, Louisa, and Culpeper Counties, a circuit of approximately 120 miles. He remained in the colony until 1791.

During his years in Virginia, Leland, a lifelong advocate of religious liberty and freedom in general, fought to end the legal incorporation of the Episcopal Church. He believed established churches had harmed Christ's church more "than all the persecutions ever did," arguing that persecution "tears the saints to death, but leaves Christianity pure." In addition, Leland urged his colleagues in the Baptist ministry to present the Gospel message in a more pious and dignified manner without the commonplace "whoops and awkward gestures." In 1789 he convinced the Baptist General Committee to condemn slavery, a position the committee later overturned. Widely read and possessed of intellectual vigor, Leland also collected materials for writing a history of the Baptists in Virginia, part of which he published in 1790 as *The Virginia Chronicle*.[1]

---

[1]John A. Garraty and Mark C. Carnes, eds., *American National Biography* (New York: Oxford University Press, 1999), 13:465–66; Edwin Scott Gaustad, *A Religious History of America: New Revised Edition* (San Francisco: Harper Collins Publishers, 1990), 48. The best study of the Church of England's disestablishment in Virginia is Thomas E. Buckley, S.J., *Church and State in Revolutionary Virginia, 1776–1787*

Leland's *Virginia Chronicle* presents a clear and rational account of the state of religion in late eighteenth-century Virginia from a Baptist perspective. The portion reprinted here relates the story of the Baptist phase of the Great Awakening in Virginia, and it presents a portrait of the persuasion very much at odds with that of many colonial Anglicans who viewed the Baptists as ignorant radicals out to overthrow both the Church and the State. Demonstrating fluency with church history and theology, Leland brings into sharp relief the points of contention between Baptists and the Church of England, thus shedding light on the controversies between the two groups and between the Baptists and Virginia's civil authorities.

During his long career, Leland preached approximately 8,000 times, baptized nearly 1,300 individuals, and claimed to have traveled a distance equivalent to three trips around the world. He described his calling, as portions of *The Virginia Chronicle* make clear, as an effort "to watch and check *clerical hierarchy*, which assumes as many shades as a chameleon."[2]

John Leland: *The Virginia Chronicle*[3]

X. HEAD

There were a few Baptists in Virginia, before the year 1760; but they did not spread, so as to be taken notice of by the people, much less by the rulers, till after that date. About the year 1764, they prevailed so much, that in the year following they formed an association, called "The Ketocton regular Baptist association."[A] From 1764 to 1774, the Baptists spread over the greatest part of the state that was peopled. Several ministers of that order came from Pennsylvania and the Jerseys, and settled in the northern parts of the state, and others were raised up in the southern parts, who travelled about, and preached like the old Baptist *John*, "Repent, for the kingdom of Heaven is at hand,"[4] and great numbers of the people went out unto them and were bap-

(Charlottesville: University Press of Virginia, 1977). See also Thomas E. Buckley, "Evangelicals Triumphant: The Baptists' Assault on the Virginia Glebes, 1786–1801," *William and Mary Quarterly*, 3d ser., 45 (1988): 33–69; Charles F. Irons, "The Spiritual Fruits of Revolution: Disestablishment and the Rise of the Virginia Baptists," *Virginia Magazine of History and Biography* 109 (2001): 159–86.

[2]Nathan O. Hatch, "The Democratization of Christianity and the Character of American Politics," in Mark A. Noll, ed., *Religion & American Politics: From the Colonial Period to the 1980s* (New York: Oxford University Press, 1990), 110–11.

[3]John Leland, *The Virginia Chronicle: with Judicious and Critical Remarks Under XXIV Heads* (Norfolk, 1790). Used by permission of the American Antiquarian Society.

[A]Ketocton, is the name of a water course, in Loudoun County that empties into the Potommack. Most of the Baptist churches, now in Virginia, take their names of distinction from the waters where they are.

[4]Matthew 3:2.

tised, confessing their sins. Many of the young converts, caught the spirit of their teachers, and zealously engaged in the work. In a course of time, the fires from the northern preachers, and those in the south met, like the two seas in St. *Paul's* shipwreck,[5] in Orange [21] county, 1767. Two or three ministers from each side assembled in conference; but did not so happily unite as candour desired. A division took place. The northern members called themselves, "regular Baptists," and the southern members called themselves, "Separate Baptists:" and if some alienation of affection did not attend this division, in some instances, it was because they were free from those temptations that have always mingled with religious divisions, and if there was not a little zeal discovered to proselyte as well as convert the people, I have been wrongly informed.

The *Regulars* adhered to a confession of faith, first published in London 1689,[6] and afterwards adopted by the Baptist association of Philadelphia in 1742; but the *Separates* had none but the bible. Just upon the spot of ground where the division took place, the members knew something of the cause; but those who lived at a distance were ignorant of the reason, and whenever they met, they loved each other as brethren, and much deplored that there should be any distinction or shyness among them. The *Separates*, who also formed an association, increased much the fastest, both in ministers and members, and occupied by far, the greatest territory. The *Regulars* were orthodox Calvanists, and the work under them was solemn and rational: but the *Separates* were the most zealous, and the work among them was very noisy. The people would cry out—fall down—and, for a time, lose the use of their limbs; which exercise made the bye-standers marvel; some thought they were deceitful, others that they were bewitched, and many convinced of all, would report, that God was with them of a truth.

XI. HEAD

Soon after the Baptist ministers began to preach in Virginia, the novelty of their doctrine; the rarity of mechanicks and planters preaching such strange things;[B] and the wonderful effect that their preaching had upon the people, called out [22] multitudes to hear them. Some out of curiosity, some in sincerity, and some in ill-will.

---

[5] Acts 27:41.
[6] The Second Confession, first published in 1677 and then again in 1689. It is based on the Presbyterians' Westminster Confession.
[B] To this day there are not more than 3 or 4 Baptist ministers in Virginia, who have received the *Diploma* M.A. which is an additional proof, that the work has been of God and not of man.

Their doctrine, influence and popularity, made them many enemies, especially among those, who value themselves most for religion in the Episcopal mode. The usual alarm of *the church and state being danger*, was echoed thro' the colony; nor were the Episcopal clergymen so modest, but what they joined the alarm; like the silversmiths of old, crying, "our craft is in danger of being set at naught."[7] Magistrates began to issue their warrants, and sheriffs had their orders to take up the *disturbers of the peace*. The county of *Spotsylvania* took the lead, and others soon followed their example. Preaching, teaching or exhorting was what disturbed the peace. A like work disturbed the peace of Satan, when he cryed out, "let us alone."[8] Sometimes when the preachers were brought before courts, they escaped the prison by giving bonds and security, that they would not preach in the county in the term of a year; but most of them preferred the dungeon to such bonds. Not only ministers were imprisoned, but others for only praying in their families with a neighbour or two.

The act of *toleration*, passed in the first of *William & Mary*,[9] afforded the suffering brethren some relief. By applying to the general court, and subscribing to all the 39 articles, saving the 34th, 35th and 36th, together with one clause in the 20th and part of the 27th,[10] they obtained liberty to preach at certain stipulated places;[C] but if they preached at any other places, they were exposed to be prosecuted.

Some [23] of the prisoners would give bonds not to preach, and as soon as they were freed, would immediately preach as before. This was done when they had reason to believe that the court would never bring suit upon the bonds. I have never heard of but one such suit in the state, and that one was dismissed. The ministers would go singing from the court-house to the

---

[7] Acts 19:27.

[8] Mark 1:24; Luke 4:34.

[9] The Act of Toleration was passed in 1689. It granted freedom of worship to some dissenters, although it excluded Roman Catholics and people who did not believe in the Trinity. Virginia's government recognized the Act of Toleration in 1699.

[10] The Articles Leland refers to address Article 34, "Of the Traditions of the Church"; Article 35, the *Book of Homilies*; Article 35, "Of the Consecration of Bishops and Ministers"; Article 20, "Of the Authority of the Church"; and Article 27, "Of Baptism."

[C] There are other parts of the 39 articles, equally exceptionable with those parts excepted. If a creed or faith, established by law was ever so short and ever so true; if I believed the whole of it with all my heart, should I subscribe to it before a magistrate, in order to get indulgence, preferment or even protection, I should be guilty of a species of idolatry, by acknowledging a power, that the head of the church, Jesus Christ, has never appointed. In this point of view, who can look over the constitutions of government adopted in most of the United States, without real sorrow? They require a religious test, to qualify an officer of state. All the good such tests do, is to keep from office the best of men: Villians make no scruple of any test. The Virginia constitution is free from this stain: If a man merits the confidence of his neighbours, in Virginia, let him worship one God, twenty Gods, or no God—be Jew, Turk, Pagan, or Infidel, he is [blurred].

prison; where they had sometimes the liberty of the bounds, and at other times they had not. They used to preach to the people thro' the grates; to prevent which, some ill-disposed men would be at the expence of erecting a high wall round the prison; others would employ half drunken strolls to beat a drum round the prison to prevent the people from hearing. Sometimes matches and pepper pods, were burnt at the prison door, and many such afflictions the dear disciples went thro'. About 30 of the preachers were honored with a dungeon, and a few others beside. Some of them were imprisoned as often as 4 times; besides all the mobs and perils they went thro'. The Dragon roared with hedious peals, but was not *red*—the beast appeared formidable, but was not *scarlet colored*. Virginia soil has never been stained with vital blood for conscience sake.[11] Heaven has restrained the wrath of man, and brought auspicious days at last. We now sit under our vines and fig-trees, and there is none too make us afraid.[12]

XII. HEAD

But why this schism? says an inquisitor. If the people were disposed to be more devotional than they had been before; why not be devout in the church in which they were raised, without renting themselves off, and procuring so much evil unto themselves? This question may be answered in part, by asking a similar one. Why did the Episcopal church rend off from the church of Rome in the reformation? Why not continue in that church and worship in her mode? What necessity for that schism, which occasioned so much war and persecution? If we are to credit *Frederick*[13] in his *memoirs of the house of Brandenburg*, the cause of the reformation, was, in England, the love of a woman— in Germany, the love of gain—in France, the love of novelty or a song. But can the church of [24] England offer no other reason for her heretical schism, but the love of a woman? Undoubtedly she can: She has done it; and we approve of her reason; but after all, she is not so pure in her worship, but what we have many reasons for dissenting from her. Some of which are as follows:

1. No national church, can, in its organization be the gospel church. A national church takes in the whole nation, and no more; whereas the gospel church, takes in no whole nation, but those who fear God and work righteousness in every nation. The notion of a christian Commonwealth, should

---

[11]It is possible that the advent of religious freedom in Virginia and the number of years that had passed since the persecution and the late 1780s, when Leland wrote *The Virginia Chronicle*, tempered his views of the earlier difficult years.

[12]Micah 4:4.

[13]Frederick II, King of Prussia (1712–1786), *Memoirs of the House of Brandenburg from the earliest accounts, to the death of Frederick I* (London, 1751).

be exploded forever, without there was a Commonwealth of real christians. Not only so, but if all the souls in a government were saints of God, should they be formed into a society by law, that society could not be a gospel church, but a creature of state.

2. The church of England in Virginia, has no discipline but the civil law. The crimes of their delinquent members are tried in a court-house, before the judges of the police, their censures are laid on at the whipping post, and their excommunications are administered at the gallows. In England if a man cast contempt upon the spiritual court, the Bishop, delegates a grave priest, who with his chancellor excommunicate him. The man thus excommunicated, is by law, disabled from being a plaintiff or witness in any suit. But for heresy, incest or adultery, the Bishop himself pronounces the exclusion. The out-cast is not only denied the company of christians, in spiritual duty, but also in temporal concerns. He not only is disabled from being plaintiff or witness in any suit (and so deprived of the protection of the law) but if he continues 40 days an excommunicant, a writ comes out against him, and he is cast into prison without bail, and there continues till he has paid the last mite. Mrs. Trask[14] was judged an Heretick, because she believed in the Jewish Sabbath, and for that she was imprisoned 16 years until she died; but a gospel church has nothing to do with corporeal punishments. If a member commits sin, the church is to exclude him, which is as far as church power extends. If the crime is cognizable by law, the culprit must bear what the [25] law inflicts. In the church of England Ecclesiastical and civil matters are so blended to-gether, that I know not who can be blamed for dissenting from her.

3. The manner of initiating members into the church of England, is arbi-trary and tyrannical. The subject (for a candidate I cannot call him) is taken by force, brought to the Priest, baptized and declared a member of the church. The little christian shews all the aversion he is capable of, by cries and struggles, but all to no purpose, ingrafted he is; and when the child grows up if he differs in judgment from his father and king, he is called a dissenter, because he is honest, and will not say that he believes what he does not be-lieve; and as such, in England, can fill no post of honor or profit. Here let it be observed, that religion is a matter entirely between God and individuals. No man has a right to force another to join a church: Nor do the legitimate powers of civil government extend so far as to disable, incapacitate, pro-scribe, or any ways distress in person, property, liberty or life, any man who

---

[14]Returne Hebdon, A Guide to the Godly, or, The Dayly Meditations of Returne Hebdon Gentleman, Who for His Conscience, (through the Tyrany of the Bishops) Suffered Many Years Imprisonment in the Kings-Bench and there Remained till Death. Being Very Usefull for Instruction of all Those that Desire to Walke in the Paths of Jesus Christ. Left to Mrs. Traske, Who Not Long Since for the Same Judgment Died in the Gate House, and Published by a Friend of Hers (London, 1646).

cannot believe and practise in the common road. A church of Christ, according to the gospel, is a congregation of faithful persons, called out of the world by divine grace, who mutually agree to live together, and execute gospel discipline among them; which government, is not national, parochial or presbyterial, but congregational.

4. The church of England has a human head. Henry VIII cast off the Pope's yoke, and was declared head of the church [in] 1533;[15] which title all the Kings of England have borne since; but the gospel church acknowledges no head but king Jesus: he is law-giver, king and judge—is a jealous God, and will not give his glory unto another.

5. The preachers of that order, in Virginia, for the most part, not only plead for theatrical amusements and what they call civil mirth, but their preaching is dry and barren, containing little else but morality. The great doctrines of universal depravity, redemption by the blood of Christ, regeneration, faith, repentance and self-denial, are but seldom preached by them, and when they meddle with them it is in such a superficial manner, as if they were nothing but things of course. [26]

6. Their manner of visiting the sick, absolving sin, administering the Lord's supper to newly married couples, burying the dead, sprinkling children with their gossips, promises, cross, &c. are no ways satisfactory, and as they were handed to us thro' the force of law, we reject them *in toto*. These are some of the reasons we have for dissenting from the Episcopalians in Virginia, and tho' they may not be sufficient to justify our conduct in the opinion of others, yet they have weight with us.[D]

XIII. HEAD

There are *three* grand, leading principles, which divide the Christian world: I say *leading* principles; for each of them is subdivided into a number of peculiarities. These *three*, I shall call *fate, free will* and *restitution*.

1st. *Fate.* Those who believe this doctrine, say, that God eternally ordained whatsoever comes to pass; that if the minutest action should be done that God did not appoint, it would not only prove a world of chance, but

---

[15]The Convocations of Canterbury and York recognized Henry VIII as the "supreme head of the Church of England" in 1531. Parliament recognized this in the Supremacy Act of 1534.

[D] What is here said of the church of England, respects them [blurred] the late revolution. Since the independence of the state, a great number of those who still prefer Episcopacy, have the most noble ideas of religious liberty, and are as far from wishing to oppress those who differ with them in judgment, as any men in the state. Experience proves, that while each man believes what he chuses, and practises as he pleases, altho' they differ widely in sentiment; yet they love each other better, than they do when they are all obliged to believe and worship in one way. The only way to live in peace and enjoy ourselves as freemen, is to think and speak freely, worship as we please, and be protected by law in our persons, property and liberty.

create an uneasiness in the divine mind; that *providence* and *grace* are stewards, to see that all God's decrees are fulfilled. Sometimes a distinction is made between God's *absolute* and *permissive* decrees; that God *absolutely* decreed the good, and *permissively* decreed the evil. Other times it is stated thus: That upon the principle of God's knowing all things, every thing comes to pass of necessity. With this sentiment, most commonly, is connected the doctrine of *particular* redemption—that Jesus Christ undertook for a certain number of *Adam's* progeny, and for them alone he died—that those for whom he died, shall be called, by irresistible grace, to the knowledge of the truth, and be [27] saved—that if one of these, whom he *chose* and *redeemed* should miss of Heaven, his will would be frustrated, and his blood lost. And as this at first view, seems to excuse the non-elect, for not believing in the Mediator; it is sometimes said that Jesus died *virtually* for all, but intentionally for a few. Others, who disdain such pitiful shifts, say, that the want of faith of God's elect, is no sin—that justice cannot require a man to have more divine life than *Adam* possest in Eden; that if we, as rational creatures, do not believe as much as *Adam* could have believed in innocency, when revealed to us, that we are guilty of the sin of unbelief; but that the law cannot require us to believe in a Mediator, and therefore the want of *that* faith is not a sin—Those who adhere to this principle, are called, *Fatalists, Predestinarians, Calvanists, Supralapsarians,*[16] &c.

2d. *Free Will.* Those who adopt this principle, affirm, that God eternally decreed to establish the freedom of the *human will*—that if men are *necessary* agents, the very idea of virtue and vice is destroyed—that the more angels and men are exalted in their creation, in the state of *free agency*, the greater was the probability of their falling—that sin could never have entered into the world, upon any other footing; that if man does what he cannot avoid, it is no rebellion in the creature; that God never offers violence to the *human will* in the process of grace—that Christ has fulfilled the law, which *all* were under—bore the curse for *all*—spilt his blood for all—makes known his grace to all; gives to each a talent; bids all improve; and finally, that if men are damned, it will not be for the want of a Saviour; but for refusing to obey him—damned for unbelief, and that those who are damned will have their torment augmented for refusing an offered Saviour. Some who adhere to this doctrine, believe that when men are once *born again*, that they can never perish, and others believe that there is no state so secure, in this world, but what men may fall from it into eter-

---

[16]Individuals who adhere to the belief that God decreed who would and would not be saved before the Fall of Adam.

nal damnation. The advocates for the above sentiment are called *Arminians*,[17] *free willers, universal provisionists, &c.*

3d. *Restitution*. Those who espouse this sentiment, declare that God eternally designed to save all men; that he made them [28] to enjoy him forever, and that he will not be frustrated; that Christ died for *all* and will not lose his blood; that if more souls are lost than saved, Satan will have the greatest triumph, and sin have a more boundless reign than grace; that if even one soul should be miserable, *world without end*, the sting of death and the victory of the grave would never be destroyed; that Jesus will reign till all his foes, even the last enemy, shall be rooted up; that he will reconcile *all things*, unto himself, and make *all things new*; that *every creature* in Heaven, in earth, and under the earth, shall join in the celestial doxology. But those who uphold this doctrine are equally perplexed and divided, with those who believe the two before mentioned principles.

Some of them extend the doctrine to fallen angels, others confine it to the human race—some believe there will be no punishment after death, others conclude that torment will be inflicted in *Hades* upon rebellious souls, even until the resurrection of the body; and others think that they will not all be restored, till the expiration of several periodical eternities. Those who avow this doctrine are called *Universalists, Hell Redemptioners, &c.*

Whether it is a blessing or a curse to mankind, it is a certain truth, that the theoretic principles of men, have but little effect upon their lives. I know men of all the beforewritten doctrines that equally seem to strive to glorify God, in the way which they conceive will do it the most effectually. It is no novelty in the world, for men of different sentiments, to stigmatize the doctrines of each other, with being pregnant with *dangerous* consequences; but it is not the doctrine or system that a man believes, that makes him either a *good* or *bad* man, but the SPIRIT he is governed by. It is a saying among lovers, that "love will triumph over reason," and it is as true that the disposition of the heart will prevail over the system of the head.

The *3d* principle mentioned above, has few, if any vouchers among the Baptists in Virginia; but the two first spoken of, divide counties, churches and families; which about the year 1775 raised a great dispute in Virginia, and finally split the separate Baptists; which division continued several years; but after [29] both parties had contested till their courage grew cool, they ceased their hostilities, grounded their arms, and formed a compromise upon the middle ground, of think and let think; and ceded to each other its territory and liberty.

---

[17]See page 68, note 144.

I am acquainted with men of all these principles, who are equally *assured* they are right. No doubt they are right in their own conceits, and they may be all right in their aims; but I am *assured* they are not all right in their systems; and far enough from being right, when they bitterly condemn each other.

XIV. HEAD

It is a question not easily answered, whether *marriage*, was appointed, by the divine parent, merely for the *propagation* of the human species, or for the *education* of children? Whether one or the other, or both were reasons of the institution, it certainly was appointed by God, honored by Jesus, and declared to be honorable unto all, by St. Paul.[18] What lies before me at present, is to consider the mode of marriage in Virginia, before the late revolution, and the alterations that have since taken place.

Under the regal government, the rites of matrimony were solemnized two ways. The first, and most reputable way, was this. From the clerk's office in the county where the bride lived, a licence was issued to the bridegroom, which cost 20s. which was a perquisite of the governor; and 50lb. of tobacco for the fee of the clerk; which raised the price to a guinea. This licence was delivered to the clergyman, on the wedding day, for his security, and for solemnizing the rites he was entitled to 20s. This way of getting wives was too expensive for the poor, and therefore another mode was prescribed by law, as an alternative. The clergyman published the banns of marriages on 3 holy days,[19] for which he was entitled to 18 pence, and for joining such couples together, he was entitled to 5s. The Presbyterian ministers sometimes solemnized the rites; but if it was by a licence, the parish preacher claimed and recovered his fee, as tho' he had solemnized the rites himself. After the declaration of independence, in 1780, an act passed the general assembly, to authorize as many as 4 ministers [30] in each county, of each denomination, to solemnize the rites; but the act was so partial, that some would not qualify, others took what indulgence the act gave, and still petitioned for equal liberty. The Episcopal clergymen were allowed to join people together in any part of the state, while others were circumscribed by county bounds.[20] In 1784, this partiallity was removed, and all ministers were set on a level.[21] By presenting credentials of their ordination, and a recommendation of their

---

[18]Hebrews 13:4.
[19]Sundays.
[20]William Waller Hening, ed., *The Statutes at Large: Being a Collection of All the Laws of Virginia . . .* , 13 Vols. (Richmond, 1809–1823), 10:361–63.
[21]Hening, *Statutes at Large*, 11:503.

good character in the society where they are members, and also giving bond and security to the court of the county where they reside; they receive testimonials signed by the senior magistrate, to join together any persons who legally apply in any part of the state. Publication is now abolished. From the county in which the bride resides, a licence is issued out of the clerk's office, which costs the groom 15 pence; this licence is given to the preacher, for his security, and for joining of them together, he is entitled to 5s. The preacher is under bonds, to certify the clerk, from whom the licence came, of the solemnization, and the clerk, for registering the certificate, is entitled to 15 pence more: So that it costs but 7s. and 6d. to get a wife in these days.

XV. HEAD

A review of XI head informs us what persecution the Baptists preachers were subject to, which continued in some counties, until the revolution. Upon the declaration of independence, and the establishment of a republican form of government, it is not to be wondered at, that the Baptists so heartily and uniformly engaged in the cause of the country against the king. The change suited their political principles, promised religious liberty, and a freedom from ministerial tax; nor have they been disappointed in their expectations. In 1776, the salaries of the Episcopal clergymen were suspended, which was so confirmed in 1779, that no legal force has ever been used since, to support any preachers in the state.[22] But as they gained this piece of freedom; so the cares of war, the spirit of trade, and moving to the western waters, seemed to bring on a general declension. The ways of Zion mourned.[23] They obtained [31] their hearts desire (freedom) but had leanness in their souls. Some of the old watchmen stumbled and fell, iniquity did abound, and the love of many waxed cold.[24] But the declension was not so total, but what God shewed himself gracious in some places; his blessings, like small showers in the drought of summer, were scattered abroad. Delegates from the churches assembled in association once or twice in each year; but so much of the time was taken up in considering what means had best be used, to obtain and preserve equal liberty with other societies, that many of the churches were discouraged in sending delegates. Many of the ministers removed from their churches to Kentuckey, and left their scattered flocks like a cottage in a vineyard, like a lodge in a garden of cucumbers. In this point of view was the Baptist society in Virginia, at the close of the war and the return of auspicious peace.

---

[22]Hening, *Statutes at Large*, 9:164–67, 312, 387–88, 469, 578–79; 10:111.
[23]Lamentations 1:4.
[24]Matthew 24:12.

Oct. 1783, was the last general association, the separate Baptists ever had.[25] They divided into 4 or 5 districts; but to maintain a friendly correspondence, and be helpers to each other, in a political way, they established a GENERAL COMMITTEE, to be composed of delegates sent from each distinct association, to meet annually. Not more than 4 delegates from one association are entitled to seats. This committee give their opinion on all queries sent to them from any of the associations, originate all petitions to be laid before the legislature of the state, and consider the good of the whole society. It may be here noted, that the general committee as well as the associations, exercise no lordship over the churches—all they attempt is advice, which is generally received by the churches in a cordial manner. Should they attempt any thing more, without *legal authority*, they will appear ridiculous; and with *legal authority*, they would grow tyrannical. Of this committee the regular Baptist association became a member.

In 1784, the Episcopal society was legally incorporated,[26] and such exertions were made for a general assessment, [to] oblige all the citizens in the state to pay *some* preacher, [and] a *bill* for that purpose passed two readings; but the final determination of the bill was postponed until November, 1785, when [32] the time came, the Presbyterians, Baptists, Quakers, Methodists,[E] Deists, and covetous, made such an effort against the bill, that it fell thro'.[27] In 1786, the act incorporating the Episcopal society was repealed;[28] but in 1788, their trustees were legalized to manage the property,[29] which is the state of things at this time.

Several attempts were made, at different times, to unite the *regular* and *separate* associations together, but all proved in vain, until August, 1787,[30] when they united upon the principle of receiving the confession of faith, beforementioned, as containing the great essential doctrines of the gospel, yet not in so strict a sense, that all are obliged to believe *every thing* therein

---

[25]The Baptist General Association of Virginia, 1771–1783.
[26]Hening, *Statutes at Large*, 11:532–37.
[E]Before *this* the Methodists petitioned for accommodation as the established religion of the state; but being organized a distinct church, they vigorously opposed the assessment; and at the same time petitioned the legislature for a general liberation of the slaves. Although the petition was rejected, as being impracticable; yet it shows their resolution, to bring to pass a noble work.
[27]Buckley, *Church and State in Revolutionary Virginia*, 90–91, 96–112.
[28]Hening, *Statutes at Large*, 12:266–67.
[29]Hening, *Statutes at Large*, 12:705–6.
[30]Reuben Edward Alley, *A History of the Baptists in Virginia* (Richmond: Virginia Baptist General Board, 1973), 60–61.

contained.[F] At the same time, it was agreed that the [33] appellations, *regular* and *separate* should be buried in oblivion, and that in future they should be called, "the united Baptist churches of Christ in Virginia."

XVI. HEAD

The first part of the last head, gives an account of the declension of religion among the baptists, which continued until 1785. In the summer of the year, the glorious work of God broke out, on the banks of the James river, and from thence has spread almost over the state. In treating of this great revival, I shall not write as a divine, philosopher, or an opposer, but solely as an historian.

In the greatest part of the meetings, where religion is low among the people, there is no unusual appearance among them; a grave countenance, a solemn sigh, or a silent tear, is as much as is seen or heard; and sometimes a great degree of inattention and carelessness; but in times of reviving, it is quite otherwise, in most places. It is nothing strange to see a great part of the congregation fall p[r]ostrate upon the floor or ground; many of whom entirely lose the use of their limbs for a season. Sometimes numbers are crying out at once, some of them in great distress, using such language as this, "God be merciful to me a sinner[31]—Lord save me or I must perish[32]—what shall I do to be saved?[33] &c." others breaking out in such rapturous expressions as these;

[F]A union seemed so necessary and desireable, that those who were somewhat scrupulous of a confession of faith, other than the bible, were willing to sacrifice their peculiarities, and those who were strenuous for the confession of faith, agreed to a *partial* reception of it. "United we stand, divided we fall," overcome, at that time, all objections; but had they united without any confession of faith, as they did in *Georgia*, perhaps it would have been better. In kingdoms and states where a system of religion is established by law, with the indulgence of toleration to *non-conformists* of restricted sentiments, it becomes necessary for such *non-conformists*, to publish a confession of their faith, to convince the rulers, that they do not exceed the bounds of toleration; but in a government like that of Virginia, where all men believe and worship as they please, where the only punishment inflicted on the enthusiastical, is *Pity*—What need of a confession of faith? Why this Virgin Mary between the sons of men and the scriptures? Had a system of religion been essential to salvation, or even to the happiness of the saints, would not Jesus, who was faithful in all his house, have left us one? If he has, it is accessible to all. If he has not, why should a man be called a heretick, because he cannot believe what he cannot believe; tho' he believes the bible with all his heart? Confessions of faith often check any further pursuit after truth, confine the mind into a particular way of reasoning, and give rise to frequent separations. To plead for their utility, because they have been common, is as good sense, as to plead for a state establishment of religion, for the same reason; and both are as bad reasoning, as to plead for sin, because it is every where. It is sometimes said, that hereticks are always averse to confessions of faith. I wish I could say as much of tyrants. But after all, if a confession of faith, upon the whole, may be advantageous, the greatest care should be taken not to sacralize; or make a *petty bible* of it.

[31]Luke 18:13.
[32]Matthew 8:25.
[33]Acts 16:30.

"bless the Lord, O my soul![34]—O sweet Jesus, how I love thee!—Let every thing that hath breath, praise the Lord![35]—O sinners! come, taste and see how good the Lord is![36] &c."

I have seen such exercise, and heard such melody for several hours together. At associations and great meetings, I have seen numbers of ministers and exhorters improving their gifts at the same time. Such a heavenly confusion among the preachers, and such a celestial discord among the people destroy all articulation, [34] so that the understanding is not edified; but the awful echo sounding in the ears, and the objects in great distress, and great raptures before their eyes, raise great emotions in the heart. Some ministers rather oppose *this* work, others call it a little in question, and some fan it with all their might. Whether it be celestial or terrestrial, or a complication of both, it is observed by the candid, that more souls get first awakened at such meetings, than at any meetings whatever; who afterwards give clear rational accounts of a divine change of heart. This exercise is not confined to the newly convicted and newly converted; but persons who have been professors a number of years, at such lively meetings, not only jump up, strike their hands together and shout aloud, but will embrace one another and fall to the floor. I have never known the rules of decency broken so far, as for persons of both sexes, thus to embrace and fall at meetings. It is not to be understood, that this exercise is seen in all parts of the state, at times when God is working on the minds of the people; no, under the preaching of the same man, in different neighbourhoods and counties, the same work, in substance, has different exterior effects.

At such times of revival, it is wonderful to hear the sweet singing among the people; when they make melody in their hearts and voices to the Lord. In the last great in-gathering, in some places, singing was more blessed among the people, than the preaching was. What Mr. *Jonathan Edwards*[37] thought might be expedient in some future day, has been true in Virginia. Bands go singing to meeting, and singing home. At meeting, as soon as preaching is over, it is common to sing a number of spiritual songs; sometimes several songs are sounding at the same time, in different parts of the congregation. I have travelled thro' neighbourhoods and counties at times of refreshing, and the spiritual songs in the fields, in the shops and houses, have made the Heavens ring with melody, over my head; but as soon as the work

---

[34]See Psalms 103 and 104.
[35]Psalm 150:6.
[36]Psalm 34:8.
[37]Jonathan Edwards (1703–1758), Calvinist minister, one of the most important leaders of the Great Awakening in the American colonies and among the most important clerics in American history.

is over, there is no more of it heard. Dr. *Watts*[38] is the general standard for the Baptists in Virginia; but they are not confined to him. Any spiritual composition answers their purpose. A number [35] of hymns originate in Virginia, although there is no established poet in the state. Some Virginia songs, have more divinity in them, than poetry or grammar; and some that I have heard have but little of either.

Candidates generally make confession of their faith before the whole assembly present; but sometimes there are so many to offer, that the church divides into several bodies, each of which acts for the whole, and receives by the right hand of fellowship. At times appointed for baptism, the people generally go singing to the water side in grand procession: I have heard many souls declare they first were convicted, or first found pardon going to, at, or coming from the water. If those who practice infant baptism, can say as much, 'tis no wonder they are so fond of it. *Forty, fifty*, or *sixty* have often been baptised in a day at one place, in Virginia, and, sometimes as many as *seventy-five*. There are some ministers now living in Virginia, who have baptized more than 2000 persons. It is said, that St. *Austin*[39] baptized 10,000 in the dead of winter, in the river *Swale*, in England, in the year 595. I have seen ice cut more than a foot thick, and people baptised in the water, and yet I have never heard of any person taking cold or any kind of sickness, in so doing. And strange it is that Mr. *Wesley*[40] should recommend *cold bathing* for such a vast number of disorders, and yet be so backward to administer it for the best purpose, viz. to fulfil righteousness. . . . [36]

XVIII. HEAD

Upon the first rise of the Baptists, in Virginia, they were very strict in their dress. Men cut off their hair, like *Cromwell's round headed Chaplains*, and women cast away all their superfluities; [37] so that they were distinguished from others, merely by their decoration. Where all were of one mind, no evil ensued; but where some did not chuse to dock and strip, and churches made it a matter of discipline, it led to great confusion. No doubt dressing, as well as eating and drinking can be carried to excess; but it appears to be a matter between God and individuals; for whenever churches take it up, the last evil is worse than the first. This principle prevailed 'till the war broke out, at which time the Baptist mode took the lead. Those who went into the army, cut off their hair, and those who staid at home, were obliged to dress in

---

[38]Isaac Watts (1674–1748), nonconformist hymn writer.
[39]St. Augustine of Canterbury (d. 604 or 605), first Archbishop of Canterbury.
[40]John Wesley (1703–1791), founder of the Methodist Movement, an evangelical movement within the Church of England.

home-spun. Since the return of peace, and the opening of the ports, the uniformity between the Baptists and others, in point of cloathing, still exists; notwithstanding the great work of conversion there has been in the state; but very little is said about rending garments; those who behave well, wear what they please and meet with no reproof.

XIX. HEAD

The principle, that civil rulers have nothing to do with religion, in their official capacities, is as much interwoven in the Baptist plan, as *Phydias's* name was in his shield. The legitimate powers of government, extend only to punish men for working ill to their neighbours, and no ways effect the rights of conscience. The nation of Israel received their civil and religious laws from Jehovah, which were binding on them and no other; and with the extirpation of that nation, were abolished. For a Christian commonwealth to be established upon the same claim, is very presumptuous, without they have the same charter from Heaven. Because the nation of Israel had a divine grant of the land of Canaan and orders to enslave the Heathen, some suppose Christians have an equal right to take away the land of the Indians, and make slaves of the Negroes. Wretched religion, that pleads for cruelty and injustice. In this point of view, the Pope offered England to the King of Spain, provided he would conquer it; after England became Protestant, and in the same view of things, on May 4, 1493, the [38] year after America was discovered, he proposed to give away the Heathen lands to his Christian subjects. If Christian nations, were nations of Christians these things would not be so. The very tendency of religious establishments by human law, is to make some hypocrites, and the rest fools; they are calculated to destroy those very virtues, that religion is designed to build up, to encourage fraud and violence over the earth. It is error alone that stands in need of government to support it; truth can and will do better without; so ignorance calls in anger in a debate, good sense scorns it. Religion in its purest ages, made its way in the world, not only without the aid of law, but against all the laws of haughty monarchs, and all the maxims of the schools. The pretended friendship of *legal* protection, and *learned* assistance, proves, often in the end, like the friendship of Joab to Amasa.[41]

Government should protect every man in thinking and speaking freely, and see that one does not abuse another. The liberty I contend for, is more than toleration. The very idea of toleration is despicable, it supposes that some have a preeminence above the rest, to grant indulgence; whereas all

---

[41]2 Samuel 20:8–10.

should be equally free, Jews, Turks, Pagans and Christians. Test oaths, and established creeds, should be avoided as the worst of evils. A general assessment (forcing all to pay some preacher) amounts to an establishment; if government says I must pay somebody, it must next describe that somebody, his doctrine and place of abode. That moment a minister is so fixed as to receive a stipend by legal force, that moment he ceases to be a gospel ambassador, and becomes a minister of state. This emolument is a temptation too great for avaricious man to withstand. This doctrine turns the gospel into merchandise, and sinks religion upon a level with other things.

As it is not the province of civil government to establish forms of religion, and force a maintenance for the preachers; so it does not belong to that power to establish fixed holy days for divine worship—that the Jewish seventh day sabbath was of divine appointment, is unquestionable; but that the Christian first day sabbath is of equal injunction, is more doubtful. If Jesus appointed the day to be observed, he did it as the head of [39] the church, and not as the King of nations; or if the apostles enjoined it, they did it in the capacity of Christian teachers, and not as human legislators. As the appointment of such days, is no part of human legislation, so the breach of the sabbath (so called) is no part of civil jurisdiction. I am not an enemy to holy days; the duties of religion cannot well be performed without fixed times; but these times should be fixed by the mutual agreement of religious societies, according to the word of God, and not by civil authority. I see no clause in the federal constitution, or the constitution of Virginia, to empower either the federal or Virginia legislature to make any sabbatical laws. . . .

~

Selected Bibliography

Primary Sources

Berkeley, Edmund and Dorothy, eds. *John Clayton: Parson With a Scientific Mind.* Chapel Hill: University of North Carolina Press, 1965.

Beverley, Robert. *The History and Present State of Virginia.* Edited by Louis B. Wright. Chapel Hill: University of North Carolina Press, 1947.

Billings, Warren M. "A Quaker in Seventeenth-Century Virginia: Four Remonstrances by George Wilson." *William and Mary Quarterly* 3d ser. 33 (1976): 127–40.

Blair, James. *Our Saviour's Divine Sermon on the Mount . . . Explained; and the Practice of it Recommended in divers Sermons and Discourses.* 5 Vols. London, 1722.

Brown, Alexander, ed. *The Genesis of the United States.* 2 Vols. New York, 1896.

Butler, Jon, ed. "Two 1642 Letters from Virginia Puritans." *Massachusetts Historical Society Proceedings* 84 (1972): 99–109.

Cabell, James Branch, ed. "A Discourse for Friends of Virginia and Carolina by Joseph Glaister." *William and Mary Quarterly* 1st ser. 25 (1916–1917): 248–53.

Camp, Ichabod. *Men Have Freedom of Will and Power, and Their Conduct, Whether Good or Evil, is of Choice.* New Haven, 1760.

Dickinson, James. *A Journal of the Life, Travels, and Labours of Love in the Work of the Ministry, of that Worthy Elder, and Faithful Servant of Jesus Christ, James Dickinson.* London, 1745. In *The Friends Library: Comprising Journals, Doctrinal Treatises, and Other Writings of Members of the Religious Society of Friends.* 14 Vols. Edited by William Evans and Thomas Evans. Philadelphia, 1837–1850.

Executive Journals of the Council of Colonial Virginia. 6 Vols. Edited by H. R. McIlwaine. Richmond: Virginia State Library, 1925.

Giberne, William. *The Duty of Living Peaceably with all Men.* Williamsburg, 1759.

Godwyn, Morgan. *The Negro's and Indian's Advocate suing for their Admission into the Church*. London: 1680.

G[reene], R[oger]. *Virginia's Cure; or an Advisive Narrative Concerning Virginia. . . .* London, 1662. In *Tracts and Other Papers, Relating Principally to the Origin, Settlement, and Progress of the Colonies in North America*, complied by Peter Force, Vol. 3, no. 15. Gloucester, Mass.: Peter Smith, 1963.

Hammond, John. *Leah and Rachel, or, The Two Fruitfull Sisters Virginia and Maryland: Their Present Condition Impartially Stated and Related*. London, 1656. In *Tracts and Other Papers, Relating Principally to the Origin, Settlement, and Progress of the Colonies in North America*, complied by Peter Force, Vol. 3, no. 14. Gloucester, Mass.: Peter Smith, 1963.

Historical Collections Relating to the American Colonial Church. Edited by William Stevens Perry. Vol. 1. Hartford, Conn.: 1870; reprint, New York: AMS Press, 1969.

Ingersoll, Thomas N. "'Release us out of this Cruell Bondegg': An Appeal from Virginia in 1723." *William and Mary Quarterly* 3d ser. 51 (1994): 777–82.

Ireland, James. *The Life of the Rev. James Ireland: who was, for many years, pastor of the Baptist Church at Buck Marsh, Waterlick and Happy Creek, in Frederick and Shenandoah Counties, Virginia*. Winchester, Va.: 1819.

The Jamestown Voyages Under the First Charter, 1606–1609. Edited by Philip L. Barbour. 2 Vols. London: Cambridge University Press, 1969.

Jarratt, Devereux. *The Life of the Reverend Devereux Jarratt*. Edited by John Coleman. Baltimore: 1806; reprint, New York: Arno Press, 1969.

Jones, Hugh. *The Present State of Virginia, From Whence is Inferred a Short View of Maryland and North Carolina*. Edited by Richard L. Morton. London, 1724; Chapel Hill: University of North Carolina Press, 1956.

The Journal of Joseph Pilmore, Methodist Itinerant, for the Years August 1, 1769, to January 2, 1774. Edited by Frederick E. Maser and Howard T. Maag. Philadelphia: Historical Society of the Philadelphia Annual Conference of the United Methodist Church, 1969.

The Laws of Virginia, Being a Supplement to Hening's The Statutes at Large, 1700–1750. Edited by Waverly K. Winfrey. Richmond: Virginia State Library, 1971.

McCulloch, Samuel Clyde, ed. "James Blair's Plan of 1699 to Reform the Clergy of Virginia." *William and Mary Quarterly* 3d ser. 4 (1947): 70–86.

Narratives of Early Virginia, 1606–1625. Edited by Lyon Gardiner Tyler. New York: Barnes & Noble, 1957.

Pead, Deuel. "A Sermon Preached at James City in Virginia, the 23rd of April 1686, Before the Loyal Society of Citizens born in and about London and inhabiting in Virginia." Edited by Richard Beale Davis. *William and Mary Quarterly* 3d ser. 17 (1960): 371–94.

Pender, Thomas. *The Divinity of the Scriptures, From Reason & External Circumstances*. New York, 1728.

The Records of the Virginia Company of London. Edited by Susan Myra Kingsbury. 4 Vols. Washington, D.C.: United States Government Printing Office, 1906–1935.

Sandys, Edwin. *A Relation of the State of Religion, and With What Hopes and Policies it Hath Been Framed, and is Maintained, in the Several States of These Western Parts of the World*. London, 1605.

The Statutes at Large: Being a Collection of All the Laws of Virginia. . . . Edited by William Waller Hening. Richmond, 1809–1823.

Story, Thomas. *A Journal of the Life of Thomas Story: Containing an Account of His Remarkable Convincement of and Embracing the Principles of Truth, as Held by the People Called Quakers.* Newcastle upon Tyme, 1747.

Strachey, William. "A True Reportory of the Wreck and Redemption of sir Thomas Gates, Knight." In *A Voyage to Virginia in 1609,* edited by Louis B. Wright, 1–102. Charlottesville: University Press of Virginia, 1964.

The Three Charters of the Virginia Company of London, with Seven Related Documents, 1606–1621. Edited by Samuel M. Bemiss. Williamsburg, 1757.

Van Horne, John C., ed. *Religious Philanthropy and Colonial Slavery: The American Correspondence of the Associates of Dr. Bray, 1717–1777.* Urbana: University of Illinois Press, 1987.

Wright, Louis B., ed. *The Prose Works of William Byrd of Westover: Narratives of a Colonial Virginia.* Cambridge, Mass.: Harvard University Press, 1966.

Secondary Sources

Anesko, Michael. "So Discreet a Zeal: Slavery and the Anglican Church in Virginia, 1680–1730." *Virginia Magazine of History and Biography* 93 (1985): 247–78.

Benedict, David. *A General History of the Baptist Denomination in America, and Other Parts of the World.* 2 Vols. Boston: Lincoln and Edmands, 1813.

———. *Virginia's Viceroy: Their Majesties' Governor General: Francis Howard, Lord Howard of Effingham.* Fairfax, Va.: George Mason University Press, 1991.

Billings, Warren M., John E. Selby, and Thad W. Tate. *Colonial Virginia: A History.* White Plains, N.Y.: KTO Press, 1986.

Bond, Edward L. *Damned Souls in a Tobacco Colony: Religion in Seventeenth-Century Virginia.* Macon, Ga.: Mercer University Press, 2000.

———. "Source of Knowledge, Source of Power: The Supernatural World of English Virginia, 1607–1624." *Virginia Magazine of History and Biography* 108 (2000): 105–38.

Bonomi, Patricia U., and Peter R. Eisenstadt. "Church Adherence in the Eighteenth-Century British American Colonies." *William and Mary Quarterly* 3d ser. 39 (1982): 245–86.

Bonomi, Patricia U. *Under the Cope of Heaven: Religion, Society, and Politics in Colonial America.* New York: Oxford University Press, 1986.

Bruce, Philip Alexander. *Institutional History of Virginia in the Seventeenth Century: An Inquiry into the Religious, Moral, Educational, Legal, Military, and Political Condition of the People, Based on Original and Contemporaneous Records.* 2 Vols. Gloucester, Mass.: Peter Smith, 1964.

Brunk, Harry Anthony. *History of Mennonites in Virginia.* Staunton, Va.: McClure Printing Company, 1959.

Brydon, George MacLaren. *Virginia's Mother Church and the Political Conditions Under Which it Grew.* 2 Vols. Richmond: Virginia Historical Society, 1947–1952.

Buckley, Thomas E., S.J. Church and State in Revolutionary Virginia, 1776–1787. Charlottesville: University Press of Virginia, 1977.

Butterfield, Kevin. "Puritans and Religious Strife in the Early Chesapeake." Virginia Magazine of History and Biography 109 (2001): 5–36.

Cross, Arthur Lyon. The Anglican Episcopate and the American Colonies. Harvard Historical Studies IX, 1902; reprint, Hamden, Conn.: Archon Books, 1964.

Davies, Horton. Worship and Theology in England. 5 Vols. Princeton, N.J.: Princeton University Press, 1961–75.

Davis, Richard Beale. Intellectual Life in the Colonial South, 1585–1763. 3 Vols. Knoxville: University of Tennessee Press, 1978.

Dreisbach, Daniel L. "George Mason's Pursuit of Religious Liberty in Revolutionary Virginia." Virginia Magazine of History and Biography 108 (2000): 3–44.

Dresbeck, Sandra. "The Episcopal Clergy in Virginia and Maryland, 1765–1805." Ph.D. dissertation: UCLA, 1976.

Eisenberg, William Edward. The Lutheran Church in Virginia, 1717–1962, including an Account of the Lutheran Church in East Tennessee. Roanoke, Va.: Trustees of the Virginia Synod, Lutheran Church in America, 1967.

Godson, Susan H., Ludwell H. Johnson, Richard B. Sherman, Thad W. Tate, and Helen C. Walker. The College of William and Mary: A History. Williamsburg: King and Queen Press, 1993.

Goodwin, Edward Lewis. The Colonial Church in Virginia, With Biographical Sketches of the First Six Bishops of the Diocese of Virginia and Other Historical Papers, Together With Brief Biographical Sketches of the Colonial Clergy of Virginia. Milwaukee, Wis.: Morehouse Publishing Company, 1927.

Gundersen, Joan R. The Anglican Ministry in Virginia, 1723–1776: A Study of a Social Class. New York: Garland Publishing, Inc., 1989.

———. "Anthony Gavin's A Master-key to Popery: A Virginia Parson's Best Seller." Virginia Magazine of History and Biography 82 (1974): 39–46.

———. "The Myth of the Independent Virginia Vestry." Historical Magazine of the Protestant Episcopal Church 44 (1975): 133–41.

———. "The Search for Good Men: Recruiting Ministers in Colonial Virginia." Anglican and Episcopal History 47 (1979): 453–64.

Gundersen, Joan Rezner. "The Huguenot Church at Manakin in Virginia, 1700–1750." Goochland County Historical Society Magazine 23 (1991): 19–40.

Hallman, Clive Raymond. "The Vestry as a Unit of Local Government in Colonial Virginia." Ph.D. dissertation: University of Georgia, 1987.

Holmes, David L. A Brief History of the Episcopal Church. Valley Forge, Penn.: Trinity Press International, 1993.

Horn, James. Adapting to a New World: English Society in the Seventeenth-Century Chesapeake. Chapel Hill: University of North Carolina Press, 1994.

Irons, Charles F. "The Spiritual Fruits of Revolution: Disestablishment and the Rise of the Virginia Baptists." Virginia Magazine of History and Biography 109 (2001): 159–86.

Isaac, Rhys. "Evangelical Revolt: The Nature of the Baptists' Challenge to the Traditional Order in Virginia, 1765–1775." William and Mary Quarterly 3d ser. 31 (1974): 345–68.

———. "Religion and Authority: Problems of the Anglican Establishment in Virginia in the Era of the Great Awakening and the Parsons' Cause." *William and Mary Quarterly* 3d ser. 30 (1973): 3–36.

———. *The Transformation of Virginia, 1740–1790.* Chapel Hill: University of North Carolina Press, 1982.

Kukla, Jon. "Order and Chaos in Early America: Political and Social Stability in Pre-Restoration Virginia." *American Historical Review* 90 (1985): 275–98.

Kupperman, Karen Ordahl. *Settling With the Indians: The Meeting of Indian and English Cultures in America, 1580–1640.* Totowa, N.J.: Rowman & Littlefield, 1980.

Levy, Babette M. "Early Puritanism in the Island and Southern Colonies." *Proceedings of the American Antiquarian Society* 70 (1960).

Lindman, Janet Moore. "Acting the Manly Christian: White Evangelical Masculinity in Revolutionary Virginia." *William and Mary Quarterly* 3d ser. 57 (2000): 393–416.

———. "A World of Baptists: Gender, Race, and Religious Community in Pennsylvania and Virginia, 1689–1925." Ph.D. dissertation: University of Minnesota, 1994.

Lohrenz, Otto. "The Virginia Clergy and the American Revolution." Ph.D. dissertation: University of Kansas, 1970.

Longmore, Paul K. "'All Matters and Things Relating to Religion and Morality': The Virginia Burgesses' Committee for Religion, 1769–1775." *Journal of Church and State* 38 (1996): 775–98.

Miller, Perry. "Religion and Society in the Early Literature of Virginia." In Perry Miller, *Errand Into the Wilderness*, 101–40. Cambridge, Mass.: Harvard University Press, 1956.

Morgan, Edmund S. *American Slavery, American Freedom: The Ordeal of Colonial Virginia.* New York: W.W. Norton, 1975.

Morton, Richard L. *Colonial Virginia.* 2 Vols. Chapel Hill: University of North Carolina Press, 1960.

Mulder, Philip N. "Converting the New Light: Presbyterian Evangelicalism in Hanover, Virginia." *Journal of Presbyterian History* 75 (1997): 141–51.

Nelson, John K. *A Blessed Company: Parishes, Parsons, and Parishioners in Anglican Virginia, 1690–1776.* Chapel Hill: University of North Carolina Press, 2001.

Owen, James Kimbrough. "The Virginia Vestry: A Study in the Decline of a Ruling Class." Ph.D. dissertation: Princeton University, 1947.

Painter, Borden W., Jr. "The Anglican Vestry in Colonial America." Ph.D. dissertation: Yale University, 1965.

Pilcher, George William. *Samuel Davies: Apostle of Dissent in Colonial Virginia.* Knoxville: University of Tennessee Press, 1971.

Rabb, Theodore K. *Jacobean Gentleman: Sir Edwin Sandys, 1561–1629.* Princeton, N.J.: Princeton University Press, 1998.

Rhoden, Nancy L. *Revolutionary Anglicanism: The Colonial Church of England Clergy During the American Revolution.* London: MacMillan Press LTD, 1999.

Robinson, W. Stitt, Jr. "Indian Education and Missions in Colonial Virginia." *Journal of Southern History* 18 (1952): 152–68.

Rouse, Parke, Jr. *James Blair of Virginia*. Chapel Hill: University of North Carolina Press, 1971.

Rutman, Darrett B. "The Evolution of Religious Life in Early Virginia." *Lex et Scientia: The International Journal of Law and Science* 14 (1978): 190–214.

Rutman, Darrett B. and Anita H. Rutman. *A Place in Time: Middlesex County Virginia, 1650–1750*. New York: W.W. Norton & Company, 1984.

Ryland, Garnett. *The Baptists of Virginia, 1699–1926*. Richmond: Virginia Baptist Board of Missions and Education, 1955.

Seiler, William H. "The Anglican Parish in Virginia." In *Seventeenth-Century America: Essays in Colonial History*, edited by James Morton Smith, 119–42. Chapel Hill: University of North Carolina Press, 1959.

———. "The Church of England as the Established Church in Seventeenth-Century Virginia." *Journal of Southern History* 15 (1949): 478–508.

———. "Land Processioning in Colonial Virginia." *William and Mary Quarterly* 3d ser. 6 (1949): 416–36.

Smits, David B. "'Abominable Mixture': Toward the Repudiation of Anglo-Indian Intermarriage in Seventeenth-Century Virginia." *Virginia Magazine of History and Biography* 95 (1987): 157–92.

Spangler, Jewel L. "Becoming Baptists: Conversion in Colonial and Early National Virginia." *Journal of Southern History* 67 (2001): 243–86.

Stuart, Karen A. "'So Good a Work': The Brafferton School, 1691–1777." M.A. thesis: College of William and Mary, 1984.

Szasz, Margaret Connell. *Indian Education in the American Colonies, 1607–1783*. Albuquerque: University of New Mexico Press, 1988.

Thompson, Earnest Trice. *The Presbyterians in the South*. 2 Vols. Richmond: John Knox Press, 1963.

Upton, Dell. *Holy Things and Profane: Anglican Parish Churches in Colonial Virginia*. Cambridge, Mass.: MIT University Press, 1986.

Walsh, James P. "'Black Cotted Raskolls': Anti-Anglican Criticism in Colonial Virginia." *Virginia Magazine of History and Biography* 88 (1980): 21–36.

Whiting, Marvin Yeomans. "Religious Literature in Virginia, 1685–1776: A Preface to a Study of the History of Ideas." M.A. thesis: Emory University, 1975.

Woolverton, John Frederick. *Colonial Anglicanism in North America*. Detroit: Wayne State University Press, 1984.

Worrall, Jay, Jr. *The Friendly Virginians: America's First Quakers*. Athens, Ga.: Iberian Publishing Company, 1994.

Wright, Louis B. "Elizabethan Politics and Colonial Enterprise." *North Carolina Historical Review* 32 (1955): 254–69.

———. "Pious Reading in Colonial Virginia." *Journal of Southern History* 6 (1940): 383–92.

~

About Edward L. Bond

Edward L. Bond was born in Newport News, Virginia, in 1961. He is currently Associate Professor of History at Alabama A&M University in Huntsville, Alabama. He holds a master's degree from the University of Chicago and a Ph.D. from Louisiana State University, where his areas of concentration included American religious history and American colonial history. He is the author of *Damned Souls in a Tobacco Colony: Religion in Seventeenth-Century Virginia* as well as several articles on religion in colonial Virginia.